JESUS,
THE GOSPELS,
AND THE CHURCH

William R. Farmer

JESUS, THE GOSPELS, AND THE CHURCH

Essays in Honor of William R. Farmer

EDITED BY

E . P . S A N D E R S

ISBN   0-86554-269-4

Jesus, the Gospels, and the Church
Copyright © 1987
Mercer University Press, Macon GA 31207
All rights reserved
Printed in the United States of America

Library of Congress Cataloging-in-Publication Data
Jesus, the gospels, and the church.

Includes bibliographies.
    1. Bible. N.T. Gospels—Criticism, interpretation, etc.
2. Farmer, William Reuben. 3. Synoptic problem.
4. Jesus Christ—Historicity. I. Farmer, William Reuben.
II. Sanders, E. P.
BS2555.2.J47   1987   226'.06   87-18473
ISBN 0-86554-269-4 (alk. paper)

Contents

Jesus and the Gospels

Early Christianity

Abbreviations

AB	Anchor Bible
ATR	*Anglican Theological Review*
BA	*Biblical Archeologist*
BASOR	*Bulletin of the American Schools of Oriental Research*
BETL	Bibliotheca ephemeridum theologicarum lovaniensium
BHT	Beiträge zur historischen Theologie
Bib	*Biblica*
BibTh	*Bible and Theology*
BJRUL	*Bulletin of the John Rylands University Library*
BR	*Biblical Research*
BTF	*Bangalore Theological Forum*
BZ	*Biblische Zeitschrift*
CBQ	*Catholic Biblical Quarterly*
CBQMS	Catholic Biblical Quarterly Monograph Series
CD	Cairo Damascus
ChH	*Church History*
ChrCent	*Christian Century*
ChrCris	*Christianity and Crisis*
CirR	*Circuit Rider*
ConBNT	Coniectanea biblica, New Testament
ConNT	*Coniectanea neotestamentica*
CTQ	*Concordia Theological Quarterly*
CTR	*Criswell Theological Review*
DR	*Downside Review*
DrewG	*Drew Gateway*
EKK	*Evangelische-Katholischer Kommentar zum NT*
ETL	*Ephemerides theologicae Lovanienses*
ExpTim	*Expository Times*
FZPT	*Freiburger Zeitschrift für Philosophie und Theologie*
HibJ	*Hibbert Journal*
HTR	*Harvard Theological Review*
Int	*Interpretation*
JAAR	*Journal of the American Academy of Religion*

JBL *Journal of Biblical Literature*
JJS *Journal of Jewish Studies*
JSNT *Journal for the Study of the New Testament*
JSNTSup Journal for the Study of the New Testament—Supplement Series
JSS *Journal of Semitic Studies*
JTS *Journal of Theological Studies*

LTQ *Lexington Theological Quarterly*

ModCh *Modern Churchman*

NTS *New Testament Studies*
NovT *Novum Testamentum*
NovTSup Novum Testamentum Supplemental Series

OBT *Overtures to Biblical Theology*

PRS *Perspectives in Religious Studies*
PSTJ *Perkins School of Theology Journal*

ReL *Religion in Life*
RevistB *Revista bíblica*
RevQ *Revue de Qumran*

SBFLA *Studii biblici franciscani liber annuus*
SBLASP *Society of Biblical Literature Abstracts and Seminar Papers*
SBLMS Society of Biblical Literature Monograph Series
SC Sources chrétiennes
SCnt *Second Century*
SD Studies and Documents
SE *Studia Evangelica*
SEcc *Sciences ecclésiastiques*
SNTS *Bulletin. Studiorum Novi Testamenti Societas*
SNTSMS Society for New Testament Studies Monograph Series

TBl *Theologische Blätter*
TGl *Theologie und Glaube*
TLZ *Theologische Literaturzeitung*
TQ *Theologische Quartalschrift*
TRu *Theologische Rundschau*
TToday *Theology Today*
TUMSR Trinity University Monograph Series in Religion
TynBul *Tyndale Bulletin*
TZ *Theologische Zeitschrift*

USQR *Union Seminary Quarterly Review*

WUNT Wissenschaftliche Untersuchungen zum Neuen Testament

ZNW *Zeitschrift für die neutestamentliche Wissenschaft*
ZSS *Zeitschrift der Savigny-Stiftung für Rechtsgeschichte*

WILLIAM REUBEN FARMER
A BIOGRAPHICAL
AND BIBLIOGRAPHICAL ESSAY

David B. Peabody

Professor W. R. Farmer embodies much of the best in good teaching. His enthusiasm for his discipline is catching. His receptivity to students, his eagerness to learn, and his willingness to allow students to pursue his research with him are some of his impressive qualities. These are not just my personal evaluations. Others, including many contributors to this volume, can testify that my experiences with him are not unique. Studying with him is an exciting enterprise.

William Reuben Farmer was born on 1 February 1921 in Needles, California, the son of William Reuben and Elsie Vaughn Farmer. His father, an employee of the railroad, was frequently away from home for long periods. Early in life Bill developed an independence of spirit that has characterized his subsequent scholarly work and sustained him through the controversies it has generated.

Bill Farmer was raised in the Methodist tradition and eventually became a United Methodist clergyman. He attended Polytechnic High School in Riverside, California from 1935-1938; and then, Occidental College in Los Angeles where he received his A.B. in Philosophy and Psychology in 1942. After graduation, he served in the United States Navy on a mine sweeper and, later, on a submarine as communications officer.

The post-war period took Farmer from the west coast of the United States to the east coast where he attended classes at Union Theological Seminary in New York during 1945. In January of 1946 he officially registered as a student in the B.D. program.

In one of Professor John Knox's summer school classes on the New Testament, Bill Farmer met Nell Cochran, a native Georgian, a Southern Baptist, and a graduate of Mercer University in Macon. These two dated and were married during the Thanksgiving holidays of 1946.

Following their marriage, Nell postponed a career of her own to raise the Farmer's four children; Richard Cochran, born 4 August 1948; William Vaughn, born 26 March 1951; Donald Guy, born 15 April 1955; and Rebecca Nell, born 26 July 1961. Now that the children are grown Nell is pursuing a second career in real estate.

Bill Farmer decided to spend his middler year of seminary, 1947-1948, at Cambridge University in England. After that first year, he decided to stay for a second in order to complete work for a Cambridge degree. He continued with his undergraduate interest in philosophy and received a B.A. degree, and later an M.A., in Philosophy of Religion and Christian Ethics. During these two years in England, Farmer first met David Daube, at that time, Regis Professor of Roman Law at Oxford, and C. F. D. Moule.[1]

Maccabees, Zealots, and Josephus

While at Cambridge, in a seminar on the Fourth Gospel with C. H. Dodd, Farmer was struck by the reference to the waving of palm branches by the crowd in John's version of Jesus' triumphal entry (John 12:13). Tracing the use of palm branches as royal symbols in antiquity, Farmer discovered that palm branches were waved by the Maccabees when they cleansed the temple of the pollutions of Antiochus IV, Epiphanes. There Farmer saw a "loose but significant parallel to Jesus' cleansing of the temple." As he read Josephus's works as the foundation documents for reconstructing Jewish history between the time of the Maccabees and that of the New Testament, Farmer came upon the idea he was to take back to New York as the basis for a doctoral dissertation. Nell affectionately refers to what followed in Bill's life as his period of "Maccabitis."

Farmer returned from England to New York City in 1949 where he entered the Th.D. program at Union. He studied with John Knox, Reinhold Niebuhr, Paul Tillich, and other distinguished members of the Union faculty at that time. Simultaneously, he continued his work for the B.D. from Union which he completed in 1950. His Th.D. was conferred two years later.

John Knox served as Farmer's *Doktorvater*. Since graduation, Farmer has twice been instrumental in highlighting Knox's scholarship. He co-edited and contributed to a *Festschrift* for Knox in 1967 and helped to plan a colloquy on New Testament Studies in honor of Knox in 1980. Farmer now has the distinctive honor of having a contribution from Knox in his own *Festschrift*.[2]

While pursuing his doctoral studies, Farmer was already publishing. His articles appeared in the *Union Seminary Quarterly Review* and the *Angli-*

---

[1]See David Daube, "Temple Tax," and C. F. D. Moule, "The Gravamen Against Jesus," in this volume.

[2]See John Knox, "Marcion's Gospel and the Synoptic Problem" in this volume.

can Theological Review.[3] In this period he also gave the scholarly world the first fruits of his research into the significance of "The Palm Branches in John 12:13."[4]

As a graduate student, Farmer was sometimes given the opportunity to entertain distinguished scholars. One such visitor was Rudolf Bultmann. As a professor himself, Farmer has continued this tradition of providing time for his students to meet with important, visiting, scholars from around the world. He also passes on to his students what he likes to call "scholarly lore." The story of how Joachim Jeremias came to write his book on the parables would be just one example.

In his doctoral dissertation, Farmer demonstrated the theretofore generally unrecognized relationship between the zeal that motivated the Maccabees during the Seleucid period and the zeal that motivated Josephus's Fourth Philosophical Sect during the later Roman period. In the published form of his dissertation, *Maccabees, Zealots, and Josephus,* Farmer concluded with a chapter on the relevance of his research to the new quest for the historical Jesus.[5] This interest in Jesus, his relevance for the contemporary world and for Christian theology, although sometimes unexpressed, continues through much of Farmer's subsequent work.

Before completing his doctoral studies, Farmer had served as visiting instructor at Emory University. But it was his view that pastoral experience was also important in making a seminary professor more effective. For that reason, following graduation in 1952, Farmer accepted a pastorate at Coatesville Methodist Church in Coatesville, Indiana. Later, in 1953, he also became a Visiting Instructor at nearby DePauw University in Greencastle, Indiana. That same year Farmer's reflections upon the arrival in Coatesville of the new Revised Standard Version of the Bible appeared in the *Union Seminary Quarterly Review.*[6]

In 1955, the Farmers moved from Indiana to Madison, New Jersey and Drew University. There Dr. Farmer served as Assistant Professor from

---

[3]"Christianity, Communism and War," *USQR* 5 (1950): 25-31; "The Patriarch Phineas: A Note on 'It was Reckoned to Him as Righteousness' [Gen. 15:6]," *ATR* 34 (1952): 26-50.

[4]"The Palm Branches in John 12:13," *JTS* 3 (1952): 62-66.

[5]*Maccabees, Zealots and Josephus: An Inquiry into Jewish Nationalism in the Greco-Roman Period* (New York: Columbia University Press, 1956; reprint edition, Westport CT: Greenwood Press, 1973). Farmer dedicates this volume "To C. H. Dodd and members of his New Testament Seminar, Cambridge, 1948-1949."

[6]"The RSV Arrives in Coatesville," *USQR* 8 (1953): 16-20.

1955-1959. He spent some of the summers of those years working as an archaeologist in Israel. From 1956-1958, Farmer helped with the excavations at Shechem. He studied the economic basis of the recently discovered Qumran community and did soundings at Khirbet Wadi Ez-Zaraniq. While visiting Israel with him in 1984, he recounted his story of Ezekiel's river of life for some of us as we stood in the ruins of the Qumran monastery. His story was as engaging as it was educational.[7]

While at Drew, Professor Farmer also chaired George Wesley Buchanan's dissertation committee. Buchanan wrote on "The Eschatological Expectations of the Qumran Community." He then became a postdoctoral research student at Hebrew Union College for three years, studying Mishnaic and modern Hebrew. Farmer and Buchanan worked together in making topographical studies of Herodion sites, at Shechem and at Wadi Ez-Zaraniq. Two of Buchanan's books, *The Consequences of the Covenant* and *Revelation and Redemption* are fruits of his early study of Jewish history and eschatology at Drew and his subsequent study at Hebrew Union College.[8]

The Synoptic Problem: A Critical Analysis

It was during his years at Drew that Professor Farmer first began to question the tradition he had received about the sequence and interrelationships among the gospels. During a visit to Germany in the summer of 1958, while in the office of Joachim Jeremias, Farmer happened upon a copy of the *Festschrift* for R. H. Lightfoot in which Austin Farrer's essay, "On Dispensing With Q," appears.[9] He did not have sufficient time to read the entire essay while Professor Jeremias excused himself for a brief ab-

---

[7]See "The Economic Basis of the Qumran Community," *TZ* 11 (1955): 295-308; "A Postscript to 'The Economic Basis of the Qumran Community,' " *TZ* 12 (1956): 56-58; "Soundings at Khirbet Wadi Ez-Zaraniq," *BASOR* 147 (1957): 34-36; "The Geography of Ezekiel's River of Life," *BA* 19 (1956): 17-22, reprinted in *Biblical Archaeologist Reader* (Garden City NY: Doubleday, 1961): 284-89.

[8]George Wesley Buchanan, *The Consequences of Covenant, NovTSup* 20 (Leiden: Brill, 1970); *Revelation and Redemption: Jewish Documents of Deliverance* (Greensboro NC: Western North Carolina Press, 1978; distributed by Mercer University Press). See also *To The Hebrews*, AB 36 (Garden City NY: Doubleday, 1972). See also n. 25 below.

[9]A. M. Farrer, "On Dispensing with Q," in *Studies in the Gospels: Essays in Memory of R. H. Lightfoot,* ed. D. E. Nineham (Oxford: Blackwell, 1955) 55-88; reprinted in *The Two-Source Hypothesis: A Critical Appraisal* ed. Arthur J. Bellinzoni, Jr. (Macon GA: Mercer University Press, 1985) 321-56.

sence from his office, but he put it on his agenda for the immediate future. He also resolved to work through Luke on the assumption that he had used Matthew as a way of testing the necessity of the "Q" hypothesis. Having completed the latter project, he concluded that "Q" was not necessary to explain the literary phenomena shared by Matthew and Luke. This discovery did not immediately lead to an additional questioning of Markan priority, however.

During the subsequent academic year at Drew, 1958-1959, Dr. Farmer set out to test the "Q" hypothesis more fully in his Graduate Seminar on the Synoptic Problem. One of the important products of that seminar was a collection of "The Agreements of Matthew and Luke Against Mark in the Triple Tradition" prepared by one of Farmer's students, Finley M. Keech. This was the most complete collection of these literary phenomena prior to the publication of Frans Neirynck's *The Minor Agreements of Matthew and Luke Against Mark with a Cumulative List.*[10] It provided Professor Farmer in 1959 with a comprehensive knowledge of some of the most important literary data which are anomalous for Markan priority, the so-called minor agreements of Matthew and Luke against Mark.

During that same graduate seminar of 1958-1959, one of Farmer's other students suggested that he read the work of B. C. Butler on *The Originality of St. Matthew: A Critique of the Two-Document Hypothesis.*[11] To comprehend Butler, Farmer found it necessary also to read the work of C. F. Burney whose work Butler had utilized.[12] Prior to reading Butler, Farmer had been prone to dismiss it as the prejudiced work of a Roman Catholic. But reading the book, Farmer discovered his own prejudice and has since built upon the work of both Butler and Burney.[13] Having previously been

---

[10]Frans Neirynck, *The Minor Agreements of Matthew and Luke Against Mark with a Cumulative List, BETL* 37 (Leuven: Leuven University Press, 1974). Neirynck utilized the work of Keech in composing his own.

[11]B. C. Butler, *The Originality of St. Matthew: A Critique of the Two-Document Hypothesis* (Cambridge: Cambridge University Press, 1951). Excerpts from this work by Butler may be found in Bellinzoni, *The Two-Source Hypothesis,* 133-42; other work by Butler is found in this same volume, 97-118.

[12]C. F. Burney, *The Poetry of Our Lord: An Examination of the Formal Elements of Hebrew Poetry in the Discourses of Jesus Christ* (Oxford: Oxford University Press, 1925).

[13]See, e.g., the relevant pages in Farmer, *The Synoptic Problem* and "Certain Results Reached by Sir John C. Hawkins and C. F. Burney Which Make More Sense if Luke Knew Matthew and Mark Knew Matthew and Luke," in *Synoptic Studies: The Ampleforth Conferences of 1982 and 1983,* ed. C. M. Tuckett, *JSNTSup* 7 (1984): 75-98.

caused to doubt the existence of "Q," the reading of Butler and Burney occasioned Farmer's first doubts about Markan priority.

Prior to the fall semester of 1959, the Farmer family moved again, this time from New Jersey to Dallas, Texas and to the Perkins School of Theology of Southern Methodist University. During Farmer's early years at Perkins, he provided a preface for an English translation of Josephus' *Jewish Wars*. He wrote an article on "Herod the Great" for the *Encyclopedia Americana* of 1962 and the editors of the original four volumes of *The Interpreter's Dictionary of the Bible* solicited articles by Farmer on the "Essenes," "John the Baptist," the "Pre-Existence of Souls," and the "Zealots." When the *IDB* was updated in 1976, Farmer was again called upon to contribute; this time, articles on "Abba," "Chreia," and the "Teaching of Jesus."[14]

It is sometimes thought that Professor Farmer brought the Synoptic Problem to the S.M.U. campus. In fact, however, Farmer's predecessor at Perkins, Edward C. Hobbs, had already suggested to Perkins students that "Q" was unnecessary prior to Bill Farmer's arrival.[15]

As he had done at Drew, now at Perkins, Bill Farmer continued with a vigorous research agenda. Rather than focusing on the archaeology of Palestine as he had done between 1955 and 1959, from 1960 to 1963 Farmer studied the history of the development of the Markan hypothesis. An early report on this research came in the form of a paper read at the Chicago Society of Biblical Research in 1961.[16] A more fully developed review of this research subsequently appeared in the first five chapters of Professor Farmer's second monograph, *The Synoptic Problem: A Critical Analysis*.[17]

---

[14]"Josephus and the Axial Age of History," in *The Great Roman-Jewish War* (New York: Harper Torchbooks, 1960); "Herod the Great," in *The Encyclopedia Americana*, 14:137; George Arthur Buttrick, et al., eds., *The Interpreter's Dictionary of the Bible*, 4 vols. (Nashville: Abingdon Press, 1962), "Essenes," 2:143-49; "John the Baptist," 2:955-62; "Pre-Existence of Souls," 3:869-70; "Zealot," 4:936-39; Keith Crim, et al., eds., *The Interpreter's Dictionary of the Bible, Supplementary Volume* (Nashville: Abingdon, 1976); "Abba," 3; "Chreia," 145-46; "Teaching of Jesus," 863-68.

[15]Edward C. Hobbs, "A Quarter-Century Without 'Q,'" *PSTJ* 33 (1980): 10-19.

[16]"A 'Skeleton in the Closet' of Gospel Research," *BR* 6 (1961): 18-42.

[17]*The Synoptic Problem: A Critical Analysis* (New York: Macmillan, 1964). Farmer dedicated this volume to "John Knox, teacher and friend"; excerpts are found in Bellinzoni, *Two-Source Hypothesis*, 163-97.

As was characteristic of his teaching then as now, Bill Farmer invited his students to join him on the front lines of scholarship, to consider carefully the primary data of New Testament study, and to come to their own conclusions based upon their evaluations of that data.

One of the seminarians that Professor Farmer encountered during his early years at Perkins was a young man by the name of E. P. Sanders, now Dean Ireland's Professor of Exegesis of Holy Scripture at the University of Oxford and editor of the present volume. Professor Farmer introduced Ed Sanders to the mysteries of the Synoptic Problem and utilized him as a research assistant during the summer of 1961. Sanders' statistical studies of vocabulary shared by Matthew and Mark confirmed what Professor Farmer had come to believe by 1961, namely, that Matthew was prior to and a source for Mark. The evidence provided by Sanders's studies of the vocabulary common to Mark and Luke, in balance, suggested that Luke also was prior to and a source for Mark. But since this evidence didn't weigh heavily in one direction, it didn't make the impression on Farmer that Sanders's studies comparing Mark with Matthew had made upon him.[18]

The following summer of 1962, with assistance from seminarians Glenn Chesnut, Bryan Forrester, Milo Thornberry, and Yves Dubois, Farmer prepared a polychrome *Synopticon* which presented the evidence of verbal agreements and similarities among the Synoptics without altering the order or context of the material in any one of the gospels. This tool was fundamental for preparing the argument of chapter 7 of *The Synoptic Problem,* "Notes for a History of the Redaction of Synoptic Tradition in Mark." The *Synopticon* itself, however, was not published until 1969, five years after *The Synoptic Problem* appeared.[19]

Another seminary student whom Farmer encountered during the early 1960s at Perkins was Philip L. Shuler, now Professor of Religion at McMurry College in Abilene, Texas. Under Farmer's guidance, Shuler first began to work on the question of the genre of the gospels. This area of New

---

[18]A study of the vocabulary shared by Matthew and Mark similar to the work carried out by Sanders can now be found in C. S. Mann, *Mark,* AB 27 (Garden City NY: Doubleday, 1986) 165-68.

[19]*Synopticon: The Verbal Agreement Between the Greek Texts of Matthew, Mark and Luke Contextually Exhibited* (Cambridge: Cambridge University Press, 1969). In dedicating this volume Farmer writes, "To the memory of my father, William Reuben Farmer, Sr., 1889-1969."

Testament study has provided a focus for much of Shuler's subsequent work.[20]

Other students in the early 1960s like Charles Reynolds, Glenn Chesnut and Tim Russell produced visual aids that are still utilized at Perkins to examine the phenomena of order of pericopes among the Synoptic gospels and the redactional characteristics of the gospel of Matthew. Anyone who has worked with Farmer for any amount of time has studied "the football" chart of Matthean redaction, so named because of its design.

Still other students from that period like Moneta Storey Speaker and Bryan Forrester were guided by Farmer through studies of the *chreiai* in antiquity while C. David Hogsett, Yoshihiro Sakaguchi, and Lee Cary collected and worked with English translations of more than 300 rabbinic parables.

When Ed Sanders graduated from Perkins School of Theology he continued his theological education at Union Theological Seminary. There he pursued a Ph.D. in New Testament with W. D. Davies and studied with Louis Martyn and Professor Farmer's own *Doktorvater,* John Knox.

Farmer also worked out a year's study abroad for Ed Sanders. He directed him to David Daube at Oxford whom Farmer had first met in C. H. Dodd's seminar at Cambridge. Ed was to establish competence in working with rabbinic texts with Daube. He was also directed to Joachim Jeremias at Göttingen and to the study of Hebrew in Israel as well as topographical study of Palestine.

From Dallas and Bill Farmer via Ed Sanders, new interest in the Synoptic Problem traveled to New York and back to Farmer's *alma mater,* Union Theological Seminary. There Farmer's work informed the authors of three doctoral dissertations which have helped to advance the contemporary discussion of the Synoptic Problem. The first, of course, was Ed Sanders's own work, completed in 1966, *The Tendencies of the Synoptic*

---

[20]See n. 27 below.

Philip L. Shuler, "The Genre of the Gospels and the Two Gospel Hypothesis," in this volume. See also *A Genre for the Gospels: The Biographical Character of Matthew* (Philadelphia: Fortress Press, 1982) which is a revised and abbreviated version of a doctoral dissertation supervised by E. P. Sanders at McMaster University in Hamilton, Ontario, Canada; "The Griesbach Hypothesis and Gospel Genre," *PSTJ* 33:4 (Summer 1980): 41-49; "Genre Criticism and the Synoptic Problem," in Farmer, *New Synoptic Studies,* 467-80. Phil Shuler studied with Professor Farmer while he was a B.D. student at Perkins School of Theology. In 1964, Shuler completed his first manuscript relating to the question of the genre of the gospels, "Encomium Characteristics in Plutarch and the Gospels."

Tradition, where he examined the adequacy of previously accepted canons of criticism for distinguishing early and late traditions within the gospels.[21]

The second and third dissertations were produced by two of Sanders's younger peers in the Union Ph.D. program. In 1971, O. Lamar Cope completed *Matthew: A Scribe Trained for the Kingdom of Heaven* and two years later Thomas R. W. Longstaff completed *Evidence of Conflation in Mark? A Study in the Synoptic Problem.*[22] Cope argued for the priority of Matthew in selected pericopes based upon evidence derived from a redaction-critical analysis of the gospels while Longstaff explored the characteristics of conflation in known examples and then examined the gospel of Mark for evidence of these characteristics. The import of Farmer's work for the authors of these three dissertations is made explicit in every case.

In October of 1971 Ed Sanders and Lamar Cope joined Bill Farmer around the table in the Seminar on Mark at the annual meeting of the Society of Biblical Literature in Atlanta, Georgia. These three were prepared to debate the Synoptic Problem with Helmut Koester and others in that seminar who were advocating the two-document hypothesis. Farmer produced a relatively brief methodological essay entitled, "Redaction Criticism and the Synoptic Problem," while Koester prepared an 85-page exegesis paper entitled, "A Test Case of Synoptic Source Theory (Mark

---

[21]E. P. Sanders, *The Tendencies of the Synoptic Tradition,* SNTSMS 9 (Cambridge: Cambridge University Press, 1969), excerpts in Bellinzoni, *The Two-Source Hypothesis,* 199-203; "The Argument from Order and the Relationship Between Matthew and Luke," *NTS* 15 (1968-1969): 249-61, reprinted in Bellinzoni, *The Two-Source Hypothesis,* 409-25. Also see "Jesus and the Kingdom: The Restoration of Israel and the New People of God" in this volume.

[22]O. Lamar Cope, *Matthew: A Scribe Trained for the Kingdom of Heaven,* CBQMS 5 (Washington DC: Catholic Biblical Association of America, 1976); see also "The Argument Revolves: The Pivotal Evidence of Markan Priority is Reversing Itself" in *New Synoptic Studies* ed. W. R. Farmer (Macon GA: Mercer University Press, 1983) 143-59. See "The Earliest Gospel Was the 'Signs Gospel'," in this volume.

T. R. W. Longstaff, *Evidence of Conflation in Mark? A Study in the Synoptic Problem,* SBLDS 28 (Missoula MT: Scholars Press, 1977); see also "Crisis and Christology: The Theology of Mark," in Farmer, *New Synoptic Studies,* 373-92; Bernard Orchard and Thomas R. W. Longstaff, *J. J. Griesbach: Synoptic and Text-Critical Studies, 1776-1976,* SNTSMS 34 (Cambridge: Cambridge University Press, 1978) esp. "Preface," xi-xv, and "At the Colloquium's Conclusion," 170-75; Thomas R. W. Longstaff and Joseph B. Tyson, *Synoptic Abstract* (Wooster OH: Biblical Research Associates, 1978).

4:1-34 and parallels)."[23] Sanders wrote on "Mark 10:17-31" and Cope produced a paper on, "The Beelzebul Controversy, Mk. 3:19-30 and Parallels: A Model Problem in Source Analysis."[24] Farmer's analysis of Matthew 13 and parallels led him to the conclusion that the Griesbach hypothesis most adequately explained the literary data within the Synoptic gospels while Koester concluded that the two-document hypothesis more adequately explained it. Cope's work tended to support the priority of Matthew to Mark within the pericope he had chosen while the evidence considered by Sanders would not, in his judgment, support the immediate priority of any one of the Synoptic gospels to any other. The papers by Sanders and Cope were never mentioned during the seminar discussion and the debate between Farmer and Koester advanced the discussion only in limited ways. At that same annual meeting, Charles Talbert and Edgar McKnight debated the Griesbach hypothesis with George Buchanan.[25]

This 1971 annual meeting of the Society of Biblical Literature marked a turning point in the discussion of the Synoptic Problem. Prior to and during this meeting, Farmer's proposal to reopen the discussion of the Synoptic Problem frequently met with hostility. After that meeting, collegiality among experts on the Synoptic Problem increased and a greater tolerance toward a variety of solutions has characterized the subsequent discussion.

Seminars, Festivals, Colloquia, and Conferences

The period following the publication of *The Synoptic Problem* in 1964 can be characterized as a period when Professor Farmer began to promote scholarly collegiality and important conferences on the gospels.

In 1966, in conjunction with Professor Albert C. Outler, Farmer helped to bring into being a post-doctoral research Seminar on the Development of Catholic Christianity. One of the purposes of that seminar was to affirm a unity in the study of early Christianity which had been lost in the wake of the information explosion of the twentieth century and increased specialization which came with it. New Testament scholars, early Church his-

---

[23]W. R. Farmer, "Redaction Criticism and the Synoptic Problem," *SBLASP*, 2 vols. (1971) 1:239-50; Helmut Koester's paper was not published in the seminar papers but was circulated when the seminar met for its closing session.

[24]E. P. Sanders, "Mark 10.17-31 and Parallels," *SBLASP*, 2 vols. (1971): 1:257-70; Lamar Cope, "The Beelzebul Controversy, Mk. 3:19-30 and Parallels: A Model Problem in Source Analysis," *SBLASP*, 2 vols. (1971): 1:251-56.

[25]Charles H. Talbert and Edgar V. McKnight, "Can the Griesbach Hypothesis Be Falsified?" *JBL* 91 (1972): 338-68; George W. Buchanan, "Has the Griesbach Hypothesis Been Falsified?" *JBL* 93 (1974): 550-72. Cf. n. 8 above.

torians, theologians, and philosophers were brought together to work on "an intelligible field of inquiry" which was too broad for any single scholar to handle adequately in detail. That seminar has continued to meet at least four times a year since its inception and continues to promote interdisciplinary and ecumenical scholarly activity in the Southwest at the time of this writing.[26]

Already during his years at Drew, in cooperation with Morton Smith, Farmer had helped to organize the Columbia University New Testament Seminar which provided the immediate model for the Southwest Seminar. But this and other cooperative seminars which Farmer has helped to bring into being took C. H. Dodd's New Testament Seminar at Cambridge as their originating model.

During the mid-1970s, Professor Farmer inaugurated and chaired the Southwest Seminar on Gospel Studies which included the graduate students in New Testament at S.M.U. at that time and a number of Professors of New Testament and Early Christianity from throughout the Southwest.[27]

Professor Farmer has also been instrumental in seeing that several major, international and ecumenical conferences on New Testament issues were carefully planned and brought to successful completion. The volumes which have come out of these conferences have been some of the most important, recent contributions to the advancement of gospel studies.

---

[26]See the "Introductory Statement" by W. R. Farmer and Albert C. Outler to *The Development of Catholic Christianity: Four Methodological Papers by Albert C. Outler, David L. Balas, Georges Florovsky, Frederick J. Streng*, reprinted from *ATR* 50 (October 1968).

[27]Members of the Southwest Seminar on Gospel Studies who have contributed essays to this volume include David B. Peabody, Philip L. Shuler, Joseph B. Tyson, William O. Walker, and Wendell Willis. Others who participated in the seminar on a regular basis included J. G. F. Collison and Dennis Gordon Tevis.

J. G. F. Collison, "Linguistic Usages in the Gospel of Luke" (Ph.D. diss., supervised by W. R. Farmer, Southern Methodist University, 1977); "Linguistic Usages in the Gospel of Luke," in Farmer, *New Synoptic Studies*, 245-60, "Eschatology in the Gospel of Luke," in Farmer, *New Synoptic Studies*, 363-71.

Dennis Gordon Tevis, "An Analysis of Words and Phrases Characteristic of the Gospel of Matthew" (Ph.D. diss., supervised by W. R. Farmer, Southern Methodist University, 1983).

Wendell Willis, "An Irenic View of Christian Origins: Theological Continuity from Jesus to Paul in W. R. Farmer's Writings" in this volume. See also *Idol Meat in Corinth*, SBLDS 68 (Chico CA: Scholars Press, 1985).

These conferences would include the Festival on the Gospels held at Pittsburgh Theological Seminary in Pittsburgh, Pennsylvania in 1970.[28] This conference celebrated the gospels from a wide range of perspectives. It was at this conference that David L. Dungan first came to international attention as a formidable opponent of the two-document hypothesis and an advocate of the neo-Griesbach hypothesis as outlined by Farmer.[29]

After 1970, Dom John Bernard Orchard joined the ranks of those publicly advocating the neo-Griesbach hypothesis. With Professors Farmer and K. H. Rengstorf in consultation with others, he helped to plan the next major conference on the gospels.[30] The Johann Jakob Griesbach Bicentenary

---

[28]David G. Buttrick, et al., eds., *Jesus and Man's Hope*, A Perspective Book, 2 vols. (Pittsburgh PA: Pittsburgh Theological Seminary, 1970).

[29]See David L. Dungan, "Jesus and Violence" in this volume; "Mark—The Abridgement of Matthew and Luke," in Buttrick, *Jesus and Man's Hope*, 1:51-97; excerpts from this article are reprinted in Bellinzoni, *The Two-Source Hypothesis*, 143-61, 427-33. Dungan became acquainted with the work of W. R. Farmer in the early 1960s through his *Doktorvater* at Harvard, Krister Stendahl, and through Glenn Chesnut and Charles Reynolds who had studied with Farmer. The published form of Dungan's doctoral dissertation (*The Sayings of Jesus in the Churches of Paul: The Use of the Synoptic Tradition in the Regulation of Early Church Life* [Oxford: Basil Blackwell, 1971]) takes account of Farmer's work and, there, Dungan concurred with Farmer in viewing Matthew's versions of the Missionary Discourse and the Sayings on Divorce as the more original forms of those traditions. Also see "Reactionary Trends in the Gospel-Producing Activity of the Early Church," in *L'evangile selon Marc: Tradition et redaction,*. ed. M. Sabbé, BETL 34 (Leuven: Leuven University Press, 1974) 179-202; "The Purpose and Provenance of the Gospel of Mark according to the 'Two Gospel' (Griesbach) Hypothesis," in Corley, *Colloquy*, 133-56, reprinted in a revised form in Farmer, *New Synoptic Studies*, 411-40. Also see n. 46 below.

[30]See J. B. Orchard, "Some Reflections on the Relationship of Luke to Matthew" in this volume. See also *Matthew, Luke & Mark*, vol. 1 of *The Griesbach Solution to the Synoptic Question* (Manchester, Koinonia Press, 1976); "Are All Gospel Synopses Biased?" *TZ* 34 (1978): 149-62; "The Making of a Synopsis," in *Wort in der Zeit: Festgabe für K. H. Rengstorf* (Leiden: E. J. Brill, 1980); "The Two-Gospel Hypothesis," *DR* 98 (October, 1980): 267-79; *A Synopsis of the Four Gospels: A New Translation Arranged according to the Two-Gospel Hypothesis* (Macon GA: Mercer University Press, 1982); *A Synopsis of the Four Gospels in Greek* (Macon GA: Mercer University Press; Edinburgh: T. & T. Clark, 1983); "The 'Common Step' Phenomenon in the Synoptic Pericopes," in Farmer, *New Synoptic Studies*, 393-407.

Colloquium was held in Münster, West Germany in 1976.[31] The conference focused upon the work of Griesbach, both as a Synoptic source critic and as a New Testament text critic. Among the papers produced for this conference was Bernard Orchard's English translation of Griesbach's "Demonstration that Mark was written after Matthew and Luke."

The Colloquy on the Relationships among the Gospels followed at Trinity University in San Antonio, Texas in 1977.[32] Farmer served on the planning committee, working closely with its key organizers, Professors Joseph B. Tyson of S.M.U. and William O. Walker of Trinity. At that time, scholars of oral traditional literature, classics, Judaica, and literary criticism were invited to share insights from their disciplines with New Testament scholars in cognate fields. Professor Farmer responded to a major paper in the "Seminar on Literary Criticism and the Gospel," which had been prepared by Roland Mushat Frye, a Shakespearean scholar from the University of Pennsylvania who had previously participated in the Pittsburgh Festival in 1970.[33]

Also in 1977, the Synoptic Problem was reopened in the German literature with the publication of Hans-Herbert Stoldt's book, *Geschichte und Kritik der Markus-hypothese.* Farmer arranged for this book to be translated into English and sponsored a Griesbach Festival at S.M.U. in 1978. At that time the Griesbachiana collected for the Münster meeting were brought to Dallas for display and Stoldt was presented the manuscript of the English translation of his book.[34] A few days later, Stoldt participated in a panel discussion in the 1978 national meeting of the Society of Biblical Literature convened in New Orleans, Louisiana. During the panel

---

[31]Orchard and Longstaff, eds., *J. J. Griesbach: Synoptic and Text-Critical Studies, 1776-1976.*

[32]William O. Walker, Jr., ed., *The Relationships Among the Gospels: An Interdisciplinary Dialogue,* TUMSR 5 (San Antonio TX: Trinity University Press, 1978). Members of the Steering Committee for this conference included Paul J. Achtemeier; William R. Farmer; Joseph A. Fitzmyer, S. J.; Reginald H. Fuller; Leander E. Keck; Joseph B. Tyson; and William O. Walker.

[33]Roland Mushat Frye, "The Synoptic Problems and Analogies in Other Literatures," in Walker, *Relationships,* 261-302; compare Roland Mushat Frye, "A Literary Perspective for the Criticism of the Gospels" in Buttrick, *Jesus and Man's Hope,* 2:193-221; W. R. Farmer, "Basic Affirmation with Some Demurrals: A Response to Roland Mushat Frye," in Walker, *Relationships,* 303-22.

[34]Hans-Herbert Stoldt, *Geschichte und Kritik der Markushypothese* (Göttingen: Vandenhoeck & Ruprecht, 1977) trans. Donald L. Niewyk, *History and Criticism of the Marcan Hypothesis* (Macon GA: Mercer University Press, 1980).

discussion, David Dungan debated the import of Stoldt's book with Howard Kee.

After participating for some years in the Consultation on the Relationships among the Gospels within the Society of Biblical Literature and as an immediate result of the debate between Kee and Dungan, Arthur J. Bellinzoni suggested that there was a need for a single volume which would bring together some of the classical and seminal essays in favor of and in opposition to Markan priority and in favor of and in opposition to the "Q" hypothesis. In 1985 such a volume appeared. It was edited by Bellinzoni himself with assistance from Joseph B. Tyson and William O. Walker.[35]

Then came the Cambridge Gospel Conference held at Pembroke College, Cambridge, England in 1979.[36] Like the Münster conference, this conference focused upon the Owen-Griesbach hypothesis. Professor Farmer reviewed the Patristic evidence relating to the gospels. Papers challenging Markan priority and advocating the Griesbach hypothesis were presented and some scholars attempted to describe the theology of the several Evan-

---

[35]See n. 9 above and n. 45 below.

Joseph B. Tyson, "Scripture, Torah, and Sabbath in Luke-Acts," in this volume. See also "Conflict as a Literary Theme in the Gospel of Luke" in Farmer, *New Synoptic Studies*, 303-27; "Sequential Parallelism in the Synoptic Gospels," *NTS* 22 (1976): 276-308 which was developed in the Southwest Seminar on Gospel Studies; "Literary Criticism and the Gospels: The Seminar" in *The Relationships among the Gospels: An Interdisciplinary Dialogue*, TUMSR 5, ed. William O. Walker (San Antonio TX: Trinity University Press, 1978) 323-41; Joseph B. Tyson and Thomas R. W. Longstaff, *Synoptic Abstract* (Wooster OH: Biblical Research Associates, 1978); *A Study of Early Christianity* (New York: Macmillan Publishing Co., 1973); *The New Testament and Early Christianity* (New York: Macmillan Publishing Co., 1984); "The Two-Source Hypothesis: A Critical Appraisal," in Bellinzoni, *The Two-Source Hypothesis*, 437-52.

William O. Walker, "'Nazareth': A Clue to Synoptic Relationships?" in this volume. See also "A Method for Identifying Redactional Passages in Matthew on Functional and Linguistic Grounds," *CBQ* 39 (1977): 76-93 which developed during the Southwest Seminar on Gospel Studies: W. O. Walker, ed., *The Relationships among the Gospels: An Interdisciplinary Dialogue*, TUMSR 5 (San Antonio TX: Trinity University Press, 1978) esp. "Introduction: The Colloquy on the Relationships among the Gospels," 1-15; "The Son of Man: Some Recent Developments," *CBQ* 45:4 (October 1983): 584-607; "The Son of Man Question and the Synoptic Problem," *NTS* 28:3 (July 1982): 374-88. The previous two entries are reprinted as a single article in Farmer, *New Synoptic Studies*, 261-301.

[36]William R. Farmer, ed., *New Synoptic Studies* (Macon GA: Mercer University Press, 1983).

gelists from the perspective of the Griesbach hypothesis. Professor Farmer's own review of scholarly developments through the conferences at Pittsburgh, Münster, San Antonio, and Cambridge can be found in his preface to *New Synoptic Studies.*[37]

In 1980 the Colloquy on New Testament Studies was held at Southwestern Baptist Theological Seminary in Fort Worth, Texas.[38] The colloquy celebrated the eightieth birthday of John Knox and included a plenary address by Ed Sanders and three working seminars; one on the Synoptic Problem, one on the genre of the gospels, and one on Pauline chronology. Helmut Koester prepared the major paper for the seminar on the Synoptic Problem. He maintained Markan priority but concluded that canonical Mark was written after Matthew and Luke. David Peabody responded from a Griesbach perspective and Professor Farmer chaired the meeting of that seminar. This conference also marked a first attempt at serious, scholarly, dialogue between conservative, Evangelical scholars and their more liberal colleagues.

The Ampleforth Conference on the gospels held at Ampleforth Abbey in England in 1983 provided Professor Farmer with an opportunity to dialogue with some British scholars who had already dispensed with "Q," following the lead of their British colleague, Austin Farrer. He then went on to suggest that approaching the gospels from a "post-Farrer" standpoint meant dispensing with Markan priority as well as with "Q." Important issues relating to the linguistic argument for solving the Synoptic problem were also highlighted at Ampleforth in the debate between Farmer and Michael Goulder.[39]

The most recent, major conference on the gospels was the *symposium de interrelatione evangeliorum* held in Jerusalem, Israel, in 1984.[40] There, scholars representing three of the currently most popular source hypotheses met to debate the Synoptic Problem for two weeks. Professor Farmer led a team advocating the Two-Gospel Hypothesis; Frans Nei-

---

[37]Farmer, *New Synoptic Studies,* vii-xxiii.

[38]Bruce C. Corley, ed., *Colloquy on New Testament Studies: A Time for Reappraisal and Fresh Approaches* (Macon GA: Mercer University Press, 1983).

[39]C. M. Tuckett, ed., *Synoptic Studies: The Ampleforth Conferences of 1982 and 1983,* JSNTSup 7 (Sheffield, England: JSOT Press, 1984).

[40]The proceedings of the Jerusalem Conference are forthcoming from Mercer University Press of Macon, Georgia and Peeters Press of Leuven, Belgium. Some reflections on this conference will be found in the April 1987 issue of the *Perkins School of Theology Journal.*

rynck, a team advocating Markan priority; and M. E. Boismard, a team advocating Multiple Stage hypotheses. Each of the three teams of scholars produced two major papers. The first was an overview of a source theory and the second, an analysis of a pericope from the perspective of that source hypothesis. In addition, each team provided written responses to all the papers produced by the other two teams. Three to five scholars composed each of the three teams and another fifteen scholars analyzed the debate and contributed other types of papers relating to gospel study. Those who participated in that conference who have also contributed to this *Festschrift* include David Daube, David L. Dungan, Birger Gerhardsson, Ben F. Meyer, J. Bernard Orchard, David B. Peabody, Bo Reicke and Philip L. Shuler.[41] Further conferences of similar scope are already in the planning stages.

In addition to David Daube, C. F. D. Moule, Joachim Jeremias and Bernard Orchard, other European scholars with whom Farmer has enjoyed close personal and professional contact include Birger Gerhardsson and Bo Reicke. Farmer and Ben F. Meyer formed a lasting friendship while working with Joachim Jeremias during their concurrent sabbatical leaves in Göttingen, 1964-1965. Pierson Parker who has also contributed to this volume was challenging the priority of canonical Mark already in 1953. He has been a close friend of Professor Farmer for many years. These two hold each other's work on the Synoptic Problem in high regard.[42]

In 1983, Professor Farmer, along with Joseph B. Tyson and others on the faculties of S.M.U. and the University of Dallas, brought into being

---

[41]For Ben Meyer, see "The World Mission and the Emergent Realization of Christian Identity" in this volume. Also see *The Aims of Jesus* (London: SCM Press, 1979). For Birger Gerhardsson, see "Agape and Imitation of Christ" in this volume and *Memory and Manuscript: Oral Tradition and Written Transmission in Rabbinic Judaism and Early Christianity,* 2nd ed. (Uppsala/Lund: C. W. K. Gleerup, 1964). Further bibliography for Gerhardsson may be found in his book, *The Origins of the Gospel Traditions* (Philadelphia: Fortress Press, 1979) 93-94. For Bo Reicke, see n. 44 below. Further bibliographical references to works by Bo Reicke may be found in *The New Testament Age: Essays in Honor of Bo Reicke,* ed. William C. Weinrich (Macon GA: Mercer University Press, 1985). Works by others in this list are discussed elsewhere in this essay.

[42]Pierson Parker, *The Gospel Before Mark* (Chicago: University of Chicago Press, 1953); "The Authorship of the Second Gospel," *PRS* 5 (1978): 4-9; "A Second Look at *The Gospel Before Mark,*" *JBL* 100 (1981): 395-405 also printed in *SBLASP* (1979) 1:151-61. Excerpts from this work appear in Bellinzoni, *Two-Source Hypothesis,* 205-17; "The Posteriority of Mark" in Farmer, *New Synoptic Studies,* 67-142; also see "Herod Antipas and the Death of Jesus" in this volume.

the Center for the Study of Religion in the Greco-Roman World. Under its auspices, several recent conferences on the gospels and a major, international colloquy on Paul have been held at S.M.U.

More recent, smaller conferences which have resulted, at least in part, from Professor Farmer's efforts would include those held at S.M.U. during the fall semesters of 1984, 1985, and 1986. The first of these addressed the topic of "Order in the Synoptic Gospels: Patterns of Agreement within Pericopes" and featured the work of T. R. W. Longstaff of Colby College in Waterville, Maine on conflation in Mark.[43] The second conference addressed the topic of "Nineteenth Century Gospel Criticism" and featured the work of Bo Reicke of the University of Basel, Switzerland and that of David Peabody.[44] The third addressed the topic of "New Critical Approaches in Synoptic Studies" featuring the work of John Drury of King's College, Cambridge; Joseph B. Tyson of S.M.U. and reviews of volumes edited by Bruce C. Corley, W. R. Farmer, and Arthur J. Bellinzoni.[45]

---

[43]See n. 22 above.

[44]Bo Reicke's paper was entitled "From Strauß to Holtzmann and Meijboom: Synoptic Theories Advanced During the Consolidation of Germany, 1830-1870"; see also "A Test of Synoptic Relationships: Matthew 10:17-23 and 24:9-14 with Parallels," in Farmer, *New Synoptic Studies*, 209-29; and "The Historical Setting of John's Baptism" in this volume. David Peabody's contribution to that conference was the essay included in this volume, "Chapters in the History of the Linguistic Argument for Solving the Synoptic Problem: The Nineteenth Century in Context." See also "A Pre-Markan Prophetic Sayings Tradition and the Synoptic Problem," *JBL* 97:3 (1978): 391-409. This paper came out of the Southwest Seminar on Gospel Studies. "Augustine and the Augustinian Hypothesis: A Reexamination of Augustine's Thought in *De consensu evangelistarum*," in Farmer, *New Synoptic Studies*, 37-64. This paper had its genesis in reading the papers from the Münster Griesbach Conference of 1976; "The Late Secondary Redaction of Mark's Gospel and the Griesbach Hypothesis: A Response to Helmut Koester," in Corley, *Colloquy*, 87-132, a response invited by W. R. Farmer; *Mark as Composer*, New Gospel Studies 1 (Macon GA: Mercer University Press, 1987). This last entry is a revision of a doctoral dissertation that was completed at S.M.U. in 1983 and supervised by W. R. Farmer.

[45]The title of Drury's paper was "Mark and Time—Secrecy and Revelation." See also John Drury, *Tradition and Design in Luke's Gospel* (Atlanta GA: John Knox Press, 1976); Joseph B. Tyson, *The Death of Jesus in Luke-Acts* (Columbia: University of South Carolina Press, 1986); Corley, *Colloquy;* Farmer, *New Synoptic Studies;* Bellinzoni, *The Two-Source Hypothesis*. Also see "Extra-Canonical Literature and the Synoptic Problem," by Bellinzoni, in this volume. The papers from the 1986 S.M.U. conference are scheduled to appear in issues of *Perkins School of Theology Journal* (Spring and Summer, 1987).

Following the 1986 meeting of the *Studiorum Novi Testamenti Societas* in Atlanta, Georgia, Professor Farmer also convened a small, international and ecumenical conference to focus on the work of David L. Dungan and to address the topic of "Text-Criticism and Synopsis Construction."[46]

Professor Farmer is not only a creative scholar in his own right but also an enabler. His efforts have helped to advance New Testament scholarship, particularly the study of the gospels, in ways that extend well beyond the bounds of his own publications.

Jesus and the Gospel:
Tradition, Scripture, and Canon

In 1967, Farmer served as one of the editors for the *Festschrift* in honor of John Knox.[47] Professor Farmer's contribution to that volume, "An Historical Essay on the Humanity of Jesus Christ," provided the necessary presuppositions and the foundation for his subsequent work on Jesus.[48] Most important was "Jesus and the Gospels: A Form Critical and Theological Essay" which appeared in the *Perkins Journal* of 1975.[49]

Building upon these and other earlier essays such as "The Provenance of Matthew," "Teaching of Jesus," "The Post-Sectarian Character of Matthew and Its Post-War Setting in Antioch of Syria," and "Who are the 'Tax Collectors and Sinners' in the Synoptic Tradition?" Farmer produced his fourth monograph in 1982, *Jesus and the Gospel: Tradition, Scripture and Canon.*[50]

---

[46]See David L. Dungan, "Theory of Synopsis Construction," *Bib* 61 (1980): 305-29; "Synopses of the Future," *Bib* 66 (1985): 457-92. Also see n. 29 above.

[47]W. R. Farmer, C. F. D. Moule, R. R. Niebuhr, eds., *Christian History and Interpretation: Studies Presented to John Knox* (Cambridge: Cambridge University Press, 1967).

[48]Farmer, Moule, Niebuhr, *Christian History,* 101-26.

[49]"Jesus and the Gospels: A Form-Critical and Theological Essay," *PSTJ* 28 (Winter 1975): 1-62.

[50]"The Provenance of Matthew," in *The Teacher's Yoke: Studies in Memory of Henry Trantham,* ed. E. J. Vardaman and J. L. Garrett, Jr. (Waco TX: Baylor University Press, 1964) 109-16; "The Post-Sectarian Character of Matthew and Its Post-War Setting in Antioch in Syria," *PRS* 3 (1976): 235-47; "Who are the 'Tax Collectors and Sinners' in the Synoptic Tradition?" in *From Faith to Faith: Essays in Honor of Donald G. Miller on His Seventieth Birthday,* ed. D. Y. Haddian (Pittsburgh: Pickwick Press, 1979) 167-74; *Jesus and the Gospel: Tradition, Scripture, and Canon* (Philadelphia: Fortress, 1982). In dedicating this volume, Farmer writes, "To my Mother, Elsie L. Farmer and to my wife, Nell C. Farmer."

Farmer's third monograph, *The Last Twelve Verses of Mark,* which developed out of his interest in the Synoptic Problem, had taken him into the realm of text criticism.[51] Farmer dedicated this volume to E. C. Colwell, Joachim Jeremias, and C. F. D. Moule as "scholars and friends of scholars." Professor Moule worked with Professor Farmer in coediting the Knox *Festschrift* along with R. R. Niebuhr and has been a longtime friend. Moule always opened his New Testament Seminar to Professor Farmer whenever he came to Cambridge and he sponsored Professor Farmer for the Cambridge B.D. He supported Professor Farmer's proposal to open a seminar on the Synoptic Problem within the Society for New Testament Studies during the 1970s and, in 1979, Professor Moule presided at the opening session of the Cambridge Griesbach Conference.[52]

It was natural that the Southwest Seminar on the Development of Catholic Christianity would bring attention to issues of New Testament canon since that seminar early began to focus on the second century, the formative period in the canon's development. Since the beginning of that seminar in 1966 one can observe Farmer's increasing interest in issues of canon. In 1969 he published "The Dynamic of Christianity—The Question of Development Between Jesus and Paul";[53] in 1976, "Matthew and the Bible: An Essay in Canonical Criticism";[54] and, in 1980, "Peter and Paul: A Constitutive Relationship for Catholic Christianity."[55] *Jesus and the Gospel* concludes with Farmer's historical reconstruction of the development of the New Testament canon.

---

[51]W. R. Farmer, *The Last Twelve Verses of Mark,* SNTSMS 25 (Cambridge University Press, 1974). In dedication, Farmer writes "PERITIS SCRIPTURARUM ATQUE AMICIS PERITORUM; E. C. COLWELL, J. JEREMIAS, C. F. D. MOULE." See also "A Note on J. N. Birdsall's Review of *The Last Twelve Verses of Mark* in *The Journal of Theological Studies* (April 1975)," in W. R. Farmer, *Occasional Notes on Some Points of Interest in New Testament Studies* (Macon GA: Mercer University Press, 1980) 15-20.

[52]Farmer, *New Synoptic Studies,* xvii. Also see C. F. D. Moule, "The Gravamen against Jesus" in this volume.

[53]"The Dynamic of Christianity—The Question of Development between Jesus and Paul," *ReL* 38 (1969-1970): 570-77.

[54]"Matthew and the Bible: An Essay in Canonical Criticism," *LTQ* 11 (1976): 57-66, 71.

[55]"Peter and Paul: A Constitutive Relationship for Catholic Christianity," in *Texts and Testaments: Critical Essays on the Bible and Early Church Fathers,* ed. W. E. March (San Antonio TX: Trinity University Press, 1980) 219-36.

After almost two decades of collegiality with Roman Catholic scholars from the University of Dallas and elsewhere, in 1983, Farmer published a developed form of his work on the canon which had appeared in *Jesus and the Gospel.* "A Study of the Development of the New Testament Canon" appeared in a volume he coauthored with his Cistercian colleague, Denis M. Farkasfalvy.[56] This topic seems to be a continuing interest of Farmer and we can probably expect more on it in the future.[57]

The Seminar on the Development of Catholic Christianity also provided numerous opportunities for Farmer to reexamine the testimonies of the early Church Fathers to the gospels. His subsequent research into this aspect of the Patristic period has borne much fruit.[58]

Professor Farmer's most recent research has focused on the material common to Matthew and Luke apart from Mark. From the two-document perspective, of course, this is "Q" material, but Professor Farmer is using evidence from his latest research to discount the "Q" hypothesis and to build his case for Luke's direct use of Matthew.[59] We hope that he will provide the scholarly world in the near future with a redactional analysis of Luke on the assumption that Luke has used Matthew.

Beyond the Study

I arrived at Perkins School of Theology as a first-year seminarian in the fall of 1968, the year Professor Farmer was awarded an honorary degree from Cambridge University for his book, *The Synoptic Problem,* two years after the institution of the Seminar on the Development of Catholic Christianity, and two years before the Pittsburgh Festival on the Gospels. I took several courses in New Testament and in New Testament Greek with Pro-

---

[56]William R. Farmer and Denis M. Farkasfalvy, O. Cist., *The Formation of the New Testament Canon: An Ecumenical Approach* (New York: Paulist Press, 1983).

[57]See "Galatians and the Second Century Development of the *Regula Fidei,*" *SCnt* 4 (1984): 143-70.

[58]See particularly "The Patristic Evidence Reexamined: A Response to George Kennedy," in Farmer, *New Synoptic Studies,* 3-15 and the work it has generated following the Cambridge Gospel Conference by Guiseppe Giov. Gamba, "A Further Reexamination of Evidence from the Early Tradition," in Farmer, *New Synoptic Studies,* 17-35. See also the appropriate sections of *Jesus and the Gospel.*

[59]See "The Church's Stake in the Question of 'Q,' " *PSTJ* 39 (July 1986): 9-19; " 'Q': State of the Question, *BibTh* 3 (1986): 202-20. Korean translation by Lee Jong-Yun.

fessor Farmer and had experiences with him that I have since come to regard as typical of him.

For instance, while studying the style and literary method of Mark in a reading course I took with him, he would ask at times that we meet off campus. One of our meetings was held at the South Dallas Y.M.C.A. where members of the Black Panther party had gathered to strategize about civil rights issues in the city of Dallas. Bill Farmer needed to be there. His commitment to the civil rights both of ethnic minorities and the poor has always been clear to all who know him. Few whites have as much credibility within the black community in Dallas as Professor Farmer. His vital interests have sometimes been threatened prior to taking part in meetings relating to civil rights issues.

On another occasion I took him orange juice to drink while he participated in a hunger strike on the steps of the Dallas city hall, protesting the lack of attention to the needs of the poor and the hungry in the city. On yet another occasion, I visited prisoners in the city jail with him. While we waited for approval to enter the jail which is granted to members of the clergy, we read the New Testament in Greek and isolated literary characteristics of the gospel of Mark.

Professor Farmer maintains membership both in the predominantly black congregation of St. Luke's Community United Methodist Church and in the predominantly white University Park United Methodist Church.

Reading John C. Bennett's biographical sketch of John Knox which opens the Knox *Festschrift* made me ask myself recently whether Bill Farmer learned more from Knox at Union than his transcript is liable to reveal. Bennett notes of Knox

> . . . [R]acial issues were always on his mind and conscience. . . . He and his family joined a small but very vital Episcopal Church a few blocks down the hill from the Seminary in Harlem, a Church which is remarkable for its interracial character and its service to the whole community.[60]

Bill Farmer's commitment to peace issues and to full participation of third world scholars in international activities has been no less evident. While visiting India during a sabbatical in 1972, Professor Farmer invited Frank Collison of Bangalore to consider the Ph.D. program in New Testament at S.M.U. Naturally, he was pleased when Collison did choose to come to S.M.U. for his doctoral studies. After Collison completed the Ph.D., Farmer continued to raise money to enable him to participate in important international planning conferences prior to the Jerusalem conference on the

---

[60]Farmer, Moule and Neibuhr, *Christian History,* xix.

Gospels in 1984. Further financial aid was secured so that he and other representatives from Asia and Africa could attend that conference.

To provide for these and other benefactions to international scholarship Professor Farmer helped to bring into being the International Institute for Renewal of Gospel Studies. Since its inception the Institute has sponsored conferences, provided travel funds for scholars who could not otherwise afford it, necessary subsidies for scholarly publications, and funds for post-doctoral research fellowships, particularly for younger scholars.

Issues of justice in Central and South America have taken Professor Farmer to those parts of the world as well.[61] In recent years he has committed himself to the discipline of learning Spanish in order to relate better with students at Perkins and others whose first language is Spanish.

That which Professor Farmer has learned in his study about the teachings of Jesus, he has sought to put into practice in the life he lives. Within the limits of human fraility, he strives for integrity.

---

[61]See, for instance, "A Statement on Sanctuary," *PSTJ* 38 (Spring 1985): 22-27, and the list of Professor Farmer's unpublished materials in this volume.

WILLIAM R. FARMER BIBLIOGRAPHY

Compiled by Page A. Thomas

Articles and Books

1950 "Christianity, Communism and War." *USQR* 5 (1950): 25-31.

1952 "The Palm Branches in John 12:13." *JTS* 3 (1952): 62-66.

"The Patriarch Phineas: A Note on 'It was Reckoned to Him as Righteousness' [Gen. 15:6]." *ATR* 34 (1952): 26-30.

1953 "The RSV Arrives in Coatesville." *USQR* 8 (1953): 16-20.

1955 "The Economic Basis of the Qumran Community." *TZ* 11 (1955): 295-308.

1956 "Cynicism and the Gospel." *DrewG* 26 (1955/1956): 14-21. Reprinted as "Cynicism and the Revival" in *ChrCris* 16 (1956): 35-38.

"The Geography of Ezekiel's River of Life." *BA* 19 (1956): 17-22. Reprinted in *BA Reader,* 284-89. Garden City: Doubleday, 1961.

Maccabees, Zealots and Josephus: An Inquiry into Jewish Nationalism in the Greco-Roman Period. New York: Columbia University Press, 1956. Reprinted 1973 by Greenwood Press. 239 pages.

"A Postscript to 'The Economic Basis of the Qumran Community.' " *TZ* 12 (1956): 56-58.

"The Teacher of Righteousness and Jesus the Christ." *DrewG* 26 (1956): 183-94.

1957 "Soundings at Khirbet Wadi Ez-Zaraniq." *BASOR* 147 (1957): 34-36.

1958 "Judas, Simon and Anthronges." *NTS* 4 (1957/1958): 147-55.

1959 "The Kerygmatic Theology and the Question of the Historical Jesus." *ReL* 29 (1959/1960): 86-97. Co-authored with Norman Perrin.

1960 "Josephus and the Axial Age of History." In *The Great Roman-Jewish War.* New York: Harper Torch Book, 1960.

"On the New Interest in Jesus." *PSTJ* 14 (Fall 1960): 5-10.

1961 "A 'Skeleton in the Closet' of Gospel Research." *BR* 6 (1961): 18-42. Reprinted in booklet form by Perkins School of Theology, 1961. 27 p.

1962 "Essenes." In *The Interpreter's Dictionary of the Bible.* George A. Buttrick, ed. New York; Nashville: Abingdon Press, 1962. 2:143-49.

"Herod the Great." In *The Encyclopedia Americana.* 14:137.

"John the Baptist." In *The Interpreter's Dictionary of the Bible.* George A. Buttrick, ed. New York; Nashville: Abingdon Press, 1962. 2:955-62.

"Notes on A Literary and Form-Critical Analysis of Some of the Synoptic Material Peculiar to Luke." *NTS* 8 (1962): 301-16.

"Pre-Existence of Souls." In *The Interpreter's Dictionary of the Bible.* George A. Buttrick, ed. New York; Nashville: Abingdon Press, 1962. 3:869-70.

"Zealot." In *The Interpreter's Dictionary of the Bible.* George A. Buttrick, ed. New York; Nashville: Abingdon Press, 1962. 4:936-39.

1963 Review of *Die Zeloten, Untersuchungen zur jüdischen Freiheitsbewegung in der Zeit von Herodes I. bis 70 n. Chr.*, by Martin Hengel (Leiden: Brill, 1961). *NTS* 9 (1963): 395-99.

1964 "The Provenance of Matthew." Pages 109-16 in *The Teacher's Yoke: Studies in Memory of Henry Trantham.* E. J. Vardaman and J. L. Garrett, Jr., eds. Waco, Tex.: Baylor University Press, 1964.

The Synoptic Problem: A Critical Analysis. New York: Macmillan, 1964; reprinted 1976 by Western North Carolina Press; distributed by Mercer University Press, Macon GA. 308 pages. "A New Introduction to the Problem" (pp. 199-232) reprinted in *The Two-Source Hypothesis: A Critical Appraisal.* A. J. Bellinzoni, Jr., ed. Macon GA: Mercer University Press, 1985. 163-97.

1966 "The Synoptic Problem and the Contemporary Theological Chaos." *ChrCent* 83 (1966): 1204-1206.

"The Two-Document Hypothesis as a Methodological Criterion in Synoptic Research." *ATR* 48 (1966): 380-96.

1967 *Christian History and Interpretation: Studies Presented to John Knox.* Ed. with C. F. D. Moule and R. R. Niebuhr. Cambridge: Cambridge University Press, 1967. 428 pages.

"An Historical Essay on the Humanity of Jesus Christ." Pages 101-26 in *Christian History and Interpretation. . . .* Cambridge: Cambridge University Press, 1967.

"The Problem of Christian Origins: A Programmatic Essay." Pages 81-89 in *Studies in the History and Text of the New Testament in Honor of Kenneth Willis Clark.* B. L. Daniels and M. J. Suggs, eds. SD 29. Salt Lake City: University of Utah Press, 1967.

1968 "Introductory Statement," with Albert C. Outler, for "The Development of Catholic Christianity: Four Methodological Papers by Albert C. Outler, David L. Balas, Georges Florovsky, Frederick J. Streng." *ATR* 50 (1968): 3-5.

"The Lachmann Fallacy." *NTS* 14 (1968): 441-43.

1969 "The Dynamic of Christianity: The Question of Development Between Jesus and Paul." *ReL* 38 (1970): 570-77.

"New Books in New Testament Reading (Bibliographical Essay)." *PSTJ* 22 (Spring 1969): 91-102.

"The New Testament Gospels." Pages 38-48 in *Theological Perspectives in Stewardship.* E. M. Briggs, ed. Evanston IL: Gen. Board of the Laity, United Methodist Church, 1969.

"The Revolutionary Character of Jesus and the Christian Revolutionary Role in American Society." *PSTJ* 22 (Spring 1969): 21-31.

Synopticon: The Verbal Agreement between the Greek Texts of Matthew, Mark, and Luke Contextually Exhibited. Cambridge: Cambridge University Press, 1969. 229 pages.

1970 "The Gospel of Mark." Pages 343-44 in vol. 2 of *Jesus and Man's Hope.* George A. Buttrick, ed. Perspective I. Pittsburgh: Pittsburgh Theological Seminary, 1970.

"How Material Common to Matthew and Luke is Viewed on the Griesbach Hypothesis: Prolegomenon to Further Discussion." Prepared at the request of M. J. Suggs, Chairman of the Gospel Seminar, for the first meeting of the Task Force on the Sequence of the Gospels, held in New York, 1970. Published in 1975 as "A Fresh Approach to Q."

"The Resurrection of Jesus Christ." *ReL* 39 (1970): 365-70.

1971 "Redaction Criticism and the Synoptic Problem." *SBLASP 1971* 1:239-50.

1973 "A Response to Robert Morgenthaler's *Statistische Synopse.*" *Bib* 54 (1973): 417-33.

1974 *The Last Twelve Verses of Mark.* SNTSMS 25. Cambridge: Cambridge University Press, 1974. 123 pages.

1975 "A Fresh Approach to Q." Pages 39-50 in *Christianity, Judaism and Other Greco-Roman Cults: Studies for Morton Smith at Sixty.* Jacob Neusner, ed. Leiden: E. J. Brill, 1975. Reprinted, pp. 397-408, in *The Two-Source Hypothesis: A Critical Appraisal.* Arthur J. Bellinzoni, Jr., ed. Macon GA: Mercer University Press, 1985.

"Jesus and the Gospels: A Form Critical and Theological Essay." *PSTJ* 28 (Winter 1975): 1-62.

1976 "Abba." In *The Interpreter's Dictionary of the Bible.* Supplementary volume. Keith Crim, ed. Nashville: Abingdon Press, 1976. Page 3.

"Chreia." In *The Interpreter's Dictionary of the Bible.* Supplementary volume. Keith Crim, ed. Nashville: Abingdon Press, 1976. 145-46.

"Teaching of Jesus." In *The Interpreter's Dictionary of the Bible.* Supplementary volume. Keith Crim, ed. Nashville: Abingdon Press, 1976. 863-68.

"Matthew and the Bible: An Essay in Canonical Criticism." *LTQ* 11 (1976): 57-66, 71.

"The Post-Sectarian Character of Matthew and Its Post-War Setting in Antioch of Syria." *PRS* 3 (1976): 235-47.

1977 "Introduction." Pages xi-xviii in *History and Criticism of the Marcan Hypothesis.* By Hans-Herbert Stoldt; Donald L. Niewyk, tr. and ed. Macon GA: Mercer University Press, 1980.

"Modern Developments of Griesbach's Hypothesis." *NTS* 23 (1977): 275-95.

"Symposium on Biblical Criticism." *TToday* 33 (1977): 360-61.

1978 "Basic Affirmation with Some Demurrals: A Response to Roland Mushat Frye." Pages 303-22 in *The Relationships among the Gospels: An Interdisciplinary Dialogue.* W. O. Walker, Jr., ed. San Antonio TX: Trinity University Press, 1978. ·

"The Genesis of the Colloquium." Pages 1-4 in *J. J. Griesbach: Synoptic and Text-Critical Studies, 1776-1976.* SNTSMS 34. B. Orchard and T. R. W. Longstaff, eds. Cambridge: Cambridge University Press, 1978.

"Kritik der Markushypothese." *TZ* 34 (1978): 172-74. Review of H.-H. Stoldt's *Geschichte und Kritik der Markushypothese.* Göttingen: Vandenhoeck & Ruprecht, 1977.

"The Present State of the Synoptic Problem." *PSTJ* 32 (Fall 1978): 1-7.

1979 "The Theological Task and the Historical Jesus." *BTF* 11 (1979): 36-64.

"Reply to Christopher Duraisingh." *BTF* 11 (1979): 70-77.

"Who are the 'Tax Collectors and Sinners' in the Synoptic Tradition?" Pages 167-74 in *From Faith to Faith: Essays in Honor of Donald G. Miller on His Seventieth Birthday.* D. Y. Hadidian, ed. Pittsburgh: Pickwick Press, 1979.

1980 *Occasional Notes on Some Points of Interest in New Testament Studies.* Macon GA: Mercer University Press, 1980. 30 pages.

"Note on the Ideological Background of the Marcan Hypothesis." Pages 1-6 in *Occasional Notes.*

"Notes for a Compositional Analysis on the Griesbach Hypothesis of the Empty Tomb Stories in the Synoptic Gospels." Pages 7-14 in *Occasional Notes.*

"A Note on J. N. Birdsall's Review of *The Last Twelve Verses of Mark,* in *The Journal of Theological Studies,* April 1975." Pages 15-20 in *Occasional Notes.*

"Critical Reflections on Werner George Kümmel's *History of New Testament Research.*" Pages 21-30 in *Occasional Notes.* Also published in *PSTJ* 34 (Fall 1980): 41-48.

Guest Editor's Preface. *PSTJ* 33 (Summer 1980): 1-2. Theme: "A Time for Reappraisal and Fresh Approaches."

"Peter and Paul: A Constitutive Relationship for Catholic Christianity." Pages 219-36 in *Texts and Testaments: Critical Essays on the Bible and Early Church Fathers*. W. E. March, ed. San Antonio TX: Trinity University Press, 1980.

"The Stoldt-Conzelmann Controversy: A Review Article." *PRS* 7 (1980): 152-62.

"The Synoptic Problem: The Inadequacies of the Generally Accepted Solution." *PSTJ* 33 (Summer 1980): 20-27.

1981 "Is Mark Really the First Gospel?" *CirR* 5 (October 1981): 6-7.

1982 *Jesus and the Gospel: Tradition, Scripture, and Canon*. Philadelphia: Fortress Press, 1982. 300 p.

1983 (Editor.) *New Synoptic Studies: The Cambridge Gospel Conference and Beyond*. Macon GA: Mercer University Press, 1983. 533 pages.

"The Patristic Evidence Reexamined: A Response to George Kennedy." Pages 3-15 in *New Synoptic Studies*.

"Appendix: A Response to Joseph Fitzmyer's Defense of the Two-Document Hypothesis." Pages 501-23 in *New Synoptic Studies*.

(Coauthored with Denis Farkasfalvy.) *The Formation of the New Testament Canon*. New York: Paulist Press, 1983. 182 pages.

Introduction to and editor of part II: "Seminar on the Synoptic Problem." Pages 29-194 in *Colloquy on New Testament Studies: A Time for Reappraisal and Fresh Approaches*. Bruce Corley, ed. Macon GA: Mercer University Press, 1983.

1984 "Certain Results Reached by Sir John C. Hawkins and C. F. Burney which Make More Sense if Luke Knew Matthew, and Mark Knew Matthew and Luke." Pages 75-98 in *Synoptic Studies: The Ampleforth Conferences of 1982 and 1983*. C. M. Tuckett, ed. JSNTSup 7. Sheffield, England: JSOT Press, 1984.

"Reply to Michael Goulder." Pages 105-109 in *Synoptic Studies: The Ampleforth Conferences of 1982 and 1983*. C. M. Tuckett, ed.

"The Import of the Two-Gospel Hypothesis." *CTQ* 48 (1984): 55-59.

"Is Streeter's Fundamental Solution to the Synoptic Problem Still Valid?" Pages 147-64 in vol. 1 of *The New Testament Age: Essays in Honor of Bo Reicke*. W. C. Weinrich, ed. Macon GA: Mercer University Press, 1984.

"A Popularization of Josephus." *Int* 38 (1984): 306-308. A major book review of *Josephus: The Jewish War*, by Gaalyah Cornfeld. Grand Rapids MI: Zondervan, 1982.

" 'Timeless Truth' and 'Apostolic Faith.' " *PSTJ* 37 (Spring 1984): 7-11.

"Albert C. Outler [a tribute]." *SCnt* 4 (1984): 131-32.

"Galatians and the Second Century Development of the *Regula Fidei*." *SCnt* 4 (1984): 143-70.

1985 "A New Introduction to the Problem." Pages 163-97 in *The Two-Source Hypothesis: A Critical Appraisal*. Arthur J. Bellinzoni, Jr., ed. Macon GA: Mercer University Press, 1985. First appeared in *The Synoptic Problem: A Critical Analysis*, 199-232. Macmillan, 1964; reprinted 1976.

"A Fresh Approach to Q." Pages 397-408 in *The Two-Source Hypothesis: A Critical Appraisal*. Arthur J. Bellinzoni, Jr., ed. Macon GA: Mercer University Press, 1985. First appeared in *Christianity, Judaism, and Other Greco-Roman Cults: Studies for Morton Smith at Sixty*, 39-50. Jacob Neusner, ed. Leiden: Brill, 1975.

"A Statement on Sanctuary." *PSTJ* 38 (Spring 1985): 22-27.

1986 "The Church's Stake in the Question of 'Q.'" *PSTJ* 39 (July 1986): 9-19.

"'Q': State of the Question." *BibTh* 3 (1986): 202-20. Korean translation by Lee Jong-Yun.

"The Sermon on the Mount: A Form Critical and Redactional Analysis of Matt 5:1-7:29." In *SBLASP 1986*, 56-87.

"Some Critical Reflections on Second Peter: A Response to a Paper on Second Peter by Denis Farkasfalvy." *SCnt* 5 (1985/1986): 30-46.

1987 Guest Editor's Preface: "Order out of Chaos." *PSTJ* 40 (April 1987).

"Luke's Use of Matthew: Some Words of Clarification." *PSTJ* 40 (July 1987).

New Gospel Studies Series Foreword. Pages ix-xiv in *Mark as Composer*, by David Barrett Peabody. William R. Farmer, series ed. Macon GA: Mercer University Press, 1987.

"Peter and Paul, and the Tradition Concerning 'The Lord's Supper' in I Cor. 11:23-26." *CTR* 2 (October 1987).

"Source Criticism: Some Comments on the Present Situation." *USQR* 41:2 (1987). Based on a presentation made at the Union Biblical Jubilee.

Selected Book Reviews

1958 *Jesus in His Homeland,* by Sherman E. Johnson. Scribners, 1957. *JBL* 77 (1958): 167-68.

"Unrolling the Scrolls." (Seven titles on the Dead Sea Scrolls.) *ChrCent* 75 (1958): 532-33.

1961 *A New Quest of the Historical Jesus,* by James M. Robinson. Allenson, 1959. *Kergyma und historischer Jesus.* Zwingli Verlag, 1960. *JBL* 80 (1961): 183-84.

The Scrolls and Christian Origins: Studies in the Jewish Background of the New Testament, by Matthew Black. Scribners, 1961. *JBL* 80 (1961): 382-83.

1963 *Die Zeloten, Untersuchungen zur jüdischen Freiheitsbewegung in der Zeit von Herodes I. bis. 70 n. Chr.*, by Martin Hengel. Brill, 1961. *JBL* 82 (1963): 128-29.

1964 *Jesus and Christian Origins*, by Hugh Anderson. Oxford University Press, 1964. *JBL* 83 (1964): 321-22.

1968 *The Gospel of Luke* (Century Bible), ed. by E. Earle Ellis. Nelson, 1967. *JBL* 87 (1968): 209-10.

Jesus and the Zealots, by S. G. F. Brandon. Scribners, 1969. A review with a rejoinder by the author entitled "Jesus and the Zealots: A Discussion." *ModCh* 11 (1968): 117-20.

1969 *Jesus and the Zealots*, by S. G. F. Brandon. Scribners, 1969. *PSTJ* 22 (Spring 1969): 131-33.

1971 *The Tendencies of the Synoptic Tradition*, by E. P. Sanders. Cambridge University Press, 1969. *JAAR* 39 (1971): 530-32.

1982 *Paulus, der Heidenapostel.* Bd. 1: *Studien zu Chronologie*, by Gerd Lüdemann. Vandenhoeck & Ruprecht, 1980. *JBL* 101 (1982): 296-97.

1986 *Conflict, Holiness, and Politics in the Teaching of Jesus*, by Marcus J. Borg. New York: E. Mellon, 1984. *JBL* 105 (1986): 723-24.

1986 *Marcion: On the Restitution of Christianity*, by R. Joseph Hoffmann. Scholars Press, 1984. *PSTJ* 40 (Jan 1987): 52-53.

New Gospel Parallels, vols. I and II, designed and edited by Robert W. Funk. Fortress Press, 1985. *PSTJ* 40 (Jan 1987): 53-56.

Selected Unpublished Papers

1950 "The Use of מַעֲשֶׂה in the Old Testament." B.D. Thesis. Union Theological Seminary (New York). 1950. 65 pages.

1957 "Field Supervisor's Report on Excavations at the Main Gate of Shechem," for the Drew University-McCormick Seminary Excavations at Shechem, Israel, 1st Season, 1957, American Schools of Oriental Research, Jerusalem.

1958- "An Abstract of the Proceedings of the Graduate Seminar on the Syn-
1959 optic Problem. Drew University, October 6, 1958–January 26, 1969." 15 pages. (Chairman and participant.)

1965 "An Address to Perkins Students on *De Revelatione*." 9 pages. Presented at a Perkins School of Theology Convocation on Vatican Council II, 1965.

"Redemption and Viet Nam: Two Sermons Preached in Perkins Chapel, March 9 and 16, 1966." 8 pages.

1967 "A Preface to Christology." Address for Honors Day Convocation, Perkins School of Theology, Southern Methodist University, Dallas, Texas, April 12, 1967. 8 pages.

Seminar on "A Review of *The Synoptic Problem* [by W. R. Farmer], Pittsburgh Theological Seminary, April 3, 1967." (Respondent to Professors Marcus Barth and William Orr). 26 pages.

1968   "Jesus and the Zealots: A Response to a paper on 'Jesus and The Zealot Option,' by Professor William Klassen, at the AAR, Dallas, October, 1968." 3 pages.

"The Synoptic Problem: A Glimpse into the Continuing Discussion." A prepared response to William C. Robinson, Jr.'s discussion of the difficulties of the Griesbach Hypothesis, given by Robinson in an open forum, Perkins School of Theology, Fall Semester, 1968. 17 pages.

1969   "A Proposed Response to 'The Black Manifesto.' " Prepared at the request of a group of ministers in Dallas during June, 1969. 3 pages.

1972   "A Celebration of Political Responsibility." A statement made at the 'Celebration of Political Responsibility' held in Perkins Chapel. 3 pages.

1975   "A Brief Progress Report on a Continuing Interest in Jesus." Prepared for a Colloquium with Schubert M. Ogden, et al. Southern Methodist University, October 2, 1975. 5 pages.

"The Relationship of SMU to the Dallas Community." Dallas, 1975. 2 pages.

1982   "To the Church in Nicaragua." Composed following a fact-finding trip by a group of Dallas citizens to investigate charges of religious persecution in Nicaragua in February 1982. 1 page.

1983   "The Role of Isaiah in the Development of the Christian Canon." A paper presented to the Southwest Biblical Seminar, Spring, 1983. 9 pages.

1984   "Some Reflections on Civil Disobedience from a Christian Perspective, prepared for, and at the request of, the Inter-Religious Task Force of Dallas, presented January 5, 1984, at the Chancery, Diocese of Dallas." 3 pages.

1987   "'A Reader' for 'Isaiah 53 and Christian Faith.'" Prepared for the Southwestern Biblical Seminar, Perkins School of Theology, Dallas, Texas, April 3, 1987. 32 pages.

Part I

LITERARY
AND HISTORICAL STUDIES
OF THE GOSPELS

EXTRA-CANONICAL LITERATURE AND THE SYNOPTIC PROBLEM[1]

Arthur J. Bellinzoni

One of the most widely accepted conclusions of synoptic studies in the twentieth century has been the hypothesis that Mark was the earliest written gospel and that Matthew and Luke used Mark and a hypothetical second source "Q," (and possibly one or more additional sources, sometimes named M and L for special-Matthew and special-Luke respectively) as the basis for the writing of their gospels. More than a century of scholarly research on the so-called synoptic problem amassed such overwhelming evidence in support of the Two-Source Hypothesis (or the Four Document Hypothesis as it is called in Burnett Hillman Streeter's classic statement[2]) that alternative solutions were virtually abandoned, even by the great majority of Roman Catholic scholars, who earlier in this century worked under what might be regarded as a Vatican proscription against the priority of Mark.[3] In 1964, however, William R. Farmer reopened the synoptic problem in a way that has been particularly painful, especially to scholars whose published research assumes and is based on the priority of Mark.[4]

Farmer subscribes to the Griesbach paradigm. Specifically, he has called for the rejection of both the priority of Mark and the whole idea of the hy-

---

[1]An earlier version of this article ("Approaching the Synoptic Problem from the Second Century: A Prolegomenon") was published in the *SBLSP* (1976): 461-65.

[2]Burnett Hillman Streeter, *The Four Gospels: A Study of Origins* (New York: Macmillan & Co., 1925).

[3]On June 19, 1911, the Biblical Commission enacted a decree affirming the traditional authorship, date of composition, and historical character of St. Matthew's Gospel. "In deciding the priority of St. Matthew's Gospel in its original language and substance, the Biblical Commission has solemnly disapproved of any form of these theories which maintains that St. Matthew's original work was not a complete Gospel or the first in order of time." Francis E. Gigot, "Synoptics," *The Catholic Encyclopedia,* ed. Charles G. Herbermann, et al. (New York: Appleton Company, 1912) 14:394.

[4]W. R. Farmer, *The Synoptic Problem: A Critical Analysis* (New York: Macmillan & Co., 1964; reprinted 1976 by Western North Carolina Press; distributed by Mercer University Press).

pothetical second source "Q," employed independently by Matthew and Luke. Instead, he has advocated a return to the hypothesis of Johann Griesbach (long since ignored or even forgotten by the authors of most standard New Testament texts) that Matthew was the first of the synoptic gospels, that Luke copied his Markan and non-Markan parallels from Matthew, and that Mark put together his gospel as a conflation of Matthew and Luke.[5]

It is far too early to predict what new hypotheses or modifications of old hypotheses will establish themselves when the evidence has been carefully and critically re-examined in light of Farmer's challenge, but it is appropriate for us to begin to test the suggestions that have disturbed, if not shaken, the critical consensus that has developed in synoptic research over the last hundred years.[6] D. Wenham in the *Tyndale Bulletin of 1972*[7] and more recently John A. T. Robinson in the July 1975 volume of *New Testament Studies*[8] have begun to re-examine specific synoptic material, although as Robinson admits his work is "but a small sample dip into the mass of material that needs to be looked at afresh."[9] Bernard Orchard in 1976 undertook a much fuller study of Matthew, Mark, and Luke based on the Griesbach Hypothesis. Specifically, Orchard, in the first full-length presentation in modern times of the Griesbach Hypothesis, has made a fresh comparison of the synoptic gospels in an effort to synthesize the existing data into the Griesbach hypothesis, the only feasible alternative to the current dominant Two-Source Hypothesis.[10]

---

[5]See Johann J. Griesbach, *Commentatio qua Marci Evangelium totum e Matthaei et Lucae commentariis decerptum esse monstratur*, I-II (Jena, 1789-1790), ET by Bernard Orchard, "A Demonstration that Mark was written after Matthew and Luke," in *J. J. Griesbach: Synoptic and Text-Critical Studies, 1776-1976*, ed. Bernard Orchard and Thomas R. W. Longstaff, SNTSMS 34 (Cambridge: Cambridge University Press, 1978) 103-35; Latin, 74-102.

[6]A collection of essays arguing the case for and against the priority of Mark and for and against the "Q" hypothesis has recently been published: ed. Arthur J. Bellinzoni *The Two-Source Hypothesis: A Critical Appraisal* (Macon: Mercer University Press, 1985).

[7]D. Wenham, "The Synoptic Problem Revisited: Some New Suggestions about the Composition of Mark iv, 1-34," *Tyn Bul* 23 (1972): 3-38.

[8]John A. T. Robinson, "The Parable of the Wicked Husbandman: A Test of Synoptic Relationships," *NTS* 21 (1975): 443-61.

[9]Ibid., 443.

[10]Bernard Orchard, *Matthew, Luke & Mark*, vol. 1 of *The Griesbach Solution to the Synoptic Question* (Manchester: Koinonia Press, 1976, [2]1977).

Rarely has the literature outside the New Testament canon been consulted for clues that might help in solving the synoptic problem. By general assent the relationship among the synoptic gospels has been established primarily, if not exclusively, by examining and comparing parallel material in the synoptics themselves. This method is surely sound; however, a close study of certain second (and perhaps even third) century synoptic-type traditions might provide new or additional evidence to help us toward a solution to the synoptic problem. What I hope to accomplish in this essay is to begin to look into some of the literature of the second and third centuries for texts that could afford us clues to the question of the literary relationships among the synoptic gospels. Frankly I view this essay as a prolegomenon to a study that might, if properly pursued, yield clues that could help in the solution of the synoptic problem. Specifically, a study of the methods of editing, redacting, harmonizing, and conflating synoptic tradition in second and third century extra-canonical literature could afford us clues about such practices in the first-century church and thereby provide an outside check on any proposed solution to the synoptic problem.

Leon E. Wright has studied the motivations of alterations in the words of Jesus in the literature of the second century and has classified these motivations under the following headings: prudential motivation, contextual adaptation, harmonistic motivation, stylistic motivation, explanatory motivation, ethical and practical motivation, dogmatic motivation, and heretical adaptation.[11] Perhaps working some of Wright's observations regarding such motivations of alterations backward from the second century literature through the synoptic gospels themselves could afford us clues as to the literary relationships among the synoptic gospels.

It would also be profitable to test in the literature of the second century the six evidences of the secondary character of a literary document outlined by Ernest DeWitt Burton and the three canons of criticism identified by Farmer. Specifically, in questions of literary dependence between two documents, Burton regards the following as evidences of a secondary character: "(1) manifest misunderstanding of what stands in one document on the part of the writer of the other; (2) insertion by one writer of material not in the other, and clearly interrupting the course of thought or symmetry of plan in the other; (3) clear omission from one document of matter which was in the other, the omission of which destroys the connection; (4) insertion of matter the motive for which can be clearly seen in the light of

---

[11]Leon E. Wright, *Alterations of the Words of Jesus as Quoted in the Literature of the Second Century* (Cambridge: Harvard University Press, 1952).

the author's general aim, while no motive can be discovered for its omission by the author if he had had it in his source; (5) vice versa omission of matter traceable to the motive natural to the writer when the insertion (of the same matter in the other Gospel) could not thus be accounted for; (6) alterations of other kinds which conform the matter to the general method or tendency of the author.''[12] Farmer adds the following three ''canons of criticism'' as evidence of the secondary character of a literary document: ''(1) That form of a particular tradition found in the Gospels, which reflects an extra-Palestinian, or non-Jewish provenance is to be judged secondary to a form of the same tradition which reflects a Palestinian or Jewish provenance. . . . (2) That form of a tradition which exhibits explanatory redactional glosses, and expansions aimed to make the tradition more applicable to the needs of the Church, is to be adjudged secondary to a form of the tradition which is free of such redactional glosses and expansions. . . . (3) That form of a tradition which exhibits words or phrases characteristic of a redactor whose hand is clearly traceable elsewhere in the same Gospel is to be adjudged secondary to a form of the same tradition which is free of such words and phrases. And as a corollary to this: That form of a tradition which exhibits words or phrases characteristic of a redactor whose hand is only traceable in another Gospel is to be adjudged secondary to the form of a parallel tradition in the Gospel where the redactor's hand can be clearly traced, provided the characteristic word or phrase occurs in the former Gospel only in passages closely paralleled in the latter, where the verbatim agreement indicates direct literary dependence.''[13] Farmer further maintains that other considerations ''which are either irrelevant or inconclusive, and therefore have little or no probative value in settling a question of literary dependence'' are ''(1) The relative length of a given passage. . . . (2) The grammar and style of a writer. . . . (3) The christology of a given passage.''[14] Does the literature of the second and third centuries confirm Burton's six and Farmer's additional three evidences of the secondary character of a literary document? And does the second and third century literature support the view that relative length,

---

[12]Ernest DeWitt Burton, *Some Principles of Literary Criticism and Their Application to the Synoptic Problem* (Chicago: University of Chicago Press, 1904) 198.

[13]Farmer, *Synoptic Problem* 227-29. In the 1964 edition of Farmer's book there were four canons; but, in the 1976 edition, on the basis of Sanders's work, Farmer withdrew the canon that there was a tendency for the Gospel tradition to become more specific.

[14]Ibid., 230-31.

grammar and style, and Christology are, indeed, irrelevant or inconclusive in settling questions of literary dependence, as Farmer maintains? These views need to be tested outside the arena of the synoptic gospels themselves, and the extra-canonical literature affords a fertile field for such an investigation.

Ed Sanders correctly points out that Rudolf Bultmann and Vincent Taylor have developed criteria for determining the primary and secondary stages in the development of the synoptic tradition by showing how Matthew and Luke have edited or redacted their Markan and Q materials.[15] Clearly such a methodology involves circular reasoning if we then proceed to use these same criteria to help us in a solution to the synoptic problem. In his study of the tendencies of the synoptic tradition, Sanders examines as possible tendencies of the tradition (1) increasing length, (2) increasing detail, (3) diminishing semitism, and (4) direct discourse and conflation, and he concludes that "There are no hard and fast laws of the development of the Synoptic tradition. . . . *Dogmatic statements that a certain characteristic proves a certain passage to be earlier than another are never justified.*"[16] The arguments of Burton, Farmer, Bultmann, Taylor, Sanders, and others need to be examined more closely and tested further before the question of the literary relationships among the synoptic gospels can be solved.

I

A first challenge for us might be to seek clues to synoptic relationships in the literature of the Apostolic Fathers. The view of Vincent Taylor that "in the Gospels the 'tradition' has attained a relatively fixed form" and "is no longer subject to change, except as it is altered by copyists or by the writers of the later Apocryphal Gospels"[17] needs clearly to be rejected. In a detailed study of synoptic tradition in the Apostolic Fathers, Helmut Koester has examined the extent of the formative period of the synoptic tradition and has argued (some would say convincingly) that in the period of the Apostolic Fathers there is dependence on both written and oral tradition.[18] Koester has argued that unaltered quotations of the words of Jesus

---

[15]E. P. Sanders, *The Tendencies of the Synoptic Tradition,* SNTSMS 9 (Cambridge: Cambridge University Press, 1969) 23.

[16]Ibid., 272.

[17]Vincent Taylor, *The Formation of the Gospel Tradition* (New York: Macmillan & Co., 1957) 1.

[18]Helmut Koester, *Synoptische Überlieferung bei den apostolischen Vätern* (Berlin: Akademie Verlag, 1957).

from the synoptic tradition are quite rare among the Apostolic Fathers and
are apparently limited to very short sentences (for example, *2 Clement* 2:4;
6:1a; *Didache* 9:5).[19] A great number of alterations in the words of Jesus
in the Apostolic Fathers depend upon the application of the sayings of Jesus to a particular situation (for example, *2 Clement* 3:2; 4:2; 9:11; 13:4;
etc.);[20] and quite frequently Koester identified in the Apostolic Fathers
synoptic-like passages which clearly harmonize parallels from Matthew and
Luke (for example, *2 Clement* 4:2, 5; 5:4; 9:11; *Didache* 1:3; 1:4),[21] a tendency which, according to Koester's view, apparently developed quite early
in the history of the synoptic tradition and which only later developed into
the full-blown harmonies of Theophilus of Antioch and Tatian. Koester
concludes that the synoptic gospels themselves play quite a subordinate role
as sources for the citation of synoptic tradition in the Apostolic Fathers.
The principal source is much more the early Christian community, which
not only transmitted and used but which, based on its own needs, also
stamped, reshaped, and enlarged upon the synoptic tradition.[22] Koester's
study is, admittedly, based on the Two-Source Hypothesis, the priority of
Mark and the hypothetical source "Q."[23] Clearly we need a fresh look at
certain key passages in the Apostolic Fathers in light of alternative solutions to the synoptic problem (for example, *1 Clement* 13:2 and 46:8, which
he believes belong to a stage behind the synoptics, possibly Q;[24] and the

---

[19]Ibid., 71, 74-75, 199-201, 264.

[20]Ibid., 71-73, 79-94, 77-79, 75-77, 199-201, 264.

[21]Ibid., 79-94, 94-99, 77-79, 220-30, 264.

[22]Ibid., 257.

[23]Ibid., 3.

[24]Ibid., 12-19, 23. With regard to the quotations in both *1 Clem* 13:2 and 46:8,
William Sanday, *The Gospels in the Second Century* (London: Macmillan & Co.,
1876), assuming the Q hypothesis, observes (65) that "doubtless light would be
thrown upon the question if we only knew what was the common original of the
two Synoptic texts"; however, he goes on to conclude (66), "Looking at the arguments on both sides, so far as we can give them, I incline on the whole to the
opinion that Clement is not quoting directly from our Gospels, but I am quite aware
of the insecure ground on which this opinion rests. It is a nice balance of proba-
bilities, and the element of ignorance is so large that the conclusion, whatever it
is, must be purely provisional. Anything like confident dogmatism on the subject
seems to me entirely out of place." For a discussion of these two passages, see
also Leon E. Wright, *Alterations*, 77-78, 58-60. See also Richard Glover, "Patristic Quotations and Gospel Sources," *NTS* 31 (1985): 234-51; Glover argues
(243-44) that *1 Clem* 46:8 and perhaps *1 Clem* 36:4 were drawn from Q.

passages in *2 Clement* and the *Didache* which, Koester believes, harmonized parallel material in Matthew and Luke).[25] It would also be profitable to examine in the Apostolic Fathers those passages which are parallel to passages in the triple tradition where it is often argued that Matthew and Luke use both Markan tradition and Q; for example: The Baptism and Temptation of Jesus (Mk 1:1-13 and parallels); The Beelzebul Controversy (Mk 3:22-27 and parallels); and The Great Commandment (Mk 12:28-34 and parallels).[26] Evidence from the Apostolic Fathers may prove to be indirect or inconclusive; but it is, I believe, worth asking if there is evidence.

II

A second challenge might be to seek clues to synoptic relationships in the Apocryphal New Testament literature, specifically in such books as the *Gospel of Thomas* and the *Gospel of Peter*. Dibelius has shown that the narrative tradition and the sayings tradition are not subject to the same law of transmission.[27] Therefore, a look at both apocryphal sayings tradition (as in the *Gospel of Thomas*) and apocryphal narrative tradition (as in the *Gospel of Peter*) is appropriate.

In the year 1908 Emil Wendling argued that the saying in Oxyrhynchus Papyrus 1, saying 6 ("No prophet is acceptable in his fatherland, and no physician performs healings among those who know him") is more primitive than the parallel passage in Mark 6:1-6.[28] This result was confirmed

---

[25]See Edouard Massaux, *Influence de l'Évangile de saint Matthieu sur la Littérature chrétienne avant saint Irenée* (Louvain: Université Catholique, 1950) 144-45 for a discussion of *2 Clem* 4:2; 608-11 for a discussion of *Did* 1:3; and 611-13 for a discussion of *Did* 1:4.

[26]See R. T. Simpson, "The Major Agreements of Matthew and Luke Against Mark," *NTS* 12 (1965-1966): 273-84 and E. P. Sanders, "Suggested Exceptions to the Priority of Mark," in Sanders, *Tendencies of the Synoptic Tradition*, 290-93; both are reprinted in Bellinzoni, *The Two-Source Hypothesis*, 381-95; 199-203.

[27]Martin Dibelius, *Die Formgeschichte des Evangeliums*, 3rd ed. (Tübingen: Mohr, 1959) 26; ET: *From Tradition to Gospel*, trans. Bertram Lee Woolf, from the German 2nd rev. ed. (New York: Scribner's, 1935) 28; Rudolf Bultmann, *History of the Synoptic Tradition*, trans. John Marsh (New York: Harper & Row, 1963).

[28]Emil Wendling, *Entstehung des Markus-Evangeliums* (Tübingen: Mohr, 1908) 54. So too H. G. Evelyn White in his edition of *The Sayings of Jesus from Oxyrhynchus* (Cambridge: Cambridge University Press, 1920).

by form-critical analysis by Rudolf Bultmann long before the discovery of the *Gospel of Thomas*.[29] Since the discovery of the complete text of the *Gospel of Thomas* to which Oxyrhynchus Papyrus 1 belongs, a number of scholars have sought to strengthen their arguments for the secondary and heretical character of the *Gospel of Thomas* by the hypothesis of its dependence on the synoptic tradition. The list of scholars who have thrown their weight on this side of the controversy is impressive: Robert M. Grant and David N. Freedman,[30] Ernst Haenchen,[31] Bertil Gärtner,[32] and H. E. W. Turner[33] to name but a few. No less impressive is the list of those who have argued in one way or another that the *Gospel of Thomas* is dependent upon a source distinct from our synoptic gospels, perhaps an independent earlier stage of the sayings tradition: Hugh Montefiore,[34] Helmut Koester,[35] James M. Robinson,[36] R. McL. Wilson,[37] R. A. Spivey,[38] as

---

[29]Rudolf Bultmann, *History*, 31-32.

[30]Robert M. Grant and David Noel Freedman, *The Secret Sayings of Jesus according to the Gospel of Thomas* (London: Collins, 1960).

[31]Ernst Haenchen, "Literatur zum Thomas-Evangelium," *TRu*, Neue Folge 27 (1961-1962): 147-78, 306-38 and *Die Botschaft des Thomas-Evangeliums* (Giessen: Töpelmann, 1961).

[32]Bertil Gärtner, *The Theology of the Gospel of Thomas*, trans. Eric J. Sharpe (New York: Harper & Row, 1961).

[33]H. E. W. Turner, "The Theology of the Gospel of Thomas," in *Thomas and the Evangelists*, ed. Hugh Montefiore and H. E. W. Turner (Naperville: Alec R. Allenson, 1962).

[34]Hugh Montefiore, "A Comparison of the Parables of the Gospel according to Thomas and of the Synoptic Gospels," in *Thomas and the Evangelists*.

[35]Helmut Koester, "Gnomai Diaphoroi: The Origin and Nature of Diversification in the History of Early Christianity," *HTR* 58 (1965): 279-318 and "One Jesus and Four Primitive Gospels," *HTR* 61 (1968): 203-47. Both reprinted in *Trajectories Through Early Christianity*, ed. Helmut Koester and James M. Robinson (Philadelphia: Fortress Press, 1971).

[36]James M. Robinson, "Logoi Sophon: On the Gattung of Q," in *Trajectories Through Early Christianity*, 114-57, 158-204.

[37]R. McL. Wilson, " 'Thomas' and the Growth of the Gospels," *HTR* 53 (1960): 231-50; "Thomas and the Synoptic Gospels," *ExpTim* 72 (1960-1961): 36-39; *Studies in the Gospel of Thomas* (London: Mowbray, 1960).

[38]R. A. Spivey, *The Origin and Milieu of the Gospel according to Thomas*. See also Ernest W. Saunders, "A Trio of Thomas Logia," *BR* 8 (1963): 43-59; Robert

representatives. Clearly the relationship of the *Gospel of Thomas* to the synoptic tradition has not been resolved. Equally clearly the decisions reached with respect to the *Gospel of Thomas* bear directly on the question of the relationship among the synoptic gospels and any proposed solutions to the synoptic problem. As Koester indicates,

> Further studies should involve a fresh analysis of the parallel sections in the synoptic gospels: the collections of parables and sayings underlying Mark 4 and Matt 13; the basis for the Marcan sayings used in Mark 2 and 3; (the so-called) Q sections underlying Matt 5-7 and Luke 6 as well as other (so-called) Q material now occurring in Matt 11:7ff.//Luke 7:42ff.; Matt 21-22 par., etc.; and, finally, the sources for the special Lucan material in Luke 12 (Luke 11:27-12:56 is paralleled by no fewer than thirteen sayings in the *Gospel of Thomas,* seven of which have parallels only in Luke).[39]

It would once again be profitable to examine, in particular, those passages in the Apocryphal Gospels that have parallels to the synoptic tradition in which it is often argued that Matthew and Luke used both Markan and Q material.[40] Such study is bound to clarify certain aspects of the controversy that now centers on the solution to the synoptic problem, especially as it enables us to identify the primary and secondary material within the synoptic gospels as well as in the *Gospel of Thomas.*

Until the end of the nineteenth century, we were only aware of the existence of a ''Gospel according to Peter.'' Although known through such ecclesiastical writers as Origen (*Commentary on Matthew* X, 17) and Eusebius (*Church History* VI, 12, 3-6), a large parchment fragment of the *Gospel of Peter* was actually discovered in the tomb of a Christian monk at Akhmim in Upper Egypt in the winter of 1886-1887. The narrative text gives an account of the Passion of Jesus from Pilate's washing of his hands to the condemnation, death, burial, and resurrection, with interesting de-

---

North, ''Chenoboskion and Q,'' *CBQ* 24 (1962): 154-70. See as well G. Quispel, ''Some Remarks on the Gospel of Thomas,'' *NTS* 5 (1958-59): 276-90 and Jacobus van Amersfoort, ''Het Evangelie van Thomas en de Pseudo-Clementinen: Een studie van de Woorden van Jezus in het Evangelie van Thomas en hun parallellen in de evangeliecitaten in de Pseudo-Clementijnse Homiliae en Recognitiones'' (diss., University of Utrecht, 1984).

[39]''Gnomai Diaphoroi,'' in *Trajectories,* 132; see also ''One Jesus and Four Primitive Gospels,'' in *Trajectories,* especially 168ff. where Koester begins to analyze some of this material.

[40]For example, Logion 35 has a parallel in Mark 3:27; Logion 48, a parallel in Mark 11:23; Logion 82, a parallel in Mark 12:34; and Logion 25, a parallel in Mark 12:31.

tails regarding the miracles that followed.[41] This mid-second century apocryphal gospel[42] is based primarily on our canonical Matthew but also uses material from both John and Luke.[43] Maurer indicates that "although Peter himself is indicated as the author (v. 26f., 60), what lies before us is a further development of the traditional material of the four canonical Gospels. These are used as remembered, whilst the oral transmission of the material in the preaching of the gospel has also told upon it (Dibelius)."[44] "Matthew with its special material forms the basis of the composition (washing of hands v. 1; guarding and sealing of the grave v. 29ff.; attempt to hush up the resurrection of Jesus by influencing the Roman soldiers and Pilate v. 47ff.). To John there go back the dating of the death (v. 5), the crurifragium (v. 14), the appearance of the risen Jesus at the sea (v. 60), as also many particular traits. Luke contributes the participation of Herod in the condemnation of Jesus (v. 2ff.) and the episode of the thief (v. 13f.)."[45] Altaner calls the *Gospel of Peter* "a very free redaction of the four canonical Gospels,"[46] and Quasten maintains that "the author seems to have worked over the narratives of the canonical gospels, adapting them freely."[47] A close study of the *Gospel of Peter's* method of redacting, editing, and conflating the canonical gospels could possibly provide us with

---

[41]According to Christian Maurer, "Ornaments at the beginning and end of the manuscript indicate that the (8th to 12th century) copyist knew no more than the text known to us. Accordingly conjectures as to the compass and contents of the whole have no foundation." Christian Maurer, "The Gospel of Peter," *New Testament Apocrypha,* ed. Edgar Hennecke and Wilhelm Schneemelcher (Philadelphia: Westminster Press, 1963) 179.

[42]Eusebius states that in about A.D. 190 Bishop Serapion of Antioch rejected the *Gospel of Peter* as being of Docetic character, but Serapion apparently dates the Gospel back at least a generation.

[43]Maurer, "Gospel of Peter," 179-87. See also Massaux, *Influence,* 358-99. Massaux argues (373-76) that vv. 52-54 of the *Gos. Pet.* have their only parallel in Mark 16:3-4.

[44]Ibid., 180.

[45]Ibid.

[46]Berthold Altaner, *Patrology,* trans. Hilda C. Graef (New York: Herder and Herder, 1960) 67.

[47]Johannes Quasten, *Patrology,* (Westminster, Maryland: The Newman Press, 1950) 1:114; Montague Rhodes James maintains that the *Gospel of Peter* "uses all four canonical Gospels" [*The Apocryphal New Testament* (Oxford: Clarendon Press, 1955) 90].

insights into methods of conflation of narrative tradition that could help us understand better the literary methods of the synoptic evangelists themselves and thereby provide us with clues to a solution to the synoptic problem.

In a recent study of the *Gospel of Thomas,* the *Secret Gospel of Mark,* the *Gospel of Peter,* and *Egerton Papyrus 2,* John Dominic Crossan argues that all four hold within their mutilated fragments traditions that are earlier than and independent of the four canonical gospels. Specifically, he maintains that (1) the *Gospel of Thomas* reflects a tradition parallel to and independent of the canonical tradition; (2) both John and Mark are dependent on *Egerton Papyrus 2;* (3) Mark is directly and John indirectly dependent on the *Secret Gospel of Mark;* and (4) the *Gospel of Peter* contains an original Passion-Resurrection source used by all four canonical gospels.[48] Crossan's study is an excellent example of the possibility of research into the literary relationships among the gospels that integrates both the canonical and the extra-canonical literature.

III

A third challenge might be to seek clues to synoptic relationships in certain post-synoptic tradition outside the Apostolic Fathers and the New Testament Apocrypha. That harmonizing of the synoptic gospels was a well-developed practice in the early church can be seen from an examination of several second century sources. Some of the papyrus fragments are well known for combining features from several gospels (cf. especially Papyrus Egerton 2). As has already been indicated, Koester believes that *2 Clement* and the *Didache* have certain harmonistic features. And in the case of Justin Martyr, as early as the nineteenth century such scholars as von Engelhardt,[49] Sanday,[50] and Lippelt[51] saw the use of a gospel harmony of some sort, a view that has now been confirmed by my own study of the sayings

---

[48]John Dominic Crossan, *Four Other Gospels: Shadows on the Contours of Canon* (Minneapolis: Seabury Press, 1985).

[49]Moritz von Engelhardt, *Das Christenthum Justins des Märtyrers* (Erlangen: Andreas Deichert, 1878) 335 ff., esp. 345.

[50]Sanday, *The Gospels,* 136ff., n. 1.

[51]Ernst Lippelt, *Quae Fuerint Justini Martyris APOMNHMONEYMATA Quaeque Ratione Cum Forma Syro-Latina Cohaeserint* (Halle: S. Korras, 1901) 35.

of Jesus in the writings of Justin Martyr.[52] And according to Jerome (*Ep.* 121. 6. 15 *ad Algasiam*), the Greek Apologist Theophilus, Bishop of Antioch composed a gospel harmony in the late second century. The *Diatessaron*, composed in the second half of the second century by Tatian, a pupil of Justin Martyr, stands, therefore, at the end of a long tradition of harmonies, not at the beginning as is often thought. The question to consider is whether the evidence of the second century fathers supports the regnant view that Matthew and Luke in their reworking of Mark and Q stand at, or at least near, the beginning of that long tradition of harmonizing, or can evidence be found among the second century witnesses to support the view that it was rather Mark who epitomized Matthew and Luke?[53] It would be especially interesting to compare passages that are paralleled in all three of the synoptic gospels to related material in Justin and other fathers who are apparently dependent upon or who reflect post-synoptic tradition. And it would be useful once again to compare in the post-synoptic tradition those passages which have parallels to synoptic passages in which it is often thought that Matthew and Luke are using both Markan and Q material. Specifically, can the tendencies in the development of the synoptic tradition in the second century witnesses instruct us with respect to the development of synoptic tradition in the first century? And what conclusions, if

---

[52]Arthur J. Bellinzoni, *The Sayings of Jesus in the Writings of Justin Martyr* (Leiden: Brill, 1967). See also Leslie Lee Kline, *The Sayings of Jesus in the Pseudo-Clementine Homilies*. SBLDS 14 (1975); Leslie Lee Kline, "Harmonized Sayings of Jesus in the Pseudo-Clementine Homilies and Justin Martyr," *ZNW*, 66 (1975): 223-41; Georg Strecker, "Eine Evangelienharmonie bei Justin und Pseudoklemens?" *NTS*, 24 (1978): 297-316.

[53]I have argued elsewhere (see my *Sayings of Jesus*) that Justin Martyr, for example, shows no knowledge of Q, an argument that has apparently won some favor by being cited elsewhere by Dungan, Borsch, Kümmel, and others. In his carelessly argued essay, "Patristic Quotations and Gospel Sources," Richard Glover maintains that Justin made use of the Q source for sayings material found in *Apology* 16:10 and its parallel *Apology* 63:5 (incorrectly identified by Glover as *Apology* 62:5), and in *Apology* 15:9 (incorrectly identified by Glover as *Apology* 9); Glover argues that Justin also "probably" made use of Q in *Apology* 16:13 and its parallel *Dialogue with Trypho* 35:3a; and that he "very possibly" made use of Q in *Apology* 15:13 and its parallel *Dialogue with Trypho* 96:3a, and in *Apology* 16:6. In his discussion of these passages in Justin and in the Apostolic Fathers, Glover shows no familiarity whatever with my *The Sayings of Jesus in the Writings of Justin Martyr*, which argues that these passages are *not* based on Q but that they are rather post-synoptic harmonized texts. Neither does Glover show any familiarity with Koester's *Synoptische Überlieferung bei den apostolischen Vätern*.

any, can be drawn from the fact that the fathers of the second and third centuries seem to prefer one or another of the synoptic gospels?

In conclusion, I am persuaded that considerable light can be cast on a solution to the synoptic problem by examining relevant second and third century material in the Apostolic Fathers, the *Gospel of Thomas* and the *Gospel of Peter,* and the post-synoptic tradition found in the harmonized texts of Justin Martyr and others. But what is needed is not simply a re-confirmation of the Streeter two-source or four-document hypothesis on a Griesbach-Farmer variation. What is needed is a more comprehensive hypothesis which seeks to incorporate the Apostolic Fathers, the *Gospel of Thomas* and the *Gospel of Peter,* Justin Martyr, and others into the fuller history of the synoptic tradition. As Walter Bauer clearly indicated in his epochal work *Orthodoxy and Heresy in Earliest Christianity,*[54] the distinctions between orthodox and heretical, canonical and non-canonical are obsolete. Only when the larger history of the synoptic tradition is written will we be paying more than lip-service to Bauer's acute observations, and in the process we may have cast additional light on the question of the relationships among the synoptic gospels.

---

[54]Walter Bauer, *Orthodoxy and Heresy in Earliest Christianity,* second German edition with added appendices by Georg Strecker, trans. by a team from the Philadelphia Seminar on Christian Origins and ed. Robert A. Kraft and Gerhard Krodel (Philadelphia: Fortress Press, 1971).

THE EARLIEST GOSPEL
WAS THE "SIGNS GOSPEL"

Lamar Cope

It seemed fitting, in preparing to write an essay for a volume honoring William R. Farmer, who has been friend and mentor and agitator to me and to so many in New Testament studies, that one should set forth a bold hypothesis and attempt to give it a forceful demonstration. For, whether we have always agreed with Bill or not, he has always been faithfully bold and forceful. Accordingly I take up a hypothesis not directly related to the Synoptic Problem but one that is vitally related to the development of the gospels as a whole. The hypothesis is this: the Johannine Signs Gospel is the earliest gospel that we know anything about and that document may have influenced the development of the Synoptic Gospels both indirectly and directly.

Research since 1938 has established the fundamental independence of the Johannine tradition from that of the Synoptic Gospels and has further established the strong possibility that two or more literary stages back from our present Gospel of John lies a rudimentary Christian writing, a book, or a "Gospel of Signs."[1]

What do we mean by the Signs Gospel? In the century's two most influential commentaries, Rudolf Bultmann and Raymond Brown have argued for a written collection of signs, signalled by 2:11, 4:54 and 20:30.[2] That is widely agreed upon today in Johannine studies. But both Bultmann and Brown limit the source to a serial account of the miracles of Jesus in

---

[1]In addition to the abundant commentary discussion of this question the following articles are important: Edwin D. Freed and Russell B. Hunt, "Fortna's Signs-Source in John" *JBL* 94 (1975): 563-79; D. M. Smith, "John and the Synoptics: Some Dimensions of the Problem," *NTS* 27 (1981): 287-94; D. A. Carson, "Current Source Criticism of the Fourth Gospel: Some Methodological Questions," *JBL* 97 (1978): 411-29; and R. Kysar, "The Source Analysis of the Fourth Gospel, A Growing Consensus?," *NovT* 15 (1973): 134-52.

[2]Rudolf Bultmann, *The Gospel of John* (Philadelphia: Fortress Press, 1971) and R. E. Brown, *The Gospel according to John (i-xii),* AB 29 (Garden City: Doubleday & Co., 1966).

the ordinary sense; that is, the changing of water into wine, the healings, the feeding of the 5,000, the raising of Lazarus, etc. If that is what the Signs Gospel contained it was not a gospel at all but a miracle collection similar to some that may lie behind the Synoptic tradition as well. But Robert Fortna's detailed source critical analysis of the Signs source shows that the set of miracles concluded with the greatest miracle of all, the resurrection, which the writer viewed as a miracle accomplished by Jesus himself.[3]

This is not the appropriate place to enter into the technical argument over Fortna's proposed source. It is, however, important to note that his critics have objected to a Signs Gospel with a Passion narrative more on the basis of preconceived ideas of the Signs Gospel's content, or for reasons connected with an overriding concept of the development of the Fourth Gospel, than on linguistic or critical grounds. No one yet has advanced sound literary criteria for denying that the Signs Gospel contained a Passion narrative. The same characteristic disruptions in the text (Fortna calls them ''aporias'') that mark the Evangelist's use of the earlier signs continue in the passion. The narrative vocabulary and the tell-tale editing of the Evangelist are often clear and distinct. Above all, the conclusion in 20:30-31, which is so fitting for a Signs Gospel and so inappropriate for the present Gospel, is very difficult to explain if the Signs Gospel did not contain the death/resurrection story. Thus I am convinced that the simplest and the most direct solution to the source evidence in John is that the Evangelist responsible for 1-14, 17-20 (less some, but few, redactional glosses) started from an existing Signs Gospel which listed the mighty deeds of Jesus the Messiah, culminating in the mightiest deed of all, the resurrection.

If that sketch is correct, then it needs to be viewed in the context of the development of the rest of early Christian literature and not just the Johannine school. Leaving aside the highly implausible reconstruction by J. A. T. Robinson, we may consider the dates that are most often posited as earliest for the Synoptic Gospels. Followers of the two document hypothesis normally date Mark about A.D. 65-75. That is usually the earliest suggestion we make for a written gospel. Even if, as I think likely, the massive tradition favoring the priority of Mark is wrong and Mark is not the Synoptic Gospel source document, one may still not date Matthew any earlier than A.D. 75-85. That is because Matthew not only very clearly reflects knowledge of, and polemical interpretation of, the fall of Jerusalem, but the first gospel also presupposes a Christian world in conflict with only

---

[3]R. T. Fortna, *The Gospel of Signs,* SNTSMS 11 (Cambridge: Cambridge University Press, 1970).

Pharisaism in a way that could not have existed before the changes wrought by the Jewish War. Hence, for the Synoptics, the earliest written gospel would be from the period A.D. 65-85.

Though the fact has not been the topic of much discussion, it follows that the Signs Gospel is likely to be the earliest gospel for several reasons. One, its use of the title Messiah is unqualified and simple. It seems to reflect the apologetics of an early Christian community appealing to the Jewish community in a non-hostile environment. Two, its naive approach to apologetics suggests an early stage of development. For it, Jesus is Messiah by virtue of his mighty deeds. That is enough that you may believe and have life. John, of course, criticized and recast this tradition, but he does so against the grain of his source. Three, the Signs Gospel lacks any clear polemic against any opponents, Christian or Jewish, except perhaps the followers of the Baptist. Thus it gives every evidence of being an early, simplistic, Palestinian/Syrian Christian document aimed at convincing Jews to believe in Jesus Messiah.

How early such a document may have come to be is of course only a guess at best. But the late forties or fifties seems likely. For, as R. E. Brown has argued, a Signs document must represent a second stage in the communities' lives after the initial preaching which established those Johannine churches.[4] For the sake of our consideration, then, any date before 60 will suffice, and a date of 55-60 seems to be a cautious and credible one.

There was, then, a document in circulation in Johannine Christianity in the period 55-70 that called for faith in Jesus by recounting his mighty deeds. It was a rudimentary gospel for it linked faith with some of the story of Jesus' life. But the linkage was incidental, secondary to the purpose for which the gospel was written. That is, all of the canonical gospels see a recasting of the "life" of Jesus as a way of promoting faith. That is even true of our John. But the Signs Gospel did not really do that. It wanted to elicit faith by reciting the mighty deeds of the Messiah. It was almost accidental that this amounted to retelling some of the story of Jesus' life.

The next step in the development of this literature would then come in the work of Mark or Matthew. One of them, and here one can make a plausible case for either (although Mark would need to be more Palestinian than the vocabulary, style, or content can probably support), moved beyond the "Jesus is Messiah because he did wondrous deeds Christology" and incorporated more material about Jesus (e.g., teachings.) and redirected the

---

[4]This position is eloquently stated both in the commentary previously cited and in the essays entitled, *The Community of the Beloved Disciple* (New York: Paulist Press, 1979).

aim of a book about Jesus. Matthew clearly produced a discipleship document, and Mark a call to faith in the crucified one. In either case "the life
story of Jesus," though artificial in terms of historicity, has become important to the presentation in a more than accidental way. Matthew and
Luke, or Luke and Mark, followed that lead. Yet the lead was in all probability the rudimentary Signs Gospel of Johannine Christian circles. Later,
too, the Evangelist John went his own unique way in adapting the Signs
Gospel to a later time of crisis in Johannine Christianity.

There are two elements of that sketch which will be revolutionary for
New Testament studies if they are adopted. The first written Gospel was
the Johannine Gospel of Signs, and if it is legitimate to speak about any of
the gospels as a foundation document, then that term properly belongs to
the Signs Gospel. Moreover, the Signs Gospel was not only the first Gospel, but set the stage for the later Synoptic Gospels, as well as the Johannine revisions, even if it did so more by accident than by design. If these
conclusions are correct, then the relationship between the Signs Gospel and
the Synoptics needs to be examined, instead of the traditional debate about
the relationship between our present Gospel of John and the other gospels.
Furthermore, much of the debate about gospel genre, though clearly not
all, would be resolved by such an understanding of the development of the
gospels. For, whatever connections with Hellenistic or Jewish hagiogra-
pha or biography the other gospels may reveal, the Signs Gospel's origin
clearly rests in a particular apologetic interest of an early Christian community, preaching the wonder-worker Messiah, and not in any literary
model.

This agenda for research deserves far more consideration than can be
given in this essay. What I would like to do here is explore briefly some
of the implications of looking at the relationships among the gospels from
the very different perspective of the Signs Gospel as the original Christian
"gospel." One realizes immediately that the classical problem, "Did John
know the Synoptics?," has been turned on its head. Now one must ask,
"Are there any indications that the Synoptic writers were familiar with the
Johannine Signs Gospel at the stage before it was revised by the Fourth
Evangelist?" So few scholars have ever considered the problem from this
perspective that one must almost immediately move into uncharted territory and/or use the results of research that was not directed exactly at this
question but may throw some light upon it. I hope that such an indirect
approach may illumine our topic.

Most treatments of the relationship between John and the Synoptics begin from the little book by P. Gardner-Smith, *St. John and the Synoptic*

Gospels.[5] It argued for the fundamental independence of the Johannine and Synoptic traditions. We may better begin, however, from consideration of C. H. Dodd's work on the subject in *Historical Tradition in the Fourth Gospel.*[6] For Dodd not only firmly anchored the argument for the independence of the Johannine tradition, but he carefully analyzed almost all of the relevant parallels.

Dodd's work is an important point of departure because it established in detail two very important facts. First, the parallels between John and the Synoptics, especially Mark, are *never* of the type to require the conclusion that the author of John knew and used Mark. Indeed, John frequently differs from Mark in ways that cannot be explained if John knew Mark.[7] But, secondly, the parallels between John and the Synoptics are close enough in several places, particularly in John 6 and in the Passion Narrative, to require the view that the two versions rest on common tradition from the oral tradition.[8] This basic understanding of the relationship may be said to be the dominant one today.[9]

In this writer's view, that general understanding of the overall relationship remains valid, but it is important to note something else that Dodd discovered but made little use of in his discussion. At several points Dodd

---

[5]P. Gardner-Smith, *St. John and the Synoptic Gospels* (Cambridge: Cambridge University Press, 1938).

[6]C. H. Dodd, *Historical Tradition in the Fourth Gospel* (Cambridge: Cambridge University Press, 1963).

[7]See particularly Dodd's treatment of the parallels in the arrest tradition, ibid., 67-81.

[8]This conclusion is often repeated, but a good example is, "there is cumulative evidence that the Johannine version represents an independent strain of common oral tradition" (ibid., 150).

[9]The only significant major dissent on John's independence of the Synoptics is the work of F. Neirynck, who holds a very narrow literary dependence view of the relationships of *all* of the gospels. In an article entitled, "John and the Synoptics: Empty Tomb Stories," *SNTS* 30:2 (1984): 161-83, Neirynck has sought to show John's dependence on the Synoptic tradition, especially Matthew 28. However, precisely the methodological problems with which Dodd wrestled trouble the article. In John 20:1-18, by Neirynck's own reckoning there are only 19 words that are directly parallel and 8 of those are prepositions or articles (179-80). Thus, while one *may* argue the possibility of Johannine knowledge of the Synoptics in the Empty Tomb stories, the argument is by no means compelling, in spite of the elaborate effort made by Neirynck to support that position. Dodd's judgment still stands.

showed, especially in the Passion Narrative, that precisely where the Lucan passages differ substantially from the tradition in Mark/Matthew, there are striking affinities with John. For example, in his discussion of the parallels in the predictions in the Passion story (of the treachery of Judas, Peter's denial, and the desertion of the twelve), Dodd says, "just as Luke reported these predictions after a tradition apparently different from that of Mark, so did John."[10] Or, in the discussion of the prayers in Gethsemane (Lk 22:42ff and Jn 12:27ff) he says, "Here we discern a third form of tradition behind John, a tradition having some more or less remote affinity with Luke's."[11] Thus, even in the process of establishing the essential independence of John from Mark, Dodd raised some serious questions about the relationship between the Johannine and the Lucan traditions.

In a 1971 article in the *Journal of Biblical Literature,* F. Lamar Cribbs took this insight a major step further.[12] Cribbs gathered an impressive amount of data comparing the Johannine and Lucan materials in detail. Perhaps the current distrust of, and even distaste for, exacting literary comparison accounts for the meager use of this article in subsequent Johannine study. At any rate, Cribbs showed that Luke does have a number of solid agreements with John against Mark/Matthew, far too many to be accidental or even the result of oral tradition. He also showed that Luke often seems to take a moderating position between John and Mark/Matthew on matters of detail, and that Luke omits a number of Mark/Matthew details that conflict with the parallels in John. Cribbs listed at least 20 cases of very close verbal parallels between Luke and John (more exact in fact than John's O.T. quotations) and also noted that all of these parallels between Luke and John occur between Luke and the narrative sections of John.[13]

There are clearly two ways to read that data. If one lumps these parallels together with the less precise parallels to Mark/Matthew, one might resurrect the argument of Johannine dependence upon the Synoptics. Or, if one defines the redactional activity of Luke by noting Luke's changes from his Marcan source, then one discovers, by definition, that the John-Luke parallels always occur between John and Lucan redaction. That is, at first

---

[10]Ibid., 64.

[11]Ibid., 70.

[12]F. Lamar Cribbs, "St. Luke and the Johannine Tradition," *JBL* 90 (1971): 422-50.

[13]"The Lukan/Johannine agreements against Matthew/Mark also occur almost entirely between Luke and the narrative sections of John" (ibid., 449).

sight, a strong argument then that the Fourth Evangelist used Luke. But such an argument is seriously flawed. One does not discover redaction in Luke simply by subtracting the Marcan, or Matthean, source. The third evangelist explicitly says that he utilized multiple sources for this story. Only if the Luke/John parallels also exhibit clearly identifiable Lucan language and motifs can they be identified as Luke's own work. For the most part, they do not. So Cribb's somewhat tentative suggestion is the far more viable one: "[A] better explanation . . . might well be the hypothesis that Luke was influenced by some early form of the developing Johannine tradition . . . rather than vice versa, . . . "[14]

If that insight is taken seriously, the study of the question has now moved in a great circle. As late as the early thirties most scholars believed that John had very freely revised the Synoptic tradition, especially Mark. Some critics still want to think that. But by the fifties the fundamental independence of John and the Synoptics seemed to have been firmly established. Now, however, further research has demonstrated a striking set of parallels between the special content of Luke and the narrative portions of the Gospel of John.

What can we make of this turn? The view that the Fourth Evangelist wrote with Luke as a source is almost impossible to support or even seriously propose. That Luke knew the Fourth Gospel as we have it is also hardly conceivable. Consequently, the likelihood is that both John and Luke utilized a narrative source other than the gospels of Mark and Matthew. There is little doubt that John used the Signs Gospel as the basis for his masterful revision. It is simplest, then, to suggest that Luke also had access to an edition of the Signs Gospel. That explains the parallels between John and Luke without the necessity of direct knowledge by either writer of the other's final work.

Both Luke and John are such clever, indeed brilliant, reshapers of the traditions that they are using that the exact details of such a source may not now be recoverable. Luke was far more sympathetic with the thrust and direction of his other sources so that it is clear that the Signs Gospel did not form a narrative framework for him, but was only a resource for enriching the Jesus story. But John (by whom I mean the editor/redactor theologian of 1-14/17-20) was a member of the community in which the Signs Gospel took shape and was not aware of, or if aware of, was unconcerned with, the Synoptic tradition. For him, the Signs Gospel was *the* starting point.

---

[14]Ibid., 450.

If the train of thought of this essay is cogent at all, we are now brought back to the initial thesis. If there is general agreement that there was a narrative source behind the Fourth Gospel, a source which consisted of the recitation of the mighty deeds of Jesus the Messiah, then that source, the Signs Gospel, must have taken shape in the decades before the Jewish War. That document preceded any of the Synoptic Gospels, on any source theory, and should therefore be understood as the earliest Christian Gospel. It is possible that the Signs Gospel was well enough known among Christian Jews even beyond Johannine circles to have provided some of the impetus for the production of the earliest Synoptic Gospel, whether Matthew or Mark. And it is highly likely that Luke had access to an edition of the Signs Gospel and that that fact accounts for the presence on the strong parallels between John and Luke.

In one sense, nothing about the preceding paragraph ought to be surprising. It is, step by step, the natural result of the research on John and on Luke over the last forty years. We have not put these ideas together as yet because of the preoccupation with the question of John's relationship to the Synoptics put in entirely the wrong way, a question about the final documents and not about their sources, a question which does not fit what we know of the literature on other grounds. We have also failed to grasp the importance of the emergence of the Signs Source in Johannine studies because we have fallen victim to such severe compartmentalization in New Testament studies: Synoptic, Johannine and Pauline areas of specialization. It is urgent that we ask the right questions today and that we seek to correlate our results in a coherent picture of Christian beginnings, especially one which recognizes the rootedness of the Gospel traditions in developing Jewish Christianity. Certainly that coherent vision has been part of the quest of William R. Farmer. Perhaps now the time is ripe for us to begin to pull together some seemingly disparate strands of gospel study. Recognition of the priority of the Signs Gospel might be an important step on that journey.

MARCION'S GOSPEL
AND THE SYNOPTIC PROBLEM

John Knox

Having been honored with an invitation to write an essay for this volume and very much wanting for many reasons to accept it, I began casting about for a subject on which I might possibly have something useful to say and which would be at least remotely relevant to the area of Professor Farmer's principal studies. That area, needless to say here, is that of the inter-relations of the first three Gospels, or what is commonly known as the Synoptic problem, in current discussions of which he has been a brilliant and most creative participant, but in which I have had, and am qualified to have, no share. The nearest I have ever come to close study of the text of any of the Gospels was in the course of my work on Marcion's Gospel forty years ago.[1] Hence my choice of the present topic. My intention is modest. I want to do little more than to ask a question: Ought this Gospel of Marcion to be regarded as having a significant place, or any place at all, in the evolution of the Synoptic Gospels?

I

So long as it is assumed, as it generally is, that Marcion's Gospel was an abridgment of canonical Luke and that it originated no earlier than late in the first half of the second century, this question, obviously, does not arise at all; and this is true whether, with the majority of New Testament scholars of my generation, one considers Mark as being earlier than Luke and one of its sources, or, with Professor Farmer and many others, regards it as the latest of the Synoptic three. On the other hand, if this assumption is questioned and one suspects that Marcion's Gospel, or (more probably) a Gospel closely resembling it, was the principal source of Luke[2] rather than a derivative from it—then, almost equally obviously, the question asked may well be quite pertinent. The question of its relevance, therefore,

---

[1]John Knox, *Marcion and the New Testament* (Chicago: University of Chicago Press, 1942; New York: AMS Press, 1980).

[2]When in this paper the word "Luke" is used without qualification, it designates the canonical Gospel.

resolves itself into the more basic question: Did the author of Luke *enlarge* the much shorter Gospel of Marcion (or some Gospel much like it) or did Marcion *abridge* the canonical Gospel?

My own conclusion forty years ago was that the former of these two possible hypotheses was the more probable, and so I still think. It would be gratuitous and inappropriate for me to repeat here in any amplitude the arguments by which I supported this conclusion, but a summary review of them may not be out of place and seems necessary to the purposes of this essay.

As I recall, a doubt about the truth of the established opinion of Marcion's derivative character was first suggested to me, as it has been to many others, by the manifest fact that Luke 3:1 indicates that at some stage in its development this Gospel began at this point—the point where, approximately, Marcion's Gospel, like Mark, also began. This fact was soon joined by another, hardly less striking; namely, the fact that the materials present in Luke but lacking in Marcion's Gospel are predominantly materials peculiar to Luke among the Synoptics. Surely, this being true, it is simpler and more natural to think of these materials as having been added than as having been excised. One rather expects a later writer to make his own peculiar contribution to a source, and the final author of Luke-Acts clearly had an invaluable contribution to make. But why, if one adopts the alternative hypothesis, should Marcion have chosen Luke among the Gospels as his own when he must eliminate what for us are the first two long chapters and when his later abridgments must cut most deeply into just those materials which give to Luke its special character and flavor? Why did he not choose Mark or John, which *ex hypothesi* were available to him and from which, it would appear, much less would have had to be expunged? This argument has not ceased to seem to me a strong one.[3]

The principal ground for my view, however, was, and is, a broader one, lying in the story of the emergence of the Catholic New Testament canon as a whole. This canon, which, with Harnack, I see to be a conscious creation of the Church between, roughly, A.D. 150 and 175, was prompted by the presence and influence of Marcion's distinctively Christian Scripture, his Gospel and Apostle. The Catholic canon's own Gospel-Apostle structure reflected that same influence. And—most important of all—the Church's method of adapting the contents of the heretical Scripture to its

---

[3]I have been charged by at least one critic with exaggerating in my book the proportion of peculiar material within the total body of Lukan material missing in Marcion. I can well believe that a margin for error should be allowed, but I am confident it should be a small one. In the particular case referred to, the critic had failed to take into account the *minor* pieces of peculiar Lukan text.

Catholic use was *expansion*. Marcion's "canon" of the ten previously collected letters of Paul was augmented with the Epistles to Timothy and Titus. Paul himself, who was for Marcion the only apostle, was joined by as many other apostles as could be found[4] (eventually by Peter, James, John and Jude). This already much fuller "Apostle" of the Catholic New Testament was headed by the book of Acts, sometimes called the "Acts of all the Apostles," which was itself the "Apostle" section of an earlier similarly structured work, the "Gospel" section of which was Luke, the very Gospel which in a shorter form Marcion acknowledged as the only true Gospel. Finally among these examples of expansion, the "Gospel" in the Catholic New Testament was four-fold, including, with Luke, Matthew, Mark, and John. My contention was that this policy of expansion or enlargement, so consistently followed, would, as a kind of *a priori,* most plausibly account for the fact that the Catholic Luke is substantially longer than Marcion's Gospel. I am far from supposing the case is proved, but I submit that the burden of proof rests with those who assert the temporal priority of the canonical Gospel.

I soon discovered, as I read the history of discussion of this issue of priority, that what seemed to many the decisive argument for Luke's precedence was that of William Sanday, who undertook to show that the characteristic vocabulary and style of Luke appeared equally in sections of Luke contained and not contained in Marcion's Gospel.[5] If this argument meant what it was thought to mean and *if it was true,* it was indeed "decisive" and the burden of proof had been easily carried. When I set myself to examine it, however, I saw to my surprise that Sanday had not taken into any account at all the *text* of Marcion's Gospel and, therefore, had succeeded only in confirming the already fully recognized unity and stylistic consistency of *canonical* Luke. As to whether Marcion's Gospel had the same Lukan style and vocabulary, he did not even ask. He simply assumed that it did. I found it not difficult to demonstrate the falseness of this assumption, at least to my own satisfaction, and thus the unreliability of the conclusions Sanday and others were building on it.[6] Since I knew of no other allegedly decisive evidence for those conclu-

---

[4]See Adolf von Harnack, *The Origin of the New Testament* (New York: Macmillan & Co., 1925) 117-18.

[5]William Sanday, *The Gospels in the Second Century* (London: Macmillan & Co., 1876) 214ff.

[6]I think now that I should have been content with this demonstration and should not have attempted to build any positive argument for Marcion's priority on so meager and uncertain a basis as the recoverable text of his Gospel provides (that

sions, I felt confirmed in my view that, in the present state of our knowledge of Marcion's Gospel, the considerations I have earlier mentioned had an evidential force strong enough to create a presumption in favor of the Marcionite Gospel's priority.

II

Before turning to a contemporary challenge to that presumption which I could hardly have anticipated in 1942, I shall briefly comment on a critical objection to the hypothesis of this priority which I *did* anticipate and which I answered to my own satisfaction, but evidently not to the satisfaction of many others. A learned friend states the objection very well in a letter: "As far as I know, no one has offered a conclusive refutation of your account of the relation of Luke to Marcion's Gospel. But it has not been widely accepted. I think the reason is that most scholars consider it, on general grounds, unlikely that one of our Gospels could have been re-edited and put into circulation in a much altered form as late as A.D. 150 without anyone's remarking on the fact." The kind of response I would make to this objection is clearly indicated in *Marcion and the New Testament*,[7] but perhaps it should be addressed more particularly and directly.

It should be observed, first, that the objection does not involve the claim that there is any evidence for the existence of Luke in its canonical form before the time of Justin Martyr. If this claim had been made, it could be most readily and convincingly refuted.[8] The question being asked, therefore, is only the social-psychological one of whether the Church in the years A.D. 125-150 would have accepted without protest or remark a form of the Gospel as different as canonical Luke would have seemed from the "Luke" it had previously known.

---

is, in its detail). If I had done so, I should have saved the reader patient enough to examine pp. 93-97 and 177-82 of my book no little unnecessary trouble and have saved myself no little unfruitful labor involving many risks of error, some of which I know I did not avoid. My conclusion (stated on p. 99) was that the linguistic evidence was not decisive "either for or against the traditional view."

[7]Ibid., 124-32, 140-57.

[8]See the pages just now cited in Knox, *Marcion*. It will be seen that there is no evidence in the Fathers or elsewhere for the existence of Luke in its canonical form until after A.D. 150. Later researches have on this particular point only confirmed long established results. Cf. Arthur J. Bellinzoni, *The Sayings of Jesus in the Writings of Justin Martyr*, NovTSup 17 (Leiden: Brill, 1967). Also see John H. Townsend, "The Date of Luke-Acts," in *New Perspectives from the SBL Seminar*, ed. Charles H. Talbert (New York: Crossroads, 1984).

In considering this question, one must be on guard against making some false assumptions. First of all, it cannot be assumed that, if Luke-Acts was first published around the middle of the second century, we have means of knowing what the reaction of the Church to that event actually was. It is true that we do not *know* of any protest or remark at the time. But obviously we cannot argue from our ignorance that none was elicited. The literature of the mid-second century is very sparse and refuses to answer many of our eager questions. We can soundly base very few, if any, negative conclusions upon its silence. For all we can know, the late appearance of canonical Luke may have given rise to a great deal of comment or it may have occurred almost without notice. I am strongly inclined toward the latter view.

Secondly, we must not assume that an earlier form of Luke was known well or widely when, according to the hypothesis, Luke-Acts came into being. We have no reason for thinking so. I have suggested elsewhere that it would seem likely *a priori* that some form of Luke was known in Bithynia-Pontus, where Marcion was reared. That fact would well account for Marcion's choice of it as "the Gospel." But that this Gospel was widely and favorably known in the emerging Catholic Church of A.D. 125-150 is much less likely than that it was only known *of*—and, even so, only to be shunned as a heretic's Gospel.

Finally, we must not ignore the importance of the fact that the making of the canon (of which the making of Luke-Acts was directly or indirectly a part) was not an unconscious process but was a deliberate official action. Canonical Luke first appeared, not only with a *nihil obstat,* stamped on it, but also with active backing from some authoritative person or body. What chance would scattered opposition have, even if it came from non-heretical sources, against such support and promotion?

III

Thus far I have done little more than to review answers to objections to the theory of Marcion's Gospel's priority to Luke-Acts which I offered and defended in my book. But now comes an objection which I did not dream of in 1942 and to which I am now prepared to make only a tentative answer. At that time I wrote about the theory: "The acceptance of it calls for no revision of the well-established results of research into the interrelations of the Synoptic Gospels. It can be harmonized with any serious theory of the sources of Luke-Acts and with any 'solution' of the Synoptic problem."[9] It was then taken for granted that, however different in other respects "solutions" of the Synoptic problem might be, they would all

---

[9]Knox, *Marcion,* 112.

agree in presuming the temporal primacy of Mark. Now, however, the view, long discredited in most circles, that Matthew, not Mark, was the earliest Gospel has become a "serious theory"; and one must ask whether the assertion of Marcion's precedence of Luke conflicts with this view.

Professor Farmer, one of its leading defenders, sees it as doing so. I quote two passages from a recent writing of his on the New Testament canon:

> . . . I have not followed John Knox in dating the completed work Luke-Acts after Marcion. The reason for this is that Knox presupposes Marcan priority at essential points in reaching this conclusion. Since I remain doubtful about this assumption, I must remain skeptical of Knox's results at this point. For those who accept Marcan priority, however, the critical discussion remains largely where Knox left it in 1942, . . . I believe that both E. C. Blackman in *Marcion and His Influence* and Hans von Campenhausen in *The Formation of the Christian Bible* are correct in not following Knox at this point. However, neither has answered Knox's arguments and evidence, and thus their own work, which presupposes, with Knox, Marcan priority, is, at this point, critically less consistent than that of Knox. . . . I see Luke-Acts as a pre-Marcionite work. Therefore, unlike Knox, I cannot credit Marcion with creating the 'Gospel-apostle' form of the New Testament. But there is no way to be sure that had Marcion not followed the 'Gospel-apostle' model of Luke-Acts in forming his New Testament, the Church would have done so. As Harnack shows, there were various shapes the New Testament might have assumed. Undoubtedly, then, the fact that Marcion followed one particular model had a decisive influence on the creation of the New Testament of the Church to the extent that the Church responded to Marcion's challenge by developing this model even further.[10]

In these passages Professor Farmer does not say that if he were able to give an early date to Mark he would be able to accept the argument for the Marcionite Gospel's priority both to canonical Luke and to Luke-Acts, but, it seems to me, he comes very near to saying it. He surely implies, at the least, that he would, in that case, see no conclusive *objection* to the argument. I am led to ask, therefore, whether the hypothesis defended in my book and in this paper is, in fact, incompatible with the late dating of Mark, of which Professor Farmer and many other scholars are persuaded. I am far from sure that it is, although I must leave to others the final determination.

It is true that in my book I spoke twice at least of Marcion's dependence on Mark;[11] but each time I did so in connection with a reference to Streeter's hypothesis that Luke was the product of a fusing of Mark with his "Proto-Luke" (which by definition excluded Mark). I was answering the contention

---

[10]"A Study of the Development of the New Testament Canon," in W. R. Farmer and Denis M. Farkasfalvy, *The Formation of the New Testament Canon* (New York: Paulist Press, 1983) 94, 90-91.

[11]Knox, *Marcion,* 106-107, 122.

of Couchoud that Marcion's Gospel might be identified with the latter.[12] I was making the point that this identification is rendered impossible by the unmistakable signs of Marcion's dependence on the so-called triple tradition, in which, it was then generally assumed, Mark was the basic element. Since it did not occur to me to question this assumption, I doubt that I made any effort to investigate Marcion's possible dependence on Mark *in particular*. Certainly I do not recall doing so. If that is true, my statement can be misleading. I would *now* ask, however, if anything with Synoptic parallels can be found in Marcion's Gospel which could not be taken as coming from Matthew as plausibly as from Mark. If this question is found to be answerable in the negative—and I should be surprised if it is not—I see no ground for a categorical denial of the compatibility of the proposal of Marcion's Gospel's priority to Luke with Professor Farmer's or any other comparable proposal as to the relative dating of the Synoptic Gospels.

It is altogether possible that someone has done the research necessary to the answering of this question, and it is also quite possible that the answer, whether already arrived at or yet to be found, is other than the negative one I should expect. But unless such an answer is forthcoming—an answer which establishes that Marcion must have depended specifically on *Mark* (and on canonical Mark, at that)—until then, I shall not disavow my earlier assertion of harmony between the theory of Marcion's priority and any possible solution of the Synoptic problem.

If what I do not expect[13] should happen, however, and I should be forced to qualify or withdraw my assertion of this harmony, the result would be, not a diminishment of my assurance of Marcion's priority, but rather a heightened doubt that any solution of the synoptic problem which denies the early date of Mark can be true.

---

[12]P. L. Couchoud, "Is Marcion's Gospel One of the Synoptics?" *HibJ* 34 (1936): 265ff.

[13]It may be objected that I ought not to have any "expectations" in such a matter as this but should wait with passive mind until what research as may be necessary has been done and all the data are in. But, agreeing as I do with that opinion in general, I submit that in this case there is some justification for expectation. Note that, according to the view Farmer accepts, Marcion's Gospel rested solely on Luke. But if Luke rested largely on Matthew and L (materials peculiar to that Gospel), why might we not expect that Matthew and some part of L (for if Marcion was prior, some part of L would belong, so to speak, to *him*) would have served the purposes of *Marcion*? In other words, if it is possible, as apparently it is, to account for Luke without any reference to Mark, it would seem likely that the Gospel of Marcion could also be explained without that reference, especially since that Gospel was much shorter than Luke and apparently contained little or nothing substantial which is not also found in the canonical Gospel.

SOME REFLECTIONS
ON THE RELATIONSHIP
OF LUKE TO MATTHEW[1]

J. B. Orchard

The problem that any discussion of the relationship of Luke to Matthew has to face today in an open forum is the difficulty of opening up the minds of contemporary scholars and exegetes to make the effort seriously to consider the arguments for the tradition that Matthew was the first written Gospel, because it involves a complete reversal of current perspectives. That is to say, they are asked to envisage that instead of Matthew and Luke being dependent on Mark and a "Q" source, the exact opposite is the case, namely that Luke is dependent on Matthew and that Mark is dependent simultaneously on both Matthew and Luke, no "Q" source being required.[2] Even John A. T. Robinson could not liberate himself from the thought of some form of the literary dependence of Matthew and Luke on Mark, in spite of his openness in other respects.[3] Nevertheless this great scholar (alas no longer with us) is now posthumously on record as preferring "to believe that the ancient testimony of the church is correct at least with respect to John the Apostle being the author of his Gospel."[4] Maybe his confession is to be regarded as a sign that the value of this testimony is now on the way to rehabilitation. For it is of little avail to attempt to discuss the relationship of Luke to Matthew unless the critics are prepared to admit at least that the priority of Matthew is now once more up for consideration.

It is, I think, worthwhile to quote from the private letter that Professor C. H. Dodd wrote to Robinson in 1972 to encourage him to write his *Re-*

---

[1]In a private discussion with Professor Farmer some time ago, he invited me to put down in writing for him not only my views, but also my further speculations, on this topic, and I promised to do so; this essay is the fulfillment of that promise.

[2]This is the essence of the Two-Gospel Hypothesis (2GH), the lineal successor of the Griesbach Hypothesis. See "The Two-Gospel Hypothesis," *DR* 33 (1980): 267-79.

[3]J. A. T. Robinson, *The Priority of John* (London: SCM Press, 1985) 34.

[4]See ibid., xiii.

dating the New Testament.[5] After admitting that "with every motive for assigning an early date to the gospels, I found this encountered too many difficulties for me to get over", Dodd went on to say:

> However, I am open to conviction. You are certainly justified in questioning the whole structure of the accepted 'critical' chronology of the NT writings, which avoids putting anything earlier than 70, so that none of them are available for anything like first-generation testimony. I should agree with you that much of this late dating is quite arbitrary, even wanton, the offspring not of any argument that can be presented, but rather of the critic's prejudice that if he appears to assent to the traditional position of the early church he will be thought no better than a stick-in-the-mud. . . . It is surely significant that when historians of the ancient world treat the gospels, they are quite unaffected by the sophistications of *Redaktionsgeschichte,* and handle the documents as if they were what they professed to be.[6]

This narrow view, still widely prevalent today, was exemplified in the attitude of the Markan priority research team at the Jerusalem Gospel Symposium of 1984,[7] who argued on the assumption that by far the most important factor for the solution of the Synoptic Problem is the internal critical evidence, wishing to leave out the historical witness and the intractable historical problems created by multiplying sources and by positing little independent Christian communities which in turn are supposed to have created the settings and the data of so many Gospel pericopes. However, the importance of "extra-critical" data was finally recognized in the ultimate agreed statement by all three research teams regarding the importance of discovering a "literary, historical, and theological explanation of the evangelists' compositional activity."[8] This was a breakthrough in the sense that it was the first occasion in modern times that a group of professional exegetes representing the whole spectrum of New Testament Scholarship, including a team of Markan priorists, had at least tacitly recognized that the ecclesiastical tradition was a factor that had to be taken seriously into consideration. In fact, of course there can be no solution of the synoptic problem worthy of the name that fails to take fully into consideration all the historical and patristic witness, and especially the Fathers, whose statements should be treated with the same respect as is ac-

---

[5]*Redating the New Testament* (London: SCM Press, 1976) 360.

[6]Cf. ibid., 360.

[7]A privately organized meeting of an independent group of scholars belonging to diverse religious traditions and diverse academic backgrounds, to reopen the question of the interrelationship of the Synoptic Gospels at Jerusalem in April 1984.

[8]A quotation from the as yet unpublished concluding communiqué issued by the Jerusalem Gospel Symposium.

corded by professional secular historians to the testimonies of the secular world.

In this short essay I propose in the first place to take note of certain guidelines and signposts provided by the tradition with regard to the formation of the Gospels; and then, in the light of these, to outline a coherent theory of the relationship of the Gospel of Luke to Matthew and to the developing apostolic church; though we shall find that it cannot be completed without also involving the Gospel of Mark.

Our first guideline is this. Eusebius of Caesarea tells us that "there is a firm tradition that they (i.e., Matthew and John) took to writing of necessity."[9] The reasons that he himself offers for this necessity may seem to us rather banal, but the statement itself is surely thoroughly sound, since there must have been very important reasons indeed for such wonderful masterpieces as Matthew and John to be brought into existence, each in its own particular church. The implication of course is that neither Gospel was the result of some private initiative based on a human whim, but that each was prepared for a particular church by a member of that church whom all trusted, for a highly relevant purpose. For if the Gospel had not grown out of the special needs of that church, there would inevitably have been some controversy, and some echo of it would have left its trace in the annals of that church; but, at least in the case of Matthew, there was never any sign of any such controversy. And what Eusebius expressly said of Matthew and John must also apply to the Gospels of Luke and Mark, at least in the sense that Paul and Peter were intimately connected with their publication.

Our second guideline is that all the evidence goes to show that the content and the preaching of the tradition was strictly and exclusively controlled by the Apostles from the very beginning.[10] For there is no evidence to be found within the canonical documents of the New Testament that either individual Christian rabbis or little Christian communities created the Gospel material in the manner suggested by the Bultmannians. It is always the authority of an apostle (in the Acts, chiefly Peter and Paul) who from his own personal eyewitness proclaims and interprets the message of the Gospel to the people, who receive it reverently and without demur. Furthermore Paul, who saw the living Christ personally on the road to Damascus but who was otherwise dependent on the tradition he received from

---

[9]Cf. Eusebius, *Eccl. Hist.* 3.24-25.

[10]Cf. Acts 2:42: "And they devoted themselves to the apostles' teaching" (RSV); Acts 4:33: "And with great power the apostles gave their testimony to the resurrection of the Lord Jesus" (RSV).

the other apostles, is always careful to distinguish between the "word of the Lord" and his own personal interpretation of the Gospel.[11] The Acts and the Letters of Paul (and of 1 Peter) make it clear that the control of the tradition remained exclusively in the hands of the Apostles, and that all deviations, like those of Simon Magus, were immediately and forcefully corrected by them.[12] The role of the Christian assembly was invariably expected to be passive as regards the reception of the tradition. The fact that all the New Testament books are attributed to one or other of the Twelve Apostles (except Mark and Luke, who were always understood to have been disciples of Peter and Paul) is a sign that the Great Church looked only to the Twelve and to Paul for the content of the written tradition. Thus the modern notion that a number of the Gospel sayings and stories were in circulation independently of the Apostles in the first forty years of the Church finds no support in the earliest scriptures. That such documents did start to circulate after the apostolic era, when there were no Apostles left to repudiate them, is of course a fact; and the gnostic literature is proof of it. But it is gratuitous and misleading to hypothecate special sources from without the apostolic circle to explain the divergencies between the Synoptic Gospels, if it is possible to explain their origin without them. Our third guideline will therefore be that our existing New Testament documents do not need to be explained by others outside the Canon.

Our fourth guideline is one that was first clearly expressed by Augustine of Hippo, but which is more or less demanded by the close-knit and fraternal nature of the apostolic church. For in his *De Consensu Evangelistarum* he asserted that no evangelist wrote his Gospel in ignorance of the work of his predecessor or predecessors, and that the order was Matthew, Mark, Luke, John.[13] The principle is again surely sound enough, since the Letters of Paul and the Acts of the Apostles reveal that all forms of communication were comparatively fast and secure in the contemporary Roman world. The fact that Paul wrote so many letters surely proves that he found writing them a very good way of communicating his knowledge and love of Jesus. And since Jesus was the center of the thoughts of all Christians, the composition of any work about him would have been a matter of eager interest to all Christians everywhere, and there were shops for copying books in every major city of the Empire. The presumption then is that

---

[11]Cf. 1 Thess 4:15; 1 Cor 7:25.

[12]Cf. Acts 8:14-24.

[13]*De Consensu Evangelistarum*, 1.2.3; but cf. 4.10.11, for some support for the order Matt-Luke-Mark-John.

all apostolic witness intended for publication in the Roman world at least got circulated at once.

Our fifth guideline is the order of the ancient formula "Matthew-Mark-Luke-John," which was current at least as early as the middle of the second century. For it seems to be the order of the Muratorian Canon (c.200), of Irenaeus, of Origen, of Eusebius (generally speaking), of Jerome and of Augustine.[14] The Gospels are of course quoted in other sequences by Clement of Alexandria (Luke second and Mark third) and by the Old Latin manuscripts (Matthew and John before Luke and Mark), by the former in the order of composition and by the latter in order of the dignity of the authors. The formula itself seems to indicate that the Gospel of Matthew has always been regarded as the first chronologically as well as first in order of importance; and because of the close literary connection between Matthew, Luke and Mark, our formula also seems to suggest that John was the last in chronological order.[15]

Our sixth guideline is the universal affirmation of the Fathers that both Matthew and John have the Apostles Matthew and John as the authors of their respective Gospels.[16] And since all agree that Matthew was the first to be written, this argues that Matthew must have been written very early and quite possibly before the persecution recorded in Acts 12, i.e. before A.D. 44.

Our seventh and final guideline is the very fact that there are just three synoptic Gospels, no fewer and no more. The correct hypothesis of synoptic origins must therefore also explain why there are exactly three of them; so far no hypothesis has offered any specific reason for this phenomenon.[17]

The value of these guidelines is considerably enhanced by the fact that Harold Riley has shown that the internal critical evidence is also heavily tilted in favor of the priority of Matthew, and that it also supports Luke's dependence on Matthew and Mark's dependence on both.[18] That is to say, although Riley's work and the guidelines are by no means probative of the

---

[14]For a fuller discussion of the historical and patristic evidence, see Bernard Orchard and Harold Riley, *The Order of the Synoptics* (Macon GA: Mercer University Press, 1987) pt. 2, chs. 2-5.

[15]But see Robinson, *Priority of John,* 33-35.

[16]Cf. Orchard and Riley, *The Order of the Synoptics,* pt. 2, chs. 3-5.

[17]Cf. ibid., pt. 3, ch. 4, conclusion.

[18]Cf. ibid., pt. 1, passim; for further recent discussion of the Synoptic Problem, see *New Synoptic Studies,* ed. W. R. Farmer (Macon: Mercer University Press, 1983).

view that the Gospels were all composed in the lifetime of the Apostles, they are fully compatible with it; and, this being the case, we are now in a position to make legitimate speculations about the thoughts and motives of the principal historical characters of this period in the light of the existing canonical writings.

I start therefore with the Gospel of Matthew in Greek, because this was the only appropriate language for use by a Church which saw the whole world as the field of its evangelization. Internal evidence also shows that Matthew was the right document to meet the needs of the Jerusalem Church as we find it in the first twelve chapters of the Acts of the Apostles.[19] For its first concern was to prove from the canonical books of the Jews that Jesus was the Christ and that he came not to destroy but to fulfill the Law of Moses. It also deals with liturgical, ritual, moral and social questions in a manner that met the anxieties and needs of a Christian minority in the midst of a hostile Jewish environment. It was written for a church that also made universalist claims (cf. 8:11-12; 28:16-20), but it was also a church that as yet had not begun in earnest its mission to the Gentiles. It was this Gospel alone that was available to Paul during his three missionary journeys to convert the Greeks. Precisely because of its orientation towards the Christian Jews of Palestine, this Gospel of Matthew came to be seen by Paul and his disciple Luke as a not wholly suitable instrument for the evangelization of the gentiles, although by virtue of its being the Gospel of the original Church of Jerusalem and of its having the authority of the Twelve Apostles it was irrevocably the fundamental document of the Christian Faith. I therefore envisage Paul, towards the end of his third missionary journey, inviting his disciple Luke to give thought how to compose a new version of the Gospel message that would cater to the intellectual and spiritual requirements of his new churches. The most appropriate time for Paul to have set Luke to work would have been during Paul's imprisonment at Caesarea c.58-60, as described in Acts 21-26, when the "we" passages indicate the presence of Luke. It will now be instructive to ask for the sort of guidelines that Paul would have laid down for Luke to observe in the construction of his new Gospel.

In the first place, given the authority wielded by the Twelve over the tradition, I believe that such a project would have been inconceivable without the personal initiative and the positive approbation and support of an apostle with the authority of Paul, who had been designated by Jesus himself as the Apostle of the Gentiles (Acts 9:15). For according to our

---

[19]Cf. Orchard and Riley, *The Order of the Synoptics*, pt. 3, ch. 1, §2.

hypothesis, the Gospel of Matthew was the Gospel of the primitive Church of Jerusalem, the Church of the Twelve Apostles, the authentic document of the tradition received from Christ himself. Written by the apostle Matthew, with the aid no doubt of the rest of the Twelve including Peter, it recorded the Person and teaching of Jesus in magisterial and monumental form. It was unthinkable that it should ever be outmoded or superseded, and by the year 58 it may well have been in circulation for as much as fifteen years, and so would have enjoyed all this time an inalienable and unassailable position not only in the Jewish Christian churches but also among all the churches established from Jerusalem, including those founded by Paul himself, since he praises highly their imitation of the Churches of God in Judea, 1 Thess 2:14. And since there is clear evidence not only of Paul's use of the Matthean tradition but also of his possession of the actual Greek text of Matthew,[20] it follows that both its strength and its weakness as an instrument for the evangelization of the Gentiles was well known to him; and we too, as a result of our hindsight, are able to understand his desire to have a new presentation of the identical message, one that would satisfy the needs and aspirations of the mass of Greek converts who had been educated outside the Mosaic Law and in an entirely different culture. Paul saw that they needed a positive presentation of Christianity in terms that would be both congenial and credible to them as Greeks. The Gospel of Matthew represented the indigenous Christianity of Judea, but what Paul was looking for was a new perspective, a manifesto that would not only respect the essential message of Matthew but would at the same time remove its preoccupation with matters of little interest or relevance to Greeks, such as Christ's attitude to the Mosaic Law or rabbinic subtleties, and would rather lay stress instead on his universal salvific mission. Yet given the invariable conservatism of Christians in favor of the tradition, no ordinary Christian would dare to claim that the Gospel of Matthew could either be improved on or that anyone might add anything to it. But if, as I believe, Paul was actually going to commission Luke to rework the whole Gospel message for the benefit of his own Greek churches, he would have to guard against the upsurge of a storm of criticism from the Circumcision Party that would be difficult to overcome, and which might even endanger the peace and unity of the whole Church. Nevertheless he must have felt justified in taking the risk, since he had received a mandate from the Lord himself to preach the Gospel to the Greeks; and after some twenty years of mission-

---

[20]Cf. J. B. Orchard, "Thessalonians and the Synoptic Gospels," *Bib* 19 (1938): 19-38.

ary endeavor he knew better than anyone else the sort of style and content this new work ought to have. Moreover there was no one alive comparable to him with the same prestige and authority, with the same vision, courage and ability to bring such a bold project to fruition. For this work would aim to give parity of esteem to the Greek approach to Christianity and to provide a manifesto that would witness that the Gospel was as much at home in the Greek world as in the Jewish. Just as the Gospel of Matthew had been the manifesto of the Church of Jerusalem and had come from within the apostolic band itself by means of a fusion of their personal memories of Jesus, so in the same way I believe that Paul was to look upon the new Gospel of Luke as the manifesto for the Greek-speaking world, the difference being that Paul had no personal memories of Jesus' earthly ministry to hand on, and had to rely on Luke to borrow what was most appropriate from the Gospel of Matthew and then to research the terrain trodden formerly by Jesus to obtain as much authentic material as was available after thirty years.

I think too that Paul had conceived the notion of preparing a Second Gospel already some time before the end of his third missionary journey; furthermore it is highly probable that a missionary of his experience and standing in the Church (cf. Gal 2:1-10) would have consulted at an early stage of his thinking with Peter, who had been presiding over the Church of Jerusalem when Matthew was produced and who was now active elsewhere in the Roman world. The very fact that Luke divides the story of the Acts into two parts, the first under the leadership of Peter, and the second under the leadership of Paul, indicates the parity of esteem that he had for both of them, and allows us to infer the reciprocal regard of Peter and Paul for each other. For after his brush with the Circumcision Party (cf. Acts 15), Paul understood very well that it was one thing to plan and to execute the writing of a new Gospel, but quite another to get it into circulation without upsetting powerful forces in the Church. We can therefore be reasonably sure that he would prudently have made certain of the support of an authority like Peter before allowing Luke to begin his task.

The hypothesis that I now wish to illustrate is that Luke was commissioned by Paul to search for authentic words and deeds of Jesus that would best suit the needs of Paul's converts. Hence with the Gospel of Matthew in his hands and as his guide, Luke was able to visit in person the scenes of Jesus' ministry and to interview individuals who had either witnessed, or even been the subject of, Jesus' miracles, and who had listened to his preaching just thirty years before. Thus he was able to gather a great deal of new material as well as striking additions to existing stories of Matthew—so much in fact that he would be forced to omit or to abbreviate some parts of the original Matthew. Among those whom Luke would have interviewed would have been all the important figures in the Church of Jerusalem at that time (58-61), including James of Jerusalem (martyred in 62), also the younger relatives of Jesus, a number of the women who had ministered to him (Luke 8:2-3), and of course scores of persons up and down Judea and Galilee, who had seen and heard and spoken to him and with him, Luke 1:1-4. However, since neither Luke nor Paul had personally known Jesus during his lifetime, neither could witness at firsthand to the truth of any of the stories told about him, nor even of the extra details he was able to add to the stories in Matthew. Thus the Gospel of Luke would never be able to possess the authority wielded by the Gospel of Matthew unless Luke or Paul could find one of the Twelve to authenticate it for him. And so far as we know the only Apostles still alive in the Mediterranean world at that time were John and Peter, around whose figure Luke was also weaving his account of the first fifteen years of the Church's life (Acts 1-12). But if he could persuade the latter of these two to confirm the truth and validity of his presentation, his Gospel could then circulate with the same authority as Matthew's. But before we record the success of his quest for approbation, we must look into Luke's method of construction when he came to write it after gathering together all the materials he had acquired by personal research during Paul's incarceration at Caesarea c.58-60.

According to the 2GH Luke had Matthew before him as his exemplar. Now the Gospel of Matthew is in fact an incredibly beautiful literary whole, and all of a piece from its opening genealogy of Christ to the final instruction of Christ to preach his message to the whole world. And of course its style and its content are definitely Hebraic, as was noted by Papias, when at the beginning of the second century he wrote that "Matthew was composed in the Hebrew style (*hebraïdi dialektō*)".[21] Luke is however a literary masterpiece of another kind. It is composed in the kind of writing that a cultured citizen of the Greco-Roman world would expect to find the biography of a great statesman or national hero. That is to say, Luke conforms to the contemporary convention of "bios" literature, to the genre of ancient biographies.[22] The biographer was expected to expound the virtues of his hero by relating how his subject had been favored at birth by the gods, how he had compelled the admiration of all men by his magnanimity and by his moral and physical excellence; how he had won the unsolicited ac-

---

[21]Cf. Eus. *Eccl.Hist.* 3.39, 15-16.

[22]Cf. P. L. Shuler, *A Genre for the Gospels: The Biographical Character of Matthew* (Philadelphia: Fortress Press, 1982) 34-57.

claim of his fellow-citizens and of foreigners too by his exploits on behalf of his nation; how he had courageously confronted his enemies jealous and envious of his noble achievements; and how in his noble death he had displayed all the qualities of his life at their best. Finally there had to be an epilogue to recount the lasting benefits his virtuous life had brought to his country, thus proving that he had not lived in vain and had left behind a glorious name. Clearly in Jesus Luke had the perfect subject and the most exciting material possible; his main problem would be to insert all he wanted to relate within the limits imposed by his use of Matthew and by the length of the normal commercial roll, since the codex was not then in normal use for books. Luke indeed found it impossible to get everything on to one roll, so he divided his work into two parts; firstly, the origin, ministry, death and resurrection of Jesus, (and he made a special point of anchoring certain key dates of his hero's life within the context of the contemporary history of the Roman Empire); and on the second roll he related the worldwide repercussions of his noble example and of his glorious victory on behalf of the human race.

With all the foregoing in mind we are now in a position to compare the structure of Luke with that of Matthew; and the similarities and dissimilarities will give us important insights into Luke's application of the principles governing the construction of his Gospel.[23] The best way for us to see what he did and how he did it, is for us to apply our Luke to our Matthew, setting them side by side and pericope by pericope without the intervention of Mark, which *ex hypothesi* was not yet in existence. But right at the beginning of the process I came across a serious obstacle caused by the column arrangement of Huck and Aland,[24] the synopses in current use, which made effective comparison almost impossible. Eventually I realized that they were both originally constructed by first applying Matthew to Mark and then adding Luke to the combination. Thus the connection between Luke and Matthew was both muddled and smudged, and I was forced to conclude that there was nothing for it but to construct my own synopsis *ab initio* to simulate the comparison of Luke with Matthew, which is the real key to the understanding of the shape of Luke.[25] By starting with the ap-

---

[23]Cf. J. B. Orchard, *Matthew, Luke and Mark* (Greater Manchester: Koinonia Press, 1976) 37-68.

[24]K. Aland, *Synopsis Quattuor Evangeliorum* (Stuttgart: Württembergische Bibelanstalt, 1963); Albert Huck—H. Greeven, *Synopse* (Tübingen: Mohr, 1981).

[25]Cf. *Synopsis of the Four Gospels in Greek* (Edinburgh: T. & T. Clark/Macon GA: Mercer University Press, 1983).

plication of Luke to Matthew I found out that in this way Luke becomes the middle term, or the mean, between Matthew and Mark, as and when Mark is added to the other two. And at the time I learnt that there is no such thing as a "neutral" synopsis, as the editors of both Huck and Aland have fondly thought their synopses to be. In fact every vertical-column synopsis is of its nature biased either for or against the 2GH according as Luke or Mark is taken as the mean or middle term between the other two Gospels.[26] The decision to adopt the column order Matthew-Luke-Mark— the first major decision—meant that this new synopsis would illustrate the 2GH in a special way, and so, if you will, be biased in its favor.

A first general glance reveals that Luke has broadly speaking respected the main structure of Matthew and conformed to it; that is to say, we find in both, in the same order, the Birth Narrative, the Mission of John the Baptist, the Galilean Ministry, the Ministry in Jerusalem, the Passion and Death, and the Resurrection Appearances.[27] The main divergences of order are not numerous but are significant and can best be followed in my new Greek Synopsis. The first problem in applying Luke to Matthew arises at Matthew 4:23, which leads up to the Sermon on the Mount; and here came my second "judgment call," namely, to decide whether to parallel Matthew's Great Sermon with Luke's Sermon on the Plain, or not, as alternative positions are possible, e.g. at Matthew 12:15-21. However, since both these Sermons have a similar beginning, middle and ending, I decided to parallel them, making Matthew 4:24-7:27 = Luke 6:12-49.[28] This decision was at once seen to have far-reaching effects on all further parallels down to Matthew 14:1. Among the consequences to be noted was that Luke had brought forward the Parables' Discourse (8:4-18), so that it is no longer parallel to Matthew's (although in both Huck and Aland they are shown as parallel). And this decision made it possible for Luke to parallel his vestigial missionary discourse (9:2-5) with Matthew's (10:5-15), and later on to parallel the other major discourses of Matthew.[29]

---

[26]Cf. J. B. Orchard, "Are All Gospel Synopses Biased?" *TZ* 34 (1978): 149-62; also, D. L. Dungan, "Theory of Synopsis Construction," *Bib* 61 (1980): 305-29; also J. B. Orchard, "Professor Neirynck and the 'Neutrality' of Vertical-Column Synopses," *ETL* (1986): fasc. 1.

[27]Cf. Orchard, *Matthew, Luke and Mark*, 41-42: "Table 1: Sequence of Gospel Topics."

[28]Cf. ibid., 149: "Chart IIA: The Great Sermon."

[29]For a visual presentation of the parallelism of the major discourses, cf. ibid., flyleaf insert: "Chart I: Unit-Sequence Comparison of Matthew-Luke-Mark."

At this point Luke very acutely observed that Matthew had divided the Galilean Ministry into three phases between the Choosing of the Twelve at 8:2 and his departure at 19:1-2; namely, firstly 8:2–11:1, secondly 11:1–14:13, (which happens to be the interval when the disciples were out preaching on their own), and thirdly the period 14:13-19:1. Luke has however made this division his own in a rather different fashion by abbreviating all three divisions in varying degrees; firstly we have his 7:1-9:6, secondly, his 9:7-10a; and thirdly his 9:10b-9:51. The most striking difference is that Luke has reduced the interval of the Apostles' absence, from Matthew's three chapters to just three verses (9:7-9), in which he described Herod's bewilderment at all the "goings on" in his kingdom. How did Luke achieve this rearrangement while remaining faithful to the general framework of Matthew? Chiefly by means of the creation of his Central Section, which he situated at 9:51 (= Matt 19:1), when according to Matthew Jesus left Galilee for good, and ultimately for Jerusalem.[30] Even for Matthew this journey was somewhat indeterminate and leisurely between Matthew 19:3 and the arrival of Jesus at Jericho (20:29-34). Luke however decided to make this Section (9:51-18:14) into a very important feature of his Gospel, for it occupies about one third of its total length. For him too it is a Journey Section, a long and indeterminate journey, it is true, but one into which he pours almost everything that he withdraws from Matthew's Great Sermon, from his Parables' Discourse, from his Missionary Discourse, from the material with which Matthew has filled up the space while the Apostles were away evangelizing (Matt 11:1-13:58 + 14:1-12), and also the material he withdraws from the discourses of Matthew 18:1-35, 23:1-39, and 24:1-25:46. Thus the Central Section has become the storehouse for all those Sayings of Jesus which Luke has taken out of their Matthean context, save for a few minor exceptions, e.g. the Lukan doublets of 8:16-18, or Matthew 10:17-22 (= Luke 21:12-19). It is clear that while Luke intended to preserve the main chronological framework of Matthew, he did not intend that in his Gospel the action of Jesus should be held up by the six long discourses that we find in Matthew. The creation of such a section was for Luke really the only way in which he could remain faithful to the tradition established by Matthew and yet be able to introduce into his Gospel the new perspectives that Paul required. Even so there was very little of Matthew that he felt he could omit, apart from duplicate stories (such as he found in Matt 14:22-16:12), also certain Mat-

---

[30]Cf. ibid., 150-51—"Chart IIB: Central Section of Luke with Matthean Parallels."

thean parables rehearsing the same theme, e.g., Matthew 13:44-50, and so on. On the other hand the Central Section gave him a number of new options; for editorially he was now free to move stories and sayings around to suit the new pattern; he could now introduce new anecdotes either into the Central Section, e.g. 9:52-56, or he could insert them into his newly streamlined narrative, e.g., the Miraculous Catch (5:1-11), or The Widow's Mite (21:1-4). The Central Section also allowed him to retain, and yet to give less prominence to, some of Jesus' strictures on his fellow Jews, e.g. their exclusion from the Kingdom (Luke 13:28,29 = Matt 8:11-12), or his Condemnation of the Scribes and Pharisees (Luke 11:37-54 = Matt 23:1-36). By streamlining his account of the Galilean Ministry, by skillful manipulation of the pericope order, by making full use of the Central Section to retain almost every saying of Jesus and by his skillful introduction of new material here and there, Luke was able to change the whole emphasis of the Gospel into a demonstration of the good fortune of the Gentiles in being given equality by Jesus with the original Chosen People, but without humiliating the Jews still further.

One of the aims of this essay has been to speculate on the thesis that Luke was splendidly right when in his Acts of the Apostles he illustrated the history of the development of the apostolic church in terms of the leadership of the two greatest of its figures, Peter and Paul. If the thesis is correct, the Gospel of Matthew is to be viewed as the manifesto of the primitive Church of Jerusalem, presided over and guided by Peter in the critical years of its formation. Matthew is then the "blueprint" or handbook for all future expansion,[31] and the Church it was written for was the model for all the churches of the world that issued from it, including those established by Paul. We have very little certain knowledge about the foundations of the other Apostles; but thanks to Luke we have a great deal of information about the churches Paul founded and about the Gospel he preached, and in their writings we have a priceless contemporary account of how they set about the evangelization of the Roman Empire. Luke's Gospel was constructed to be Paul's special teaching instrument, and in the Acts (and in the Letters of Paul) we have the background necessary to understand the connection between Luke and Matthew. Under the guidance of Paul and in the light of his experience among the Greeks, Luke was able to restate the main teaching of Matthew in a form and style that appealed to the Greek mind and heart.

---

[31]Cf. K. Stendahl, "Commentary on Matthew," *Peake's Commentary on the Bible* (1962) §673c.

Thus the complementarity of Luke to Matthew is the mirror of the complementarity of the mission of Paul to that of Peter, as we see them focussed in the Acts. And in our view the document that binds together these two distinct yet complementary Gospels is the Gospel of Mark, who according to the most ancient tradition was the *hermēneutēs* of Peter. J. J. Griesbach, to his great honor, saw this in a brilliant insight, but at the literary level only; he failed to understand what lay behind and underneath the bare literary relationship, namely the union of heart and mind of the two founders and the completion of their grand strategy for the Church. But the unifying role of the Gospel of Mark is a separate topic and is beyond the scope of the present essay. The logical continuation would be to go on to show that because of its secondary character Luke needed the approval of an eyewitness apostle to gain proper accreditation in the Church. Clement of Alexandria has recorded the very ancient tradition that the Gospel of Mark is neither more nor less than the discourses of Peter given in Rome and recorded by his disciple Mark. And if we were to go on to combine this piece of information with the insight of Griesbach that Mark had the Gospel of Matthew and Luke in his hands when composing his Gospel, we would have found what looks like the final piece that completes the "jigsaw" of the Synoptic Problem. That is to say, Peter himself was the apostolic eyewitness who provided the accreditation for the Gospel of Luke by personally comparing it with the Gospel of Matthew as he gave his own oral version of the stories common to both, at which he himself had been present in person. And this would be why there are just three Synoptic Gospels, no fewer and no more!

CHAPTERS IN THE HISTORY
OF THE LINGUISTIC ARGUMENT
FOR SOLVING THE SYNOPTIC PROBLEM
THE NINETEENTH CENTURY IN CONTEXT

David B. Peabody

Werner Georg Kümmel has claimed that the two document hypothesis was proven by H. J. Holtzmann, in part, on the basis of linguistic arguments.[1] More recently, C. M. Tuckett has claimed that the Griesbach hypothesis was disproven, in part, on the basis of linguistic arguments.[2] Both of these scholars appeal to work done in the nineteenth century. Together their claims represent a serious challenge to those who would revive the Griesbach or "Two Gospel" hypothesis today.

The purpose of this study is to reexamine the work of Holtzmann and his predecessors and to suggest a more adequate reading of the history of the linguistic argument, a reading which also views the work of the nineteenth century as but one chapter in a much longer history. A full account of the linguistic argument begins at least in the second century BCE.[3]

At that time in pre-Christian Alexandria, Homer's *Iliad* and *Odyssey* were being subjected to rather thorough literary analysis. These classical Greek texts were the basis for education but variations in the manuscripts had developed by that time. Educators felt a need to provide a standard text for educational purposes in the Hellenistic schools.

It became necessary to establish sound canons of literary criticism for reconstructing a text of the *Iliad* and *Odyssey* which would be closest to the actual words of Homer. One such canon prescribed a preference for the reading which most conformed to the literary style of the author.

---

[1] Werner Georg Kümmel, *The New Testament: The History of the Investigation of Its Problems,* trans. S. McLean Gilmour and Howard C. Kee (Nashville: Abingdon Press, 1972).

[2] C. M. Tuckett, "The Griesbach Hypothesis in the 19th Century," *JSNT* 3 (1979): 29-60.

[3] Bruce Manning Metzger, *The Text of the New Testament: Its Transmission, Corruption, and Restoration,* 2nd ed. (Oxford: Oxford University Press, 1968) esp. ch. 5: "The Origins of Textual Criticism as a Scholarly Discipline," 149-55.

The literary style of every author is distinctive if not unique. While authors may share any number of literary characteristics, no two will have exactly the same combination. Like the human personalities they reflect, styles cannot be duplicated though elements may be imitated.

An author's literary characteristics may be isolated by studying the words, phrases, and grammatical constructions which reoccur within the total body of his or her work. An author's literary style is the composite of these characteristics. Passages not conforming to it may reflect the style of the copyist of that text.

Students of the history of text criticism of the Greek New Testament have noted that the text critical signs which were utilized by the pre-Christian text critics of Homer in Alexandria were also used by Origen in his famous *Hexapla.*[4] This continuity in technique extending to the critics of the Christian scriptures in the third century CE suggests that other pre-Christian techniques would have been known to Christian scholars in Alexandria.

It can be demonstrated that Dionysius of Alexandria, a student of Origen, used recurrent words and phrases which he found within the Johannine corpus of the New Testament, in order to identify the author of the Fourth Gospel with the author of the first ''Johannine'' Epistle and to distinguish the author of these books from the author of the Apocalypse.

Eusebius quoted this detailed work of Dionysius in order to discount the canonical authority of the Apocalypse and, more importantly, the Millenarianism which that text tended to support.[5]

For Eusebius, canonical authority included the requirement of apostolic authorship. Dionysius had demonstrated that the Apocalypse had a different author from the Gospel and the first Epistle of John. Since Eusebius assumed that the apostle John wrote the Gospel and the first Epistle of John which reflected the same literary style, (and since he could think of only one apostle named John, the son of Zebedee), Eusebius concluded that the Apocalypse was not authored by the apostle, John. It therefore had no claim to canonical authority as derived from known apostolic authorship.

Although there are no known comparable lists of literary characteristics of other New Testament documents collected by the ancient Church Fathers, we do know that similar challenges to the apostolic authority of 2 Peter and Hebrews were made in antiquity at least through the time of

---

[4]W. R. Farmer, *The Last Twelve Verses of Mark,* SNTSMS 25 (Cambridge: Cambridge University Press, 1974) 14 and the works cited in 14n1.

[5]Eusebius, *Hist. eccl.* 7.24-25.

Jerome. Differences in literary style were perceived when 1 Peter was compared with 2 Peter, and when Hebrews was compared with the balance of the Pauline corpus, including the Pastorals.[6]

Clement of Alexandria, Origen, Dionysius, Eusebius, Jerome and some later students of the Christian canon isolated the linguistic characteristics within New Testament documents to determine authorship because, according to the ancients, the author gave any text its authority.

My research thus far has not revealed any significant use of this type of linguistic argument among students of the New Testament in the West after Jerome and before Erasmus. At present, I account for this by the rise in popularity of the Latin versions prior to Jerome and the ultimate dominance of the Vulgate in the West after Jerome completed his translation. Of course, study of the literary characteristics of an author writing in Greek cannot be pursued in translations. It may be that this type of work survived in the East where the Scripture continued to be read in Greek but, as yet, I am unaware of it.

Not until Erasmus's critical edition of the Greek New Testament appeared in the wake of Renaissance interest in classical learning was it again popular to study the literary styles of New Testament authors in Greek.[7] Erasmus also popularized the work of Jerome by publishing the first critical edition of his works.[8] At that time, students of the New Testament were reintroduced to the ancient controversies over the authorship of various New Testament books based on perceived differences in literary style since Jerome had preserved comments about these controversies in his writings. Martin Luther made use of some of these in discounting the canonical authority of Hebrews and the Apocalypse.[9]

---

[6]Discussion of the authorship of 1 Peter and 2 Peter may be found in Jerome, *De Viris Illustribus,* 1. Discussions of the authorship of Hebrews and the balance of the Pauline corpus may be found in Clement of Alexandria quoted in Eusebius, *Hist. eccl.* 6.14.1-2; in Origen, also quoted in Eusebius *Hist. eccl.* 6.25.11-14; in Jerome, *De Viris Illustribus* 5 and 15.

[7]Erasmus, *Novum Instrumentum omne . . .* (Basel, 1516). See Erasmus's comments on the authorship of 2 Peter at paragraph 617 and his comments on the authorship of Hebrews at paragraph 600.

[8]In 9 vols. (Basel, 1516).

[9]Martin Luther, "Prefaces to the New Testament," in *Luther's Works,* vol. 35: American Edition: *Word and Sacrament* 1, trans. and ed. E. Theodore Bachmann and Charles M. Jacobs (Philadelphia: Muhlenberg Press, 1960) 355-411 esp. 390-92 on 1-2 Peter, 394-95 on Hebrews, 395-98 on James and Jude, and 398-411 on Revelation.

But there was also a Catholic voice early in the sixteenth century who was conversant with this type of argumentation. Cardinal Cajetan, in replying to the linguistic argument against the apostolic authorship of 2 Peter, pointed out the logical flaw in the argument. He agreed that 1 and 2 Peter were different in literary style but noted that, if only one of the letters could be by the apostle, then it might just as well be 2 Peter as 1 Peter. In the end, however, Cajetan objected to the validity of this whole type of argumentation noting that works by Gregory differed in literary style in spite of their authorship by one person.[10]

It was in the early decades of the nineteenth century that the first serious work on the linguistic characteristics of the Synoptic gospels was carried out. This was done in order to respond to two different but not unrelated challenges to the canonical authority of parts of these gospels. Since the time of John Calvin, Protestants had been reacting to the tradition of the Church which stated that Mark was the abbreviator of Matthew. This, of course, is a tradition which may be traced back to a statement in Book 1 of Augustine's *de Consensu Evangelistarum* but does not represent any part of what Augustine himself described as the more probable view of Mark and its relationship to the other canonical gospels in his concluding statement about Synoptic relationships in Book 4.10.11.[11]

Some of the traditions of the Church Fathers about the gospels were received by the Reformers through the Catenae of the Medieval schoolmen. The most important of these catenae, the so-called *Catena Aurea* of Thomas Aquinas, does not record the relevant passage from Book 4 of Augustine's *de Consensu*.[12]

Whatever the explanation may be, some of the Reformers had an imperfect picture of the tradition. This can be seen in the fact that Calvin ascribes the view that Mark was the abbreviator of Matthew to Jerome rather than Augustine. As far as I know, Jerome never passed on this view anywhere in his work.

[10]Cardinal Cajetan (Thomas de Vio), *Epistola Pauli et Aliorum Apostolorum* (1532) ¶189 and ¶217.

[11]David B. Peabody, "Augustine and the Augustinian Hypothesis: A Reexamination of Augustine's Thought in *de Consensu Evangelistarum*," in *New Synoptic Studies,* ed. W. R. Farmer (Macon GA: Mercer University Press, 1983) 37-64.

[12]S. Thomas Aquinas, *Catena Aurea: Commentary on the Four Gospels, Collected out of the Works of the Fathers,* vol. 2: *St. Mark,* trans. John Dobree Dalgairns (Oxford: John Henry Parker, 1842).

Calvin disputed this tradition by postulating that the Synoptic gospels stood in no literary relationship to one another at all.[13] Presumably this returned to Mark a certain dignity not accorded him as the abbreviator of Matthew.

Later critics like John Mill and J. J. Wetstein,[14] two eighteenth century editors of the Greek New Testament, could not deny something which Augustine had affirmed at the turn of the fifth century, namely, that no one of the Evangelists did his work as if in ignorance of that of his predecessor(s). While admitting that the evidence within the gospels supported this, they could not agree that Mark was the abbreviator of Matthew. John Mill cited a significant amount of text where Mark represented an expansion or elaboration of Matthew. This evidence, of course, contradicted the view of Mark as an abbreviator. The material isolated by Mill was adopted by J. D. Koppe and expanded in his article "Marcus non Epitomator Matthaei" in 1782.[15] More evidence was marshalled by Bartus van Willes in a dissertation prepared at Utrecht, where literary analysis of the Johannine materials, like that of Dionysius, appeared in early dissertations also supervised by van Willes's *Doktorvater,* Jodocus Heringa.[16]

---

[13]John Calvin, *A Harmony of the Gospels: Matthew, Mark and Luke (and the Epistles of James and Jude),* trans. A. W. Harrison (Grand Rapids: Eerdmans, 1972) xxxviii.

[14]John Mill, *Novum Testamentum Graecum . . . ,* editio secunda (Lipsiae: Sumptibus Filii J. Friderici Gleditschii, 1723) prolegomena, 101-11; J. J. Wetstein, 'Η ΚΑΙΝΗ ΔΙΑΘΗΚΗ, *Novum Testamentum Graecum . . .* (Amstelaedami: Ex Officina Dommeriana, 1751) 1:551.

[15]J. B. Koppe, *Marcus non epitomator Matthaei,* Programme, University of Göttingen (Helmstadii, 1782); reprinted: ed. D. J. Pott and G. A. Ruperti, *Sylloge commentationum theologicarum* 1 (Helmstadii, 1800) 35-69.

[16]Bartus van Willes (praes. Jodocus Heringa), *Specimen hermeneuticum de iis, quae ab uno Marco sunt narrata, aut copiosus et explicatius ab eo, quam a caeteris evangelistis, exposita* (Traiecti ad Rhenum, 1811): Car. Wilh. Stronk (praes. Jodocus Heringa) *Specimen hermeneutico-theolo. de doctrina et dictione Johannis apostoli ad Jesu magistri doctrinam dictionemque exacte composita* (Traiecti ad Rhenum, 1797); Hendrick Herman Donker-Curtius (praes. Jodocus Heringa) *Specimen hermeneutico-theologicum de Apocalypsi ale indole doctrina et scribendi genere Johannis apostoli no abhorrente* (Traiecti ad Rhenum, n.d.) [1799]; Adr. Christianse (praes. Jodocus Heringa) *Specimen hermeneutico-theologicum exhibens vindicias facultatis, apostolis J. Chr. alim datae, peregrinis loquendi sermonibus* (Traiecti ad Rhenum, 1801); Jac. Ju. Scholten (praes. Jodocus Heringa) *Specimen hermeneuticum de diversis significationibus vocis* χαρις *in NT*

If the view of Mark as an abbreviator of Matthew tended to discount the value of Mark, matters could only get worse with the advent of the Owen-Griesbach hypothesis.[17] If there was very little material in Mark which was not also in Matthew, there was even less distinctive material in Mark when his gospel was compared to both Matthew and Luke.

Griesbach himself claimed that there were but 24 verses in Mark which did not derive from Matthew and Luke.[18] Whereas the uniform tradition of the Church had always affirmed the chronological priority of Matthew, G. C. Storr (in 1786) was already advocating the priority of Mark. He protested against Griesbach's hypothesis by claiming that these 24 verses left very little room for the Petrine influence on Mark which the tradition of the Church had affirmed since Papias.[19]

Griesbach's response to Storr was to agree with him, and, making a virtue out of a necessity, he discounted this tradition of the Church as worthless along with most of the other traditions of the Fathers.[20] This attitude toward the external evidence marks an important difference between the original position of Griesbach and that of the neo-Griesbachians who put equal weight on both the external and the internal evidence in coming to their conclusions about Synoptic relationships.

On the other hand, J. D. Schulze was not so ready to discount the whole of the tradition about Mark's relationship to Peter.[21] Yet he could not deny,

---

(Traiecti ad Rhenum, 1805). See also the following dissertation supervised by Heringa's colleague at Utrecht, D. H. Wildshutt (praes. Hm. J. Royaards), *Specimen acad. de vi dictionis et sermonis elegantia en ep. P. ad Philem. conspicuus* (Traiecti ad Rhenum, 1809). With the exception of the dissertation by van Willes to which I have had direct access, all of these titles follow the citations given by Georg Benedict Winer, *Handbuch der theologischen Literatur hauptsachlich der protestantischen nebst kurzen biographischen Notizen über die theologischen Schriftsteller,* 3rd ed., 2 vols. (Lepizig: Carl Heinrich Reclam, 1838).

[17]Henry Owen, *Observations on the Four Gospels* (London, 1764); J. B. Orchard and T. R. W. Longstaff, eds. *J. J. Griesbach: Synoptic and Text-Critical Studies 1776-1976* (Cambridge: Cambridge University Press, 1978).

[18]Orchard and Longstaff, *Griesbach Studies,* 80; ET 111.

[19]Orchard and Longstaff, *Griesbach Studies,* 84-87; ET 114-18.

[20]Orchard and Longstaff, *Griesbach Studies,* 84-87; ET 114-18.

[21]Johann Daniel Schulze, "Über den schriftstellerischen Charakter und Werth des Evangelisten Marcus: Ein Beitrag zur Special hermeneutik des N.T." in *Analekten für das Studium der exegetischen und systematischen Theologie,* ed. Karl August Gottlieb Keil and Heinrich Gottlieb Tzschirner, 4 vols. (Leipzig: J. A.

on the basis of his own research, the validity of the view that Mark was third. Schulze set out to demonstrate that one could hold to the Griesbach hypothesis and, at the same time, maintain the Tradition of the Fathers about Mark's relationship to Peter.

Like Mill, Koppe, and van Willes before him, Schulze carefully studied the text of Mark in comparison with those of Matthew and Luke. Unlike Griesbach, however, he found a great deal more than 24 verses in Mark which were not paralleled in Matthew or Luke or both. To be sure, this material did not consist of whole pericopes unique to Mark like the Two Healing stories of Mark 7:32-37 and 8:22-26 or the Parable of the Seed Growing Automatically in Mark 4:26-28; it consisted primarily of additions of words or phrases within pericopes which Mark shared with one or both of the others.[22] By concentrating on these Markan supplements, Schulze was able to discover an impressive number of words and phrases which reoccur within Mark, some of them confined to the supplemental material.

In Schulze's view, this material not only contained identifiable literary characteristics but also reflected a consistency such as would be found in the work of a single author. Here, in Schulze's judgment, was the hand of the author of Mark. Schulze was not willing to speculate about the material's source in the main body of his work, but he did speculate in a footnote that this was the type of material which John Mark could have heard from Peter in the house of his mother, Mary, in Jerusalem.[23]

Of course, Schulze was not surprised at his findings because he began by assuming that Mark had used materials from Matthew and Luke as his sources. Mark's additions would then most likely reflect the hand of the author.

Whatever problems one may have with Schulze's conclusions, one will find his analysis impressive in volume and detail. No wonder his work was the standard on the topic for the first half of the nineteenth century. It was cited as such by Georg Benedict Winer in 1828 and by authors of Introductions to the New Testament during that period, even those produced by

---

Barth) "Erster Abschnitt," 2:2 (1814), 104-51, "Zweiter Abschnitt: Erster Halfte," 2:3 (1815) 69-132, "Zweiter Abschnitt: Zweiter Halfte," 3:1 (1816) 88-127.

[22]For lists of this type of material see Hans-Herbert Stoldt, *History and Criticism of the Marcan Hypothesis,* trans. Donald L. Niewyk (Macon GA: Mercer University Press, 1980) 7-21.

[23]Schulze, "Marcus," Erster Abschnitt, 105-106, n. 5.

critics like Credner who did not share Schulze's source hypothesis.[24] But in 1863 Holtzmann dismissed its significance in one sentence. Since that time it has not been critically reviewed.[25] Holtzmann made no direct use of what earlier critics considered the definitive work on the linguistic characteristics of Mark, but this may not be as serious an omission as it first appears because Holtzmann did make use of Credner's list of the linguistic characteristics of Mark, and Credner learned virtually everything he knew about them from the work of J. D. Schulze.

A second development in New Testament studies which led to a detailed study of the linguistic characteristics of the other two synoptic gospels, Matthew and Luke, was the rise of rationalistic interpretation, particularly as that was expressed in English deism. In 1771, John Williams, an English deist, published a work challenging the authenticity of the first two chapters of Matthew.[26] Williams's work set off a lively exchange of publications between the deists and more orthodox Christians. The challenge of authenticity soon spread to other sections of the canonical gospels including the first two chapters of Luke, the account of Pilate's wife's prophetic dream [Matt 27:9], the resurrection of many saints [Matt 27:52-53], and the guard set at the tomb [Matt 27:62-66, 28:4, 11-15], all features of the gospel narratives which might cause offense to the rationalistic mind. Another feature which unites all these verses is that none of them appear in Mark.

One of the critics who brought the challenge of the authenticity of these verses to German soil was Friedrich Andreas Stroth.[27] Having prepared a critical edition of Eusebius's *Church History,* Stroth was acquainted with the methods of text criticism and he apparently approached the texts of the

---

[24]Winer, *Handbuch;* Karl August Credner, *Einleitung in das Neue Testament* (Halle: Waisenhaus, 1836) 63-69, 102-109, 130-42, 222-35.

[25]Heinrich Julius Holtzmann, *Die Synoptischen Evangelien. Ihr Ursprung und ihr geschichtlicher Charakter* (Leipzig, 1863) 271.

[26]John Williams, *A Free Enquiry into the authenticity of The First and Second Chapters of St. Matthew's Gospel* (London, 1771).

[27][Friedrich Andreas Stroth], "Von Interpolationen im Evangelium Matthaei," in *Repertorium für biblische und morgenlandische Literatur,* 9, ed. J. G. Eichhorn (Leipzig: Weidmann, 1781) 99-156. Stroth was identified as the author of this article by J. G. Eichhorn who was the editor of this journal some years after the article appeared. See J. G. Eichhorn, *Einleitung in das Neue Testament,* vol. 1, 2nd ed. (Leipzig: Weidmann, 1820) 465n1.

Synoptic gospels as if they were something like variant manuscripts of a single original.[28] He wrote

> The evangelist Mark did not have the dubious pericopes to which reference was made above in his exemplar of Matthew. For this, I presuppose that which perhaps no one can deny, that Mark had Matthew in front of him and epitomized him with a drawing in of Luke. Now, not only does Mark begin his gospel precisely with the third chapter of Matthew, but he also omits the other three suspicious pericopes in the passion narrative of Christ [Matt 27:9; Matt 27:52-53; Matt 27:62-66, 28:4, 11-15]. He who certainly omits speeches of Christ but does not easily omit narrative in the rest of his gospel, is also so complete, especially in his passion narrative, that he has each and every circumstance that Matthew has. At least, he narrates and does not omit anything of any importance. How would it be possible, since Mark narrates the rest of the miracles about the death of Jesus and hardly leaves out anything else in the passion narrative which Matthew has, that he would have left out precisely the greatest miracle of all [the raising of many dead at Mt 27:52-53] if he had it in his source, Matthew? This is almost unthinkable. The same thing applies to the story of the guards at the grave [Mt 27:62-66, 28:4, 11-15]. Now in the history of the text of an author one cannot easily find in all of literature a witness which is as old as the witness of Mark in relation to Matthew, a witness which is more than one hundred years older than the text of all our manuscripts [of Matthew] which, in any case, with reference to these main interpolations, can only be of value as witnesses to the Matthew which was translated [into Greek] from the Hebrew. So one must judge which of these two must have the greater weight: Mark or our manuscripts?[29]

This passage from Stroth is noteworthy on several counts:

(1) The use of "epitomized" to describe Mark's use of Matthew, in spite of the additional comment, "with a drawing in of Luke," demonstrates how influential Augustine's "less probable" view remained in this period. Here is the best evidence of which I am aware that the Griesbach hypothesis originated as a modified version of the so-called "Augustinian" hypothesis.

(2) This text provides good evidence that the Synoptic Problem was perceived at least by some critics in Germany in the eighteenth century as a problem of text criticism and canon criticism. That is, one must separate the work of the apostolic authority, Matthew, from that of the apocryphal "Pseudo-Matthew" as Stroth refers to the author of these "interpolations" in Matthew. Since the problem is one of text criticism, it is to be solved by using the canons of the text critics. One must examine the manuscript evidence which in this case turns out to be the texts of other Synoptic

---

[28]See Eusebius, *The Ecclesiastical History*, trans. by Kirsopp Lake, LCL 153 (Cambridge: Harvard University Press, 1965) introduction, xxxi, where it is noted that Stroth's edition of Eusebius appeared in 1779.

[29]Stroth, "Interpolationen," 144-45. The English translation is my own.

gospels and one may use linguistic characteristics to distinguish authors from one another. Stroth appealed to the concentrated use of κατ' ὄναρ within the first two chapters of Matthew and the dream of Pilate's wife in order to distinguish the author of these sections from the author of the balance of Matthew.

(3) Stroth claims that some omissions from Matthew on the part of Mark would be "almost unthinkable." In our own time, the idea that the gospel tradition always grew by means of incremental gain is a feature which characterizes some Multi-Stage theories of Synoptic relationships.

(4) Here is evidence from an advocate of the Griesbach hypothesis that the text of *Mark* should be normative for establishing the text of Matthew.

From here it is not a long road to the priority of Mark (Storr, 1786),[30] or to Eichhorn's *Ur-gospel* (reconstructed from the Triple Tradition, 1794, 1804),[31] or to the priority of *Ur-Marcus* reconstructed from the Triple Tradition plus what Mark shares with Matthew apart from Luke and that which Mark shares with Luke apart from Matthew (Wilke, 1838).[32]

It appears that a liberal Protestant rationalist precursor of Griesbach may be due a place among the founding fathers of Markan priority in the ideological history of the Synoptic Problem.

It is clear from Stroth that his work was apologetic as well as literary, for he closed his article by saying

Our religion gains ground against its opponents if we are able to demonstrate that those pericopes, or even the greatest part of them, are inauthentic.[33]

In 1801 Griesbach himself entered this fray over the authenticity of certain verses in Matthew and Luke.[34] After consulting with Griesbach and gaining his encouragement, another German text critic, Christoph Gotthelf Gersdorf, published the collections he had been compiling since 1786 of

---

[30]G. C. Storr, *Über den Zweck der evangelische Geschichte* (Tübingen, 1786).

[31]Eichhorn, *Einleitung*.

[32]C. G. Wilke, *Der Urevangelist oder exegetisch kritische Untersuchung über das Verwandtschaftsverhältniss der drei ersten Evangelien* (Dresden/Leipzig: Gerhard Fleischer, 1838). See also C. G. Wilke, *Die neutestamentliche Rhetorik, ein Seitenstuck zur Grammatik des neutestamentlichen Sprachidioms* (Dresden/Leipzig: Arnoldische Buchhandlung, 1843).

[33]Stroth, "Interpolationen," 156. The translation is my own.

[34]J. J. Griesbach, "Ἐπιμετρον ad Commentarium Criticum in Matthaei Textum," in D. Io. Iac. Griesbachii, *Commentarius Criticus in Textum Graecum novi Testamenti,* Particula 2 (Jenae: I. C. G. Goepferdt, 1811) 45-64.

linguistic characteristics of Matthew and Luke.[35] Gersdorf wished to demonstrate the unity of literary style in the dubious pericopes and the balance of the gospels being challenged. His work of 1816 must have been convincing because interpolation theories for discounting the apostolic authority of passages like these faded from view after that time. What grew in their place was the theory of Markan priority which was able to achieve the same results by a shift in the source theory about the gospels.

In Kümmel's history of New Testament research and in those by Meijboom, Farmer and Stoldt, the figure of H. J. Holtzmann looms large as the great synthesizer of previous critical opinion.[36] He is the person most to be credited for the general acceptance of the two document hypothesis. But a great deal of the actual spade work which led to Holtzmann's conclusions was done by his predecessors. (See the appendix below, p. 68.) The same can be said of Holtzmann's linguistic data. The first literary characteristic of Holtzmann's Source A (*Ur-Marcus*) is what he calls "the characteristic 'echo'," the repetition of words within a few verses in Mark.[37] Frans Neirynck has now labeled this literary characteristic "Duality in Mark."[38] Holtzmann's presentation of this data (280) corresponds exactly to C. G. Wilke's *Die neutestamentliche Rhetorik* (Dresden/Leipzig: Arnold, 1843) 436-38.

Other examples might be cited but this is sufficient to show that Holtzmann adopts large sections of others' works into his own argument, sometimes ignoring the original context for the data or the method used in marshalling it. Therefore, if one wishes to critique the best in Holtzmann, one would do well to check out Holtzmann's sources. Three of Holtzmann's predecessors, C. G. Wilke (1838), Eduard Zeller (1843), and Bernhard Weiss (1861) will be considered here. In his linguistic argument for solving the Synoptic Problem, Holtzmann relies heavily upon the work of C. G. Wilke, both the data in *Der Urevangelist* (1838) and the more

---

[35]Christoph Gotthelf Gersdorf, *Beiträge zur Sprach-Characteristik der Schriftsteller des neuen Testaments,* Erster Theil (Leipzig: Weidmannischen Buchhandlung, 1816).

[36]Hajo Uden Meijboom, *Geschiedenis en kritiek der Marcus-hypothese* (Amsterdam, 1866) trans. John J. Kiwiet (Fort Worth TX, unpublished manuscript); W. R. Farmer, *The Synoptic Problem: A Critical Analysis* (New York: Macmillan & Co., 1964); Stoldt, *History and Criticism of the Marcan Hypothesis.*

[37]Holtzmann, *Synoptischen Evangelien,* 280.

[38]Frans Neirynck, *Duality in Mark: Contributions to the Study of the Markan Redaction,* BETL 31 (Leuven: Leuven University Press, 1972).

precise presentation of much of the same material in *Die neutestamentliche Rhetorik* (1843).

Tuckett has claimed that a valid argument against the Griesbach hypothesis which makes use of "characteristic words" appears in the earlier work of Wilke. Let us examine this claim.

One may best understand Wilke's linguistic argument if one understands the basic structure of his book. Wilke says his basic purpose in *Der Urevangelist* was to conduct "a critical-exegetical investigation of the origin of the 'gospel-harmony' (26)." In short, he wanted to solve the Synoptic Problem. The linguistic characteristics of the three synoptic Evangelists which he would isolate in his book would be used both as evidence for his own source theory and as evidence against certain alternative theories.

The argumentation in *Der Urevangelist* proceeds along two parallel lines. While presenting evidence from the Synoptic Gospels in support of his own theory, he is also utilizing that evidence to argue against the source theories of Gieseler (the oral theory), Schleiermacher (the fragment theory), Eichhorn (an *Ur-Gospel* theory) and Griesbach (the Two Gospel theory).[39]

Wilke divides his book into two main parts: "I: Points relating to a single non-written (oral) norm for the gospel story" (26-161) and "II: Points relating to a written norm for the agreement in the gospel story" (162-694). Part II may be divided into three divisions which give the whole book the following four-fold structure:

In Part I, Wilke argues against Gieseler's idea that the norm for the harmony of the gospels was a single oral norm (26-161). Having discounted this possibility, in Part II, Wilke turns to a consideration of a literary norm for the agreement among the Synoptic Gospels. If the norm for the agreement was literary, then that norm might consist of several sources or of a single source. Wilke next responds to Schleiermacher (several sources) and Eichhorn (a single source) as representatives of these alternatives.

Wilke argues against Schleiermacher's idea that the literary norm was a collection of fragments and for his own idea that this literary norm was a single literary work (162-555). He then argues against Eichhorn's idea that this single literary norm was to be reconstructed only from the material within the Synoptic Gospels to which all three of the Synoptic Evangelists bear concurrent testimony. Instead, he argues, this norm should be recon-

---

[39]Johann Carl Ludwig Gieseler, *Historisch-kritischer Versuch über die Entstehung und die fruhesten Schicksale der schriftlichen Evangelien* (Leipzig, 1818); Friedrich Daniel Ernst Schleiermacher, *Einleitung ins neue Testaments* (Berlin: G. Reimer, 1845). Eichhorn, *Einleitung*.

structed from all of the material in Mark to which one or both of the other Synoptic Evangelists bear concurrent testimony (556-658). Having established that the norm for the agreement among the Synoptic gospels was a written (26-162), single (162-555), *Ur-gospel* including all of the material in Mark to which one or both of the other Synoptic Evangelists bear concurrent testimony (556-658), on page 659 Wilke poses his "Third", and final, "Point in Question: Could Mark himself have been the author of the *Urschrift?*" Wilke's book concludes when he believes that he has provided an affirmative answer to this question, some thirty-five pages later.

For the greatest part of his book (1-659), Wilke presupposes, in agreement with Gieseler, Schleiermacher and Eichhorn, that the gospels stand in an indirect relationship to one another. That is, he presupposes that no Evangelist made direct use of any other canonical gospel but rather they each made mutual but independent use of common source material. It is only in the last thirty-five pages of his book (659-694) that Wilke begins to consider the possibility of a direct literary relationship among the gospels.

It is important here to distinguish Wilke's arguments for his own source hypothesis from Wilke's arguments against alternative source hypotheses.

All of Wilke's arguments against alternative source hypotheses are found prior to page 659. That is, all of his arguments against Gieseler, Schleiermacher, Eichhorn, and Griesbach. After page 659, Wilke only argues for his own hypothesis, not against any others.

Although the source hypotheses of Gieseler, Schleiermacher and Eichhorn varied considerably, all three did share at least one presupposition: an indirect relationship among the gospels. They all presupposed that no canonical Evangelist made direct use of any other canonical gospel as a source. It was, therefore, appropriate for Wilke to debate these alternative source hypotheses at points in his book, when, in arguing for his own source hypothesis, he was able to share this presupposition with them (prior to page 659).

If Wilke would have debated on common ground with Griesbach as he did with Gieseler, Schleiermacher and Eichhorn, it would have been appropriate to begin when he began to consider the possibility of a direct literary relationship among the gospels (659 and thereafter). But this was not Wilke's procedure. He debates with Griesbach at points where the two do not share common ground (prior to page 659), with the result that one must question the adequacy his arguments against Griesbach, including, of course, arguments which make use of the linguistic characteristics of the Synoptic Evangelists.

In isolating the linguistic characteristics of all three Synoptic Evangelists, like Stroth before him, Wilke approached the texts of the Synoptic gospels as if they were variants of a single lost original manuscript. By presupposing that all three made mutual but independent use of a lost original, he could reason that where two gospels were in agreement against the third that those gospels which were in agreement preserved the wording and therefore the literary characteristics of the original while the third who differed may preserve literary characteristics of a copyist who changed that original.

Given Wilke's overall literary procedure in his book and his historical context where the texts of the Synoptic gospels could be treated as if they were variant manuscripts, one can understand why his procedure for isolating the linguistic characteristics of all three Synoptics might seem plausible to him.

But if one reflects upon this procedure for a moment one will see its limitations. First, in order to distinguish a departure from the original text one must have a norm for isolating the original text (those places where at least two evangelists agree) and a norm for determining a departure from the original (those places where one differs from two). This, of course, limits one's view to the Triple Tradition and, within that material, only to those points where the wording of two agree against the third. None of the *Sondergut* of any gospel will receive any attention nor will any section where two gospels share material and the third is lacking, nor any of the Triple Tradition where all three are in agreement, nor any of the Triple Tradition where all three differ. The amount of text in any one of the Synoptics which will ever be given consideration will be very limited and accordingly the procedure will produce limited results.

Wilke's method for isolating the linguistic characteristics of all three Synoptic Evangelists began by focusing on those words and phrases where one Evangelist differed from the common wording of the two others. He then searched the text of the Evangelist who differed for other occurrences of the same literary phenomenon. If he found one or more usages elsewhere in that gospel he concluded that the literary phenomenon was a linguistic characteristic of that Evangelist. By beginning with peculiar matter in each gospel Wilke's collections of the linguistic characteristics of each Evangelist tended to be collections of the linguistic peculiarities of each gospel.

When Wilke concluded that the Griesbach hypothesis could not be true because none of the linguistic characteristics of Matthew or Luke appeared in the text of Mark, as one would expect if Mark were utilizing those gospels as sources, his conclusion was unwarranted because his method for isolating the literary characteristics of all three Synoptic Evangelists tended to isolate linguistic peculiarities of each gospel in the first place.

Tuckett is mistaken in his claim that the Griesbach hypothesis was disproven by Wilke in the nineteenth century on the basis of linguistic arguments. Wilke's method of isolating the data base he used in his argument against Griesbach was inadequate so his conclusions drawn from that data must also be considered inadequate.

In addition, Wilke's argument against the Griesbach hypothesis was based upon material which did not appear in the shared texts of the gospels. It was, therefore, an argument from silence. As such, it has all the weaknesses of any argument from silence.

In contrast to his argument against the Griesbach hypothesis which was based upon negative evidence, what did not appear in the shared texts of the gospels, Wilke's argument for his own theory did make use of positive evidence, linguistic characteristics of Mark which did appear in the shared texts of the other gospels. These linguistic data were called "the characteristic echo" by Holtzmann and Frans Neirynck has labeled them "dualisms," namely, the repeated use of language within a relatively limited literary context, usually no more than a few verses.

This material was marshalled at the end of Wilke's book when he asked, "Could Mark be the author of the *Urschrift*?" Wilke found that "dualisms" appeared both in the sections of Mark shared with the others and in sections which he did not share with others. Given the unity of literary style which Wilke demonstrated within the gospel of Mark, the answer could have been "Yes." But Wilke never asked whether Luke or Matthew could have been the author of the *Urschrift*. Since both Matthew and Luke can use dualisms apart from a Markan parallel as well as in parallel with him the answer would also have been "Yes." But Wilke never asked these questions. He marshalled some data consistent with his source hypothesis and ignored its potential relevance to other source theories as the very formulation of his last point in question makes clear.

There seems to be a consensus among contemporary experts on the Synoptic Problem that an argument using linguistic data can be of service in solving that problem, but there does not seem to be any agreement, now or in the past, as to what makes such an argument decisive.

The issue is not whether any particular literary evidence can be interpreted as consistent with a source hypothesis. The issue is whether there are linguistic phenomena within the Synoptic gospels which have decisive value for solving the Synoptic Problem—data which would unambiguously indicate the direction of literary dependence between any two of the three Synoptic Evangelists.

Five years after Wilke published his first book and in the same year that his second book, *Die neutestamentliche Rhetorik* (1843), appeared, Eduard Zeller published an article in which he outlined the necessary conditions for a linguistic feature to be a decisive indicator of the direction of literary dependence. Zeller first establishes that a similarity exists among the gospels which can only be explained if one accepts the literary usage of one by the author of another. He continues:

> If we then pursue this connection more precisely, a relationship among these writings comes to light also with respect to the vocabulary (which is the only respect which can be taken into consideration here) which is similar to what can be demonstrated also from a consideration of their contents, in spite of the most recently revived preference for Mark. That is, Luke has the most of that which is peculiar, Mark has the least. But with respect to what is common the greatest originality seems to lie on the side of Matthew. The least, on the side of Mark. However, isolated exceptions always provide something unsteadying in this relationship. With regard to what is common, certainly it is often difficult to decide to whom an expression may have belonged originally. If a word is found in all the gospels with equal frequency or in all of them with equal rarity or even in one gospel but not in the same narrative context as another gospel, then there is no criterion for making this decision. On the other hand, however, the circumstance may be discovered not too infrequently that the one evangelist uses an expression *only* [italics mine] in such narrative contexts where another evangelist also has it, while the latter, by contrast, uses the same expression also in yet further literary contexts for which the first provides no parallel. In this situation, it is probable that the expression belonged to the characteristic vocabulary of the second evangelist, and, should such cases be repeated a number of times in a manner such that the greater originality of expression falls to one and the same evangelist in all or in the majority of cases, then we would be justified in assuming that he had been the source from which the other had drawn.[40]

Zeller does not say that all words which occur more frequently in one gospel than they do in another have value for solving the Synoptic problem, only some of them which meet other more stringent conditions. Although the words to which he assigns value occur more frequently in one gospel than another, that alone does not give them value.

Zeller's more refined conditions for value are as follows: Every occurrence of a word in a gospel which uses the word *less* frequently must appear *only* in pericopes where the word is present in the parallel passage of another gospel. At the same time, that parallel gospel must include usages of the same word not *only* in passages parallel to the first gospel but also in passages for which that first gospel provides no parallel.

---

[40]Eduard Zeller, "Studien zur neutestamentlichen Theologie 4: Vergleichende Übersicht über den Wörtervorrath der neutestamentlichen Schriftsteller," *Theologische Jahrbücher* 2 (1843): 443-543. Quotation is from 527-28. English translation is my own.

Zeller does not spell out why he believes he can draw conclusions about sources from this type of evidence but, from what he does say, one can infer he probably reasoned like this:

Condition 1: If a word appears in one gospel *only* where it is paralleled in another gospel then every occurrence of that word could be explained as the result of copying.

Condition 2: If a word appears both where it is paralleled and in contexts where it is not paralleled, then at least some occurrences (the unparalleled ones) cannot be the result of any direct copying.

If every occurrence of a word in gospel A is shared with gospel B so that the word qualifies for condition 1 when gospel A is taken into consideration but that same word qualifies for condition 2 when gospel B is taken into consideration then one may conclude the following about this single word.

Every occurrence of this word in Gospel A could be the result of A copying it from gospel B. But the reverse is not true.

Every occurrence of the word in gospel B could not be the result of B copying it from gospel A since B can utilize the word not only in contexts parallel to A but also in contexts independent of A. Hence, the argument may be labeled "non-reversible" for any single linguistic phenomenon.

But Zeller's actual work with shared vocabulary items and selected phrases in the gospels demonstrated to him that the evidence did not all indicate the same thing. That is, when he applied the test to lists of shared vocabulary items, he discovered some cases suggesting the direction of literary dependence went from Matthew to Mark; other instances suggested the reverse. And so it was for every possible direction between any two of the three documents: Matthew to Mark, Mark to Matthew, Mark to Luke, Luke to Mark, Matthew to Luke and Luke to Matthew. At this point the argument appears to be "reversible."

But Zeller suggested that the argument could have value if the evidence is weighed. This could lead to some solid conclusions about the direction of literary dependence between any two.

From the linguistic data within the Synoptic Gospels, Zeller concluded that Griesbach was most likely correct, i. e. that it was more likely that Luke had used Matthew rather than the reverse, and that Mark had used both Matthew and Luke rather than that either Matthew or Luke had used Mark.

Once Zeller had collected his evidence and weighed it in the balance, he was obligated to provide an explanation for the lesser amount of evidence which remained on the lighter side of his scale, evidence which seemed to contradict his central thesis.

Zeller produced a list of 78 words and phrases which, on the basis of his method, suggested that Matthew was used by Mark. He also produced three lists of potential counterexamples but discounted the value of some words for various reasons. The first list included 19 items favoring Mark's priority to Matthew. The second included nine items and the third, three. Although some were discounted, Zeller marshalled a total of 31 words or phrases which supported Mark's priority to Matthew. The 31 items could be compared with the 78 items supporting Matthew's priority to Mark. The weight of the evidence favored Matthew's priority to Mark over Mark's priority to Matthew by a proportion of about 2 to 1, if one allows for the difference between Matthew and Mark in overall length.

In discussing these two lists which related to Matthew and Mark, Zeller provided the following explanation of the items which represented anomalies for the Griesbach hypothesis.

> But even the words which were cited first [in favor of Mark's priority to Matthew] can prove nothing against the greater originality of Matthew; not only because their number stands in hardly any proportion to those cited for Matthew but also because one may discover also something which is very noteworthy, [namely, that] almost none of the expressions in Mark's list would be designated as favorite words of the author on the basis of the frequency with which they are repeated like these in Matthew: ἀναχωρεῖν, ἀποδιδόναι, γέεννα, εἰσέρχεσθαι εἰς τὴν ζωήν, θησαυρός, καλεῖν, κόσμος, μισθός, ναί, ὅμοιος and ὁμοιοῦν, ὅπως, ὄχλοι, ὁ πατὴρ ὁ ἐν τοῖς οὐρανοῖς (ὁ οὐράνιος), πονηρός, πρόβατον, προφήτης, προσφέρειν, πρόσωπον, υἱὸς Δαυίδ. And on this ground too they cannot be used as an appeal against the general canon which we are employing here. That a copyist, who is not entirely dependent [upon his source(s)] may find isolated expressions in his original which are otherwise already current with him and which he, therefore, also employs where they are lacking in the original comes as no surprise. However, if this [disproportionate] relation takes place not simply in isolated cases, if it is extended to quite an overburdening proportion of the points of literary contact [between two Evangelists], if a long list of the favorite expressions of one author are supposed to have been borrowed from a few scattered expressions of another, then one would probably call this a reversal of the natural connection between cause and effect and a forced labeling of something as earlier which shows off its [literary] dependence in all places.[41]

In spite of Zeller's warning here, this is precisely what Holtzmann did in his *Die Synoptischen Evangelien* twenty years after Zeller published his findings (Zeller—1843; Holtzmann—1863). He took Zeller's explanation of evidence on the lighter side of his scale and used it to explain the great bulk of evidence on the heavier side of Zeller's scale, while using the evidence on the light side as support for his own two source theory.[42]

---

[41]Zeller, "Wortervorrath," 531-32. English translation is my own.

[42]See esp. Holtzmann, *Synoptischen Evangelien,* 346-57.

Zeller did not emphasize the word "only" but it has been emphasized here because its importance seems to have been missed by those who have attempted to respond to Zeller's work. Holtzmann offered words from Mark which simply occurred more frequently in Mark than in Matthew as counter evidence against Zeller. But, as may be seen by taking note of the word "only" in Zeller's methodological statement for making the linguistic characteristics of the Synoptics of service in solving the Synoptic Problem, this response was not to the point. This inappropriate response gives the reader the impression that the weight of the evidence favors Mark's priority to Matthew which, as Zeller's more refined lists indicate, is simply not the case. Neither Holtzmann nor his contemporary defender, C. M. Tuckett, realizes his response is not to the point.

Another way to respond to Zeller's conclusion favoring the Griesbach Hypothesis is to recall that literary dependence seems to run in opposite directions. This could be used as evidence that the gospels do not stand in a relationship of direct literary dependence. This was the road traveled by Bernhard Weiss and the road being traveled by some contemporary advocates of Multi-Stage theories of Synoptic relationships.[43] That is, those words and phrases which lend support to Matthew's priority to Mark are assigned by these critics to *Ur-Matthaus* upon which Mark is supposedly literarily dependent. At the same time, those words and phrases which lend support to Mark's priority to Matthew are assigned to *Ur-Marcus* upon which Matthew is supposedly literarily dependent. The unanswered question to date is whether there is sufficient linguistic evidence which is anomalous for the Griesbach hypothesis to warrant hypothecating sources to explain it.

Finally, let us look at the organization of Holtzmann's own work. His *Die Synoptischen Evangelien* is divided into four chapters: Chapter 1: "The Problem [of Synoptic Origins] and its Historical Development;" Chapter 2: "The Composition of Mark—Source ℵ—*Ur-Marcus*;" Chapter 3: "The Composition of Matthew and Luke—Source Λ—*Ur-Matthaus*;" Chapter 4: "Tests;" and Chapter 5: "The Synoptic Gospels as Historical Sources."

---

[43]Bernhard Weiß, "Zur Entstehungsgeschichte der drei synoptischen Evangelien" in *Theologischen Studien und Kritiken* 34 (1861): 29-100, 646-713. Multiple Stage theories of Synoptic relationships are represented in the works of M. E. Boismard, Rainer Reisner, and Ph. Rolland. In a paper authored by Boismard, "Groupe C: theorie des Niveaux Multiples," this team recently defended these source hypotheses at the Jerusalem Symposium on the Interrelationships of the Gospels, April 1984. The papers and proceedings of this conference will be published by Mercer University Press and Peeters Press, Leuven.

It is in "Tests" that one finds a long section entitled "*Der Sprachchar-akter der Synoptiker*" (271-357). If there is a linguistic argument for solving the Synoptic Problem anywhere in Holtzmann, here would be the most likely place to find it. Kümmel has claimed that Holtzmann "based his Proof [*Nachweis*] of the two document hypothesis mainly on the linguistic characteristics/peculiarities of the sources and on the connection of the accounts" thereby "grounding the two source hypothesis so carefully that the study of Jesus henceforth could not again dispense with this firm base." But Holtzmann places his discourse on linguistic data in the Synoptics in a chapter he labels "*Proben*" in contrast to Kümmel's claim that there in Holtzmann one will find a "*Nachweis*."

If one has doubts about the significance of this semantic difference in the German one may appeal to Holtzmann's own words in the opening paragraph of Chapter 4:

> Since we took our departure from the gospels in their present form and in the course of an internal investigation, we were simply led to distinguish two sources, we have traveled a course which is opposed to the usual one. Namely, it is customary to take one's departure from certain other essential points, among which the Tradition and Internal Testimony of the gospels about themselves and about the state of their mutual relationships take the first place. The Prologue of Luke qualifies as one such essential point which we may now take up as a first member in a whole series of such phenomena by which other critics almost exclusively have been willing to let themselves be led to the first clue whereas these same things have been taken up in the course of *our* investigations only as just so many tests of the correctness of results which have already been achieved [nur als eben so viele Proben für die Richtigkeit des schon gewonnenen Resultates auftreten werden] (p. 243).

One would think that such a statement would raise serious questions in the mind of the reader about the adequacy of Kümmel's claims about Holtzmann's work. Holtzmann himself does not seem to have put the stress on his work with the linguistic characteristics of the Synoptic Evangelists which Kümmel claims for him. Holtzmann seems to stress argumentation elsewhere in his book or in the work of his predecessors as proof for his hypothesis. Greater questions may be raised about the adequacy of Holtzmann's argumentation if Meijboom is correct in his analysis of him.

> Let us ask first of all for the major arguments which Holtzmann presents as a justification of his hypothesis. . . . we are continually referred back by Holtzmann and finally find ourselves outside of his book with a reference to contemporary scholarship. The fourth chapter, entitled "test cases," opens with a declaration that all the phenomena which will come under discussion will be welcome as confirmations of the already achieved result. These test cases are not needed as witnesses which have to be heard before the decision is made. Indeed, their fate had been decided already on p. 167. We therefore go back further and discover in paragraph ten a "proof of existence" for a second source in addition to the Logia [p. 126]. At this point Holtzmann

calls it sufficient to separate the remaining obscure portions from that which was explained before. His conclusion is thus contingent upon an earlier statement and, indeed, in paragraph five we do come across "the establishment of Source A." [p. 67]. But we did not ask for the establishment of a source, but rather for the justification of its existence. We are then referred to the form which the quest of Gospel criticism has taken in the present development of critical investigation [pp. 1-66]. Does a contemporary situation actually provide a justification for a hypothesis?[44]

Contrary to the judgment of Kümmel, Holtzmann did not even attempt to "prove" the validity of his two source theory on the basis of the linguistic peculiarities of the sources. Rather, he calls his work with the linguistic data within the Synoptic gospels only so many "tests" of a hypothesis he claims to have been established on other grounds. Much of the data Holtzmann used in these "tests" were vocabulary items, phrases, and syntactical/grammatical constructions which had been labeled characteristic of the various synoptics by his predecessors, C. G. Wilke and Eduard Zeller. As we have seen, Wilke's method for isolating the linguistic characteristics of all the various Synoptic Evangelists was inadequate and his argument against the Griesbach hypothesis utilizing this material was circular and/ or inconclusive.

Whatever Holtzmann adopted from Wilke without refinement or modification,—and there appears to be an abundance of this type of material in Holtzmann—is just as inadequate in its new literary context in Holtzmann as it was found to be in its original context in Wilke.

As we have already noted, Holtzmann's response to Zeller's linguistic argument in favor of the Griesbach hypothesis was also inappropriate.

C. M. Tuckett is mistaken when he suggests that Wilke's and Holtzmann's arguments against the Griesbach hypothesis in the nineteenth century which made use of characteristic words still have relevance today. The only adequate linguistic argument for solving the Synoptic Problem in the nineteenth century was that of Zeller and he concluded that the weight of the evidence supported the Griesbach hypothesis.

---

[44]Meijboom, *Marcus-hypothese,* trans. Kiwiet, 73-74.

Appendix
Holtzmann and His Sources

Philosophotos Alethias [Christian Adolf Hasert], *Die Evangelien, ihr Geist, ihre Verfasser und ihr Verhältniss zu einander* (Leipzig, Otto Wigand, 1845) 265-66.

Heinrich Julius Holtzmann, *Die Synoptischen Evangelien, Ihr Ursprung und ihr geschichtlicher Charakter* (Leipzig, 1863) 271.

Holtzmann cited Hasert's work, but did not mark (with quotation marks or italics) the words he adopted.

Und soll der Grundsatz, dass der Stil der Mensch sei, richtig verstanden und richtig angewandt sein, so darf er nur gelten von den bleibenden, weder von einer besonderen Stimmung noch von der besonderen stilistischen Gattung, in der man gerade arbeitet, abhängigen, sondern in jeder stilistischen Gattung, gleich möglichen Spracheigenthümlichkeiten. Unter diese gehört in Stil und Ausdruck einmal Alles das,	Denn soll der Grundsatz, dass der Styl der Mensch ist, richtig verstanden und richtig angewandt werden, so darf er nur gelten von den bleibenden, in jeder Stimmung und bei jedweder Art von Darstellung
worin sich das eigenthümliche Geisteswesen des Schreibenden zu Tage legt und zweitens alle die Constructions- und Rede-Weisen und alle die eigenthümlichen Worte, welche sich der Mensch aus dem allgemeinen Sprachvorrathe heraus nach und nach zugeeignet hat und welche so gerade ihm zur Bezeichnung bestimmter Lieblingsgedanken geläufig ihm eigenthümlich werden und endlich gleichsam seinen eigenen Sprachkreis bilden.	gleich möglichen, Eigenthümlichkeiten. Es wird also besonders auf solche Elemente des Ausdrucks und der schriftstellerischen Manier ankommen, worin sich das eigenthümliche Geisteswesen des Schreibenden offenbart, zugleich aber auch alle die Constructions- und Redenweisen, sowie auf alle die eigenthümlichen Worte, welche sich der Mensch aus dem allgemeinen Sprachvorrathe heraus nach und nach zugeeignet und behufs der Bezeichnung seiner eigenen originalen Gedanke auserwählt hat.

THE GENRE OF THE GOSPELS
AND THE TWO GOSPEL HYPOTHESIS

Philip L. Shuler

The present paper attempts two essential tasks. The first is to relate the gospels to hellenistic biography. The second is to explain the emergence of the synoptic gospels, understood as hellenistic biographies, in the sequence of Matthew, Luke, and Mark. The format consists of a discussion of four basic theses, the first three of which are directly related to the question of genre. The fourth thesis identifies the synoptic gospels with encomium-type hellenistic biography. Whereas the four theses are equally valid for understanding the formation of any *bios* narrative, the present work focuses upon gospel formation within the New Testament canon.

THESIS 1: *The shift from individual sources, whether circulating as individual or collected traditions, to the form of a "story" about Jesus constitutes a literary, genre decision of the redactors/authors/evangelists.* That traditions related to Jesus circulated prior to their incorporation into a "gospel" is not a point of contention. Indeed, the consensus of gospel research confirms the presence of such traditions and attributes to them the character of orally transmitted material. It is clear, however, that what we find in the canonical gospels is more than collections of material or random duplication of individual Jesus traditions. New Testament studies currently employ references to "structure," "outline," "purpose," "milieu," "redactor," and even "theology" with regard to *each* of the four evangelists' works. Consequently, one can no longer speak of the gospels as accidental products of random selection. Rather are they works reflecting redactional and authorial intent. Norman Petersen believes that the recognition of such intent automatically compels one to address the question of genre. He writes:

> The bridge between collection and another genre is crossed, descriptively and normatively, at the moment when an *intent* beyond the explicit claims of the component material is given either formal (structural, compositional) or material (simple editorial) expression in a text. That is to say, a collection becomes something else at that moment when mere concatenation is replaced by composition at whatever level of sophistication.[1]

---

[1]Norman Petersen, "So-called Gnostic Type Gospels and the Question of the Genre 'Gospel' " (The Task Force on Gospel Genre, 1970 SBL Gospels Seminar) 25.

One can conclude that current gospel research is based on a view of the gospels as more than literary accidents. Genre, therefore, *is* an important issue for gospel studies. Furthermore, the question of the genre of the gospels is the problem of identifying the literary pattern behind the evangelists' use of those sources which comprise their present narratives.

THESIS 2: *It is unlikely that this decision would have resulted in the creation/choice of a totally non-existent and therefore completely unique literary form.* At the heart of the second thesis is the presupposition that behind the present form of the gospels is the evangelist's desire to communicate. It is reasonable to expect that the evangelist would utilize whatever native abilities and literary resources were available to him in order to be understood. Paul did not invent the personal letter form. Similarly, the evangelists desired to be understood and interpreted properly.

Fundamental to interpreting the gospels is the presupposition of the compositional care explicit in Bernard Lonergan's hermeneutic circle.

> Heuristically, then, the context of the word is the sentence. The context of the sentence is the paragraph. The context of the paragraph is the chapter. The context of the chapter is the book. The context of the book is the author's *opera omnia,* his life and times, the state of the question in his day, his problems, prospective readers, scope and aim.[2]

Given the author's desire to communicate, a desire which leads to the choice of the medium of communication, it is unlikely that a genre would emerge from a literary vacuum. Thus Wellek and Warren write: "The totally familiar and repetitive pattern is boring; the totally novel form will be unintelligible—is indeed unthinkable."[3] Further, "the genre represents, so to speak, a sum of aesthetic devices at hand, *available to the writer and already intelligible to the reader.*"[4]

No doubt this basic principle explains why the question of the genre for the gospels as literature continues to surface again and again within scholarly circles. Karl Ludwig Schmidt's postulation of the gospels as *sui generis* is not a satisfactory answer to the problem: nor are those theoretical explanations of how they could be *sui generis* and still display form; e.g., explanations of the gospels as expansions of the kerygma. In order to communicate, forms must be accessible not only to the writer, but also to the audience. Thus E. D. Hirsch writes:

---

[2]Bernard Lonergan, *Method in Theology* (New York: Seabury, 1972) 163.

[3]René Wellek and Austin Warren, *Theory of Literature,* 3rd ed. (New York: Harcourt Brace Jovanovich, 1962) 235.

[4]Ibid.

This is one of the many penetrating observations that E. H. Gombrich makes in his book, *Art and Illusion*. He quotes approvingly Quintilian's remark, "Which craftsman has not made a vessel of a shape he has never seen?" and comments: "It is an important reminder, but it does not account for the fact that even the shape of the new vessel will somehow belong to the same family of forms as those the craftsman has seen." This tendency of the mind to use old types as the foundation for new ones is, of course, even more pronounced when communication or representation is involved. Not every convention could be changed all at once, even if the craftsman were capable of such divine creativity, because then his creation would be totally incommunicable, radically ambiguous.[5]

THESIS 3: *The gospels were no doubt received as popular "lives" of Jesus, and the Jesus tradition by being so incorporated became more powerful in authenticating the person of Jesus within the life of the community.* Even a cursory reading of any one of the gospels confirms the conclusion that traditions attributed to Jesus have been presented so as to give emphasis not merely to the traditions themselves but also to the person of Jesus. There is emphasis upon the function, character, and nature of the glorified Christ, an emphasis upon the total event that bears testimony of God's soteriological activity. This emphasis upon the person of Jesus, which is developed by the use of traditions associated with Jesus, constitutes the *bios* character of the evangelists' work.

The recognition of this *bios* factor produced the impression, even among contemporary readers, that the gospels are biographies, and genre discussions have correctly focused upon ancient biographical works.[6] Such investigations, however, have been complicated by the fact that biography, as we moderns understand it, did not exist in antiquity. This does not mean that the ancients did not celebrate the lives of esteemed personages in their literature. Indeed, the opposite was the case, and further work in the area of ancient *bios* narratives makes clearer the exact relation of the gospels to ancient *bios* literature.

References in Polybius (*Histories* X. 21.8), Cicero (*Epistulae ad Familiares* V. xii. 3), Lucian (*History* 7), Cornelius Nepos (*Pelopidas* XVI. 1.1) and Plutarch (*Alexander* I. 1-3) give evidence for a popular form of *bios* literature where the purpose was primarily that of praise. In these ref-

---

[5]E. D. Hirsch, *Validity in Interpretation* (New Haven CT: Yale University Press, 1967) 104.

[6] See, for example, Moses Hadas and Morton Smith, *Heroes and Gods: Spiritual Biographies in Antiquity* (New York: Harper & Row, 1965); Charles H. Talbert, *What Is a Gospel?: The Genre of the Canonical Gospels* (Philadelphia: Fortress Press, 1977); and Philip L. Shuler, *A Genre for the Gospels: The Biographical Character of Matthew* (Philadelphia: Fortress Press, 1982).

erences, this literature is consistently contrasted with history. Several of these references employ the term encomium as a designation, and a reading of the rules for this rhetorical device helps one to understand more clearly this ubiquitous literary type, genre.[7] Encomium biographies included the topics one expects to find in biographies: family background, birth (and events surrounding birth), accounts of childhood and youth, the career, manner of death, and events following death. It is to be noted, however, that the primary focus was upon the "adult," and all topics tended to be used to serve the author's portrayal of the adult. In addition, two literary techniques were employed: amplification and comparison. Amplification is the process by which the author "amplifies" those points he is trying to make through a process of selection, an emphasis upon a few aspects of the character at the expense of a complete account, an account (or more than one account) of what a person "might have" done regardless of whether or not he actually did it, and/or the omission of material that does not fit in with the praiseworthy purposes of the author. Comparison demonstrates how the chosen subject excels those with whom he comes into contact or with whom he may be compared.

Authors who write in this medium display various, though closely related, purposes. Some works are exercises in literary models, others attempt to defend, while still others are very close to funeral eulogies. The common thread is that of praise. Each work intends to enlist a praise response from the reader/hearer, one that could range anywhere from mere pleasure to emulation. All of the topics and literary techniques were employed in the author's accepted task; i.e., the favorable portrayal of persons whose significance was clearly demonstrable in his adult life and death.

Into this literary milieu the gospels make their appearance. With this kind of first century C.E. backdrop, it is not difficult to understand how Jewish religious traditions and concepts could have been appreciated by Gentile readers (a recognition that none of the gospels pre-date the Gentile mission made official in Acts 15). A unique proclamation has been transmitted in

---

[7]The Polybius and Lucian treatises specifically refer to "encomium" in contrast with "history." Representative of the rhetorical rules for writing encomia are Aristotle, *Rhetorica* 1.6.9; *Rhetorica ad Alexandrum* 3-4; Cicero, *Rhetorica ad Herennium* and *De Partitione Oratorica* 21; and Quintilian, *Institutio oratoria* 3.7.10-18. Classical examples of encomia are *Helen, Busiris,* and *Evagoras* by Isocrates and *Agesilaus* by Xenophon. For relevant discussions, see D. R. Stuart, *Epochs of Greek and Roman Biography* (Berkeley: University of California Press, 1928); Arnaldo Momigliano, *The Development of Greek Biography* (Cambridge MA: Harvard University Press, 1971); and Shuler, *A Genre*, 36-87.

a relatively common praise form. No doubt, the gospels were received by their original readers as biographies containing the summons to faith in the Messiah, Jesus of Nazareth.

THESIS 4: *The best way of viewing the emergence of the synoptic gospels from the perspective of genre is that they belong to the hellenistic biography classification; more specifically, encomium biography.* According to H. I. Marrou, the encomium was an elementary exercise in the educational systems throughout the Greco-Roman world. As such, its rules for composition were rigidly set forth and rigorously applied at the beginning of the student's exposure to compositional skills. Whereas encomia written as "models" in the ancient world reflect this literary rigor, most of the works which fall within the encomium biography classification are less restricted by strict adherence to the rhetorical rules of composition. *Bios* works from the period roughly contemporary with Jesus tend to reflect, on the one hand, evidence of the impact of encomium writing, while, on the other hand, considerable variety when authorial intent rather than rhetorical rules shape the narrative. Such examples as Suetonius's *Deified Julius,* Tacitus's *Agricola,* Lucian's *Demonax,* Philo's *Moses* (also his *Abraham* and *Joseph*), and several of Plutarch's *Lives* come to mind.

For gospel critics, the largest problem is associating the gospels with any existing genre of antiquity. This is true for two reasons. First, the methodology followed has usually involved one-to-one comparisons. Such comparisons tend to accent the differences at the expense of genre affinities.[8] Unfortunately, the variety within *bios* literature complicates the recognition of gospel genre identity. Second, most genre discussions begin with the presupposition that Mark is the earliest gospel. Reinforced by Mark's perceived incompleteness, Mark is understood as the original compiler of Jesus tradition (or some earlier version of our canonical Mark). Matthew and Luke are secondary productions which carry on Mark's ini-

---

[8]See, e.g., Karl Ludwig Schmidt's response to C. W. Votaw's *The Gospels and Contemporary Biographies in the Greco-Roman World* (Philadelphia: Fortress Press, 1970) in his "Die Stellung der Evangelien in der allgemeinen Literaturgeschichte," *EUCHARISTERION: Studien zur Religion und Literatur des Alten und Neuen Testaments, Hermann Gunkel zum 60 Geburtstag,* ed. Hans Schmidt (Göttingen: Vandenhoeck & Ruprecht, 1923) 2:50-134. The failure of such one-to-one comparisons has led to the general view that there are simply no examples with which the gospels may be compared. The view of the present paper is that the problem is with the methodology of comparison and not with the absence of literary examples.

tial activities out of loyalty to the tradition more than any genre motive.[9] Without denying loyalty to tradition, the picture for gospel genre changes significantly if the synoptic gospels are recognized as hellenistic biographies and Mark is not *a priori* the earliest of the three. The remainder of this paper will attempt to demonstrate genre affinities. This will be attempted not by one-to-one comparisons but through the analysis of *topoi*, literary techniques, and authorial intent. The reader will also be invited to view the emergence of these "biographical" works from the perspective of the Two Gospel Hypothesis (formerly called the Griesbach Hypothesis).

The relationship of Matthew's gospel to encomium biographical literature has been discussed in an earlier book previously cited.[10] Here, it was demonstrated that the basis for identifying Matthew as an example of encomium biography is a consideration of *topoi*, literary techniques, and authorial intent. For the present, a summary of the research will suffice.

Clearly, many of the *topoi* common to encomium biographies are present in Matthew. Further, Matthew uses the *topoi* in the same manner and for the same reasons that they were incorporated by writers of encomium biographies. For example, Matthew presents Jesus' illustrious family background—illustrious, that is, from the perspective of Jewish messianic expectation. The genealogy (Matt 1:1-17) gives emphasis both to God as creator (four women and a multiple of seven in the number of generations separating the three periods) and to Jesus as a descendant of David (DVD: $4+6+4=14$). The designation of Joseph as *dikaios* represents an encomium-type emphasis upon the character of Joseph's role as Jesus' "earthly" father (1:19). In chapter 2, Matthew identifies the place of Jesus' birth. At the same time, he reconciles those Old Testament traditions that would point to the birth place of the one who is to come as Bethlehem with reference to his being a "Nazarene". Also, the subject, "king of the Jews," is raised with reference to Jesus in contrast with Herod; and there is the soteriological allusion to Moses. In addition, one notes the reference to dreams and the role of the "star" for the Magi, again common features of encomium biographies. In chapter 4, Matthew presents the temptation of Jesus which occurs at the transition point between his youth and the beginning of his adult ministry. Jesus is here displayed as a young man of obvious moral perseverance who is fully capable of and prepared for the tasks ahead.

---

[9]An example of this view is found in James M. Robinson and Helmut Koester, *Trajectories Through Early Christianity* (Philadelphia: Fortress Press, 1971). Helmut Koester's article "One Jesus and Four Primitive Gospels" in this book is representative of more recent *sui generis* positions.

[10]Shuler, *A Genre,* 36ff.

The combination of these common *topoi* in the first four chapters of Matthew is also instructive, because the result is Matthew's way of convincingly preparing for the presentation of Jesus' career. This kind of literary procedure is precisely the manner in which these and similar *topoi* are utilized in encomium biographies. Presupposed in all ancient biographical works is the adult portrait. Preliminary events such as birth, childhood, and youth accounts prepare the reader for the adult career. In Matthew's gospel, the identity is the crucial point, and it is developed in an ascending manner. Chapter one points to Jesus as "son of David." Chapter two points to his kingly and soteriological role. Chapter three builds to his identification after baptism as "son", and the first eleven verses of chapter four specifically include his title, "son of God" (two times). Matthew's procedures here are exemplary of encomium biography.

For the most part, the career is presented in a manner consistent with the nature of Jesus as Messiah. Words and deeds (the forms of proclamation and miracle stories) are the proper subjects just as orations are to the orator, laws and actions to the statesman, or battles to the soldier. The material is well-structured and the emphases carefully presented. Still, there does not seem to be a forcing of rhetorical device. It is the nature of the subject and the evangelical purposes of Matthew that guide his hand. There are no rhetoric *vs.* theology motifs in Matthew's work; rather, a devout Christian writer is conveying his account of Jesus in the most compelling manner of which he is capable.

Two additional *topoi* utilized by Matthew are worthy of note: death and resurrection. The manner of Jesus' death would not have been the easiest death for a writer of encomium biography to treat. In fact, had it not been for the crucial role it played in early Christian proclamation (e.g., Phil 2:6-11 and speeches in Acts), Matthew might have omitted an account of Jesus' death altogether (as rhetorical rules for such ancient praise works allow). As Matthew's story unfolds, however, it is clear that he has chosen not to avoid the issue; but, instead, he has so incorporated it into his narrative as to make it worthy of praise. Jesus is the victim of the opponents' plot (e.g., 26:3-5; 27:1). Supernatural events surround his death just as in the case of his birth. The wife of his judge, Pilate, warns him to have nothing to do with this "righteous" man following a dream (27:19). His betrayer hangs himself; his judge washes his hands of what is taking place (27:24-26); and the centurion acknowledges Jesus as "son of God" (27:54).

Proof of the resurrection comes from those who were hired to guard the tomb: that is, having been made fully aware of the resurrection rumor, this event could not be stopped. Of course, testimony of the resurrection also comes from those who visited the empty tomb. Thus, in his treatment of death and resurrection, Matthew transforms the lowliest of deaths into a victorious glorification of Jesus. This kind of testimony and literary procedure is fundamental to the apologetic motive often found in encomium biography. Literary *topoi*, and Matthew's use thereof, point to the encomium biography genre.

The two most common literary techniques employed in this genre are amplification and comparison. Both are utilized by Matthew. Previously discussed was Matthew's "amplification" of the preliminary episodes by which the identity of Jesus is presented. Also, a process of selection is surely evident in the manner by which Matthew presents Jesus' death in strictly positive and praiseworthy terms. The length of the passion account alone demonstrates Matthew's use of amplification of this most important event in Jesus' career. Finally, the decisions involved in the presentation of Jesus' ministry reflect Matthew's amplification of these teachings and actions which instruct the reader in the nature and significance of this soteriological event. It is evident that Matthew has chosen his sources and utilized his traditions in such a way as to create *his* portrait for the purpose of enlisting the response of faith.

Comparison is also important to Matthew. It is functional in his clarification of the relationship between John the Baptist and Jesus. After identifying the message of John with that of Jesus (3:2 and 4:17) and after the reader notes that John's opponents are those of Jesus (3:7), it is John himself who declares his unworthiness to participate in the baptism. If John is one deserving of the reader's attention, how much more so is Jesus! Elsewhere, comparison is evident in Matthew's portrayal of Jesus and his opponents. From chapter 12 on, the conflicts produce no victories for Jesus' opponents. In fact, in chapter 22, Jesus' generally passive and controlled character becomes aggressive. The opponents are unable to respond to Jesus' question, a fact that reduces them to sinister silence. Jesus far surpasses his opponents. What has been noted of John the Baptist and the opponents is equally true of all the personages with whom Jesus may be compared. Such comparisons as developed by Matthew call attention to Jesus' far superior qualities when viewed along side of the other characters in his narrative.

The primary purpose of encomium biographies is praise. At times this purpose incorporated apologetic concerns while at other times emulation seems to have been important to the writer. Matthew surely desires both. Even more, however, he desires the response of faith. He is writing for faith and for the edification of faith. To believe is to become a part of the church's mission of baptism and making disciples (16:20). Matthew's purpose, therefore, is to work not only toward the recognized goals of encomium biography, but to move beyond them for faith, edification, and training. The analysis of Matthew's over all structure reflects this didactic emphasis: instruction of the believer in the exacting demands of discipleship (1-11, especially chapters 4:23-10:42) is followed by Jesus' ministry presented as the paradigm of true discipleship even unto death and beyond (12-28).[11] In view of our consideration of *topoi*, literary techniques, and authorial intent, one can understand Matthew's appeal within the Christian community of the first century C.E., both Jew and Gentile. "Gospel" has been transmitted in a recognized and easily received literary pattern.

If the genre critic can begin with the assumption that the evangelists decided to incorporate traditions related to Jesus in a *bios* context in which the traditions are enriched by the person of Jesus, then Matthew represents the pattern of least variation from encomium biography. Since, as previously noted, the synoptic texts possess such direct interrelatedness, Matthew's close proximity to the encomium biography pattern could point to Matthew as the first or primary gospel; the narrative from which the other two take their departure. This conclusion is not so much based upon a statistical count of *topoi* and techniques as it is upon the significant manner in which Luke and Mark deviate from the encomium biographical pattern. Though by no means conclusive, the remaining discussions of Luke and Mark tend to reinforce this preliminary conclusion.

The problem of the genre of Luke is complicated by the relationship of Luke to Acts. Charles Talbert has rightly noted that the genre of Luke must be one that accounts for the totality of Luke and Acts as one work. This means that Luke-Acts does not reflect the encomium biographical pattern in the same way that Matthew exemplifies the genre. Talbert argues that Luke-Acts belongs to that genre consisting of the biographical accounts of philosophers and their schools as is evident in the works of Diogenes Laertius.[12] Whereas the present author tends to agree with Talbert's general view, one should note the encomiastic character of the whole of Luke-Acts. The discussion of Luke as encomium biography, therefore, will be preceded by a few remarks concerning the encomiastic nature of Acts.

That Acts was intended to be read as a history of the early church is not at issue in the present work. One clearly sees the author's results as "interpreted" history writing: i.e., history written from particular theological perspectives. Without being exhaustive, several examples may be cited.

---

[11]Ibid., 103-106.

[12]Charles H. Talbert, *Literary Patterns, Theological Themes, and the Genre of Luke-Acts* (Missoula MT: Scholars Press, 1974).

Acts depicts the harmonious account of the expansion of the church from Jerusalem (the place of Jesus' death) to Rome (the center of the ancient world). The earliest phase of ministry was under the illustrious leadership of Peter: the second phase, marked by the effective and rapid expansion among the Gentiles, was the result of the model work of Paul. The opening of the Gentile mission was initiated by the Holy Spirit in the conversions of the Ethiopian Eunuch (with the assistance of Philip), Saul, and Cornelius (with the assistance of Peter); affirmed at the Jerusalem conference through the efforts of Peter and James; and only then carried out by Paul (the so-called "first" journey of Acts 13-14 understood as the period during which Paul emerges as a leader in the church and rightful participant in the Jerusalem council). Throughout the transition of power from Peter and the apostles to James and the elders (chapter 15), the harmonious positions and relationships among the leaders are clearly evident. For Luke, Acts is the account of the development of a praiseworthy institution, the church. It is the church that has now become the proper vehicle for true Christian discipleship, and the development and expansion of the church among the Jews and Gentiles is directed by the Spirit of the glorified Christ. The church continues Jesus' ministry in the world, a ministry of word and deed. Throughout the narrative, therefore, one can see that the objectives of the author are encomiastic; and the *topoi,* techniques, and authorial intent point to encomiastic history.[13] This development by Luke clearly goes beyond Matthew's work in that the time of the church is kept distinct from, though fundamentally related to, the time of Jesus.

Analysis of Luke's gospel convinces one of the encomium biographical character of this work. As with Matthew, Luke uses *topoi* common to the encomium biography. His use of the *topoi* surrounding birth now includes that of John the Baptist as well as Jesus. Clearly, John's birth is that of forerunner to the Messiah; and the angelic visitation, summaries of nurture (Luke 1:80; 2:40, 52), and prophetic statements of Zechariah and Simeon accent God's soteriological actions throughout the narrative. Luke also includes an account of Jesus as a twelve-year old boy visiting the temple (2:41-51). This event, which depicts Jesus in meaningful dialogue with teachers (2:46), impresses one with his exceptional insight and understanding while preparing the reader in a special way for Jesus' divine mission ("... I must be in my Father's house," 2:49). Other *topoi* in the

---

[13]It should be noted that encomia were written about many topics which included gods, people, and cities to mention only a few. Given Lucian's "How to Write History," one notes how encomiastic intent became a part of the writing of history (much to Lucian's consternation). See also Josephus, *Jewish War,* 1.2.

preliminary section include the place of birth (2:1ff.) and familial relationships (genealogy, 3:23ff.).

In Luke, the presentation of Jesus' ministry employs *topoi* identical with those of Matthew; namely, words and deeds. Luke tends to emphasize the balance of the two more than does Matthew. The call to discipleship is a call to the balanced totality of Jesus' ministry (cf. 24:19). This balance/emphasis is made especially clear at two points critical to the narratives: (1) the call of Peter who responds to the miraculous catch in the context of the proclaimed word (Luke 5:1-11); and, (2) the beginning of the church at which time 3,000 people respond to Peter's proclamation preceded by the miracle of language (Acts 2:1-21).

The *topoi* surrounding death focus upon Jesus' innocence. The charges are false and yet designed to incur a sentence of death from civil authorities (Luke 23:1-2). The contrast of Jesus' innocence (23:4, 14, 22) with Barabbas's guilt aptly characterizes Jesus as upright victim. A similar contrast occurs in the crucifixion of Jesus with two other criminals (23:79ff.). Also, illustrations of Jesus' character in death are the prayer for the forgiveness of those crucifying him (23:34) and his committal into the Father's hands (23:46). The *topoi* surrounding what happens after Jesus' death consist of the road to Emmaus story and appearances in Jerusalem, a divine commentary on the vindication of Jesus and his ministry. Luke's gospel, too, may effectively be classified as encomium biography when the *topoi* employed are considered.

Luke also includes literary techniques common to encomium biography. We have previously mentioned Luke's amplification of John's birth in God's soteriological plan (evidenced by the obvious association with Abraham and Sarah). Perhaps the best example of amplification is Luke's technique of creating a special, final journey to Jerusalem between 9:51-18:27 with an emphasis upon Jesus' rendezvous with death (cf. esp. 9:51; 13:22, 33; 17:11; 19:28). This amplified journey serves as the vehicle for material unique to Luke.[14] One also notices the correspondence between this view of Jesus' journey in Luke's gospel and the journeys of Paul in Acts.

---

[14]Aristotle's words regarding amplification come to mind: " . . . for we should praise even a man who had not achieved anything, if we felt confident that he was likely to do so" (*Rhetorica* 1.9.33). Whether or not Jesus made the journey *as Luke* describes, Jesus did make a final journey to Jerusalem and Luke's emphasis upon Jesus' teaching throughout the journey account is consistent with Jesus' character and what he might have done.

Luke uses comparison initially in order to keep the persons of John the Baptist and Jesus distinct while, at the same time, acknowledging the significant contribution both ministries make to God's soteriological design. One notices the close parallelism of the stories of conception (1:5-25//1:26-38) and birth (1:57-79//2:1-39). Also to be noted are the two parallel statements of nurture (1:80//2:40). Throughout, however, Luke is careful to keep the two distinct thereby avoiding a possible confusion of allegiance. John has his function: so does Jesus. John's is a ministry of expectation, pointing ahead to one who is to come. Jesus is the expected one as indicated by the third nurture summary (2:52) and the traditions of chapter 3 (see also 4:17-21). John's secondary character and that of his ministry in Luke (cf. also Acts 18:24f.; 19:24f.; 19:1f.) serves to enhance the central importance of Jesus. Additional comparative work could be done with other persons included in Luke's gospel; however, such endeavors are not necessary at this writing. For Luke, Jesus is the one whose identity, accomplishments, and faith are second to none.

Two things need to be kept in view when viewing Luke from the perspective of authorial intent. First, Luke 1:1-4 contains the author's statement which is generally understood to mean that Luke is writing an "orderly account." While it is not absolutely clear what this means, the passage is a truth claim, though not a claim to exclusivity. Second, as previously stated, Luke's purpose for writing his gospel must be viewed in conjunction with his writing Acts. With these two aspects in mind, the question is, what did Luke intend when he wrote his gospel?

When viewed separately from Acts, Luke's intentions are closely associated with those of Matthew; namely, to write convincingly of the praiseworthiness of Jesus that enlists a faith response. For this reason, assuming the validity of the description of Luke as "historian," he cannot simply describe the events of Jesus' life. He thus chooses to incorporate those *topoi* and literary techniques by which he can both edify and effectively confront the reader with the advent of the Messiah. In this regard, the results may be classified, as with Matthew, as encomium biography.

When viewed from the larger perspective of Luke-Acts, one finds the same literary decisions applicable. Luke wants to relate the story of Jesus in a convincing way, but he also wants to convey the impact of this soteriological event upon the community of faith derived therefrom. For Luke, the critical issue is clear: it is impossible to do literary justice as a historian to the development and life of the church without first doing literary justice to the soteriological event out of which the church emerged. To incorporate a life of Jesus in a history of the church as a Polybius would incorporate a life into a larger history (e.g., Polybius, *Histories*, X. 21.8) would not adequately convey the impact of the soteriological event upon the committed life of the disciple or upon the rapid expansion of the church. Thus, Luke composes a ''gospel'' similar to Matthew in a manner that classifies it as encomium biography in order to adequately fulfill his larger purpose of relating the development and life of the church to God's continuing, saving activity.

Whereas taken separately, Luke may be regarded as encomium biography, Luke-Acts is much more. The addition of Acts to Luke provides the genre critic with a special situation. Though Talbert's observations of the similarity of Luke-Acts to the works of Diogenes Laertius cannot be ignored, the encomiastic character of both Luke and Acts does not have a parallel in the lives of Diogenes. The best explanation for Luke's literary procedure is that his historical and encomiastic literary objectives have led him, on the one hand, to separate the period of Jesus' ministry from that of the church while, on the other hand, to confront the reader in a decisive way with the significance of both the person of Jesus (his work, death, and glorification) and the church (as the continuation of Jesus' work on earth). Luke, therefore, has taken his point of departure from Matthew. This separation of the church from the time of Jesus constitutes a major variation which is best explained, according to the Two Gospel Hypothesis, by Luke's knowledge of Matthew's gospel. His retention of the encomium biographical form for the presentation of the period of Jesus is indicative of his correct view that the reader cannot fully understand or appreciate the development of the church (through which the reader is now to fulfill his own Christian commitment) apart from the impact of the soteriological event which gave it birth. Luke, therefore, has retained the encomium biographical model in his gospel and has modified it significantly by supplementing the traditions of Jesus and by adding an encomiastic history of the early development of the church, Acts.

It is more difficult to see Mark as a part of the encomium biography genre when one considers the *topoi* common to the genre. Mark says nothing about the birth and genealogical history of Jesus. He omits references to childhood and youthful excellence. The popular association of such *topoi* with ''biography'' in general and with ancient biography in particular has led scholars to declare Mark incapable of being classified as a biographical genre. Such arbitrariness does not do justice to ancient writing for several reasons. First, such *topoi* comprise the preliminary portion of the narrative and, because of the preoccupation with the ''adult career,'' are not integral to biographical literature of the ancient world. They appear only to serve the author's purposes in his portrait of the adult. Consequently, ancient authors are granted considerable freedom in the use of such *topoi*.[15] Second, to deny Mark biographical genre classification, one would have to argue that functionally Mark has no alternative preliminary section which contributes to an adult literary portrait consistent with Marcan intentions. Otherwise, one may argue, as will be the case in this paper, that Mark has chosen an alternative literary route to arrive at the same destination. Such a decision would not automatically deny Mark's gospel encomium biographical status. Third, the total structure along with Mark's use of other *topoi* common to the encomium biography actually argues for his inclusion therein. The latter two reasons deserve further comment.

To the modern reader, the manner by which Mark opens his narrative is both abrupt and unusual when viewed alongside the other canonical gospels and other ancient biographical works. But, close examination reveals that his procedure is not without precedent[16] or intent. Mark's work in the first chapter is carefully structured. After stating the thesis in Mark 1:1, he moves directly into his narrative. His starting point is at the "beginning" (1:1); namely, John the Baptist and Isaiah's passage fulfilled by John's ministry (1:2). John truly "prepares" for the ministry of Jesus, and Mark's references to John and the baptism of Jesus serve simultaneously as a preliminary account pointing ahead to Jesus' ministry. To this preliminary material Mark adds a mere reference to Jesus' temptation, a reference which, by the omission of detail, is designed not so much to call attention to the account itself as to provide the necessary credentials which undergird Jesus' ministry and passion. The introductory section (1:1-13), therefore, functions as a preliminary section which prepares the reader for Jesus' ministry. Though avoiding the more common *topoi* and moving quickly and concisely through this preliminary task, Mark's work does reflect encomium biography procedure.

Mark moves to the ministry without delay. What Jesus preached is summarized in 1:15 followed by the selection of four disciples (vv. 16ff.). An unclean spirit recognizes Jesus' authority (v. 24) and his fame spreads (vv. 28, 29, 45). Thus, in the brief span of one chapter, Mark has set the stage for his work in a preliminary section and then revealed several important themes: Jesus' identity, his call to discipleship, the content of his preaching and view of his deeds, and testimony to his success throughout Galilee. Such literary procedure is common to encomium biography. Contrary to

---

[15]Shuler, *A Genre*, 34-57.

[16]Plutarch, e.g., does not record the events of birth and/or youth excellences of Camillus.

more commonly held opinion, this chapter of Mark is more than a collection of random, unrelated traditions which have fallen accidentally into place.

Further confirmation of the above conclusion may be derived from a cursory examination of Mark's use of εὐθύς, a use which indicates that Mark *intends* to present a simple, rapidly moving narrative. It is one that confronts the reader with the urgency of Jesus' messianic mission. The use of εὐθύς is characteristic of Mark. This term is found seven times in Matthew, two times in Luke-Acts and three times in John while Mark uses it some forty-two times. In the first two chapters alone, Mark uses the term seventeen times, eleven of which occur in chapter one. Thus, Mark's intention is to create a rapidly moving narrative depicting Jesus' intense activities. In fact, Lightfoot sees 1:1-32 as Mark's presentation of the first day (v. 32) of Jesus' manifestation.[17]

It is this view of Mark's redactional activity that accounts for his omission of more commonly found *topoi* such as those noted in Matthew and Luke. Furthermore, given his intention, his use of birth or youth accounts would only interfere with the very effect Mark is clearly attempting to achieve. Rather than moving Mark out of the encomium biography category, the effect he creates is to be seen as complying with the broader goals of encomiastic literature.

Other common *topoi* are to be noted in Mark's presentation of a ministry of words and deeds. This portion is designed to bring the reader to the point of Jesus' death which is viewed by Mark as that of the suffering Messiah locked in a cosmic struggle against evil.[18] In addition to the *topos* of death, his gospel concludes in a manner which leaves the reader with the inference and anticipation of things that are to happen after Jesus' death.

Mark, too, employs literary techniques found in encomium biography. One notices, for example, the way by which he has, through a process of selection, given emphasis to or amplified Jesus' deeds thereby presenting more of the ''miracle worker'' than the preacher/teacher. Also, his deci-

---

[17]R. H. Lightfoot, taking note of the impression Mark creates in ch. 1, suggests that ''St. Mark desires to give at the outset a picture of typical activities of Jesus Christ under the form of events loosely represented as occurring more or less within twenty-four hours; . . . it is the day of the manifestation, or epiphany, of our Saviour Jesus Christ; . . . It is one of intense activity and unceasing strain for the Lord.'' R. H. Lightfoot, *The Gospel Message of St. Mark* (Oxford: Clarendon Press, 1950) 24ff.

[18]See James M. Robinson, *The Problem of History in Mark* (London: SCM Press, 1957).

sion to begin with John the Baptist and end with death also reflects Mark's amplification of this portion of God's soteriological event. One final example may be noted in Theodore Weeden's discussion of Marcan characterization.[19] In his discussion of Mark's use of "crowds," it is clear that Mark amplifies the response to Jesus' ministry. Weeden writes:

> That role [scil., the role played by the crowd] is to dramatize, by contrast with the religious leaders, the positive response to Jesus. The crowds flock to him with eagerness (1:32ff., 37; 3:7-12; 4:1; 6:53-56; 9:15; 11:8ff.), listen to his teaching enthusiastically (1:22, 27; 12:37b) and respond to his healing powers with anticipation (1:32ff.; 3:7ff.; 6:53ff.).[20]

One cannot fail to note the manner in which Mark depicts Jesus as far superior to all the personages in his work. John the Baptist comes closest to a position of comparison, but the two are kept far apart and John receives less attention than in the other canonical texts. Also, long noted among New Testament scholars is the superiority of Jesus over all of his disciples. Of all the gospels, Mark is the hardest on the disciples and Jesus, by comparison, towers over them. Finally, Jesus' control over demons and spirits signifies his power over evil.

Consideration of Mark's authorial intent reveals literary purposes similar to those of Matthew and Luke. Mark portrays the Messiah whose identity cannot be suppressed and who is locked in a cosmic struggle against evil. Faith is the response intended by Mark, for to the believer belongs the final victory anticipated at the time of the suffering Messiah's return. Mark tells his story persuasively and, as a result, Mark's gospel has been recently characterized as one sermon (Marxsen).[21] Such evangelistic purposes are truly compatible with encomium-type biography, and Mark's use of the *topoi* and literary technique warrants the inclusion of this "gospel" therein.

With the background of encomium biography clearly in view, a different view of Mark as author emerges. To that segment of the gospel genre discussion which has viewed Mark's gospel as primitive and possessive of very little literary design, the present discussion has offered a very different view. It is unlikely that Mark omitted traditions of birth and youth because they were not important or because none were available to him. Such

---

[19]Theodore Weeden, *Mark: Traditions in Conflict* (Philadelphia: Fortress Press, 1971) 13ff.

[20]Ibid., 22.

[21]W. Marxsen, *Introduction to the New Testament* (Philadelphia: Fortress Press, 1968) 144.

omissions are now to be viewed as points at which Mark consciously departs (as an author in the ancient world could and often did) from stories or texts which preceded his own. Whereas the Two Source Hypothesis credits Mark with very little "literary" activity, the Two Gospel Hypothesis elevates Mark's role as an author both in terms of the traditions he has chosen to incorporate into his narrative and in terms of what he has chosen to omit. Mark is indeed responsible for the content of his gospel.

Although one can not with absolute certainty relate the reason Mark would write as he has if he had Matthew and Luke before him, some plausible reasons have been offered which deserve careful consideration. Perhaps the most convincing, based on the Two Gospel Hypothesis, is the one offered by David Dungan. He argues that one of the major concerns of the early Christian community was to preserve harmony within the church.[22] The presence of two such compelling works as Matthew and Luke-Acts would surely have created theological difficulties for those who would focus on the points at which the two gospels are different. Obviously, one of the most immediate problems confronting the reader are the different birth narratives. In both the gospels of Matthew and Luke, however, the point of convergence is that of John the Baptist. If Mark viewed his task as one of mediation as Dungan and others have suggested (and as the Two Gospel Hypothesis would indicate), then Mark's omission of the more common *topoi* surrounding birth and early childhood is to be understood in terms of Mark's theological and literary restraint. Indeed, his alternative approach is to be seen as quite a creative one: i.e., his substitution of the tone of urgency for the self-defeating task of choosing one gospel birth account over another or of opting for some kind of conflated narrative uniting both accounts. Mark's procedures minimize the obvious problems while focussing upon the common point of departure; i.e., John the Baptist. Additional follow-up on Tom Longstaff's study of conflation in Mark (from the point of Mark's position as third in the synoptic sequence) could further support the view that Mark plays a mediating role between the Matthean and Lukan synoptic texts.[23] Therefore, from the standpoint of the encomium biography genre to which all three synoptic gospels are related,

---

[22]David L. Dungan, "Reactionary Trends in the Gospel-Producing Activity of the Early Church: Marcion, Tatian, Mark," in *L'Evangile Selon Marc: Tradition et Redaction,* ed. M. Sabbé (Gembloux, Belgium: Leuven University Press, 1974) 179-83.

[23]T. R. W. Longstaff, *Evidence of Conflation in Mark? A Study in the Synoptic Problem* (Missoula MT: Scholars Press, 1977).

Mark's work is best understood and his literary contributions appreciated more fully when one is freed to seriously consider the possibility of Mark's gospel having been written third in the synoptic sequence with both Matthew and Luke at his disposal.

The research of noted literary critic, Roland Mushat Frye, tends to further identify the secondary character of Mark to Matthew and Luke. In "The Synoptic Problems and Analogies in Other Literatures," a paper delivered at the colloquy on the gospels held in San Antonio, Texas, and later published in *The Relationships Among the Gospels: An Interdisciplinary Dialogue,* Fry treats three criteria for determining the secondary nature of documents that are as closely related as are the gospels.[24] In the discussion of "the criterion of language," Frye observes that the argument for "an earlier date for Mark because it is closer to the spoken versions of *koine* Greek in the time of Jesus" is not convincing in view of his own comparative literary research.[25] Examination of the works of Lucian, tendencies of the "Old French" language following the Roman conquest of Gaul, and the linguistic tendencies in the development of black English reveals that the creolization of language (evident in the above argument for Marcan priority) is more often evidence for later development than for primary writing. On the contrary, non-creolized writing tends to be early and more closely related to acceptable, existing patterns of literature especially for colonized or conquered people. Frye's conclusion parallels our earlier preliminary suggestion that Matthew is possibly earlier because of his closer conformity to the literary pattern (above, p. 77). It also conforms to the present research involving the placing of Mark as third in sequence precisely because of its distance from the more standard Greek of Matthew and Luke. Frye's second criterion is that of comparative length. Here Frye observes that secondary documents reveal two striking characteristics: the length of secondary documents tended to be shorter due to processes of selection and/or omission, but the individual pericopes included in the secondary document frequently underwent expansion. Citing several examples of these two characteristics in the history of literature, Frye correctly observes the identical phenomena in Mark's gospel. The criterion of comparative length, therefore, supports Mark's position as third in sequence rather than the reverse. The third criterion Frye discusses is that of confla-

---

[24]Roland Mushat Frye, "The Synoptic Problems and Analogies in Other Literatures," *The Relationships Among the Gospels,* ed. William O. Walker (San Antonio TX: Trinity University Press, 1978) 261-302.

[25]Ibid., 264ff.

tion. In addition to the comparative literature cited by Longstaff in his work previously mentioned[26], one must include Frye's insightful work on Shakespeare and on Old English literature.[27] In this research, Frye documents the expansion of pericopes coupled with the abbreviation of the narrative as a whole; attention to immediacy, impact, and vivid detail; and the writer's "wiggling back and forth" between *Vorlagen* for reasons known only to the writer himself.[28] Here again, such characteristics are especially associated with Mark and support his secondary character to Matthew and Luke.

Based upon the above considerations, the present genre critic concludes that the arguments for the sequence of Matthew, Luke, and Mark are impressive. After all, the alternatives are far from satisfactory. The Two Source Hypothesis portrays Mark as working in a literary vacuum, as lacking in authorial purpose or design, and as lacking in literary skill and talent. One has to struggle to appreciate the significant contribution Mark has made to his reading/listening audience. When placed third in sequence, on the other hand, Mark's contributions and mediating role become more evident, and his native abilities and inspired faith more recognizable. While such comments are important, however, they are not entirely convincing. What is more persuasive is the evidence from the standpoint of genre and comparative literature. Having identified a genre for the gospels and having noted the work of Dungan, Longstaff, and Frye, one can see a developing pattern of the sequence of the synoptic gospels within encomium biography. Such is not the case with the Two Source Hypothesis sequence. The *crucial* question for those who accept the traditional Two Source position is this: where in the history of literature does one find an example of two related documents (as closely related as Matthew and Luke appear to be) that have emerged from the same *two* sources (Mark and Q) and, though *independent* of one another, have preserved not only a vast majority of the same traditions but also virtually the same *order* of one of the sources (Mark)? At issue is a convincing explanation of the independent development of Matthew and Luke from Mark and Q *supported* by examples from the history of literature and/or tradition (oral or written!).

By way of summary, we have presented the thesis that the canonical gospels, because they are preserved in text form, are the products of "authors" and may be referred to as examples of literature. This was done by

---

[26]Above, n. 23.

[27]Frye, *The Relationships*, 274ff.

[28]Ibid., 281.

offering four theses for consideration: (1) that the shift from sources, whether in individual or collected form, to story constitutes a genre and hence literary decision of the redactor/author/evangelist; (2) it is probable that this "literary" decision did not take place in a vacuum; (3) the gospels were no doubt received as popular "lives" of Jesus thereby authenticating within the Christian community the person as well as the tradition of Jesus; and (4) the most productive way of viewing the emergence of the synoptic gospels is from the perspective of hellenistic biography, more specifically, encomium biography. With these theses in view, the explanation for the emergence of the sequence of the gospels from the standpoints of genre and comparative literature is more easily understood when considered from the perspective of the Two Gospel Hypothesis: i.e., Matthew, Luke, and then Mark.

SCRIPTURE, TORAH, AND SABBATH IN LUKE-ACTS

Joseph B. Tyson

The purpose of this essay is to raise certain questions about the concept of authority in Luke-Acts. The specific problem to be dealt with is posed by the recognition that, although scripture and Torah appear to be accepted as authoritative in Luke-Acts, there are particular aspects within the scriptures that, for Luke, require some qualifications. The qualifications are of such a nature as to require us to make a careful examination of the concept of authority in Luke-Acts and its relationship to scripture and Torah. One such particular element is the requirement of Sabbath observance.

Although NT scholars have shown a good deal of interest in the use of the OT in the NT,[1] relatively little attention has been devoted either to Luke-Acts in particular or to the broader question of religious authority in these writings.[2] This question inevitably brings us face to face with Luke's understanding of Torah. A whole host of questions need to be faced. Despite the affirmation of Jesus in Luke 16:17 ("But it is easier for heaven and earth to pass away, than for one dot of the law to become void"), we need to ask if Luke really conceded that the validity of Torah extended on into the age after Jesus. Despite Luke's references to Torah as a component part

---

[1]Cf., e.g., Barnabas Lindars, *New Testament Apologetic* (Philadelphia: Westminster Press, 1961); C. K. Barrett, "The Bible in the New Testament Period," in *The Church's Use of the Bible Past and Present,* ed. D. E. Nineham (London: S.P.C.K., 1963) 1-24; idem, "The Interpretation of the Old Testament in the New," in *The Cambridge History of the Bible,* ed. P. R. Ackroyd and C. F. Evans (London: Cambridge University Press, 1970) 1:377-411. On the OT quotations in the passion narratives of the gospels, cf. Douglas J. Moo, *The Old Testament in the Gospel Passion Narratives* (Sheffield: Almond Press, 1983).

[2]Cf., however, S. G. Wilson, *Luke and the Law* (Cambridge: Cambridge University Press, 1983); cf. also Jacob Jervell, "The Center of Scripture in Luke," in *The Unknown Paul* (Minneapolis: Augsburg Publishing House, 1984) 122-37. Space does not permit an analysis of *exousia* and related terms in Luke-Acts. It is, nevertheless, useful to note that, although the word is used in a number of different contexts, it is never explicitly connected with Torah or scripture.

of scripture, we need to examine his understanding of its relationships to the prophets and the writings.

These and other questions are acute, because it is frequently maintained that Luke wanted to emphasize the continuity between Judaism and Christianity. If he did, we should expect that he would understand there to be some compatibility between Christian and Jewish views on basic questions of authority. We should expect that he would have a keen interest in questions about the proper ways to interpret scripture and the correct ways to observe its commandments.

The view that Luke emphasized the continuity between Judaism and Christianity is widespread but not universal. John Knox was impressed with the continuity. He was led to wonder why Marcion, who emphasized the discontinuity between Judaism and Christianity, would have chosen Luke as his gospel. He wrote:

> That the one work among early Christian documents whose primary purpose was to demonstrate the continuity of Christianity with Judaism should have been deliberately selected and adopted by the one church leader whose primary interest was to deny that continuity is to me almost incredible.[3]

This recognition tended to confirm Knox's contention that Marcion did not accept and abbreviate canonical Luke. Rather, according to Knox, Luke-Acts in its present form was produced out of reaction against Marcion.

Jacob Jervell has also been impressed with the sense of continuity between Judaism and Christianity in Luke-Acts. In his approach, the Jewish Christians in Acts form, for Luke, the necessary link:

> The promises to Israel are fulfilled in the only Israel of which Luke is aware, the Jewish Christians. Then, because the church is the direct continuation of the history of God's people, and itself the bearer of the promises, Luke must indicate that the Messiah Jesus is the genuine and true Messiah.[4]

Jervell is convinced that the Jewish-Christian element was a powerful one in Luke's church toward the end of the first century. In order not to offend this group, Luke was required to portray a Christian movement that was in fundamental harmony with Judaism.[5]

In contrast to scholars such as Knox and Jervell, Ernst Haenchen thinks that there was a deep enmity between Luke's community and the non-be-

---

[3]John Knox, *Marcion and the New Testament* (Chicago: University of Chicago Press, 1942) 139.

[4]Jacob Jervell, "The Circumcised Messiah," trans. Roy A. Harrisville, in *The Unknown Paul*, 145.

[5]Cf. Jervell, "The Mighty Minority," in *The Unknown Paul*, 26-51.

lieving Jews.[6] He agrees that Luke conceived of the Christian community as accepting the basic tenets of the Hebrew scriptures, but he calls attention to the deep rift that, for Luke, lies between the two communities. In the speech of Stephen in Acts 7, for example, there are expressions of hostility and scorn directed at the Jewish people. Haenchen thinks that these expressions are not from a pre-Lukan source; rather they represent the views of Luke himself. In connection with this speech, Haenchen writes, "Hier spricht Lukas selbst, und zwar nicht im Kostüm einer judenfreundlichen Vergangenheit, sondern in Haltung und Stimmung der eigenen, heidenchristlichen Gegenwart."[7] The continuity that Luke wants to emphasize is with the scriptures, not with Judaism. In Haenchen's interpretation of Luke-Acts, the earlier Christian mission to the Jews was essentially a failure, and the existence of a Jewish-Christian community was of no consequence, once the gospel had taken root among Gentiles.

The work of scholars such as Knox, Jervell, and Haenchen should serve to illustrate the complexity of the problem of continuity in Luke-Acts. Despite their differences, they all seem to agree that Luke wanted to emphasize the relationship of the Christian faith to the OT and the conformity of this faith with Moses and the prophets. The scriptures appear to be fundamentally authoritative for Luke. This essay will suggest that this proposition needs to be more carefully nuanced.

The approach that will be taken in this essay has been indirectly facilitated by recent studies in the relationships among the synoptic gospels, an enterprise closely associated with the name of my colleague, William R. Farmer. The approach may best be described as holistic. Its indebtedness to studies of the synoptic problem may need some explanation.

The various challenges to the two-document hypothesis have tended to raise serious questions about the adequacy of most redaction-critical work on the synoptic gospels. Farmer has himself pointed out, on a number of occasions, that redaction criticism depends upon a particular solution to the synoptic problem, namely the two-document hypothesis.[8] Redaction critics generally assume that this hypothesis is, if not an assured result of criticism, at least a workable and fruitful hypothesis. Thus, in those places

---

[6]Cf. Ernst Haenchen, "Judentum und Christentum in der Apostelgeschichte," *ZNTW* 54 (1963): 155-87.

[7]Ibid., 165.

[8]Cf. esp. W. R. Farmer, "Redaction Criticism and the Synoptic Problem," *SBLASP* (1971) 1:239-50; "Modern Developments of Griesbach's Hypothesis," *NTS* 23 (1977): 275-95.

where, for example, Luke and Mark have similar material, it should be possible to identify redactional elements in Luke, since the author of the third gospel made use of Mark. But if confidence in the two-document hypothesis as the correct solution to the synoptic problem begins to erode, confidence in a form of redaction criticism that depends on this hypothesis likewise begins to diminish.

If one takes these challenges seriously but is not willing to adopt an alternative solution to the synoptic problem, some consideration needs to be given to the implications for future redaction-critical work. Although a number of alternative implications have been proposed, a potentially fruitful approach has been introduced by some NT scholars who are sensitive to the lessons to be learned from secular literary criticism.[9] Although their studies vary in a number of particulars and in their results, in general these NT scholars look upon the gospels as products of individual authors, and they concentrate upon each gospel as a whole. To be sure, such scholars do not deny that the various synoptic evangelists had sources, which they used and sometimes altered, nor do they deny that there is a documentary relationship among them. Indeed, most continue to hold to the two-document hypothesis. But they do not make use of this hypothesis in the attempt to practice a kind of surgery on the gospels in which tradition and redaction are separated. At least, they do not do this in the first instance. The initial effort is to understand the work of a particular evangelist by examining his gospel as a whole. The principle is that whatever a gospel writer used, he finally made it his own by including it within a particular kind of literary structure and by making each element serve a certain narrative purpose.

The literary-critical interest in these studies also means that historical-critical questions receive little if any attention. The first task in exploring the gospels is to understand the world that the text itself describes. This

---

[9]Cf., e.g., Norman R. Petersen, *Literary Criticism for New Testament Critics* (Philadelphia: Fortress Press, 1978). Several studies of the gospel of Mark have been influential. Cf., e.g., David Rhoads, "Narrative Criticism and the Gospel of Mark," *JAAR* 50 (1982): 411-34; David Rhoads and Donald Michie, *Mark as Story* (Philadelphia: Fortress Press, 1982). On Luke and Luke-Acts, cf. Charles H. Talbert, *Literary Patterns, Theological Themes and the Genre of Luke-Acts* (Missoula MT: Scholars Press, 1974); Eckhard Plümacher, *Lukas als hellenistischer Schriftsteller* (Göttingen: Vandenhoeck & Ruprecht, 1972). For studies of specific literary themes in Luke-Acts, cf. Luke T. Johnson, *The Literary Function of Possessions in Luke-Acts* (Missoula MT: Scholars Press, 1977); David L. Tiede, *Prophecy and History in Luke-Acts* (Philadelphia: Fortress Press, 1980).

effort requires the scholar to become immersed in the world of the text. Questions about the correspondence between the world of the text and the "real" world, i. e., historical questions, are not the same as questions about the meaning of the text.

The problems that plague the study of the synoptic gospels do not greatly affect the study of Acts. Indeed, source criticism of Acts has just about been abandoned. Thus, if it is appropriate to approach the synoptic gospels without making use of a source hypothesis, then surely it is appropriate to study the entire Lukan corpus as a whole. Facilitated by studies of the synoptic problem and by interest in literary criticism, the holistic study of Luke-Acts promises to be a fruitful area of NT criticism.

The intent of this essay, therefore, will be to examine the concept of authority in Luke-Acts by raising questions about the meaning and relationship of scripture, Torah, and Sabbath observance in these documents. Due to the nature of the material, our attention will be focused on the gospel, but full use will be made of the relevant data from Acts. The method of study will be holistic, and the objective will be to understand the ways in which scripture, Torah, and Sabbath observance relate to each other in the text of Luke-Acts.

Luke's View of Scripture and Torah in General

Although Luke does not use the word *graphē* with great frequency (four times in the gospel; seven times in Acts), his uses are sufficient to show that for him the word connoted a sense of authority. In his post-resurrection appearance to the two disciples on the way to Emmaus, Jesus assumes the role of the authoritative interpreter of scripture and shows that it was necessary for the Christ to suffer. He interprets "all the scriptures," "beginning with Moses and all the prophets" (Luke 24:27; cf. 24:32,45). Although it is clear that an authoritative interpreter is required for the scriptures to be understood by the disciples, the interpreter does not confer authority on the scriptures. Scripture has priority over the interpreter. It is scripture, not the interpretation of scripture, that makes the suffering of the Christ necessary (Luke 24:26). Nor is Jesus the only authoritative interpreter. His apostles may interpret the scriptures correctly, as Philip does in his contact with the Ethiopian (cf. esp. Acts 8:32-35). On the basis of the scriptures Paul attempts to persuade the Jews about Jesus (Acts 17:2), as does Apollos after being instructed by Priscilla and Aquila (Acts 18:28). One might understand Acts 1:16 as embodying the essence of Luke's view of the authority of scripture, although it is used here in specific reference to Judas: "The scripture had to be fulfilled."

The verb *graphō* almost always refers to the Hebrew scriptures in Luke-Acts and has the same general connotation of authority as the noun *graphē*.

The debates between the devil and Jesus in Luke 4:1-13, with quotations from the scriptures on both sides, show that the authority of these documents is assumed. The phrase that introduced these and other quotations in Luke-Acts, "It is written," appears tantamount to saying, "God has said."[10] In one place a quotation from scripture even serves to condemn an action of Paul, the hero of the last half of Acts (cf. Acts 23:5). Paul himself seems to represent the Lukan point of view when he says to Felix, "I worship the God of our fathers, believing everything laid down by the law or written in the prophets" (Acts 24:14). There seems to be no equivocation on the question of the authority of scripture.

Moreover, there are several indications that Luke is aware of divisions within the scriptures. He speaks of the law (of Moses) and the prophets (Luke 16:16; Acts 13:15; 24:14; 28:23; cf. Luke 16:29,31; 24:27) and once of the law of Moses, prophets, and Psalms (Luke 24:44).

In general, Luke makes more use of the prophets and writings than he does of the Torah. The prophets and writings are most frequently used in predictive ways, to show that what occurred in the life of Jesus or in the experience of the apostles was known and announced beforehand. They serve as ways of understanding things that would have been perplexing to Luke's community, such as the treachery of Judas (Acts 1:16), the death of Jesus (Luke 22:37; 24:46), or the rejection of the Christian message by Jews (Acts 28:25-28).

Torah may also be thought of as having the same sort of predictive power as the prophets. For example, in his defense before Herod Agrippa, Paul speaks of the predictions of both Moses and the prophets (Acts 26:22). Torah may also have paradigmatic significance. In Luke 17:26-32, for example, incidents from the stories of Noah and Lot in Genesis are cited as models for what will occur at the coming of the Son of man.

Most references to Torah, however, consist of quotations or allusions to the legal materials. Many of these are intended to be explanatory. In the infancy narratives, Luke appears to stress the piety of the families of John and Jesus by calling attention to their adherence to the law of Moses. Both John (Luke 1:59) and Jesus (2:21) are circumcised on the eighth day. When the family brings Jesus to be presented in the Temple, Luke explains that this is done in accordance with the law of Moses, and he quotes from Exodus 13:2,12,15 (Luke 2:22-23). Similarly, he explains a sacrificial ritual in terms of a quotation from Leviticus 12:8 (Luke 2:24). Luke summarizes

------

[10]Cf. Luke 4:4,8,10. Cf. also Luke 4:12, where the expression is, "It is said" (εἴρηται).

the religious observances connected with the birth of Jesus in 2:39, "And when they had performed everything according to the law of the Lord, they returned into Galilee, to their own city, Nazareth." It is generally recognized that the Lukan infancy narratives are marked by a keen interest in Jewish religious practices and that they breathe the air of pious Judaism. Elizabeth and Zechariah walk "in all the commandments and ordinances of the Lord blameless" (Luke 1:6). The birth of John means that God has remembered "his holy covenant, the oath which he swore to our father Abraham" (Luke 1:72-73). Jesus' parents go to Jerusalem every year for Passover (2:41). Here there appears to be no question about the value of Torah observance.

In a number of pericopes dealing with the teaching and ministry of Jesus, the authority of Torah seems to be made clear. When Jesus heals a leper, he tells him to show himself to the priest and to make an offering "as Moses commanded" (Luke 5:14; cf. Lev 14:2-3). Ten lepers are told to do the same in Luke 17:12. A lawyer who asks about eternal life is referred to the Torah, and his quotations from Deuteronomy and Leviticus are approved by Jesus, whose words allude to Leviticus (Luke 10:25-28). A ruler who asks about eternal life is told to observe the commandments (Luke 18:18-20).

In general, Luke's heroes in Acts are shown to be fully observant Jews. Although Stephen is accused of speaking against the Temple and the law, Luke maintains that this was an accusation by false witnesses (Acts 6:13).[11] Similarly, Paul is accused of persuading people to act contrary to the Law (Acts 18:13; 21:28), but this charge is denied by James (21:24) and by Paul (22:3; 25:8).

Probably the most forceful statement in the gospel of Luke is in the pronouncement of Jesus, "But it is easier for heaven and earth to pass away, than for one dot of the law to become void" (*pesein,* Luke 16:17; cf. Matt 5:18). But the verse has its problems. The pronouncement directly follows a statement that seems to put a limit upon the authority of both prophets and law: "The law and the prophets were until John" (Luke 16:16). Commentators have achieved no unanimity in addressing the apparent problems. I. H. Marshall says that Luke 16:16 refers to the period in which law and prophecy were produced and 16:17 refers to the period of their validity. The stress, therefore, is on the continuing validity of law and proph-

---

[11]Jervell regards Acts 6:13 as a clue to the Lukan *Sitz im Leben.* Cf. his "The History of Early Christianity and the Acts of the Apostles," in *Unknown Paul,* 13-25.

ets.[12] Others comment that Luke thinks of law and prophets only in the sense in which they are predictive of the life of Jesus. That is, law is fulfilled in Jesus' life, death, and resurrection, and so its validity has not ceased.[13] Still others look upon Luke 16:17 as ironic. George Caird writes,

> Any rabbi might have said this [Luke 16:17], but we cannot imagine it on the lips of Jesus, especially in view of the fact that the very next verse contains an alteration of the Mosaic law of divorce. This being so, the simplest expedient is to regard the saying as an ironical attack on the pedantic conservatism of the scribes: it was easier for heaven and earth to pass away than for the scribes to surrender that scrupulosity which could not see the Law for the letters.[14]

Moreover, the connection between Luke 16:17 and 16:18, the statement about divorce, has puzzled many interpreters. Caird takes the latter verse as an annulment of the law of divorce. David Daube has, however, contended that the statement about divorce is an illustration about the eternal validity of Torah in the age of the gospel. He understands Luke 16:18 as an expansion of the precept for royalty, "He shall not multiply wives to himself" (Deut 17:17). Daube writes:

> John [the Baptist, cf. Luke 16:16], whatever his powers may be, has not abrogated the Law. The faithful will not disregard even the *yodh* in the precept 'He shall not multiply wives to himself.' It is a precept for royalty, but the true members of the kingdom will cherish it the more on this account. Man and woman by sexual union return to, or re-approach, the ideal androgynous state. A husband remarrying after divorce, or a man marrying a divorced wife, commits adultery.[15]

Although the passage, Luke 16:16-18, is not without problems, Daube has gone a long way toward explaining the collocation of ideas contained in it. Under his interpretation, the central affirmation is one that speaks of the eternal validity of *nomos*.

All of these considerations suggest that Luke wants to show that authority continues to reside in scripture and Torah and, hence, that there is a fundamental continuity between Judaism and Christianity.

---

[12]Cf. I. Howard Marshall, *The Gospel of Luke: A Commentary on the Greek Text* (Grand Rapids: Eerdmans, 1978) 626-30.

[13]Cf., e.g., E. E. Ellis, *The Gospel of Luke* (Greenwood SC: Attic Press, 1977); Walter Grundmann, *Das Evangelium nach Lukas*, 2nd ed. (Berlin: Evanglische Verlagsanstalt, 1966); K. H. Rengstorf, *Das Evangelium nach Lukas,* 5th ed. (Göttingen: Vandenhoeck & Ruprecht, 1949).

[14]George B. Caird, *Saint Luke* (New York: Penguin, 1963) 190.

[15]David Daube, *The New Testament and Rabbinic Judaism* (London: Athlone Press, 1956) 300.

There are, however, two important considerations that hold us back from a whole-hearted acceptance of this proposition. One consideration relates to terminology. We have already observed that Luke frequently connects the law with Moses, and so the phraseology, the law of Moses, is familiar. Of course, there are many uses of the word *nomos* without a following genitive. But the only times the law is explicitly connected with God are in the infancy narratives. Here we have the phrases, *en nomō kyriou* (Luke 2:23); *kata to eirēmenon en tō nomō kyriou* (2:24); and *kata ton nomon kyriou* (2:39; cf. also 1:6). The absence of this, or any similar expression, in the narratives and discourses outside Luke 1-2 might be insignificant if there were no other grounds for thinking that Luke is hesitant to grant ultimate authority to Torah. As we shall see below, however, there are such grounds. The terminology in the infancy narratives might be explained by the generally positive image of Jewish piety that Luke wants to convey in these chapters. The absence of any explicit connection between law and God in great stretches of Luke-Acts tends to diminish the positive impression conveyed in Luke 1-2.

The other matter that makes us cautious is a statement attributed to Paul in Acts 13:38. Here Paul announces the possibility of forgiveness of sins and freedom "from everything from which you could not be justified in the law of Moses (*apo pantōn hōn ouk ēdynēthēte en nomō Mōuseōs dikaiōthēnai*)." This verse, which contains some words that remind readers of Paul's letters, serves to qualify the more affirmative aspects of Luke's treatment of Torah. These qualifications become more significant as we examine Luke's understanding of one aspect of Torah, namely Sabbath observance.

Luke's View of Sabbath Observance in Particular

Although the view of scripture and Torah in Luke-Acts is, on the whole, positive, an examination of certain related particulars shows that Luke assumes an extensive qualification of the authority of Torah. Such particulars include Sabbath observance, circumcision, and dietary regulations. Due to the restrictions of space, only the first of these can be dealt with here. Suffice it to say that Luke-Acts gives a basis for questioning the authority of Torah and scripture in the case of both the requirement of circumcision and the laws of *kashrut*. Consideration of these particulars shows that the question of authority and the role of scripture and Torah are exceedingly complex matters in Luke's writings.

One must, however, be cautious in dealing with the relationship between Torah and any particular matter relating to it. In the first place, we cannot be certain in every case that Luke was able or willing to recognize a connection between these particulars and Torah itself. In a few places, he speaks of the custom(s) (*ethos*) of the Jews (Acts 26:3), or Moses (Acts 6:14; 15:1), or the fathers (28:17). In Luke 2:27, he connects custom and law (*kata to eithismenon tou nomou peri autou*). *Ethos* clearly refers to circumcision in Acts 15:1. But in other places *ethos* seems to refer to traditional observances that may or may not be related to *nomos*. It is not at all certain that Luke thought of all these customs as required by Torah or scripture.[16]

Another factor that must give us pause is the recognition that there is no one normative Jewish approach to these particulars. Not only was there variation among the Jewish sects of the first century, but even among the Tannaites there was a wealth of discussion about points relating to the various observances and, in some cases, a myriad of qualifications. These considerations make it extremely difficult to settle questions about the distinctiveness of Luke's concepts.

We must, therefore, form our questions as sharply as possible. In view of the fact that Luke has affirmed the general authority of scripture and Torah, is the observance of Sabbath a particular matter which, in his mind, requires a qualification of this authority? If so, what authority does he recognize for altering the ways in which the Sabbath should be observed?

Clearly Luke has emphasized the customary observance of the Sabbath by Jesus (Luke 4:16,31; 6:6; 13:10) and his followers (Luke 23:54,56; Acts 1:12; 13:14; 16:13). He also knows something about the nature of the synagogue Sabbath service, and he refers to the reading of scripture on these occasions (Luke 4:17-19; Acts 13:15,27; 15:21).

Nevertheless, a number of these occasions do not emphasize piety and Sabbath rest but controversy. In the first narrative in which Jesus attends a synagogue service on the Sabbath (Luke 4:16-30), we have a kind of model for his entire ministry.[17] Luke uses this occasion to present a programmatic narrative in which some of the themes that will be developed later are introduced. Jesus reads from the book of Isaiah and announces the

---

[16]Cf. the discussion of *ethos* in S. G. Wilson, *Luke and the Law*, 1-11. Wilson thinks that Luke may have been influenced by Josephus's apologetic use of *ethos* to describe for a Gentile audience such Jewish practices as Sabbath observance, circumcision, and dietary regulations. He observes that for Luke to describe the law as custom "is to view it as a cultural as much as a religious phenomenon and indicates an ability to view it either from something of a distance or within a broad perspective" (p.11).

[17]Cf., e.g., the essays in *Jesus in Nazareth*, ed. W. Eltester (Berlin: Walter de Gruyter, 1972).

fulfillment of the passage in his own ministry. As we have seen, for Luke this is a customary use of scripture as predictive of the life and ministry of Jesus. But Jesus goes on to speak of the work of Elijah and Elisha, who passed by widows and lepers in Israel and offered help to Gentiles. The audience in attendance at the Sabbath service was initially favorable to Jesus' announcement about the fulfillment of the Isaianic scripture. But with the words about Elijah and Elisha and their work among Gentiles, the people turned against Jesus, threw him out of the city, and almost killed him.[18]

Similarly, the narrative in Acts 13:13-52 tells of Paul's first missionary sermon in a synagogue on the Sabbath. Here there is no reaction against what Paul said, even when he talks about the impossibility of being justified by the law of Moses. Only when the Jews observe the interest of Gentiles is there a problem. The result is that Paul and Barnabas are driven out of Pisidian Antioch.

These narratives are not used by Luke simply to illustrate the piety of Jesus and Paul in their observance of the Sabbath. Rather they are paradigms for the life of Jesus and for the Christian missionaries. Jesus attempts to heal in the synagogue and is rejected (cf. Luke 6:6-11; 13:10-17; 14:1-6). Paul attempts to proclaim the fulfillment of scripture in Jesus; he is rejected by the Jews and goes to the Gentiles (cf. Acts 17:2-9). In both Luke and Acts the Sabbath synagogue service is more frequently an occasion for controversy and Jewish rejection than for worship.

In the gospel of Luke there are four occasions on which there is a controversy between Jesus and the Jewish leaders in regard to the Sabbath: Luke 6:1-5; 6:6-11; 13:10-17; and 14:1-6. The first deals with the question of plucking and rubbing grain, and the other three are questions of healing. The form for all four is basically the same and involves a criticism by Jewish leaders and a defense by Jesus of his or his disciples' actions.

In Luke 6:1-5, the narrative begins with an action on the part of Jesus' disciples: they pluck, rub, and eat some of the grain from a field. Some Pharisees accuse them of doing something unlawful (*ouk exestin*) on the Sabbath, and Jesus responds to the criticism. His defense is two-fold. First, he cites a precedent, not explicitly for violating the Sabbath, but for eating the bread of the presence in the house of God. The precedent was, according to Luke, supplied by David, who ate bread that was not lawful for any but priests to eat. The precedent is, however, problematic on several counts. In the first place, in the narrative in 1 Samuel 21:1-6, which is evoked here,

---

[18]Cf. my essay, "The Jewish Public in Luke-Acts," *NTS* 30 (1984): 575-83.

the action of David is not set on the Sabbath.[19] Second, nothing is said in the narrative of 1 Samuel about the exclusive right of priests to eat the bread of the presence. Ahimelech, the priest of the shrine at Nob, to whom David appeals for bread, simply inquires if the men who are to eat it have kept themselves from women. When he finds that they have, he gives them the bread. Although Leviticus 24:9 restricts the holy bread to Aaron and his sons, there is no explicit or implicit reference to that verse in 1 Samuel 21:1-6. Thirdly, it is possible that Luke meant to evoke images of the Temple by his use of the phrase, "house of God" (6:4). He speaks of it as "my house" in an OT quotation in Luke 19:46. To speak of the "house of God" as the Temple in Jerusalem would be anachronistic from the perspective of David, but this point should probably not be pressed.

Despite these problems, we must take the precedent in the sense which Luke probably intended. It means that there are occasions on which it is permissible to violate laws that are given in Torah. To be sure, the Rabbis sometimes entertain interpretations of the Sabbath commandment that might appear to qualify it, but Luke does not display any awareness of this mode of interpretation. He only wants to stress the point that Jesus and the Pharisees differed sharply on the interpretation of the Sabbath commandment and its elasticity. For Jesus, a basic human need, such as hunger, takes precedence over the commandment to observe the Sabbath. Luke's Pharisees do not agree.

The other defense that Jesus offers to the Pharisaic objection is the pronouncement, "The Son of man is lord of the sabbath" (Luke 6:5). In the context of Luke's developing picture of Jesus, this becomes an announcement that Jesus himself is Lord of the Sabbath.[20]

The two defenses shed light on Luke's sense of authority. To take the second first, we are to conclude that Jesus himself has authority to determine the proper ways to observe Sabbath. The first defense might have been more readily acceptable to Pharisaic interpreters, since it involved an appeal to another part of scripture. David Daube, however, has shown that the kind of citation in Luke 6:3-4 is not the best kind of citation to provide. It is *haggadic* rather than *halakhic*. He maintains that haggadic citations

---

[19]There is, however, evidence that some Rabbis thought that this narrative was set on the Sabbath. Cf. the references in H. L. Strack and P. Billerbeck, *Kommentar zum Neuen Testament aus Talmud und Midrasch* (Munich: Beck, 1922) 1:618-19.

[20]Not all references to the "Son of man" in Luke unquestionably refer to Jesus. But the only one prior to Luke 6 is clear. In 5:24, Jesus heals a paralytic in order to demonstrate the authority of the Son of man to forgive sins.

are regarded as helpful and suggestive, but, for the interpretation of law, they do not take the place of legal citations. The principle is: "Laws must be ordained, their character as commands, prohibitions or concessions must be clearly recognizable."[21] Daube concludes that Luke 6:3-4 would not have been taken as a serious interpretation by the Rabbis.

The second controversy is set in a synagogue on another Sabbath and involves the healing of a man whose right hand was withered (Luke 6:6-11). The scribes and Pharisees are cast in the role of critics, but they actually have no speaking parts. Jesus' defense in the case is to ask, "Is it lawful [*exestin*] on the sabbath to do good or to do harm, to save life or to destroy it?" (6:9). Then he proceeds to restore the withered hand, presumably an act of doing good. The implication is that, according to Jesus, it is lawful to do good and to save life on the Sabbath. That Luke understands this position to be radically different from that of the scribes and Pharisees is indicated in the closing verse of the pericope, where the opponents furiously discuss what to do with Jesus (6:11). Notably, no scriptural authority is referred to here, nor is there any claim about the authority of Jesus. There is a kind of appeal to general humane considerations, which would, according to the Lukan Jesus, carry an authority greater than that of the Sabbath commandment.

The third controversy also occurs in a synagogue and involves healing (13:10-17). This pericope, about a woman who was unable to straighten up, is unique to Luke, but it has the same general form as other controversies about the Sabbath. In this case, Jesus heals the woman, and then an objection is raised by the ruler of the synagogue. Addressing himself to the healed woman and the congregation, he says, "There are six days on which work ought to be done; come on those days and be healed, and not on the sabbath day" (Luke 13:14). A reader familiar with the OT would observe the allusion to Exodus 20:9 "Six days you shall labor, and do all your work." Jesus' response is to call attention to the practice of feeding animals on the Sabbath. Although Pharisaic practice in regard to feeding domestic animals was probably highly qualified, Luke seems to know nothing about any restrictions.[22] He simply presupposes that domestic animals were fed seven days a week, without any sense of violating Torah.

---

[21]Daube, *New Testament*, 69. Daube adds that the citation in Matt 12:5 about the activities of priests in the Temple on the Sabbath is, from a rabbinic point of view, more acceptable.

[22]For references to rabbinic restrictions on the care and feeding of domestic animals on the Sabbath, cf. Strack and Billerbeck, *Kommentar*, 2:198-200.

On that principle, it would be perfectly permissible to heal a handicapped woman on any day of the week. It is notable here that Jesus does not defend his practice by appeal to scripture, nor does Luke assert Jesus' personal authority, unless the use of *kyrios* in 13:15 is meant to signify it. The only appeal is to allegedly common practice. The form of interpretation is similar to that which in rabbinic literature is called *qal wahomer,* i. e., arguing from the lesser to the greater. If it is permissible on the Sabbath to perform work that is necessary for the care of domestic animals, then surely such work is lawful in the case of human beings. It is also worth noting that, in contrast to Jesus, the ruler of the synagogue appeals to the authority of scripture in his allusion to Exodus 20:9.

The fourth Sabbath controversy in the gospel of Luke is in 14:1-6, another pericope that is unique to the third gospel. The setting is in the house of a Pharisee, and the narrative is about the healing of a man with dropsy. When he sees the man, Jesus asks the lawyers and Pharisees who are present, "Is it lawful [*exestin*] to heal on the sabbath, or not?" (Luke 14:3), and he heals the man. Although no verbal challenge is contained in this passage, Jesus defends his action in much the same way he did in 13:10-17. He calls attention to the practice with respect to domestic animals. The owner of an animal that has fallen into a well will pull it out immediately, even on the Sabbath. The implication is that if it is lawful to save endangered animals on the Sabbath, then (by *qal wahomer*) it is certainly lawful to save endangered humans.

It is important to keep in mind the fact that these four pericopes are essentially controversy dialogues. That is, these are occasions that the evangelist has used to portray various conflicts between Jesus and his opponents. There are no occasions on which Jesus abstractly discourses on the meaning of scripture, Torah, or Sabbath. All is done in the midst of controversy, and this gives the reader the sense that the position of Jesus is to be contrasted with that of the Pharisees and the other Jewish leaders, not with the Hebrew scriptures. Despite these observations, it is still legitimate to raise questions about Luke's view of Torah as implied in these narratives, since the fundamental authority for observing Sabbath is found in Torah.

In these four pericopes, two of which are unique to Luke, there appear to be four sources of authority to which appeal is made. One is an appeal to common practice, which appears to need no further explanation. Luke seems to assume that his readers will immediately see the rightness of feeding and caring for domestic animals as a matter of common sense and routine practice. A second is an appeal to humane considerations, which likewise appear to need no defense: it is lawful to do good and heal on the Sabbath. The third is an appeal to scripture, not, however, to the Torah, but to the prophets (1 Sam), viz. to the example of David. Finally, appeal is made to the authority of Jesus himself, who, as Son of man, is Lord of the Sabbath.

What is notable in its absence is an appeal to the meaning of Torah. The Rabbis frequently made their case by appealing to scripture against scripture, by citing one passage in Torah to clarify another, by building a family of supposedly similar texts, or by making inferences based on the context of a difficult passage. The purpose of the rabbinic argument was to determine the meaning of a Mosaic commandment. But in the discussion of Sabbath observance in Luke, these forms of argument play no role. The only possible exception is in Luke 6:3-4, where a passage of scripture is cited. The problems in these verses have been noted. Luke-Acts never asks what the Mosaic commandment about Sabbath observance meant, as judged by its wording, its relation to other parts of Torah, or its context. Indeed, there is not even a quotation of the commandment about Sabbath observance anywhere in Luke-Acts. Although the list of commandments given by Jesus in Luke 18:20 is almost certainly not meant to be exhaustive, it should be observed that the Sabbath commandment is absent from the list. The only allusion to the commandment in Luke-Acts is that provided by a ruler of a synagogue (Luke 13:14), one who is cast in the role of an opponent of Jesus.

These facts would seem to suggest that Luke had no interest in drawing attention to the connection between scripture, Torah, and Sabbath observance. By de-emphasizing this connection, he could affirm the authority of Torah and scripture but qualify some of its basic content. Nor was Luke interested in associating the commandment to observe the Sabbath with the message of Jesus or the apostles. Although he frequently noted that they did in fact observe the Sabbath, he more readily associated that observance with conflict than with rest. The Lukan Jesus affirmed that there are considerations that override the Sabbath and that these considerations do not need to be determined on the basis of authoritative Torah. At least in respect to the Sabbath commandment, Torah, and hence, scripture cannot be regarded as having unqualified, plenary authority for Luke.

Although the question of Luke's view of the relationships between Judaism and Christianity is by no means simple, this limited study suggests that Luke-Acts is pervaded by a sense of tension. On the one hand, Luke wants to affirm that authority resides in the Hebrew scriptures and that Jesus and his followers were pious, observant Jews. On the other, he feels compelled to show that there are significant qualifications to the authority of scripture and Torah, at least in respect to the observance of the Sabbath. Moreover, Torah is not an authoritative resource for determining what qualifications need to be made. It is plausible to think that Luke and his community did not recognize the full significance or implications of this understanding of Sabbath observance and that Luke did not think that he was challenging scriptural authority. The tension that we see here in reference to the treatment of Torah, scripture, and Sabbath carries over into the broader aspects of the relationships between Judaism and Christianity. There is a sense in which Luke wanted to emphasize both continuity and discontinuity. Any attempt to resolve the tension in favor of either would be misleading.

"NAZARETH": A CLUE TO SYNOPTIC RELATIONSHIPS?

William O. Walker, Jr.

The Gospel of Luke places Jesus' rejection at Nazareth immediately after his temptations by the devil, that is, at the very beginning of his public ministry (Luke 4:16-30); the Gospels of Matthew and Mark, however, place it considerably later in the narrative—Mark after the raising of Jairus's daughter (Mark 6:1-6a) and Matthew still later, after a series of parables (Matt 13:53-58).[1] Furthermore, Matthew and Mark have essentially the same account of the episode, but Luke's account is significantly different. Because of these differences in placement and content, a few scholars have assumed that Jesus was rejected twice in Nazareth and that Luke reports the earlier rejection and Matthew and Mark the later.[2] Others, without nec-

---

[1]An interesting and important question—not, however, to be explored in this paper—is why Matthew and Mark have the episode at different points in their respective narratives, particularly in light of the fact that neither of them is in agreement with Luke.

[2]See, e.g., William L. Lane, *The Gospel according to Mark: The English Text with Introduction, Exposition, and Notes* (Grand Rapids MI: Eerdmans, 1974) 201n2: "An examination of a synopsis . . . indicates that the parallel between Mk. 6:1-6a and Lk. 4:16-30 is extremely slight. The key point of parallelism is the traditional word (in different formulations) that 'a prophet is not accepted in his own country.' This is merely a traditional aphorism that can exist without context (as in the Oxyrhynchus Papyrus 1 No. 6 = the Coptic Gospel of Thomas, Logion 31) or in a different context (as John 4:44). The conclusion seems probable that Mk. 6:1-6a and Lk. 4:16-30 describe two distinct visits to Nazareth. They do not narrate the same visit from merely different points of view." The chief difficulty with such a view, of course, is what would appear to be the inherent improbability that two such similar episodes should occur. For another example of the same type of problem, compare Matthew's and Mark's accounts of the anointing at Bethany (Matt 26:6-13; Mark 14:3-9; cf. John 12:1-8) with Luke's earlier account of an anointing in an unnamed city (Luke 7:36-50). It may be, indeed, that the modern scholar should refrain from asking such historical questions as whether there were one or two rejections at Nazareth and simply explore the literary relations among the accounts and the literary/theological interests of the respective authors.

essarily assuming two rejections, have argued for a distinctive source or sources, reflecting a variant version of the rejection episode, underlying the Lukan account.[3] Most recent commentators, however, maintain that Matthew and Mark reflect the earlier tradition and that Luke[4] has himself altered both the sequence and the content for theological and/or literary reasons, perhaps making use of distinctive source material for certain of the details of his version. The view of Joseph A. Fitzmyer is typical:

> From v. 23 it is clear that Luke was aware of a period of Jesus' ministry in Capernaum prior to this visit to Nazareth. He is, then, consciously making this episode the first of the ministry, knowing that it was not really such. . . . Here Luke has transposed the account of Jesus' visit to his hometown from later on in the gospel tradition (see Mark 6:1-6a; Matt 13:53-58), where it is recounted shortly before the end of the Galilean ministry. . . . Though there is little similarity in the details or in the wording of the Lucan and Marcan form of the account of this visit, the substance of the two stories is the same. . . . The Lucan form of the story of the Nazareth visit owes its inspiration to Mark 6:1-6a. . . . It is better to regard the Lucan story as a reworking of the Marcan source . . . a reworking with the sources suggested . . . by Bultmann.[5]

---

[3]See, e.g., Burnett Hillman Streeter, *The Four Gospels: A Study of Origins,* rev. ed. (London: Macmillan & Co., 1930) 209-10; J. Schmid, *Das Evangelium nach Lukas,* 4th ed. (Regensburg: Pustet, 1960) 110; and H. Schürman, "Zur Traditionsgeschichte der Nazareth-Perikope Lk 4,16-30," in *Mélanges bibliques en hommage au R. P. Béda-Rigaux,* ed. A. Descamps and A. de Halleux (Gembloux: Duculot, 1970) 191-205. Hans Conzelmann notes the difficulty of determining whether such a passage as Luke 4:16-30 is "derived from a special source" or represents "a free adaptation by Luke" of a source such as Mark (or perhaps Matthew): "If the latter could be proved, we should possess not only a striking illustration of his own theological outlook, but also of the degree to which he has modified his sources. But we are in a vicious circle, for the requisite proof presupposes a knowledge of these very factors, i.e., of Luke's own views and of the degree to which he has adapted the sources." *The Theology of St. Luke,* trans. Geoffrey Buswell (New York: Harper & Row, 1960) 32.

[4]For the sake of convenience, the authors of the four Gospels are here referred to as "Matthew," "Mark," "Luke," and "John." This by no means, however, implies acceptance of the traditional views regarding actual authorship.

[5]Joseph A. Fitzmyer, *The Gospel according to Luke (I-IX): Introduction, Translation, and Notes* (Garden City: Doubleday & Co., 1981) 526-27; cf. 71: "Jesus' visit to Nazareth (Mark 6:1-6) is transferred by Luke to the beginning of Jesus' Galilean ministry (4:16-30) to serve a programmatic purpose: it presents in capsule form the theme of fulfillment and symbolizes the rejection that will mark the ministry as a whole." In agreement with most scholars, Fitzmyer presupposes that Luke's primary source, at this point as well as elsewhere, is Mark (advocates of the Griesbach Hypothesis, of course, would assume that Luke has departed from

Occasionally, however, it has been suggested that Matthew (but not Mark), while placing his own rejection story later in the narrative, nevertheless reflects a tradition that also (like Luke) placed Jesus' rejection at Nazareth immediately after his temptation[6] (indeed, it has even been suggested that this order might be closer to the actual historical facts than that followed by Matthew and Mark[7]). The purpose of the present paper is to argue that Matthew does, in fact, reflect such a tradition and that the relation between Luke's rejection story (including the two verses immediately preceding and the two immediately following: Luke 4:14-32) and Matthean material at the same point in the narrative (Matt 4:12-17) is such as to suggest that Matthew and Luke are, at this point in the narrative, making use of common (or, at least, similar) source material—perhaps what modern scholarship has called "Q." It appears, too, that Luke is here following the source material more closely than is Matthew.

A careful examination of the two passages reveals at least seven clues pointing to such a relation between Matthew and Luke. These clues appear most clearly when the passages are printed in parallel columns as follows:

Matthew 4:12-17	Luke 4:14-32
And having heard that John had been arrested,	(Cf. Luke 3:19-20: But Herod the tetrarch, being reproved by him concerning Herodias the wife of his brother and concerning all the evil things that Herod had done, added also this to them all, that he shut up John in prison.)

Matthew in essentially the same ways as advocates of the Two-Source Hypothesis see him departing from Mark). The "sources suggested . . . by Bultmann" relate to Luke 4:23, 25-27; see Rudolf Bultmann, *The History of the Synoptic Tradition,* trans. John Marsh (New York: Harper & Row, 1963) 32: "Vv. 25-27 clearly came to Luke from the tradition (originally Aramaic? cp. Wellhausen). . . . In order to fit vv. 25-27 in, Luke has, as I suppose, constructed a scene on the pattern of Mk. 6[1-6], and at the same time in v. 23 used the παραβολή which had been handed down in another context."

[6]See, e.g., Eduard Schweizer, *The Good News according to Matthew,* trans. David E. Green (Atlanta: John Knox Press, 1975) 67; *The Good News according to Luke,* trans. David E. Green (Atlanta: John Knox Press, 1984) 86; and Robert H. Gundry, *Matthew: A Commentary on His Literary and Theological Art* (Grand Rapids MI: Eerdmans, 1982) 59-60.

[7]According to both Schweizer and Gundry (see n. 6 above), "such a rejection might explain why Jesus moved to Capernaum with his family (John 2:12), so that only his (married) sisters stayed in Nazareth (Mark 6:3)"; Schweizer, *Matthew,* p. 67. In addition, it might be expected that, immediately after his baptism and temptations, Jesus would return to Nazareth to begin his public ministry.

he withdrew into Galilee;

And Jesus returned in the power of the Spirit into Galilee, and a report concerning him went out through all the surrounding country. And he was teaching in their synagogue, being glorified by all.

And he came into Nazareth, where he had been brought up, and he entered the synagogue, as was his custom, on the sabbath day, and he stood up to read, and the book of the prophet Isaiah was given to him, and having opened the book he found the place where it was written: "The Spirit of the Lord is upon me, because he has anointed me to preach good news to the poor. He has sent me to proclaim release to the captives and recovering of sight to the blind, to set at liberty those who are oppressed, to proclaim the acceptable year of the Lord." And he closed the book, and gave it back to the attendant, and sat down; and the eyes of all in the synagogue were fixed on him. And he began to say to them, "Today this scripture has been fulfilled in your hearing." And all spoke well of him, and wondered at the gracious words which proceeded out of his mouth; and they said, "Is not this Joseph's son?" And he said to them, "Doubtless you will quote to me this proverb, 'Physician, heal yourself; what we have heard you did at Capernaum, do here also in your own country.' " And he said, "Truly, I say to you, no prophet is acceptable in his own country. But in truth, I tell you, there were many widows in Israel in the days of Elijah, when the heaven was shut up three years and six months, when there came a great famine over all the land; and Elijah was sent to none of them but only to Zarephath, in the land of Sidon, to a woman who was a widow. And there were many lepers in Israel in the time of the prophet Elisha; and none of them was cleansed, but only Naaman the Syrian." When they heard this, all in the synagogue were filled with wrath. And they rose up and put him out of the city, and led him to the brow of the hill on which their city was built, that they might throw him down headlong.

and having left Nazareth,

But he, passing through the midst of them, was going.

having come, he dwelt in Capernaum, which is by the sea in the region of Zebulun and Naphtali;
in order that what was spoken by the prophet Isaiah might be fulfilled: "The land of Zebulun and the land of Naphtali, toward the sea, across the Jordan, Galilee of the Gentiles—the people who sat in darkness have seen a great light, and for those who sat in the region and shadow of death light has dawned."
From that time Jesus began to preach, saying, "Repent, for the kingdom of heaven is at hand."

(Cf. Matt 7:28-29: And when Jesus finished these words, the crowds were astonished at his teaching, for he was teaching them as one having authority, and not as their scribes.)

And he went down to Capernaum, a city of Galilee;

and he was teaching them

on the sabbath;
and they were astonished at his teaching, for his word was with authority.

The first clue that Matthew and Luke may be using common (or similar) source material appears in Matthew's reference to Jesus leaving Nazareth (Matt 4:13). Matthew has not previously indicated that Jesus went to Nazareth after his temptations (he only has him going into "Galilee"), but here Jesus leaves Nazareth. Commentators have attempted in various and sometimes interesting ways to smooth over the difficulty,[8] but the problem

---

[8]See, e.g., Alexander Balmain Bruce, "The Synoptic Gospels," in *The Expositor's Greek Testament,* ed. W. Robertson Nicoll (Grand Rapids: Eerdmans, 1951 reprint) 1:91: "Jesus naturally went to Nazareth first, but He did not tarry there"; and R. C. H. Lenski, *The Interpretation of St. Matthew's Gospel* (Columbia: Wartburg Press, 1943) 163: "John 2:12 reports that Jesus transferred his home from Nazareth to Capernaum shortly after he first returned to Galilee from the Jordan. When Matthew writes, 'and having left Nazareth, having come, he dwelt in Capernaum,' these aorists merely mark facts without particular reference to the exact past moment of time. We are simply to know that, when the Baptist was imprisoned, Jesus no longer lived in Nazareth but in Capernaum." Perhaps the most interesting suggestion is that of Jack Dean Kingsbury that Matt 4:13 "is directly associated both formally and materially with 2:23": "We can observe how flawlessly the one passage picks up on the other: ' . . . *and he came and dwelled in a city which is called Nazareth,* in order that what was spoken by the prophets might be fulfilled . . . ' (2:23); ' . . . *and he left Nazareth and came and dwelled in Capernaum beside the sea,* in the regions of Zebulun and Naphtali, in order that what was spoken by Isaiah the prophet might be fulfilled . . . ' (4:13-14). From this we learn that the 'divinely ordained' travels of Jesus, which began in ch. 2, do not, as Matthew tells it, come to an end until Jesus settles in Galilee, which is

remains. Furthermore, the participial construction in Greek appears to suggest a merely passing or incidental reference to something presumably already known to the readers. It would appear, therefore, according to Matthew, that Jesus did, in fact, go to Nazareth after his temptations (as in Luke), but nothing is said in Matthew about anything that happened while he was there—there is only the bare mention of his leaving. The Greek root of the participle referring to his leaving, however, is a compound root, carrying the idea of "leaving behind," "abandoning," "forsaking," or "deserting."[9] Thus, there may well be more than meets the eye in Mat-

---

the region in which God has decreed he should embark upon his public ministry to Israel. To signal the termination of these travels and to ready Jesus for the beginning of his public ministry is the dual purpose of 4:12-16." *Matthew: Structure, Christology, Kingdom* (Philadelphia, Fortress Press, 1975) 16. The most obvious problem with this interpretation is, of course, the fact that, between Matt 2:23 and Matt 4:13, it is clear that Jesus has been away from Nazareth (see Matt 3:13: "Then Jesus came from Galilee to the Jordan to John, to be baptized by him"; 4:1: "Then Jesus was led up by the Spirit into the wilderness to be tempted by the devil"; 4:12: "Now when he heard that John had been arrested, he withdrew into Galilee." A further difficulty is the fact that the spelling of "Nazareth" is different in the two passages (on this, see my "second clue" below). It is true that the crucial words in Matt 2:23 and Matt 4:13 are parallel (Matt 2:23: "And having gone, he dwelt in a city called Nazareth, in order that what was spoken by the prophets might be fulfilled"; Matt 4:13: "And . . . having gone, he dwelt in Capernaum . . . in order that what was spoken by Isaiah the prophet might be fulfilled"). Such parallelism clearly reflects the editorial hand of Matthew (or perhaps of Matthew's source materials), but it does not eliminate the problem in Matthew's reference to Jesus leaving Nazareth.

[9]The verb is καταλείπειν. See, e.g., Matthew 19:5: "a man shall *leave* his father and mother and be joined to his wife." In only two other passages does Matthew use the verb: 16:4b (after refusing to give any sign to "an evil and adulterous generation" "except the sign of Jonah"): "So he *left* them and departed"; and 21:17 (after being rebuked by the chief priests and scribes for allowing children to cry out, "Hosanna to the Son of David!"): "And *leaving* them, he went out of the city to Bethany and lodged there." See Francis Wright Beare, *The Gospel according to Matthew: Translation, Introduction, and Commentary* (New York: Harper & Row, 1981) 114: "Matthew alone tells us of a definitive move from Nazareth, from the home of Jesus' childhood and youth where his mother and his brothers and sisters were still living (Mt. 13:55), to Capernaum. To our evangelist, this change of abode is not an incidental item of topographical interest. It is a fulfillment of prophecy, and it establishes Jesus in a region where a mission to Israel can be carried on in an environment which includes Gentiles. It is a foreshadowing of the great Gentile mission that is to come. There is perhaps also a

thew's apparently passing reference to Jesus leaving Nazareth. The root suggests some strong reason for leaving—perhaps a reason such as rejection by the people of Nazareth (as is spelled out at this point in the Lukan narrative). It is important to observe, too, that Luke (unlike both Matthew and Mark in their later accounts of the rejection) makes specific reference to Jesus leaving Nazareth after his rejection (Luke 4:30).

It is possible, of course, that Luke, using Matthew as a source and noting Matthew's obscure reference to Jesus leaving Nazareth, has seized the occasion to introduce a rejection story at this point and then has omitted Matthew's later (somewhat different) account. This possibility, however, leaves unexplained Matthew's reference to Jesus leaving Nazareth. More likely, Matthew, using a source that (like Luke) included a rejection story at this point, has eliminated the rejection story (perhaps because he chooses to include a somewhat different rejection story later in the narrative), retaining only an obscure allusion to it. It is possible that the source used by Matthew is the Gospel of Luke itself. This appears unlikely, however, in light of general arguments that have been advanced against Matthew's use of Luke as a source.[10] Apparently, then, Matthew and Luke are here using either different sources, both of which include a rejection story at this point, or the same source. Although certainty is by no means possible, the application of "Ockham's Razor" (*Entia non sunt multiplicanda praeter necessitatem*), if nothing else, would favor the latter hypothesis: Matthew and Luke are here using the same source material. In any case, some type of relation between Matthew and Luke appears clear at this point—a relation in which Luke reflects a primary and Matthew a secondary version of the tradition.

A second clue that Matthew and Luke may be using common (or, at least, similar) source material appears in the spelling of the place name, "Naz-

---

suggestion of the breaking of family ties. Not merely is the time of tutelage over, and the security of the family circle removed, but the service of the kingdom of God takes precedence over the closest domestic bonds of affection.''

[10]Even Robert L. Lindsey, who argues that Luke was the earliest Gospel, does not believe that Matthew made direct use of Luke; rather, in his view, Matthew and Luke used some of the same source material (i.e., Q and a so-called Proto-Narrative or "PN"), and Matthew also used Mark, which, in turn, had used Luke. See Lindsey's "A Modified Two-Document Theory of Synoptic Dependence and Interdependence," *NovT* 6 (1963): 239-63; *A New Approach to the Synoptic Gospels* (Jerusalem: Dugwith Publishers, 1971); and *A Hebrew Translation of the Gospel of Mark* (n.d. and n.p.) 44-45. Cf. Werner Georg Kümmel, *Introduction to the New Testament*, trans. Howard Clark Kee, rev. ed. (Nashville and New York: Abingdon Press, 1975) 64: "The dependence of Mt on Lk is no longer defended today and can drop from consideration."

areth.'' The name occurs three times in the Gospel of Matthew. Twice, the best textual evidence points to a spelling of either Ναζαρέτ (Matt 2:23) or Ναζαρέθ (Matt 21:11), which are by far the more common spellings in the New Testament as a whole.[11] At Matthew 4:13 (the text now under consideration), however, the spelling is the unusual Ναζαρά.[12] In light of the fact that Matthew elsewhere uses the more common spelling, it is unlikely that he has himself introduced the unusual spelling at this point;[13] more likely, use of a source is reflected. This likelihood is strengthened by the observation that the only other occurrence in the New Testament of the unusual spelling, Ναζαρά, is precisely in Luke's account of Jesus' rejection at Nazareth (Luke 4:16). Initially, this might suggest that the source being followed by Matthew at this point is, in fact, the Gospel of Luke. In light of the fact that Luke elsewhere is completely consistent in his use of the spelling, Ναζαρέθ, however, it appears that Luke, too, is here using

---

[11]The name occurs twelve times in the Gospels and Acts and nowhere in the remainder of the New Testament. The references are: Ναζαρέτ (Matt 2:23; Mark 1:9; John 1:45, 46); Ναζαρέθ (Matt 21:11; Luke 1:26; 2:4, 39, 51; Acts 10:38); and Ναζαρά (Matt 4:13; Luke 4:16). It should be noted that none of the Gospel passages mentioning ''Nazareth'' is parallel to any other passage containing the name, at least not explicitly so.

[12]To be sure, there is significant manuscript evidence for Ναζαρέθ at Matt 4:13, including the original reading of Codex Sinaiticus. The correction of Sinaiticus and the original of Codex Vaticanus read Ναζαρά, however, and, in light of the fact that the spelling elsewhere in the New Testament, except for Luke 4:16, is consistently Ναζαρέθ or Ναζαρέτ, it must be assumed that Vaticanus is correct and that Sinaiticus initially reflects an assimilating tendency that also appears in the majority of later manuscripts but was then corrected to conform to Vaticanus or some other manuscript with the same reading. Unless Ναζαρά is original, it is difficult to understand why Sinaiticus would have been changed from the much more common Ναζαρέθ to the much rarer Ναζαρά. On variations in the Greek spelling generally, see Walter Bauer, *A Greek-English Lexicon of the New Testament and Other Early Christian Literature*, trans. William F. Arndt and F. Wilbur Gingrich, 2nd rev. ed. (Chicago: University of Chicago Press, 1979) 532; Raymond E. Brown, *The Birth of the Messiah: A Commentary on the Infancy Narratives in Matthew and Luke* (Garden City: Doubleday & Co., 1977) 207-208; and Joseph W. Fitzmyer, *Luke*, 530.

[13]It is possible, of course, but not probable, that Matthew's more usual spelling elsewhere reflects use of source material and that Ναζαρά is his own preferred spelling.

a Greek source with the spelling, Ναζαρά.[14] Again, it is possible that Luke is here using Matthew as a source, but this would imply that Matthew, in turn, is also using a source containing the unusual spelling. For reasons already suggested in connection with the first clue, however, it is unlikely that Luke is using Matthew. It is also unlikely, for reasons cited above, that Matthew is using Luke as a source. Thus, as in the case of the first clue, the evidence appears to indicate that Matthew and Luke are here using either different sources, both of which contain the unusual spelling of "Nazareth," or the same source, with the latter the more likely possibility.

A *third clue* that Matthew and Luke may be using common (or similar) source material appears in Matthew's reference to the arrest of John the Baptist (Matt 4:12). Matthew has not previously mentioned John's arrest (he reports it later at Matthew 14:1-12—interestingly enough, immediately after his account of Jesus' rejection at Nazareth;[15] cf. also Mark 6:14-29, where it is separated from the rejection story by the report of Jesus sending out the Twelve); Luke, however, has mentioned it (Luke 3:19-20, just prior to the story of Jesus' baptism, as the conclusion to the John-the-Baptist material). At 4:12, however, Matthew mentions the arrest—again, as in the case of his reference to Jesus leaving Nazareth, almost in passing,[16] as though it would already be known to the readers.[17] It is barely possible that Luke, seeing Matthew's obscure allusion at this point, would introduce an account of John's arrest earlier in his own narrative, thus making Matthew's reference intelligible; this would imply, however, that Luke then eliminated the reference to John's arrest at the point where Matthew has it, thus, in fact, removing the need for introducing his own account of the arrest earlier in the narrative. More likely, Matthew is here using a source that (like Luke) reports the arrest of John before it reports

---

[14]See Luke 1:26; 2:4, 39, 51; Acts 10:38. It is unlikely that Ναζαρά reflects an older Semitic form of the name, as has been argued by some; see Brown, *The Birth of the Messiah*, 207-208.

[15]At this later point, Matthew reports not only the arrest but also the death of John (as does Mark). At 4:12, however, he mentions only the arrest, even as only the arrest is reported in Luke 3:19-20.

[16]ἀκούσας δὲ ὅτι Ἰωάννης παρεδόθη.

[17]Mark 1:14 also refers at this point to the arrest of John without having previously mentioned it, but his reference is perhaps a bit more direct and categorical than is Matthew's (μετὰ δὲ τὸ παραδοθῆναι τὸν Ἰωάννην). Clearly, Matthew and Mark are related at this point, either directly or indirectly, but the nature of the relation is not immediately apparent.

the beginning of Jesus's public ministry. If so, as in the case of the rejection story, Matthew has eliminated the account of John's arrest (perhaps because he chooses to include a somewhat different and more expanded account later in the narrative), retaining only an obscure allusion to it. Again, the source used by Matthew could be the Gospel of Luke, but, for reasons already cited, this appears unlikely. Apparently, then, Matthew and Luke are using the same (or similar) source material at this point.

A *fourth clue* that Matthew and Luke may be using common (or similar) source material appears in their common reference to Jesus going to Capernaum upon leaving Nazareth (Matt 4:13; Luke 4:31) and in the fact that both Matthew and Luke (unlike Mark) append some further characterization of Capernaum—Matthew with the words, "which is by the sea in the region of Zebulun and Naphtali," followed by a fulfillment-of-prophecy formula, and Luke simply with the words, "a city of Galilee." It should be noted, at this point, that while Matthew (like Luke) has Jesus proceeding immediately to Capernaum after leaving Nazareth, Mark (who, of course, has no reference to Jesus being in or leaving Nazareth) interjects the call of the four disciples (Mark 1:16) before indicating that Jesus went to Capernaum (Mark 1:21); Matthew, on the other hand, has the call of the disciples after the move to Capernaum (Matt 4:18-22; Luke, of course, has a somewhat similar call story later in the narrative, at Luke 5:1-11).

A *fifth clue* that Matthew and Luke may be using common (or similar) source material appears in the fact that each has two references to "Galilee"—the first at the beginning of the pericope (Matt 4:12; Luke 4:14) and the second in connection with the reference to Capernaum (Matt 4:15; Luke 4:31)—and that the two references in each are parallel as regards content. In Luke, of course, the two references are separated by the account of Jesus' rejection at Nazareth. Mark, it should be noted, has only the former reference (Mark 1:14).

A *sixth clue* that Matthew and Luke may be using common (or similar) source material appears in the fact that each includes a fulfillment-of-prophecy formula and each appeals to a passage (different passages, to be sure) from Isaiah (Matt 4:14-16; Luke 4:17-21). (Mark has no such fulfillment-of-prophecy formula or scriptural reference.) It is true that, while Luke has the appeal to prophecy as a part of the rejection story, Matthew associates it with the move to Capernaum. If Matthew is familiar with an account similar to Luke's however, but has chosen to eliminate the actual rejection story at this point, he may well have decided, nevertheless, to preserve an appeal to prophecy (indeed, to the prophet Isaiah), changing the specific passage in light of his omission of the rejection story.

A *seventh clue* that Matthew and Luke may be using common (or similar) source material appears in the fact that each concludes his account with a reference to Jesus preaching (Matt 4:17) or teaching (Luke 4:31b-32). The difference between "preaching" and "teaching" may be insignificant, indicating only the literary and/or theological preferences of the two writers. It may well be, however, that Matthew has, at this point in his narrative, turned to a different source: as already noted, his next pericope is the call of the four disciples (Matt 4:18-22; cf. Mark 1:16-22), which does not appear in Luke, where, instead, there is the account of the miraculous catch of fish and call of three disciples (Luke 5:1-11).

On the basis of these seven clues, it is possible to build a very strong case that Matthew and Luke are using common (or similar) source material for the parallel passages under consideration and, indeed, that Luke reflects the source material more closely than does Matthew. Specifically, it appears that Matthew was familiar with a rejection story similar or identical to that included by Luke and that, in Matthew's source material, this rejection story appeared at the same point in the narrative as it now appears in Luke. This raises a question about the possibility of a similar relation between Matthew and Luke at other points in the two Gospels where such a relation has not generally been recognized. It is beyond the scope of this paper to explore the matter in detail, but an examination of the two narratives about John the Baptist (Matt 3:1-17; Luke 3:1-22) does reveal phenomena that are strikingly similar to those that have been observed in Matthew 4:12-17 and Luke 4:14-32.

One such phenomenon occurs at the beginning of the two John-the-Baptist reports. Matthew begins with the words, "In those days," with no indication as to just which "days" are intended (clearly, however, the reference cannot be to the immediately preceding passage, which speaks of Joseph, Mary, and the young Jesus settling in Nazareth). Robert H. Gundry, among others, suggests that Matthew has brought the words forward from Mark 1:9 in order to "weld together John's ministry and Jesus' baptism in a single episode."[18] On the face of it, however, it appears more likely that Mark would have moved the words to a later point in the narrative—a point where they are, indeed, more intelligible—than that Matthew would have moved them forward in such a way as to leave them without any clear reference. So far as possible links between Matthew and Luke are concerned, however, it is important to note that the parallel passage in Luke begins with the words, "In the fifteenth year of the reign of Tiberius Caesar, Pontius Pilate being governor of Judea, and Herod being tetrarch of Galilee, and his brother Philip tetrarch of the region of Iturea

---

[18]Gundry, *Matthew*, 41.

and Trachonitis, and Lysanias tetrarch of Abilene, in the high-priesthood of Annas and Caiaphas . . . '' In other words, Luke supplies a possible reference for Matthew's ''In those days.'' It is possible, of course, that Luke, using Matthew as a source and noting the latter's obscure ''In those days,'' has decided to amplify and clarify the reference; it is also possible that Matthew has simply abbreviated Luke's reference. It is at least equally possible, however, that both Matthew and Luke are here using a source that begins the narrative about John's preaching with some indication of the date. If so, Matthew has apparently shortened the reference in such a way as to make it virtually meaningless, and it may be that Luke has expanded or otherwise revised the reference. In any case, this represents yet another instance in which Matthew has some type of obscure reference that becomes intelligible only in light of parallel material in Luke.

Further examination of the Matthean and Lukan materials on John the Baptist, particularly when compared with the parallel Markan material (Mark 1:2-11), discloses other possible links between Matthew and Luke—links involving both sequence and content. The following are noteworthy: (1) As already noted, both Matthew (3:1) and Luke (3:1-2), but not Mark (1:1), begin the narrative with a chronological reference. (2) Both Matthew (3:1) and Luke (3:2-3) proceed immediately to a direct statement about John and his preaching, while Mark (1:2-3) begins with a quotation from Malachi 3:1 and Isaiah 40:3. (3) Both Matthew (3:3) and Luke (3:4-6) then introduce the quotation from Isaiah (Luke in an expanded form), and both omit the quotation from Malachi. (4) Both Matthew (3:7-10) and Luke (3:7-9) include John's ''brood of vipers'' message, but Mark does not.[19] To be sure, there are also indications of links between Matthew and Mark and between Luke and Mark, but it is clear that, for much of the material, Matthew and Luke are related to each other, either directly or indirectly, quite independently of the relation of each to Mark. This, of course, has long been noted by commentators and has been explained on the basis of the various source theories held by the respective commentators (e.g., both Matthew and Luke are here dependent upon the hypothetical source, Q; Luke is here dependent upon Matthew; or Matthew is here dependent upon Luke). Sometimes, it is argued that sheer coincidence is the explanation. On the basis of the earlier examination of Matthew 4:12-17 and Luke 4:14-32, however, it appears likely that Matthew and Luke are here using com-

[19]For a convenient outline that illustrates these data, see Albert B. Lord, ''The Gospels as Oral Traditional Literature,'' in *The Relationships among the Gospels: An Interdisciplinary Dialogue,* ed. William O. Walker, Jr. (San Antonio TX: Trinity University Press, 1978) 60-61.

mon (or similar) source material (perhaps Q) and, indeed, that Luke follows this source material more closely than does Matthew.

Standing between the narratives about John the Baptist and Luke's account of the rejection at Nazareth (and Matthew's obscure reference to Jesus leaving Nazareth), in both Matthew and Luke, is the story of Jesus' temptations by the devil (Matt 4:1-11; Luke 4:1-13). Despite significant differences between the two accounts, virtually all scholars agree that the accounts are related, either directly or indirectly.[20] Again, the specific explanation depends upon the particular source theory held by the commentator, but, as in the case of the materials about John the Baptist, it appears most likely that Matthew and Luke are here using common (or similar) source material.

Preceding the narratives about John the Baptist, in both Matthew and Luke, are the birth and infancy narratives (Matt 1:18-2:23; Luke 1:5-2:52). Virtually all modern scholars have agreed that Matthew and Luke here reflect different source materials.[21] Gundry, however, has recently made a much more persuasive argument than most scholars would have thought possible that, in his birth and infancy narratives, "Matthew used haggadic and midrashic techniques on the very tradition later appearing in the early chapters of Luke,"[22] and, indeed, that Q should be expanded to include "not only the material usually designated as Q, but also the nativity story and some of the materials usually regarded as peculiar to Matthew (M) and Luke (L)." His argument is that "Q included much more than is usually thought . . . but at times Matthew redacted it so freely that his drawing on Q has gone unrecognized and separate traditions have wrongly been posited."[23] Although much further study of the birth and infancy narratives is needed, the conclusions drawn in the present paper tend to suggest that Gundry may be correct. If so, then it would appear that Matthew and Luke are drawing on common (or similar) source material from the beginning of their Gospels (except, perhaps, for the John-the-Baptist material in Luke 1) at least as far as Luke's account of Jesus' rejection at Nazareth and his move to Capernaum. It would also appear that, at least for much of the material, Luke more closely follows the source than does Matthew.

---

[20]See R. Schnackenburg, "Der Sinn der Versuchung Jesu bei den Synoptikern," *TQ* 132 (1952): 297-326.

[21]For a discussion of sources, see Brown, *The Birth of the Messiah,* 104-19, 244-50.

[22]Gundry, *Matthew,* xi.

[23]Ibid., 4-5.

Whether the same is true in later sections of the two Gospels requires considerable additional investigation. I have suggested elsewhere, for example, that all of the Synoptic "Son of Man" sayings, even those that are unique to Matthew and to Luke, are to be traced to the Q source material used by both Matthew and Luke.[24]

> Whether this Q was written or oral, whether Matthew and Luke made independent use of it or one of the two also knew the other, and whether Matthew and/or Luke also used other sources, perhaps even one or more sources common to both, are not important for our purposes.[25]

What is important is an apparently growing body of evidence indicating that the source material common to Matthew and Luke was more extensive than is generally supposed. Specifically, so far as the reports of the preaching of John and the early preaching of Jesus are concerned, it now appears likely that Matthew and Luke had access to some common (or similar) non-Markan source material beyond what is usually included under the heading of Q. Additional study may well uncover additional evidence supporting such a hypothesis, and, if so, the generally accepted solutions to the Synoptic Problem will require reexamination.

---

[24]William O. Walker, Jr., "The Son of Man Question and the Synoptic Problem," *NTS* 28:3 (July 1982): 374-88; reprinted in slightly revised version as the second part of "The Son of Man Question and the Synoptic Problem," in *New Synoptic Studies: The Cambridge Gospel Conference and Beyond,* ed. William R. Farmer (Macon GA: Mercer University Press, 1983) 261-301.

[25]Walker, "The Son of Man Question," 380.

Part II

JESUS
AND THE GOSPELS

TEMPLE TAX

David Daube

Matthew's four verses about this subject[1] do not rate high in the prevalent opinion, chiefly because the introduction of the fish is uncomprehended—to say the least.[2] A further reason is the neglect of a controversy within Jewry certainly very intense in the thirties but going on right until A.D. 70. The following pages are intended to show that the little section forms a well-constructed whole; that it is definitely part of *Ur*-Christian lore and, indeed, most probably harks back to an actual occurrence; and that the fish makes perfect sense in a directive of eminent practical and spiritual importance for the earliest believers.

The collectors of the Temple tax accost Peter. What they say is translatable in two ways between which it is fortunately not necessary to decide: "Your teacher does not pay the half-shekel" or "Does your teacher not pay the half-shekel?". If we go by the first alternative, they assume resistance; but even the second presupposes suspicion, they would not be surprised by Jesus opting out, they are on the attack. The challenging of a disciple for his master's aberrations is a universal phenomenon. A Jungian is expected to defend Jung's response to the Third Reich, a devotee of Est, Werner Erhard's socializing. In the first two gospels Jesus's disciples are interrogated why he eats with publicans and sinners.[3] Peter's "Yes," however, quickly stops the confrontation. No doubt he thinks that Jesus cannot be remiss though he may be far from sure about the ins and outs. It

---

[1]Matt 17:24ff. See D. Daube, "Responsibilities of Master and Disciples in the Gospels," *NTS* 19 (1972) 13ff.; and Fraud No. 3, in *The Legal Mind, Essays for Tony Honoré*, ed. N. MacCormick and P. Birks (1986) 15.

[2]It might be worthwhile, as a contribution to *Wissenschaftsgeschichte*, to study the diverse methods (including silence) of dealing with this embarrassment. Even authors who, as far as the rest is concerned, come close to the approach of this paper—e.g., G. A. Buttrick, "The Gospel according to St. Matthew: Exposition," *The Interpreter's Bible*, vol. 7 (1951) 465ff.; and E. Schweizer, *Das Evangelium nach Matthäus* (1976) 231ff.—are at a loss when it comes to the haul.

[3]Matt 9:10ff., Mark 2:15ff., restructured in Luke 5:29ff. See D. Daube, "Responsibilities," 11ff.

is likely, moreover, that his desire to get rid of the officers without ado plays a part in the terse affirmation.

As he returns from the encounter, ere he can report, Jesus divines his perplexity and enlightens him. At first sight, one might infer that we have to do with the type of disciple who does not dare or know to ask and whose interest is to be aroused by the teacher. This type figures in the ancient Seder, from where it is taken over into Mark's day of questions: "And no one dared any longer ask him, and Jesus, commencing the discourse, said."[4] Yet the set-up before us is not quite the same. For one thing, whereas both in the Seder and in the Marcan analogue, the problem does not enter the disciple's mind till his attention is called to it, in the Temple tax story, he comes upon it himself. Again, whereas both in the Seder and in the Marcan analogue, the master refrains from unravelling the knot— his task being to get the disciple to cogitate—in the Temple tax story, Jesus does so. Lastly, maybe Peter would have asked, only that Jesus "anticipates him," gets in first. This action, as we shall see, is indeed of no mean import. It sets the tone: he has rare powers at his command. We may compare his spontaneous taking up of the dispute among his disciples as to which of them will be the greatest in the kingdom—found in Mark and Luke[5]; also, though it is less close, his precise acquaintance with the home life of the Samaritan woman in John.[6]

The handling of the Temple tax, he explains to Peter, is a far from simple matter and the "Yes" stands in need of a vital qualification. He begins his instruction by setting out the latter: ideally, he and his are not bound at all. He reasons that earthly kings exact tribute from strangers only and not from their sons. By analogy, as he and his are sons—scil. of the heavenly King, the Temple's sovereign—they must be free.

The antithesis son or member of a family vs. stranger is common both in Greek and in Hebrew. Herodotus[7] tells of a woman whose entire kins-

---

[4]Mark 12:34f. See D. Daube, *The New Testament and Rabbinic Judaism* (1956) 148ff.; "The Earliest Structure of the Gospels," *NTS* 5 (1959): 180ff.; *He That Cometh* (1966): 8ff.; and "Zukunftsmusik," *BJRUL* 68 (1985) 58ff.

[5]Mark 9:33f., Luke 9:46ff. Not in Matt 18:1ff.: the display of extraordinary perception in the Temple tax piece suffices. It has long been seen that there is a genetic tie between "And when they were come to Capernaum . . . and when he (Peter) was come into the house" in Matt 17:24f. and "And he came to Capernaum and being in the house he said to them" in Mark 9:33. (None of it in Luke.) Which of the two descends from which may here be left open.

[6]John 4:17ff.

[7]Herodotus, *History* 3.119.

folk are under sentence of death. Darius, moved by her continual laments (one is reminded of the Lucan judge[8]), allows her to pick one of the lot to live. She names a brother, whereupon he enquires why she chooses one who is "more a stranger than your children." Hosea speaks of bastards as "sons that are strangers",[9] and the stricken Job is accounted "a stranger" by his own household.[10] Particularly relevant, however, is the attachment in Jewish religion of the label stranger to a non-priest, frequent from Exodus, "a stranger shall not eat thereof,"[11] through Sirach, "but strangers (Korah, Dathan and Abiram) were incensed against him (Aaron),"[12] to the Talmud where, indeed, we find a derivative added, an abstract, strangeness, signifying the quality of being a non-priest.[13] Such a formation testifies to considerable reflection and discussion upon the area. The point here is that, in Jesus's time, the priests insisted on exemption from the Temple tax,[14] doubtless as "belonging" in a fashion incompatible with this obligation on strangers. The reverberations of this issue in fragmentary reports and allusions—several of which will be inspected—give us an idea of just how hotly and widely it was debated. To some degree, it appears, he is casting himself and his followers in a similar role.

Several other groups were immune: women, slaves, minors, gentiles and Samaritans. In all five cases, we have to do with a *privilegium odiosum*, a benefit that is really a degradation.[15] A specimen from our day is the non-conscription of asthmatics and homosexuals. There was, moreover, within the five a division into two ranks. Women, slaves and minors, though under no duty, yet might make payment of their own will; whereas none was accepted from gentiles and Samaritans—they were right outside, with no stake in the community. (No need here to go into fluctuations with respect to Samaritans.) To this, too, there are modern parallels. An asthmatic, not

---

[8]Luke 18:1ff.

[9]Hos 5:7.

[10]Job 19:15, 17.

[11]Exod 29:33.

[12]Sir 45:18.

[13]E.g., Babylonian Yebamoth 68b, toward the beginning.

[14]Mishnah Sheqalim 1.3f. See H. L. Strack and P. Billerbeck, *Kommentar zum Neuen Testament aus Talmud und Midrasch*, vol. 1 (1926) 762f.

[15]See D. Daube, "Enfant Terrible," *HTR* 68 (1975) 371ff.; "Johanan ben Beroqa and Women's Rights," *ZSS* 99 (1982); *Rom. Abt.*, pp. 27ff.; and Fraud No. 3, pp. 4ff.

too sick, if offering to serve, will not necessarily be rejected; but the army has no room for a homosexual. The priests' contention was on a radically different level from any of these categories: for a privilege in the proper sense, a mark of excellence. They regarded themselves as intimates of the Revered one at whose feet the levy was laid. They were almost recipients of it, standing apart from, above, all the rest, whether payers or non-payers. So essentially tied to their calling, in their eyes, was the exercise of this distinction that they—or at least the extremists among them—declared unenforced payment by a priest to be a sin, an abdication of their special relationship. Persons dispensed from the draft because of their absolutely vital work in thermonuclear development would be something of a present-age counterpart. Or better, in 1914, the young man at Oxford who, unlike most of his contemporaries, did not volunteer. When a patriotic lady, passing him in the street, reproved him, "What are you doing here? Why are you not with your comrades in the trenches, defending civilization against the Huns?," he replied: "Madam, I am civilization."

It is against this background that the reaction of the Pharisees becomes understandable. To them, the attitude summarized was one more instance of unwarranted priestly pretensions—smacking of Sadducean exclusivity. At the academy of Jabneh, one Ben Bukri reported a predestruction tradition to the effect that a priest paying voluntarily was committing no sin.[16] Johanan ben Zaccai, the academy's head, now as before advocated an even stronger line: it was sinful for a priest to abstain from paying. The Mishnah's legal ruling, which must have prevailed in the final years of the State whenever the Pharisees had the upper hand, agrees with Johanan, that is, priests ought to pay, nonetheless "one does not compel them, for the sake of the ways of peace."[17] Relaxations in order to avoid ill-feeling are no rarity in Rabbinic—or New Testament—teaching[18]; the very pericope here studied ends up with one, on the part of those who feel unjustly taxed. It is worth noting, however, that, possibly, a variant of the Mishna's compromise, preserved in the Jerusalemite Talmud, reflects a stage when the priests' aspirations still enjoyed a measure of recognition. Instead of "the ways of peace," we meet here the far less usual term "the ways of honor": indicating, possibly, less a mitigation of a principle than a genuine relief

---

[16]Ben Bukri is known only for this testimony, cited, besides Mishnah Sheqalim 1.4, in Babylonian Menahoth 21b f., 46b, and Arakin 4a.

[17]Mishnah Sheqalim 1.3f. and, consistent with it, 1.6.

[18]See D. Daube, "Pauline Contributions to a Pluralistic Culture," in *Jesus and Man's Hope*, ed. D. G. Miller and D. Y. Hadidian (1971) 2:233ff.

on account of exalted vocation.[19] After all, vestiges of their past glory survive in fairly late statements—for example, a fourth-century one, that the priests, when officiating, were representatives, not of the congregation before God, but of God before the congregation.[20]

In debate with Johanan ben Zaccai, prior to the catastrophe, the priests appealed to an injunction in Leviticus[21] according to which offerings brought by them for themselves must be totally burnt, without any portion being eaten. Quite a few offerings, their argument went, as for example the showbread, the ingredients of which the Temple purchases with its revenue,[22] are expressly given over to them as food in the Pentateuch.[23] If they contributed to the revenue, they would be helping purchase these offerings,[24] ergo be bringing them—in part at least—for themselves, ergo be precluded from eating them. Seeing that, on the contrary, they are encouraged to do so, it follows that they must have no hand in the purchase. The conclusion: they may not lawfully participate in the tax. It would be naive to think that the provision in Leviticus and the tortuous ratiocination taking off from it were the actual root of their claim. The latter came first and was perhaps in existence for centuries before being pegged to the Pentateuch.[25] Roughly, from Hillel on, any regulation, to be fully binding, had to be based on a Scriptural law. Mattathias, for instance, and his entourage, had allowed their troops to fight on a Sabbath if attacked after experience showed that, otherwise, the Syrians would simply annihilate them; and there is no indication that they invoked a Mosaic ordinance. Some hundred-and-fifty years later, however, Hillel managed to prove from Deuteronomy that a Jewish army need not interrupt a siege on a Sabbath.

---

[19]Such distinctions as that between interrupting one's prayer to greet somebody from fear and doing the same in acknowledgement of his honor are pertinent: Mishnah Berakoth 2.1 and accompanying Gemara. "The honor of kings" occurs in Babylonian Berakoth 19a.

[20]Babylonian Yoma 19a f., Qiddushin 23b, Nedarim 35b. See Strack-Billerbeck, *Kommentar,* vol. 3 (1926) 4; vol. 4, pt. 1 (1928) 150.

[21]Lev 6:16.

[22]Confirmed by Josephus, *Jewish Antiquities* 3.10.7.255.

[23]Lev 24:9.

[24]It would be interesting to examine this construction within a history of legal personality in Jewish law.

[25]The Roman priests who protested against being taxed in 196 B.C.—Livy, *From the Founding of the City* 33.52.4—had no Pentateuch to support them.

This code forbids the use of fruitbearing trees for siegeworks, adding: "only those not for food, with them you shall build bulwarks against the city until it be subdued." "Until it be subdued": that is to say, according to Hillel, without desisting on a Sabbath.[26] An interpretation manifestly superimposed on, not generated by, the original tenor—just like the priests'. Again, when Jesus's disciples pluck corn on a Sabbath, in all three Synoptics he supports them by referring to David and his band who, as they suffered hunger, ate the showbread reserved for the sanctuary. In Matthew, he appends a justification from what may be read "in the law." In the Book of Numbers, the Temple priests are supposed to break the Sabbath, say, for the slaughter of sacrifices. What is now involved, he urges, is greater than the Temple, ergo plainly supersedes those rules. The conclusion: the plucking of the corn is licit. Once more, a highly refined syllogism, employing the technical step *a minori ad maius*, not at all envisaged by the old text.[27] The derivation from the Torah of the prohibition of suicide (subscribed to by Hamlet when he deplores "the Everlasting's canon 'gainst self-slaughter") and the duty of procreation (in the Bible, a blessing) are of the same nature.[28] The number of these cases is large; enormous if we include all the slightly less extreme ones, where the passage resorted to contains some element at least of what is made of it. A systematic exploration would throw much new light on the evolution of the Rabbinic edifice.

The assumption by Jesus and his circle of priestly status of some sort is traceable from early on in so many different strata of the New Testament that—discounting any reinforcement from the Dead Sea Scrolls—its beginnings may safely be ascribed to his lifetime. It is indeed met in his quotation, just adverted to, of the precedent set by David and his retinue who, in an emergency, ate the priests' showbread. The implication is that their overriding task entitled them, even obliged them, to act thus, they were

---

[26]1 Macc 2:39ff., Josephus, *Jewish Antiquities* 12.6.2.276f., 13.1.3.12f., Deuteronomy 20:20, Tosephta Erubin 4.7. See D. Daube "Texts and Interpretation in Roman and Jewish Law," *JJS* 3 (1961) 9, 15.

[27]Matt 12:1ff., Mark 2:23ff., Luke 6:1ff., 1 Sam 21:1ff., Num 28:9f. See D. Daube, *Rabbinic Judaism*, 67ff.

[28]See D. Daube, "Das Alte Testament im Neuen—aus jüdischer Sicht," *Xenia*, vol. 10, p. 7 (German translation by W. Schuller of an as yet unpublished English lecture "The Old Testament in the New: A Jewish Perspective," where the reading back of the ban on suicide into the Ten Commandments is noted in section 1); and *The Duty of Procreation* (1977) 1ff., 42.

directly engaged in executing God's Messianic plan,[29] and now it is Jesus and his faithful who occupy this place. The additional plea, from precept (the Book of Numbers) instead of from example (David's boldness), puts the notion in more explicit terms: the Sabbath restrictions, suspended for the priests serving in the Temple, must *a fortiori* not stand in the way of a greater service, greater priests. The "cleansing" of the Temple, with, in Mark, prominence accorded to a technical detail of the daily priestly business,[30] is another strong piece of evidence.

Jesus is not willing to waive the prerogative: this is the major premise he impresses on Peter. From here, however, he goes on to a formidable complication. A downright refusal of the administration's demand might put off[31] people not otherwise hostile—interfering with his mission. No doubt there are conditions in which a path must be continued regardless. But the Temple tax does not fall under them, hence creates a dilemma. He solves it by devising a course which formally, in semblance, amounts to perfect compliance, so will avoid any discord, while, in reality, they part with nothing that is genuinely their own, so are not subjecting themselves to the impost. The latter is to be satisfied with a coin Peter will take from the mouth of the first fish he catches. Whosesoever it was in the past, it became ownerless when the fish carried it off, and now it falls to the finder. It can, therefore, be validly employed to discharge a debt and—equally important—no uninitiated will be aware of anything out of the ordinary. Nevertheless, as far as substance is concerned rather than image, no concession is made. Economically and psychologically, the passing on of money coming from nowhere and the group's property for a fleeting moment only, just long enough to fulfill the purpose of appeasing an environment of deficient insight, is not a true contribution on their part.

---

[29]It would not be surprising if pious scribes of Jesus' era had taken David's declaration in 1 Sam 21:3, "The king has commanded me a business," in the sense not of "Saul has commanded me" but of "God has commanded me." For one thing, on this basis, David would not be guilty of deception. That the interpretation is not preserved may be due precisely to the use made of the episode in the gospels. But, of course, one cannot build on this speculation.

[30]Mark 11:16, a provision singled out by the priest Josephus, *Against Apion* 2.8.106.

[31]*Skandalizo:* when it has its full weight, "to give offense to somebody leading to his alienation, missing the right way, stumbling"; at times, little more than "to give offense to somebody"—our modern "to scandalize." See G. Stählin, art. "Skandalon, Skandalizo," in *Theologisches Wörterbuch zum Neuen Testament,* founded G. Kittel, ed G. Friedrich and others, vol. 7 (1964) 343ff.

Dodges of this pattern were familiar in that period. Here is one[32] dating from before the middle of the first century B.C. and going on for hundreds of years. Under the austere Roman reglement of insolvency, infamy befell not only an actual bankrupt but also a debtor who got his creditor to be content with a percentage. A creditor wishing to spare his debtor this punishment would cooperate in the following procedure. Say, the debtor owed 1,200 and all he had was 200. He paid 200 and the creditor immediately returned it, by way of gift. The debtor then paid it again, to get it back again as a gift. And so on—and only the sixth payment was kept by the creditor. Formally, in semblance, the debtor had now paid in full. But 1,000 out of the 1,200 were, so to speak, brought along by a fish, provided to him for just the brief hour of the transaction, economically and psychologically not a true disbursement by him. A Talmudic anecdote,[33] where it is not payment that is simulated but acceptance of a gift, is worth quoting here because the reason for staging the make-believe is to forestall the would-be donor's resentment: reminiscent of Jesus's reason for feigning conformity. On a pagan festival, Jews were to refrain from any dealings that might boost the thanksgiving to idols—such as lending or making a present to a pagan. Some Rabbis worried even about receiving a present since even this might make the pagan rejoice and bless his gods. When Judah II (grandson of Judah the Prince) on such a festival was sent a gold piece by a pagan acquaintance, he asked Resh Laquish who happened to be with him: "If I do accept, he may render thanks to his idol, if I do not, he will conceive enmity against me." At Resh Laquish's advice, he took the piece but at once, while the messenger was still there, dropped it into a well as if by accident. Thus the donor, on being told, could not be insulted—since his gift was accepted—but neither would he be moved to praise his idol—since no sooner was it accepted than lost. It was "accepted" in inverted commas, for a few seconds, so no animosity would ensue.

Modern commentators tend to overlook the fact that Jesus is supplying an illustration, a model, and that it is offered not for literal imitation but for imitation as to its substantive content, its message—namely, that while the position of this special priesthood is inabdicable, it must be exercised gently. Au fond, it accords with the counsel: "Be subtle as the serpents

---

[32]Digest 46.3.67, Marcellus XIII digestorum. See D. Daube, *Roman Law* (1969) 93f.; and Fraud No. 3, p. 14.

[33]Babylonian Aboda Zara 6a, cited by Strack-Billerbeck, *Kommentar*, vol. 1, p. 885.

and harmless as the doves,'' which, curiously, like the Temple tax narrative, is preserved only in Matthew.[34] His sending out of Peter for a coin the first fish will present draws on his superior capacity of being informed about odd circumstances, certainly not meant to be reproduced. As noticed above, the session opens by his realizing what has occurred without being told. This is a peculiar knowing of past and present. His mandate regarding the coin actually implies a foreknowing—such as he manifests when he predicts to the disciples preparing his entry into Jerusalem that they will find a colt tied for his use[35] and to those looking for a room for his Passover meal that they will meet a guide.[36] Of course, once he is gone, the community cannot rely on a magical haul. But this does not dispense them from heeding the core of the lesson. They will have to contrive mundane, ever varying ruses enabling them to reconcile the conflicting requirements—to live up to their election at once and not upset the ignorant. It is the master alone who may choose a shortcut bordering on the miraculous for the exemplary precedent. For one thing, in this way, it can be flawless—as even the best-intentioned schemes lacking supernatural assistance seldom are.[37] It should be observed that this mode of instruction is evidenced among the Tannaites. The clearing up of a complex of questions by Gamaliel II, successor of Johanan ben Zaccai as president of Jabneh, involved his astounding identification of a person he had never seen before: "He recognized him through the holy spirit and from his words we learnt three things."[38]

In the most fundamental respect, Jesus's attitude to tribute to Caesar is at one with that just outlined. Caesar does occupy an elevated rank, but when his bidding clashes with God's, God must prevail: in the maxim to pay "what is Caesar's to Caesar and what is God's to God," the emphasis is on the final words. Often, here too, the best course will be to be serpent

---

[34]Matt 10:16.

[35]Matt 21:2ff, Mark 11:2ff., Luke 19:30ff.

[36]Mark 14:13ff., Luke 22:10ff., considerably reduced in Matt 26:18f.

[37]Take the one mentioned above, where creditor and debtor colluded to save the latter from infamy. The earlier jurists did not pass it: they decided that, as 1,000 came in effect from the creditor's funds, it remained a case of insolvency. By contrast, even these diehards would have had no complaint about money furnished to the debtor by a god or, for that matter, discovered inside a fish.

[38]Tosephta Pesahim 1.27, Palestinian Aboda Zara 40a, Babylonian Erubin 64b, Leviticus Rabba on 27:2.

as well as dove, to get along by means of loopholes.[39] Indeed, the reply itself is "subtle," serpent-like, so framed that while sympathizers will appreciate where priority is placed, no easy pretext for intervention is handed to the government. Significantly, in Mark, this section corresponds to that of the Seder exhibiting the type of disciple concerned about law, and he also receives a cryptic answer.[40] The opacity of the saying is underlined by the contradictory meanings attributed to it already in New Testament times. According to Luke,[41] it was used in Jesus's arraignment before Pilate, distorted into an unambiguous No to Roman taxation. In Romans,[42] it is pretty much the opposite. (Admittedly, juristic acumen can turn around the clearest dictum. A forthright Mishnaic paragraph treats murderers, robbers and excise-gatherers as equally deserving to be misled. The Gemara transmits an exegesis of it which, deferring to Caesar like Romans, virtually annuls

---

[39]Wolfgang Kunkel lived up to it in the second world war. [A sketch of his personality by Dieter Nörr may be found in *Gedächtnisschrift für Wolfgang Kunkel*, ed. D. Nörr and D. Simon (1984) pp. 9ff.] He was a military judge in the East. In 1943, one captain denounced another one for having listened to the Moscow radio a year previously: a capital crime. What prompted him to come forward at that moment was that the culprit had just been appointed *Bahnhofskommandant*, i.e., was given charge of a little railstation. (The degree by which this put him ahead of the accuser was minuscule; and so, of course, was either's life expectancy.) Kunkel did not want to pronounce sentence of death. The trouble was that his verdict would have to be approved by higher-ups behind the front, and they were ruthless. It would have been no use, for example, to point to the promotion as proof that the man was doing his duty to the full. Yet he found a way. The decree which ordained the death penalty was issued *für den grossdeutschen Raum*, "for the greater German realm." The area around Moscow was not part of this, but again, to simply state this and acquit would not have sufficed: the Berlin authorities would have rejected it as formalistic and weak-kneed. Kunkel declared the decree inapplicable because the Moscow area was *noch nicht,* "not yet," incorporated in the *grossdeutsche Raum.* By phrasing it thus, he appeared to be absolutely confident of the outcome: it was only a matter of a few clean-up operations. To make doubly sure, and no doubt also to teach the informer a lesson, he added a rider in which he severely censured the latter for waiting so long before bringing so serious an offense to the attention of his superiors. The judgment was duly confirmed.

[40]Mark 12:13ff. See the writings listed in n. 4 above.

[41]Luke 23:2, prepared for by 20:20. See J. M. Creed, *The Gospel according to St. Luke* (1930) 247. The historicity or otherwise of the notice is immaterial in the present connection.

[42]Rom 13:6f.

the part as to publicans.[43]) Of course, notwithstanding the profound affinity, there are bound to be major dissimilarities between the two cases. One is that, Caesar being a heathen tyrant, whatever may speak against submitting to his tribute, it cannot be his fatherhood; nor can we expect from Jesus a warning against "putting him off." Another, that, in the gospel framework, the question respecting Caesar emanates from hostile outsiders whereas that respecting the Temple is gone into within the inner circle. As a result, the answer to the former has to remain on a general level whereas that to the latter follows up the governing principle with specific, practical guidance.

In conclusion, some remarks on setting. Few nowadays deny that the first half of the pericope goes back to before the destruction. After it, the conquerors appropriated the tax, diverting it to heathen worship.[44] To take the argument as envisaging this *Fiscus Judaicus* will not do. No first-century Christian author can have thought of the saved ones as sons of the Emperor to whom it went, and to be sons of the Highest would be irrelevant if the tax was not his.

The second half is mostly treated as an eccentric appendage. There is a tendency, moreover, to postulate relatively late elements both in it and in the first. If the foregoing exposition is approved, the pre-destruction date holds good for the pericope in toto, including the catch—essential to the complete, down-to-earth teaching. As for the late elements, the arguments are unconvincing. Jesus's repudiation of liability is alleged to evince a disdain for the Temple at variance with his zeal as he "cleanses" it.[45] In reality, his stand founds on the conviction that he and his are its truest priests. The view here combated would mean (unless the comparison he draws is quite off, *hinkend*) that the sons of earthly kings are left untroubled by the

---

[43]Mishnah Nedarim 3.4; Babylonian Nedarim 28a.

[44]Josephus, *Jewish Wars* 7.6.6.218; Suetonius, *Lives of the Caesars, Domitian* 12.2; Dio Cassius, *Roman History Epit.* 65.7.2.

[45]See e.g., E. Lohmeyer, *Das Evangelium des Matthäus*, ed. W. Schmauch (1956) 275; F. V. Filson, *A Commentary on the Gospel according to St. Matthew* (1960) 195; G. Stählin, "Skandalon, Skandalizo," 350f. Basically similar is the position of C. H. Dodd, *History and the Gospel* (1938) 90ff.: The story "of the Coin in the Fish's mouth is pertinent to the question of the payment of the Temple tax by Jewish Christians who no longer felt themselves to be within the Jewish community. That question is hardly likely to have become acute in the stage of church life represented by the early chapters of Acts, and still less likely during the lifetime of Jesus. The story is suspected, not without good reason, of being a later accretion."

treasury because they despise the throne; whereas, palpably, the reason is their closeness to it, their share in it. It would mean also that, when Jesus, in defence of his disciples, cites the eating of hallowed food by David and his men, he is depicting them as scornful of the sanctuary—not credible. They were, indeed, at this moment its most devoted fighters, precursors of Jesus's group. This is not to exclude the possibility that the preservation (precarious, via Matthew only) of the incident owes something to precisely this misinterpretation of it as documenting contempt. Again, the prominence of Pauline ideas is noted as militating against the first half of the century: the Christian's freedom from the law as a child of God and the yielding in order not to cause the weak to stumble.[46] But it may be Paul who is secondary. The freedom theme in the Temple tax story is far less developed than in his writings; and all the three Synoptics carry strong pronouncements by Jesus against putting off the little ones.[47]

W. D. Davies lists the second half among the Matthean revisions by which a Jesuanic absolute is toned down, to make it livable with; it is akin, as he sees it, to Paul's procedure anent tribute to Caesar.[48] The parallel, however, is illusory. Jesus's saying about the tribute guardedly (since ill-wishers are listening) recommends a bending which, however, must never be such as to detract from the principal allegiance; Paul bids us pay.[49] By contrast, Jesus's saying about Temple tax openly (since he is addressing a confidant) denies its bindingness and the practical solution following on it (again, not needing to be veiled) is in line, not with Paul, but with the original, cautious word about the tribute: do make the requisite gesture without, however, any surrender of substance. This latter agreement, already mentioned above, sets the case apart from others where Davies is right. He takes no account of the fish. It may be worth observing that, even if it were due to Matthew, this manner of procuring the tax ought to be credited with the goal here postulated: appeasement but no stepping down. It would still be, not some extravaganza, but a standard for an embattled community to emulate. To this extent, that is, the gist of my thesis would remain unaffected.

A number of traits do strongly favor a very early origin of the whole—the nature of the band in particular. As already pointed out, the collectors

---

[46]See, e.g., S. E. Johnson, "The Gospel according to St. Matthew: Exegesis," *Interpreter's Bible*, vol. 7 (1951) 465f.

[47]Matt 18:6, Mark 9:42, Luke 17:2.

[48]W. D. Davies, *The Setting of the Sermon on the Mount* (1964) 389ff.

[49]With a powerful underpinning, so there be no breach.

expect Peter to account for Jesus's conduct. Furthermore, they speak of "your teacher" with "your" in the plural: any one of the disciples represents all the others. Nor is this all. In expounding the situation, Jesus does not differentiate between himself and his followers: they are all equally of the family of the Temple's Lord. By the same token, the coin he foresees will be a *stater*, a full shekel, to serve in one go on behalf of both himself and Peter;[50] and doubtless, qua recipient of the model advice how to cope, Peter once more stands for his fellows as well. Such a presentation suggests a time when the group was small and close-knit and before the crucifixion had rendered the master more distant. Perhaps the latter point can be made more concrete by adducing again the Matthean expansion with Jesus's statement[51] that "here is something greater than the Temple." From the sixth century on, we meet the reading "somebody greater." The Temple Tax episode is unmistakably conceived in terms of "something greater."

Peter's appearance may have to be taken seriously. If he were singled out just for retrieving a bonus from a fish, that might be brushed aside by reference to his former trade. But he is on stage from the first, when probed by the officials. There is reason to believe that Mark's day of questions derives from a Seder where Peter fitted sayings of Jesus into the pre-established liturgy.[52] The opening topic is tribute to Caesar. Quite possibly, then, Peter heard about the related topic of the Temple tax, too, from Je-

---

[50]For B. H. Streeter, *The Four Gospels,* new ed. (1930) 504, the *stater* supports an Antiochene provenance of the pericope: it seems that only at Antioch and Damascus was this coin worth exactly two half-shekels. But, first, the evidence is shaky. Secondly, the *stater* is customarily equated with a full shekel, so at any rate near enough. Third, the half-shekel being seldom coined in Jesus's time, it may indeed have been quite usual for two persons to combine and pay with a *stater:* see A. H. McNeile, *The Gospel according to St. Matthew* (1955) 257. Lastly and above all, even if the *stater* hails from Antioch, by itself it proves nothing for the bulk of the narrative. "When I worked on fables, I was amused by the transformation of animals in the course of migration. The longbeaked bird that removes a bone from the wolf's throat is a heron in Babrius, a crane in Phaedrus, a stork in La Fontaine. Joshua ben Hananiah speaks of an Egyptian partridge; and the wolf becomes a lion—symbolizing Rome or the Emperor Hadrian. None the less the body of the paradigm stays the same throughout": see D. Daube, *Ancient Jewish Law* (1981) 22. Valuta is at least equally exchangeable. Streeter himself describes the point as of merely "infinitesimal" significance.

[51]Matt 12:6.

[52]See Daube, "Zukunftsmusik," 61ff.

sus. First Peter, it should be recalled,[53] contains what sounds like an echo of the scene here analyzed: the Christians are looked upon as the choice Temple and priesthood and as such, indeed (by now Jesus has been crucified and the battle-lines are drawn), a rock putting off[54] unbelievers.

At any rate, two basic considerations seem scarcely disputable. One, the Temple tax problem must have been terribly hard, on every level, for Jesus and those around him. Two, whatever Jesuanic tradition existed concerning it is likely to have crystallized, say, around A.D. 40, in those years, that is, when the community would badly want to hear about what it owed to the foreign regime and the native Temple rulers an unholy alliance between whom had just contrived the death of its head. Even Paul, preaching obedience to the State, still focuses on tax as the ultimate criterion.[55] For one who disagrees with Bill's affirmation of the overall priority of Matthew, it is gratifying to be able to write up for his *Festschrift* an occurrence as authentic as anything in Mark. It is one of very few such instances, left-overs, one imagines, from the Hebrew precursor.[56]

---

[53]1 Pet 2:4ff.

[54]*Petra skandalou.*

[55]Rom 13:1-7.

[56]I am deeply grateful to William David Davies for criticizing the first draft of this paper. Whether he is less skeptical about the present one, I dare not guess.

JESUS AND VIOLENCE[1]

David L. Dungan

In view of the long history of the Christian Church's massive commitment to the use of violence in every form, ranging from bloodthirsty crusades, to horrible torture of heretics, to vindictive pogroms and lynchings, to mass witch-burnings, to American church leaders blessing the nuclear bombs that devastated Hiroshima and Nagasaki, all *ad maioram gloriae dei Christianorum,* it could seem terribly dense to ask at this late date what connection there might have been between this bloody history of Christian violence and the Jesus of the Gospels. Is it not extraordinarily difficult to reconcile this chronicle of death and destruction with sayings of Jesus such as: "love your enemy?" Whence cometh this righteous and vindictive hatred? From an alien spirit, masquerading as Christianity? Yes, although by now most western Christians know no other spirit. I agree with those who say that this spirit of murder in the name of God came into the Church with the Emperor Constantine's transvaluation of Christianity and his typically Roman, warlike motto: *in hoc signo vinces.*

Of course, there has been a centuries-long series of attempts to protest against the Christian use of violence, founded on these very same words: "love your enemy." In modern times, Jesus' nonretaliation sayings have buttressed numerous campaigns of nonviolent resistance. But here again, it must be pointed out that *resistance* of any kind—violent or nonviolent— is not recommended by these sayings of Jesus. *"Do not resist evil"* does not mean to resist evil nonviolently. In plain terms it means *do not retaliate* when attacked by evil and injustice.

---

[1] I am delighted to be able to pay tribute in this way to my dear friend and colleague William Farmer, whose research on the Synoptic Problem has helped to invigorate New Testament studies around the world. I hope he will find this application of the Two Gospel Hypothesis to the Synoptic evidence on nonretaliation helpful to his thinking about civil rights. In addition, I would like to mention that my doctoral father, Krister Stendahl, provided the basic starting point for this essay, and the book of my dear friend and mentor, David Daube, *Civil Disobedience in Antiquity* (Edinburgh: University Press, 1972), encouraged me to take up two extremely tender issues ordinarily left out of the discussion. My interest in this question stems from my father, who was a lifelong conscientious objector.

In either case, I see no warrant in the Gospels for any Christian organization, whether the Moral Majority or the World Council of Churches,[2] to use *violent* methods to resist evil and injustice, nor do I see any warrant for claiming that Jesus advocated using *nonviolent* methods to resist evil and injustice. "Do not resist evil; turn the other cheek" simply means: do not resist—at all.

If I may pursue the issue a step further, recent pacifist studies create an exceedingly misleading impression when they say that "nonviolence was central to Jesus' ethics," or that "forgiving love was central in Jesus' teachings."[3] Those who make such generalizations apparently do not realize what they are saying. To say that someone advocates not resisting evil, that someone urges people to "forgive evil-doers," obviously makes him party to the doing of evil. To permit evil to happen, to not resist it if one has the power to do so, to "forgive" it after it has been done, is a *crime* under our legal statutes. Such persons are contributory to the perpetration

---

[2]For reports on the World Council's activity along these lines, see *The Christian Science Monitor* (23 February 1971 and 14 August 1978). By 1977 approximately $2,640,000 had been channeled into its "Programme to Combat Racism." For American conservative and liberal reactions, see the *Presbyterian Layman* (December 1978 and January 1979), and "Killing for Christ," *New Rupublic* (21 October 1978).

[3]Out of many examples which could be cited, I will only draw attention to those studies which have focused on the Gospel of Luke see especially, Richard J. Cassidy, *Jesus, Politics and Society. A Study of Luke's Gospel* (Maryknoll NY: Orbis Books, 1983); Paul W. Walaskay, *"And So We Came to Rome." The Political Perspective of St Luke,* SNTSMS 49 (Cambridge: Cambridge University Press, 1983); Josephine M. Ford, *My Enemy Is My Guest. Jesus and Violence in Luke* (Maryknoll NY: Orbis Books, 1984); and the collection of papers ed. R. J. Cassidy and P. J. Scharper, *Political Issues in Luke-Acts* (Maryknoll NY: Orbis Books, 1983). For a wider perspective, see William Klassen, *Love of Enemies. The Way to Peace,* OBT 15 (Philadelphia: Fortress Press, 1984); also John Piper, *Love Your Enemies; Jesus' Love Command in the Synoptic Gospels and the Early Christian Parenesis,* SNTSMS 38 (Cambridge: Cambridge University Press, 1979); John H. Yoder, *The Politics of Jesus* (Grand Rapids MI: Eerdmans, 1972) and *He Came Preaching Peace* (Scottdale PA: Herald Press, 1985). For a thorough bibliographical review and excellent critical discussion of recent New Testament studies on this subject, see Richard A. Horsley, "Ethics and Exegesis: 'Love Your Enemies' and the Doctrine of Nonviolence," *JAAR* 54 (1986): 3-31. For the view that "forgiving love is at the heart of Jesus' ethics," see among many others, Stanley Hauerwas, *The Peaceable Kingdom. A Primer in Christian Ethics* (Notre Dame IN: University of Notre Dame Press, 1983).

of evil and wrongdoing; our law books have all sorts of penalties for such dereliction of civil obligation.

Perhaps centuries of gold and incense have caused us to forget how shockingly *immoral* these teachings of Jesus originally were. I detect a faint echo of the distaste, not to say outrage, that these sayings caused his original hearers, in the following reaction of Baruch Spinoza, many centuries later:

> It is certain that duties towards one's country are the highest that man can fulfil; for, if government be taken away, no good thing can last, all falls into dispute, anger and anarchy reign unchecked amid universal fear. . . . It is in the abstract my duty when my neighbor . . . wishes to take my cloak to give him my coat also; but if it be thought that such conduct is hurtful to the maintenance of the state, I ought to bring him to trial, even at the risk of his being condemned to death.[4]

And again,

> When Christ says: "But if a man strike you on the right cheek, turn to him the left also," . . . [he did not give] such a command as a lawgiver . . . for he would have thereby abrogated the law of Moses which he expressly says he did not intend to do [Matt 5:17]. [Rather,] these words were spoken to men who were oppressed, who lived in a corrupt commonwealth on the brink of ruin, where justice was utterly neglected. [It was a doctrine] also taught by Jeremiah before the first destruction of Jerusalem, . . . as we can see in Lam. 3:25-30.[5]

Spinoza's reaction is most instructive, for it points to the pivotal issue: what is the larger context within which one should deviate from a strict righteousness for oneself and for others? Or, to put it in more modern language: assuming that breaking the law is morally wrong, what is the larger political context within which not retaliating for wrongdoing is morally justifiable? It is this question which most if not all recent studies of Jesus' ethics of nonviolence fail to address, resulting in a skewed caricature of his teachings. I would like in the present essay to focus on this issue of the larger context.

The Gospels' Context of Jesus' Teachings
Regarding Nonretaliation

I should insist at the outset that whenever these sayings are lifted out of their original contexts and turned into moral absolutes, they instantly lose all ethical validity. Time and again, one finds generalizations to the effect that "Jesus taught us not to resist evil," with little apparent realization of

---

[4]Benedict de Spinoza, *A Theologico-political Treatise* (1670); trans. Elwes (New York: Dover Publications, 1951) 249.

[5]Ibid., 105.

what that means, if taken at face value. It means precisely to permit evil to occur.

Not only is that foolish ethics, it isn't good exegesis. All around Jesus' nonretaliation sayings are stories in which he is depicted as eagerly anticipating God's catastrophic, violent destruction of evil in all forms. What of the numerous Synoptic accounts portraying Jesus engaged in vigorous, aggressive assaults on evil demons, evil persons and evil institutions? Do they not exude Jesus' confident hope in God's violence?

When Jesus sent out the Twelve Disciples, he specifically correlated whatever treatment they received in the towns and villages to which they went with the decision they would receive on the Day of Judgment (Matt 10:11-15/Luke 10:10-12).[6]

What of the Temptation Story? Baptized, that is, fully empowered by the Holy Spirit and *at its prompting,* the Gospels tell how Jesus Christ went into "the desert" to confront Satan in his own "house." This story with its emphatic location at the very head of the narrative of Jesus' public ministry obviously meant to signify something very important. Why not the obvious idea that God, using Jesus as his "agent," launched an outright attack upon Satan? Satan comes forward, drawn by the lure of the human "bait," and the momentous struggle ensues. Three tremendous blows are hurled at Jesus by Satan, insidious temptations which we all constantly fall prey to, but Jesus valiantly parries them one after the other.[7] Momentarily thwarted, Satan backs off. Or as Luke ominously put it, "the Devil left him until the opportune moment" (4:13 New Jerusalem Bible). How can we overlook the dangerous boldness of Jesus' actions in this story? And did he not gloriously resist evil, nay, The Evil One?

Luke, "the pacifist Gospel,"[8] carries the initial onslaught of Jesus from the Temptation scene straight on into subsequent scenes.

---

[6]See further David Dungan, *Sayings of Jesus in the Churches of Paul* (Philadelphia: Fortress Press, 1971) 56ff.

[7]The most profound exegesis of this enormously undervalued narrative is still that by Fyodor Dostoyevski in the "Grand Inquisitor" scene from *Brothers Karamazov.* For a good brief discussion, see Anne Freemantle, *Fyodor Dostoyevsky, The Grand Inquisitor* (New York: Ungar, 1978). The best recent exegetical discussion is by Birger Gerhardsson, *The Testing of God's Son (Matthew 4:1-11 & Parallels): An Analysis of an Early Christian Midrash,* trans. J. Toy, CBNTS 2 (Lund: Gleerup, 1966).

[8]See Ford, *My Enemy Is My Guest,* 137: "It is not my contention that all the evangelists teach what we now call 'pacifism' but that this is one of the special features of Luke (and John)."

Then Jesus, with the power of the Spirit in him, returned to Galilee, and his reputation spread throughout the countryside. He taught in their synagogues and everyone glorified him. (Luke 4:14, New Jerusalem Bible)

This is followed by the story of the clash between Jesus and a demon in the synagogue at Capernaum. When the demon sees Jesus coming, it shouts, "Ha! What do you want with us Jesus of Nazareth? Have you come to destroy us?" (Luke 4:33/Mark 1:24, New Jerusalem Bible). To which Jesus responds, "Silence! Come out of him!" and the man heals immediately. Does that seem nonresisting? Pacifist?

Many concur with James Robinson who noted that these stories portray Jesus moving from his clash with Satan to a series of combats against the lesser demons under Satan's sway. What the evangelists are trying to describe, said Robinson, is the drama of the final, step by step destruction of Satan, evil and death.[9] Observe the "fight" terminology in the Beelzebul Controversy, where Jesus speaks of "plundering" the "strong man's house" (Satan's domain?), something he can do because he has already "attacked" the strong man and "defeated" him (Luke 11:22, cf. Mark 3:27/Matt 12:29). So also when the "Seventy" return, according to a tradition recorded in Luke, they tell Jesus joyously, "Master, even the demons are subject to us in your name!" to which he replies, just as fervently, "And I saw Satan fall like lightning from Heaven (i.e., his throne). Behold, I have given you authority . . . *over all the power of the Enemy!*" (Luke 10:17-19, RSV). Who hurled Satan out of Heaven?

We need not belabor the point. All of the healing stories in the Synoptic Gospels are "signs" pointing to the unexpected eruption of eschatological Judgment into human history. This is how these accounts were *meant to be understood* by the original Gospel authors. We are clearly in the presence of such a massive feature of the Jesus tradition that I find it astonishing for trained historians to dismiss them all as "legendary." Even the Talmud records this about Jesus, that he had potent black magic.[10] To the

---

[9]See the discussion in James M. Robinson, *The Problem of History in Mark* (London: SCM Press, 1954) 35f.

[10]Of course, many of these references stem from the Tannaitic campaign to discredit the Christian faith, but some may contain valid historical truth, such as the famous passage in the Babylonian Sanhedrin 43a:

On the evening of Passover, Yeshu ha-Notzri was hanged. For forty days before the execution took place, a herald went forth and cried, "He is going to be stoned because he practiced sorcery and enticed Israel to apostasy. Anyone who can say anything in his favor, let him come forward and plead on his behalf." But since nothing was brought

degree that we reject these accounts as pious legends or superstitious fantasies invented by the Christian community to glorify Jesus, we will never understand how the early Church saw him. To the degree that we ignore these accounts in our analyses of the nonretaliation sayings, we will miss a whole side of Jesus' ministry where he was strikingly retaliatory, in fact the one area where he was truly awesome as a fighter, showing no mercy and giving no quarter: "Jesus Christ, our Savior and Defender against Death and the Devil."

What about the threat Matthew records that Jesus leveled at the High Priest during his trial; a threat so frightening and offensive it caused the latter to go berserk with rage?[11] What of the Cleansing of the Temple? Coming as it does immediately following the Triumphal Entry, how can this be described as a nonaggressive act? All attempts I have seen to gloss over the violence implicit in the Cleansing of the Temple are patently unconvincing. (Now we learn, for instance, that the real reason Jesus made the whip was to guide the bulls with it so as to keep people from being trampled.)[12] What about the closely related Cursing of the Fig Tree—was this also something merciful, a gentle act of nonretaliation?

Noting this anxious desire to see love and forgiveness in everything Jesus did, David Daube asks, "It would be interesting to find out at what moment, at what place, in what milieu, it was first felt desirable to tone down or eliminate the violence of the Cleansing."[13] I will have a suggestion to make on this question below.

---

forward in his favor, he was hanged on the eve of Passover [ed. Soncino]. See further Herman L. Strack and Paul Billerbeck, *Kommentar zum NT aus Talmud und Midrasch* (München: Oscar Beck, 1922) 1:631ff.

[11]For the interpretation of Jesus' reply to the High Priest adopted here, see J. A. T. Robinson, *Jesus and His Coming* (London: SCM Press, 1957) 43-51.

[12]See Klassen, *Love of Enemies*, 77: "The fact that Jesus hastily made a whip from the cords that bound the animals, far from indicating that he had lost his cool and was prepared to begin thrashing the merchants, indicates rather his profound respect for all the people there and his desire to protect them from the trampling of the bulls. As every farm boy can tell you, a whip can control bulls."

[13]See David Daube, *Civil Disobedience in Antiquity* (Edinburgh: University Press, 1972) 108. Daube continues: "The inquiry would, of course, reach right into the present." As a contrast, he cites the comments of J. Gossip, *The Interpreter's Bible*, ed. George Arthur Buttrick, 12 vols. (Nashville: Abingdon Press, 1952) 8:497f. I keep wondering what exactly is supposed to have happened. Anyone who has stood on the immense plaza of the Haram al-Sharif can't help but wonder how Jesus could have done it so quickly and without any help. If he came

What About the Nonretaliation Sayings?

Jesus' instructions never to return evil for evil were vividly enacted during his own last days. I will first consider his teachings as such and then see how they might have been implemented in his own last moments. But here we encounter a major methodological choice. It is common to use the Two Document Hypothesis as a guide through the Synoptic material. However, my experience here as elsewhere is that to do so only compounds confusion. Therefore, I will use the Two Gospel Hypothesis, which means that I must begin by examining the earliest Gospel, Matthew, first. Luke will then be considered as a careful revision of Matthew. Mark and John will have to wait for another occasion.

The chief riddle confronting any attempt to reconstruct the original historical context has always been to guess correctly Jesus' specific motivation or purpose for saying these words. Before I examine the Matthean context, however, the discovery of astonishingly similar instructions in the Dead Sea Scrolls adds an unexpected dimension to the range of motivations for us to consider. Let us therefore turn to the Essene material first.

Nonretaliation Based on Hatred of the Enemy (Qumran)

Passages in the *Scroll of the Rule* reveal that a strategy of strict nonretaliation was in force upon all members of the Sect. It played an integral role in a comprehensive policy of total secrecy regarding all things pertaining to "salvation" as understood by the Sect: the correct interpretation of Torah, the true calendar and proper feast days, the correct design of the Temple, etc. The strategy of nonretaliation can be seen in the following passage:

---

in through the triple Huldah gate and went back out the same way, as Richard Mackowski thinks (see *Jerusalem. City of Jesus* [Grand Rapids MI: Eerdmans, 1980] 163, fig. 28), he would not have gone into the Temple area proper, but only the Portico of Solomon, where the money changers were. But I thought that the cattle and birds were all at the far end of the temple compound. How did Jesus clear them all out single-handedly, without taking all day? If he had help, then what are we talking about, that he came sweeping into the Temple with all the people who followed him into the "City of David" and they *all* cleansed the Temple? Now it begins to sound like a raid. Or did he come in alone, ahead of the crowd, and, taking his stand in some prominent place, hold up a little symbolic whip, and shout out the dire words from Isa. 56:7 and Jer. 7:11? Being who he was perceived to be at that moment, such an action would doubtless have struck terror into everyone. I can envision the ensuing panic, as one and all cleared out of the place, knocking over tables and dragging their precious livestock out with them.

These are the norms of conduct for the man of understanding in these times, concerning what he must love and how he must hate. Everlasting hatred for all men of the Pit in a spirit of concealment.[14] He shall surrender his property to them and the wages of the work of his hands, as a slave to his master and as a poor man in the presence of his overlord. But he shall be a man full of zeal for the Commandment, whose time is the Day of Vengeance. To no man will I render the reward of evil, with goodness will I pursue each one; for the judgment of all the living is with God, and He it is who will pay to each man his reward. As for the multitude of the men of the Pit, I will not lay hands on them until the Day of Judgment. But I will not withdraw my anger from perverse men nor will I be content until He begins the Judgment! (1QS IX.21-23; X.18-20, Dupont-Sommer)

This passage forbids any retaliation for personal injury or property damage, sustained at the hands of outsiders. The reason given is that divine wrath is about to strike. Let the wicked alone; let them continue to heap up their sins; by so doing they will make their eventual punishment all the worse!

But why the secrecy? The Essenes saw themselves as an army outpost in a condition of "red alert," that is, full battle-readiness. The Messiahs of Aaron and David were due to come any minute and then the climactic Battle of Armageddon would begin. "Then I *will* lay my hands on the men of the Pit!" The battle plans were all ready. This state of military preparedness was being carried out according to the ancient regulations of Holy Warfare as set forth in Deuteronomy, and these regulations explain many other features of the whole Essene operation: their location, their exclusively male membership, their ideal of total celibacy, their individual propertylessness, their daily cleansings, and so on. These were all typical features of traditional Israelite holy war behavior, not the result of any "Persian dualistic influences." In this context of battle-readiness, non-retaliation for day-to-day insults or injuries would have been an important *interim strategy* whose essential purpose was to keep the full contours of the main Essene fighting force from being spotted by the Enemy (human and supernatural). It was part of a "total blackout" that would be thrown off as soon as the fighting began. Clearly hostile in motivation, it was camouflage over the Army of God; they were trying to be invisible.

---

[14]Adopting the translation given these words by K. Stendahl, "Hate, Nonretaliation, and Love. 1QS X, 17-20 and Romans 12:19-21," *HTR* 55 (1962) 349; see also the translation of Dupont-Sommer, *The Essene Writings from Qumran* (New York: Scribner's, 1962) 96n2.

Essenes, Paul and Jesus

In a ground-breaking study of these Essene passages and their possible kinship with nonretaliation sayings in the New Testament,[15] Krister Stendahl asked whether the motivation behind Paul's words in Romans 12:19-21 might not be based on the same kind of secret hostility as found in 1QS:

> Beloved, never avenge yourselves, but leave it to the wrath of God. For it is written, "Vengeance is mine; I will repay, says the Lord." No, "if your enemy is hungry, feed him; if he is thirsty, give him drink, for by so doing you will heap coals of fire upon his head." Do not overcome evil with evil, but overcome evil with good. (Romans 12:19-21, RSV)

Stendahl concluded that Paul's motivation in this passage seemed to have much in common with the Essene outlook. He found little positive regard for the welfare of the "enemy" in these words.[16] On the contrary, in this and other passages in the Catholic Epistles, Stendahl sensed a general attitude of avoidance of outsiders (especially the government), coupled with a fervent hope that divine Retribution would begin soon.

However, when Stendahl turned to the sayings of Jesus in the Sermon on the Mount concerning love for the enemy and prayer "for those who persecute you," he concluded that these sayings were different. He decided that they contained "elements which transcended such an interpretation."[17] Is it anything more than pious prejudice that prompted Stendahl to distinguish the nonretaliation sayings of Jesus from those of Paul and others in the New Testament?

I believe that Stendahl was right to draw the line where he did. Jesus' teachings on nonresistance to evil and love of the enemy mainly occur in the Beatitudes and Antitheses in Matthew 5 (and parallels), and I have the impression that many of these antithetical teachings reflect key points of disagreement between Jesus and other powerful Jewish groups at the time. For example, if we step back and compare Jesus and his followers with the Essenes, we can see a number of ways in which these two groups differed from each other. The Essenes were an exclusive, priestly-oriented, all-male, secret army; as such they were very conscious of each man's rank and office. The Essenes were fanatically concerned about ritual purity; they had intentionally removed themselves as far as possible from all contact with the "sons of Darkness," at least in their central headquarters, and they spent a considerable portion of each day keeping themselves free from ritual im-

---

[15]Stendahl, "Hate, Nonretaliation, and Love," 343-55.

[16]Ibid., 348.

[17]Ibid., 355.

purity. This was to enable them, at a moment's notice, to join with the Messiah(s) and the angelic armies to fight against the Sons of Darkness.

Jesus, on the other hand, publicly gathered a high profile band of men and women around a nucleus of twelve "inner disciples," who were not particularly noted for their ritual fastidiousness. He did not attempt to conceal the Way of Truth from anyone,[18] but publicly warned everyone of the impending Judgment. So far from insisting upon rank and order, he abolished titles and insisted that those who led should be the servants of others. Nor did he dwell on being ready to destroy evil-doers; just the reverse. Many other important differences between Jesus and the Essenes could be mentioned.

Jesus' Nonretaliation Sayings in Matthew

I wish to focus on the last difference mentioned, namely, the prominent note of forgiveness—God's forgiveness—toward Israel's outcasts, found in many of Jesus' parables and actions, as recorded by Matthew. This public offering of forgivensss to sinners outside the elect community is quite the opposite of the Essene outlook.

It is important not to psychologize or sentimentalize this aspect of Jesus' teaching, for these outsiders were rejected for strong reasons. These people were the religiously apathetic, the backsliders, the unbelievers ("harlots"; this word should not be taken sociologically but, as in the Old Testament, as a metaphor for those within Israel who "whored after heathen gods"), chronically immoral people, and, worst of all, those who sold God's People for money, the tax collectors. They had all cut themselves off from the Covenant of Abraham by their chronic sinfulness.

However, in sharp contrast to the Qumran sectarians, but squarely in line with Elijah's task as envisioned in Mal. 4, and as enacted by John the Baptist, Matthew portrays Jesus making numerous efforts to warn these "lost sheep of the house of Israel" of the danger they faced, offering them a sort of eleventh-hour reprieve if they repented and changed their lives. It was as if, and here we encounter solid Pharisaic tradition also, the God of Israel were especially worried about those in Israel who were going to be lost. In a characteristic hyperbole, Jesus says according to one tradition that there will be more joy in Heaven at the recovery of one of these sinners than over the safe entry into the Age to Come of ninety-nine righteous.

---

[18]On the problem posed for this interpretation by the saying of Jesus in Mark 4:11 par., see Joachim Jeremias, *The Parables of Jesus,* 2nd ed. (New York: Scribner's, 1962) 16ff.

Nor is it hard for us to understand why Jesus would have had to defend himself at this point against the outraged protests of these "99 righteous." We can see the same situation today when a governor pardons some axe-murderer or habitual criminal. Protests break out immediately. Policemen ask why they bother to arrest these criminals if the governor is just going to pardon them. Law and order groups write letters to newspapers denouncing the governor's decision. Jesus ran into precisely the same thing. His message of special mercy toward Israel's criminal element clearly offended stricter Jews; certainly the Essenes would have objected. As we can see from the Dead Sea Scrolls, in their eyes the time for mercy was past; God was no longer offering "one last chance." Now it was time for the punishment to begin.

It is in this bias toward mercy for those on Israel's "death row" that we find the source of the generous character of Jesus' counsels regarding nonresistance and nonretaliation. As Stendahl said, Jesus really did call for genuine mercy and nonretaliation, from the heart. This would be poles apart from the Essene nonretaliation based on a secret lust for vengeance. The sayings in Matthew specifically disallow the thought of hatred; "pray for your enemy." Extend God's "come back!"—seventy-times seven times if necessary—for the time is short. Furthermore, I agree with Richard Horsley that the sociological context of these sayings is not some sort of universal brotherhood, but the everyday, common life of the Galilean villages.[19]

But even here Jesus scandalously extended the admonition to be merciful to the hated occupation forces, as we can see from the special case of Matthew 5:41. This saying unambiguously refers to the privilege Roman soldiers had to force local inhabitants to carry their gear for them. The Roman Senate had interposed the reasonable restriction: one "mile" per inhabitant. Here again, Jesus' hyperbole emerges: "What if a Roman soldier orders you to carry his pack? Don't run away; do what he says. Do extra; carry his pack *two* miles!" I see the same intention at work even here. It is as if Jesus were saying: "Do *nothing* that might hinder anyone's reconciliation with the God of Israel." Stated positively: "Do everything you can to help others find (or rediscover) God. There isn't much time left."

The "time" factor, the awareness that there is only a short time left, flavors everything in Matthew. If this all-pervading eschatological expectation be ignored, and Jesus' admonitions not to resist evil are turned into timeless absolutes, they lose all ethical integrity immediately. They sim-

---

[19]See Horsley, "Ethics and Exegesis," 22f.

ply become advice to allow evil to do its work. Stripped of the intense eschatological framework of Matthew, Jesus' teaching, "Do not resist evil," means no more than "let evil do what it will." These teachings were perceived as expressions of God's grace precisely because they were so unexpected. They seemed to indicate a scandalous relaxation of God's Norm, an outrageous disregard for everything Israel had learned about divine justice. Those of us who, centuries and generations later, like to feel gloriously uplifted by these sayings, have certainly lost any sense of their original terrible disregard for normal rules of proper religious behavior. Krister Stendahl aptly described this quality of Jesus' behavior as "messianic license."

How Matthew's Gospel Relates Jesus' Divine Power to Destroy Evil to His Nonretaliation in His Last Days

The discovery of the Essene practice of nonretaliation based on hatred of the outsider should warn us that we are venturing into exceedingly deceptive terrain. But perhaps the Essene material can help us spy out other details, ordinarily overlooked, that also bear on this issue. We will begin by looking at passages unique to Matthew.

The Qumran scroll of *The War Between the Sons of Light and the Sons of Darkness* bears a distinct similarity to the statement recorded only in Matthew 26:51-54, where Jesus says that he can request God to send a huge angel army to defend him from harm, but he is not going to ask for it. This posture of nonretaliation while being confident of angelic power just around the corner seems to resemble rather closely the Essene stance, does it not? Are there any other passages in Matthew that convey the same impression? That say: I am not at the mercy of anyone in what I am about to do, least of all my opponents. I can think of three more:

a. Jesus' explanation to his disciples, stated *on the way to Gethsemane,* that after being crucified and raised he would meet them all in Galilee (26:30-32).

b. The passage in question in which he tells his followers he could call thousands of angels to his defense and instantly stop the arrest, if he wanted to.

c. The way Jesus threatens Caiaphas with divine retribution at the very climax of his Trial (Matt 26:24).

Perhaps a paraphrase of Matthew 26:53f. can express more vividly what these passages intend to convey.

[Jesus turns to the person who has just cut off the ear of the High priest's lieutenant and says,] "Does it seem to you that I am helpless? That I can not request of my Father and He would send me—right now—thousands of angels, to defend me? To fight with your sword is the world's way, futile. But what if I do successfully escape from these men? How would the Scriptures ever be fulfilled, that I must suffer and die so that many are forgiven?''

These three passages all seem intended to reassure the listener (or reader) that Jesus' death was anything but that of a weak, unarmed, impotent man. On the contrary, Matthew repeatedly stresses that Jesus was fully aware of being part of a larger divine plan. As the designated Ruler of Israel in the Age to Come, his present nonresistance and nonretaliation was purposeful, voluntary and, above all, temporary.

However, not everything fits neatly into this interpretation. If Jesus was so confident of his divine destiny, then why does Matthew's narrative mention Jesus' extreme grief in the Garden of Gethsemane? What is the ''Cry of Dereliction'' intended to mean—a cry that was so traumatic to the followers that Matthew records it in two languages?[20] In the Garden scene, Matthew says that, when Jesus went to pray, ''he fell on his face in prayer;'' hardly the normal Jewish posture. The text says that he told his dearest disciples, ''My heart is ready to break with grief'' (26:38 RSV). Why? What was causing him such intense despair? If Matthew's Jesus is elsewhere portrayed as being confident of God's plan, if he is otherwise portrayed as totally certain of divine protection, why does Matthew portray him in such tremendous anguish in Gethsemane and on the Cross? Are these stylistic touches meant to create sympathy for Jesus, as if the Lord dreaded the physical pain that lay ahead? Is it intended to suggest that the Lord feared death? How could that be since He was not going to remain dead? Somehow these descriptions of Jesus' anguish in Matthew do not fit the rest of the picture. They seem strangely jarring.

Finding no way to resolve this puzzle from evidence close at hand, I must beg the reader's indulgence if I go rather far afield for parallels. Perhaps the experiences and writings of Mohandas K. Gandhi and others may help us understand the situation behind the scenes of Matthew's carefully structured narrative. Gandhi's fully worked out, mature strategy of nonviolent resistance may provide some clues to help us piece together the fragments of the story of Jesus' own final moments.

---

[20]Although it is far too complex a question to discuss here, I do not lean toward the ''positive'' interpretation of the Cry from the Cross, whereby it is suggested that as Jesus quoted the opening words of Psalm 22, he meant the whole psalm, particularly its hopeful ending. It may be that Jesus quoted that psalm while on the Cross; the anguish and despair in the Gethsemane scenes convinces me that he was feeling real terror on the Cross, not confident hope (see below).

The Example of Mohandas K. Gandhi

Not long after Gandhi had successfully conducted his first nonviolent protest against the mill industry in Ahmedabad, India, in 1918, he unexpectedly promised the British Viceroy that he would help to recruit 500,000 Indians for the war effort against Germany. When news of this decision reached his faithful millhands, they were doubly shocked and furious. One day he was demanding that they nonviolently resist the British Raj to the death if need be, and the very next he was going around urging everyone to join the British army to fight the Germans! It seemed like a double hypocrisy and he did not get more than a handful of recruits. At first, he was shocked and surprised. But, as he argued heatedly with his followers, an unsuspected side of his millhands began to emerge, one that disturbed him deeply. He began to wonder if the real reason why they did not want to enlist was because they were *afraid to fight in a war.*[21] This caused him to see that his recent success with "peaceful protest" had been founded on little more than rhetoric and fortuitous circumstances.

As this insight cut through his earlier euphoria, Gandhi saw his grandiose hopes for a free and independent India fall to the ground; they had been founded upon a fatal illusion regarding the bravery of the Indian people. Unable to take this crushing blow to all his hopes, he suffered a nervous breakdown.[22] Now he had to endure the agony of realizing that, all along, his wonderful talk about *ahimsa* (nonviolence), within the context of *satyagraha* (the active quest for truth in relationships), had been nothing more than rhetorical flourishes covering up the true weakness and cowardice of his followers.[23]

After he had recovered, Gandhi's subsequent statements about nonviolent resistance differed markedly from his earlier simplistic absolutisms. He began to insist that nonviolence was the most moral form of resistance

---

[21]Erik Erikson, *Gandhi's Truth* (New York: Norton, 1969) 372-78.

[22]Ibid., 371f.

[23]"When friends told me here that passive resistance was taken up by the people as a weapon of the weak, I laughed at the libel, as I called it then. But they were right and I was wrong. With me alone and a few other coworkers it came out of our strength and truly was *satyagraha,* but with the majority it was purely and simply passive resistance that they resorted to, because they were too weak to undertake methods of violence." Ibid., 372.

only if the capacity for violent retribution is truly there as well.[24] He even asserted, for the first time, that there were *ethical limits* to the applicability of nonviolent resistance. He put this in the form of the following paradox:

> There can be nonviolence in violence. This is the big change that has come about [in my thinking]. I had not fully realized the duty of restraining a drunkard from doing evil, of killing a dog in agony or one infected with rabies. In all of these instances, violence is in fact nonviolence.[25]

Thus Gandhi came to the view that nonviolent resistance was morally acceptable *as a strategy of resistance* if and only if it could reasonably be expected to penetrate successfully the hard crust of hatred and estrangement, breaking through to the common humanity beneath. If it succeeded in awakening the pangs of conscience within the opponent, by accepting voluntary suffering at his hands, it was in fact the best and quickest way to work toward better relationships in the future.[26]

But if there was nothing beneath the crust except more hatred, fear and loathing, then unarmed resistance only invited catastrophic violence from the opponent. This is the "mad dog" situation, and one must be prepared to kill as quickly as possible, even while recognizing that it is a tragic situation.[27]

Martin Luther King, Jr.

Let us compare this carefully nuanced position of Gandhi's to another well-known advocate of peaceful opposition to injustice: Martin Luther King, Jr.

There was bitter criticism of King's constant reliance upon nonviolent resistance by Malcolm X and other militant Afro-Americans. He was accused of looking the other way when blatant evidence confronted him that

---

[24]"What am I to advise a man to do who wants to kill but is unable to, owing to his being maimed? Before I can make him feel the virtue of not killing, I must restore to him the arm he has lost. . . . A nation that is unfit to fight cannot from experience prove the virtue of not fighting. I do not infer from this that India must fight. But I do say that India must know how to fight." Ibid., 374.

[25]Ibid.; see further p. 422. He could also see that there had been "violence" in some of his former nonviolent campaigns; see p. 372.

[26]See Erikson's discussion, ibid., 434ff.

[27]Gandhi warned on one occasion that, having learned military discipline and technique from the English, Indians would be more than a match for them when fighting in their own country. "We may even fight the Empire, should it play foul with us!" See ibid., 374; further p. 376.

racial hatred went so deep in certain parts of America that there simply was no underlying sense of common humanity to work with. Being peaceful *and at the same time actively resisting* racial hatred in places like Birmingham, or Selma, or Cicero, just infuriated the racists who lived there, causing them to resort to all sorts of terrible things. As Bull Connor said, "I hope one of them damn niggers does lay down in front of my police car!"

This was the important distinction that King was accused of ignoring: what are the practical and moral limits to nonviolent resistance? What is the larger political context within which illegal, nonviolent resistance is morally acceptable? And when is nonviolent resistance to evil both irrational and immoral? Malcolm X once asked his audience why they were so unwilling to be violent, when Americans all around them were being violent about everything.

> If violence is wrong in America, violence is wrong abroad. If it is wrong to be violent defending black women and black children and black babies and black men, then it is wrong for America to draft us and make us violent abroad in defense of her. And if it is right for America to draft us and to teach us how to be violent in defense of her, then it is right for you and me to do whatever is necessary to defend our own people right here in this country. . . . You can't have a turn-the-other-cheek revolution! There's no such thing as a nonviolent revolution. The only kind of revolution that is nonviolent is the "Negro" revolution. The only revolution in which the goal is loving your enemy is the "Negro" revolution. It's the only revolution in which the goal is a desegregated lunch counter, a desegregated theater, a desegregated park, a desegregated public toilet. You can sit down next to white folks—on the toilet! That's no revolution. . . . Revolution is bloody, revolution is hostile, revolution knows no compromise, revolution overturns and destroys everything that gets in its way. And you, sitting around like a knot on the wall, saying, "I'm going to love these folks no matter how much they hate me." No, you need a revolution. Whoever heard of a revolution where they lock arms . . . singing, "We Shall Overcome?" You don't do that in a revolution! You don't do any singing, you're too busy swinging![28]

It seems evident now that King was able to achieve as much as he did because of a credibility loaned to him by the militant Black Muslims and Black Panthers. The white racists dealing with King knew he was weak, though not lacking in courage, but they also knew that, if they did not come to terms with King and the Southern Leadership Conference or the NAACP, they would soon have to face far more destructive reprisals from armed factions like the Black Panthers. Nor am I aware that King ever fully acknowledged this debt to his more militant Afro-American brothers and sisters.

---

[28]*Malcolm X Speaks: Selected Speeches and Statements* (New York: Grove Press, 1965) 8-9.

The Jewish Tradition of the Death of the Righteous Man

These latter-day parallels shed light on the situation in Matthew in two major respects. First of all, they make it crystal clear that nonretaliation is always a strategy pursued for a definite purpose; it can never be an end in itself, for then it is simply immoral. Therefore, whether it is morally acceptable as a strategy always depends on whether it can reasonably be expected to achieve the purpose in mind, which is reconciliation and renewal of relationships. Otherwise, to be nonretaliatory or to pursue a strategy of nonviolent resistance is morally worse than doing nothing at all because any kind of resistance invariably inflames evil, and if one does not have any coercive measures at hand to constrain the evil thus aroused, it freely wreaks havoc and mayhem, resulting in a net increase of injustice and misery. Matthew's portrayal of Jesus clearly indicates that this important practical and moral limitation to Jesus' nonretaliation was very clearly understood. In a word: Jesus counted on God's violence to set the limits to evil's duration.

Thus considered, we can see how Matthew's portrait of Jesus fits perfectly within an honored Jewish tradition: the death and vindication of the righteous man. George Nickelsburg has observed the close similarities in structure between the Gospel portraits of Jesus and earlier Jewish stories of "the vindication and exaltation of the persecuted righteous one."[29]

Among numerous similar stories Nickelsburg mentions in 1 and 2 Maccabees and Jubilees, I would like to draw attention to the story of Taxo and his sons, recorded in the *Testament of Moses*. Originally written during the period of the persecution under Antiochus Epiphanes, it adopts the Deuteronomic conception of Israel's history (sin-punishment-renewal). Within this context, however, it inserts a new element, drawn from the experience of the generation that returned from Exile (2 Isaiah). If the innocent *voluntarily suffer* (are "punished"), this will serve to excite God's righteous anger, and he will speedily save Israel from her oppressors. Thus "Taxo" says to his sons:

> Let us fast for a three day period and on the fourth day go into a cave . . . There let us die rather than transgress the commandments of the Lord of Lords, the God of our fathers. For if we do this, and do die, our blood will be avenged before the Lord. Then his kingdom will appear throughout the whole creation. Then the devil will come

---

[29]George W. E. Nickelsburg and Michael E. Stone, *Faith and Piety in Early Judaism. Texts and Documents* (Philadelphia: Fortress Press, 1983) 151. See also George W. E. Nickelsburg, *Jewish Literature between the Bible and the Mishnah* (Philadelphia: Fortress Press, 1981) 80-83, 94f., 114ff., 119-21.

to an end; yea, sorrow will be led away with him. (Testament of Moses 9:6-10:1; trans. J. Priest, ed. Charlesworth)

Nickelsburg comments:

They die with an appeal that God will avenge their blood. Taxo's words echo Deuteronomy 32:43,

"Praise his people, O ye nations, for he avenges the blood of his servants and takes vengeance on his adversaries."

The repetition of this theme in 10:2 indicates that God will hear their prayer. Their innocent deaths and their cry for vengeance will trigger the wrath of God and move the drama into its final act [i.e., the Day of Universal Judgment].[30]

The desired effect of Taxo's and his sons' deaths, namely, bringing about the immediate appearance of God's "kingdom" and the destruction of Satan, seems to be precisely the point of Jesus' menacing response to Caiaphas at the climax of his Trial: "[God will let you kill me now] . . . but henceforth you will see the 'Son of Man seated at the right hand of the Power' and 'coming on the clouds of Heaven' " (Matt 26:64, New Jerusalem Bible). As John A. T. Robinson has shown, Jesus was telling the High Priest Caiaphas and everyone else present that they were intentionally being permitted by God to misuse him all they wanted (to give everyone one last chance to repent), but "before long" (*ap' arti*) their positions would be reversed and they would all be before *him*, the Son of Man, and he would be *their* judge.

This story of Taxo and his sons may throw some light on another of Matthew's peculiar stories, namely, the mention, in the middle of the crucifixion account, of the earthquake which caused "the tombs to be opened and the bodies of many holy people to arise from the dead, and, after his resurrection, to appear to a number of people" in Jerusalem (Matt 27: 52f.). Scholars have recognized that this is an explicit, if clumsy, attempt on Matthew's part to link Jesus' resurrection with the general resurrection.[31] But why would Matthew wish to do that?

Perhaps the story of Taxo will give us the solution: Matthew wished to show that God was indeed so totally angered at the brutal death of his Righteous One that he immediately began the great drama of Judgment. First there would be the general resurrection as forecast by Ezekiel, and then the Great Judgment as described by Daniel. The prime clue comes from Taxo and similar traditions, where the suffering righteous one is no

---

[30]Nickelsburg, *Jewish Literature*, 82.

[31]In this passage, Matthew gives in visual narrative form precisely what Paul speaks of in the metaphor: Christ's resurrection was "the first fruits of all who have fallen asleep" (1 Cor. 15:20).

sooner dead than he is *instantly* vindicated by the eruption of these tre-mendous cosmic events, signaling the beginning of the destruction of Sa-tan and the renewal of all creation. This chain of events is invariably said to be *triggered by* the death of the Righteous One.[32]

With this, the final bit falls into place in our puzzle regarding the rela-tionship between Jesus' divine power to retaliate and his self-imposed re-straint and temporary nonresistance to the evil heaped upon him. Now these unique passages in Matthew fit together to present a unified portrait of Je-sus Christ as the suffering/vindicated Righteous King of the Age to Come. It is a firm, clearcut portrayal, full of deep meaning and value in terms of the Jewish apocalyptic context out of which it emerged.

I also mentioned a second conclusion to be drawn from studying these latter-day parallels. The nervous breakdown of Gandhi makes me look more closely at Jesus' final moments. What happened to Jesus? Why did Mat-thew portray him as suffering such anguish? In none of these other writings do I see any mention of *dread* on the part of the suffering/vindicated Righ-teous One prior to his self-sacrifice. There is no sign of grief, anguish, misgiving, uncertainty or despair in the story of Taxo. Josephus records nothing like this about Ben Ya'ir in the last days of Masada. The Tannaitic account of Rabbi Akiba's last moments, reciting the Shema while he was having his flesh pulled off his body with hooks, indicate nothing like de-spair; quite the opposite. Why is Jesus described as being heart-broken in Gethsemane? Even more atypical from the point of view of this tradition is the total absence of any heavenly sign or *bath qol* in response to Jesus' cry from the cross. To be more precise, why does Matthew say that God's answer to Jesus' cry was *silence*?[33]

Luke's Bias Toward an Irenic Portrait of Jesus

The recent study by Josephine Ford demonstrates quite convincingly that the author of the Gospel of Luke went to extraordinary lengths to include traditions depicting Jesus Christ as rising above the rivalries, disputes and

---

[32]This crucial element of the *timing* of God's vindication immediately follow-ing the death of the Righteous One is a feature of several of these apocalypses; see Nickelsburg, *Jewish Literature,* 81f.

[33]This feature of the passion narrative has not, in my knowledge of the history of New Testament interpretation, ever received anything like the powerful un-derstanding given it in the recent novel by Shusaku Endo, *Silence,* trans. W. John-ston (New York: Taplinger, 1980); and worked out fully in his subsequent *A Life of Jesus,* trans. R. A. Schuchert (New York: Paulist Press, 1973); esp. 143ff. and 156ff.

conflicts of early first-century Palestine.[34] Interestingly, an application of
the Two Gospel Hypothesis (instead of the Two Document Hypothesis)
would have made the picture even sharper.

Perhaps I may briefly illustrate. If we look at the process by which Luke
combined certain stories from the first half of Matthew to build the first
part of his own narrative, we can easily see the author methodically shaping a narrative about a peace-loving, irenic Lord. First, Luke starts with
the distinctive Inaugural Sermon and its prominent display of the messianic prophecy from Isaiah, (Luke 4:16-30). Then a few healings are described (drawn from Matt 8:14-17), followed by a redactional passage
mentioning an intended preaching tour, all of which are meant to validate
the original claim: ''The Spirit of the Lord is upon me'' (Luke 4:18).

Having given a brief demonstration of his own divine powers, Luke next
has Jesus begin to pick his disciples. Hence we next encounter the unique
Lukan scene where Jesus chooses his first three disciples. Now accompanied by a small circle of followers, Luke portrays Jesus' activity in a series of healings and a debate. These Luke has carefully picked out of the
abundance of material in Matthew 8, 9 and 12. His purpose in choosing
just these stories is that they have as their common theme the hostile reaction of the Pharisees toward the things Jesus does. So, following the inaugural sermon, Jesus' demonstration of power, and the selection of a few
disciples, Luke has set the stage for the initial series of confrontations between Jesus and his adversaries, the ''scribes and Pharisees.''

Next Luke tells how Jesus enlarges the circle to a core group which he
pointedly names ''the twelve apostles'' (Luke 6:12-16). This is clearly a major turning point in Luke's narrative, for here he describes the creation of the
nucleus of the cult that will later become so important in Acts, that is, in the
history of the mission to the wider world. Appropriately (according to the dic-
tates of hellenistic historiography), on this historic occasion, the Hero makes
a speech to tell everyone what his intentions are. This means that we should
look with especial care at what Luke has decided to put into this address, out
of all the material available to him from Matthew 5, 6 and 7.

The content of Luke's ''Sermon on the Plain'' may be characterized
briefly as follows:

a. Blessing upon the poor and downtrodden (his audience) and Woe to
the rich and powerful (their oppressors).

b. Do not retaliate against those who wrong you, nor condemn them.

c. Be doers of this teaching, not just hearers.

---

[34]See Ford, *My Enemy Is My Guest*.

It is striking to see what Luke has decided to emphasize, out of all the sayings he could have chosen from the Sermon on the Mount. It is quite clear that Luke has put *nonretaliation* and *divine retribution* at the very top of the list of the teachings of the Lord Jesus. In other words, the additional evidence we have generated by using the Two Gospel Hypothesis fits fairly well into Ford's contention that it was Luke's purpose to give a highly slanted, irenic portrait of Jesus Christ.

Luke's Description of the Final Week[35]

Scholars have long recognized that Luke's passion narrative differs from the other Synoptics in a number of ways. Thus we are amply forewarned that Luke placed a very different interpretation upon Jesus' final moments. This, in turn, would mean that he understood the sayings counseling non-retaliation in a different way also. Although this cannot be more than a sketch, let us examine the evidence for this supposition. We will do so by focusing on passages which clearly diverge from Matthew's account.

The entry into Jerusalem scene is notable for Jesus' striking addition of the prediction of the destruction of Jerusalem, with the pivotal saying, "Would that even today you knew the things that make for peace!" (Luke 19:41) The Cleansing of the Temple is too ambiguous for Luke's irenic theme, so he reduces it to two short verses. In fact, what is left is not so much a cleansing as a passing swipe at the Temple (19:45-46). And Luke will have nothing to do with the Cursing of the Fig Tree story.

Moving on to the Garden of Gethsemane scene, we note that Luke has shortened and augmented Matthew's account, joining together the prayer scene and the description of Jesus' arrest. The result intensifies the pathos of Luke's tableau: "Savior set upon by brutal mob while in anguished prayer."

As for the prayer scene itself, Luke's version moves more quickly than Matthew's by removing the three-fold repetition. Luke also introduces the strong term *agonia* (only here in the N.T.) for Jesus' state of mind. The addition of the comforting angel is Luke's revision of the Matthean bit where Jesus says he could call upon legions of angels to defend him if he wanted to. This jars against Luke's irenic Christ portrait, so instead Heaven goes ahead and sends Jesus one angel to *comfort* him; you might call this "defense" of the Lukan variety. If this hypothetical suggestion be correct, this could be another illustration of Luke's recasting of an apocalyptic idea in Matthew into a more well-known, nonapocalyptic, Hellenistic motif.

---

[35]See ibid., 108-35.

The differences between Luke's version of the Trial and Matthew's are numerous and important. I will only mention Luke's version of Jesus' reply to the High Priest (22:69): "From now on the Son of Man will be seated at the right hand of the Power of God." If we did not have Matthew to influence us, we would undoubtedly interpret Luke's version to mean that Jesus counted on being raised, as soon as he had died, to a position of honor in the next world. There need be no apocalyptic assumptions to the answer at all. Nor is there any sign that the High Priest acted as if he had been threatened, because he hadn't.

The Crucifixion in Luke is a gold mine of unique elements. We note first Jesus' word of forgiveness to his tormentors, and second, his answer to the thief who says, "Remember me when you come into your kingly power;" Jesus replies, "Today, you will be with me in Paradise." (Luke 23:34, 42f.)[36] These additions would clearly have told Luke's audience not to worry, that Jesus (a) was in perfect control of the situation, and (b) was that very day going back to "Paradise," a place with which they would have been quite familiar.

The "Cry of Dereliction" recorded by Matthew is nowhere to be seen in Luke's account, nor any reference to Jesus' final wordless scream. Far too ambiguous. In their place Luke depicts a Lord who forgives his tormentors, reassures a fellow sufferer and then dies with a pious prayer on his lips: "Father, into thy hands I commit my spirit;" nonretaliatory to the last. Also omitted is the reference to the resurrection of "the holy ones." Luke has no intention of using Matthew's apocalyptic symbology for interpreting Jesus' resurrection as part of the universal raising of the dead. Accordingly, when Luke begins describing Jesus' resurrection appearances, he breaks cleanly away from the Matthean narrative in order to prepare for the next major part of his writing, the story of the growth of this new cult of Jesus the Savior.

The Tradition Behind Luke's Portrayal of Jesus Christ

What is guiding Luke in making all these changes? Although the Matthean apocalyptic flavor is still undeniably present in many sayings and scenes utilized by Luke, their surrounding context and the general framework of Luke-Acts is in its essence nonapocalyptic. Instead, we encounter a totally different intellectual tradition. As Charles Talbert has convincingly shown, Luke-Acts belongs to the genre of Hellenistic biographies of

---

[36]For the sake of this discussion, I accept Luke 22:43-44 and 23:34 as authentic.

the founders of philosophical schools.[37] Many other scholars have noted this as well, but I would like to draw attention to two in particular that have been largely passed over by our colleagues.

Several years ago, Arnold Toynbee suggested that the skilled narratives of Luke-Acts were composed of a whole series of set-pieces or *tableaux* readily identifiable in contemporary Greco-Roman literature: the Hero is surrounded by a group of trusting but naive disciples; the Hero publicly denounces tyrannical authorities for perverting the ancient laws; the Hero demonstrates extraordinary powers over nature; at the Hero's final meal he is surrounded by disconsolate companions, one of whom leans upon his breast; the Hero is manacled and led through the city streets to jeers and taunts; etc., etc. According to these and other themes, Toynbee gathered a wealth of comparative material.[38]

Even more impressive, in my judgment, is the research of Isadore Levy, who did much to identify the particular philosophical tradition we encounter in Luke-Acts: the *Pythagorean* bios-tradition.[39]

In this tradition, confrontation with tyranny is a prominent feature, often leading to the martyrdom of the Hero. A good example of philosophical martyrdom in Hellenistic Judaism is the story of Eleazar and the Mother

---

[37]His first book set the direction for two later ones: *Literary Patterns, Theological Themes, and the Genre of Luke-Acts* (Missoula MT: Scholars Press, 1974); followed by the very powerful refutation of the Bultmannian school: *What Is A Gospel? The Genre of the Canonical Gospels* (Philadelphia: Fortress Press, 1977) 126. Talbert is currently at work on a new typology of ancient biographies, including the Gospels.

[38]Arnold Toynbee, *A Study of History* (Oxford: Oxford University Press, 1939) 6:376-539, esp. 377-406, where he has collected hundreds of parallels and analogies to Gospel scenes.

[39]Levy's studies on the origin and influence of the Pythagorean tradition have not been sufficiently considered by American biblical scholars. *Recherches sur les sources de la légende de Pythagore,* Bibliothèque de l'école des hautes études. sciences religieuses 42 (Paris, 1926) contains an exhaustive analysis of the references to Pythagoras in the sayings and writings of Herekleitos, Herodotos, Pherekydes, Empedocles, Xenophon, Plato and especially Aristotle. *La Légende de Pythagore de Grèce en Palestine* (Paris, 1927) follows out the later developments of the Pythagorean tradition in the cult brotherhoods in Pontus and Kroton, among the Alexandrian Jews (esp. Philo), among the Hellenized Egyptians, among the Palestinian Pharisees and Essenes, and finally in the Christian Gospels. His final book, *Recherches esséniennes et pythagoriciennes,* Hautes Études du Monde Gréco-Romain 1 (Genève, 1965) contains essays completing earlier discussions.

with her Seven Sons (2 Maccabees 6, 7 and 4 Maccabees). Since 4 Maccabees was probably composed during the first quarter of the first century in one of the coastal cities of Asia Minor,[40] I do not doubt that the author of Luke-Acts as well as his readers were familiar with it.

Moreover, in the tradition of the philosopher-martyr, the posture of nonretaliation was central. The true philosopher never sought to defend himself by force, only through moral persuasion. This conviction rested on the assumption that man's higher nature was rational, and therefore the "higher way" to live was to follow the rational virtues of courage and temperance and justice and freedom; not enslavement to irrational passions. When opposition arose, nonretaliation was the only rational response, and examples and teachings advocating nonretaliation for evil are to be found scattered up and down the philosophical literature, from Socrates to Epictetus.[41] Violent death was viewed with disdain. If the body be destroyed, has anything of value been lost? Plato's eloquent portrait of Socrates' final moments in the *Phaedo* was widely known and admired in this tradition. Scholars have long recognized a number of Orphic and Pythagorean doctrines in Socrates' last dialogue, such as Socrates' picture of the afterworld at the end of the dialogue, or the use of reminiscence as a proof for the preexistence of the soul, and transmigration. So it was that Socrates was quite unafraid to die, since he was convinced that he was going to a far better world. "I know that I am going to other Gods both wise and good, and to men departed who are better than those here. Otherwise I should be wrong in not being grieved at death."[42]

This Pythagorean image of the martyr-philosopher, a man believed in those times to be half divine in origin, rested upon some important assumptions regarding human history. Apart from some rather vague ideas about slowly evolving (or devolving) Ages of the World (from Gold to Silver to Iron), the real time-consciousness of this outlook is best described as static or unchanging. The upper realm of Light and Reason exists forever above, while the earthly realm of Darkness, irrationality and suffer-

---

[40]See most recently H. Anderson, "4 Maccabees," in *The Old Testament Pseudepigrapha,* ed. James Charlesworth (Garden City: Doubleday & Co., 1985) 2:534, 537. Cf. M. Hadas, *The Third and Fourth Books of Maccabees* (New York: Harper & Brothers, 1953) who suggests a date of approx. A.D. 40 and provenance of Antioch, 96, 111.

[41]See W. Klassen, *Love of Enemies* (Philadelphia: Fortress Press, 1984) 12-26 for a collection of references.

[42]*Phaedo* 63B; cf. 107A-114D. See also *Apology* 40E-41D.

ing exists forever here below. In such a two or three-story cosmos, divine men would periodically appear from the realms above to become national champions, commanders of armies, healers of the sick, and religious reformers. They were called "saviors and benefactors of the inhabited world." At death they were thought to be rewarded by being taken back to their original place among the Gods.[43]

This is the thought framework we encounter in Luke-Acts. Largely gone is the Jewish apocalyptic frame of reference found in Matthew, with its impending cosmic Day of Judgment. For Luke-Acts (and this philosophical tradition generally) *death* is the universal time of judgment on each person's life, precisely as described in the unique Lukan parable of Dives and Lazarus. If one's life is filled with suffering and evil in this world, then at death one will go to a place of happiness and freedom from pain: "Paradise." This is precisely the reason Luke's Jesus is able to pronounce a blessing upon all the poor, disenfranchised, outcast, and downtrodden who listen to him in the Sermon on the Plain. At death, they will go to a wonderful abode of angelic bliss. Those who have been oppressing them, on the other hand, "have had their reward" and will go into the place of eternal torment, just as Dives did.

In this context of static-time consciousness, that is, where "the coming of the Kingdom" is not much more than a pious memory, nonretaliation is *the more divine way to act*. When Jesus is asked by one of his disciples as he is about to be arrested, "Shall we use the sword?"—and before he can answer the disciple hacks off someone's ear—Jesus sternly admonishes, "No more of this!" (Luke 22:49-51). At the moment of his own death, Jesus is perfectly nonretaliatory, even forgiving those who were killing him.

In Luke, therefore, Jesus' actions and teachings regarding nonretaliation are all essentially *pedagogical* in intention. Not to strike back is the superior moral way. Luke's Jesus Christ says, "Be ye merciful, even as your Heavenly Father is merciful" (6:36; cf. Matt 5:48). Likewise, Luke portrays Jesus in the Gospel as the perfect martyr, and then in Acts, he portrays Stephen as the first perfect follower (Acts 7). Stephen's final speech before being put to death is full of philosophical themes. Most significant for our purposes is the element where he forgives his killers as he lies dying

---

[43]For numerous examples of this conception, see David Cartlidge and David Dungan, *Documents for the Study of the Gospels* (Philadelphia: Fortress Press, 1980), esp. the introductory essay, "Savior Gods of the Mediterranean World," as well as the prefaces to Philo's *Life of Moses* and Philostratus of Lemnos's *Life of Apollonios of Tyana*.

(Acts 7:60). Of course, a moment before, Stephen—and the reader—has just been granted a vision of the Paradise to which *he* will be privileged to enter in a minute or two (in contrast to all those who are busily stoning him). That is, there is not meant to be any doubt on the reader's part what Stephen thinks will happen to him next, or where he will go in the next world. Moreover, Luke's portrait of Paul fits the same mold.

Finally, Luke's narrative of Jesus' resurrection activities (in Jerusalem, *contra* Matthew) belong to the same outlook. Far from being apocalyptic in meaning, Jesus' resurrection is treated as an isolated miracle in Hellenistic style, indeed, as the miracle *par excellence* founding and validating the new cult. Immediately after being raised, in contrast to Matthew and the other Gospels, Jesus is portrayed as spending "forty days" teaching his disciples many divine truths. Then he is lifted up into Heaven, i.e., to Paradise. Immediately, another divine manifestation descends upon the disciples, giving them the ability to speak foreign languages, an obvious divine assistance in spreading the new cult far and wide.

One aspect of Luke's portrait does not fit the tradition of the martyr-philosopher, however. In Plato's account, on the day Socrates is to die he is serenely confident; it is his disciples who break down in tears. Likewise, when Philostratus speaks of Apollonios in prison and facing death, he portrays him calmly assuring his fellow prisoners that the tyrant can do nothing to him. Again, in 4 Maccabees there is no mention of fear or anxiety on the part of Eleazar, the Seven Sons, or the Mother. Whence then comes this reference to Jesus' *agonia* in the Garden of Gethsemane in Luke? Obviously from Matthew, but, interestingly enough, it clearly does not accord at all well with the philosophical tradition underlying Luke's portrait of Jesus.

Conclusions

This essay has attempted to demonstrate the importance of the specific gospel orientation for understanding the particular meaning-in-context of Jesus' counsels regarding nonretaliation in Matthew and Luke.

In Matthew, Jesus' teachings and example are part of a consistent pattern according to which Jesus Christ is portrayed as offering a last-minute pardon to all who would repent and turn to God. Unexpected, scandalous to some, it represented a loving entreaty on the part of Israel's God to come back before it was too late. Likewise, in Matthew's description of Jesus' last days, Jesus did not retaliate against those seeking to destroy him, although Matthew makes it clear that Jesus could have. Instead, he suffered, while consistently warning those abusing him of God's revenge. As such, Matthew's picture of Jesus Christ rests squarely within the apocalyptic

Jewish tradition (going back to II Isaiah) of the suffering/vindicated Righteous One.

Luke's portrayal of Jesus Christ belongs to an entirely different intellectual and religious tradition: the Pythagorean bios-literature. This popular and wide-spread tradition contained within it the ideal of the martyr-philosopher who lived a life of perfect self-control, poverty, freedom of speech, courage, justice and piety toward God or the Gods. Whenever this person encountered injustice, impiety, oppression or corruption, he fearlessly pointed it out in public, regardless of the cost to his person. If attacked for it, he disdained to retaliate in kind, preferring to win over his enemies (or reduce them to silence) by moral persuasion. If unsuccessful, he cheerfully suffered torture and/or death in the confidence that he was immediately going to a far better world anyway, while those persecuting him would be severely punished in the next world for their sins.

Politically speaking, Matthew's portrait is nationalistic (with some universalist overtones), and apocalyptic; Israel's God will come soon to violently punish evil. Luke's portrait is universalist, that is, individualistic, and only vaguely apocalyptic. In Luke, the God of the universe judges all people at death to see what fate they deserve. In Matthew's context, Jesus' acts of forgiveness and nonretaliation are God's last-minute grace toward ''the lost sheep of the House of Israel.'' In Luke, the same stories become the vehicle for teaching a morally superior (i.e., pleasing to God) way of life for all who want to be rewarded with Paradise after death. Thus Luke consistently softens the harsh apocalyptic edges of Matthew's stories, removing ambiguous elements whenever he can. At this point, we are in a position to suggest an answer to Daube's question as to when the softening of Jesus' violence (in the Cleansing) first began: with the Gospel of Luke.

In both cases, the larger context, that is God's corresponding action, is in clear evidence. Gandhi is particularly instructive in this regard because he worked out a nonmetaphysical, ethical context, composed of a mixture of psychological and political considerations. *Any discussion recommending the adoption of Jesus' counsels on nonretaliation that does not include a careful discussion of the larger ethical or metaphysical context within which the nonretaliation makes ethical sense, is a half-truth and becomes the functional equivalent of recommending collusion with injustice and evil.*

On comparing the two, we may marvel at Luke's skill in transposing the stark and gripping Matthean portrait of Jesus Christ, Son of David, into concepts and symbols more accessible to the wider Hellenistic-*oikoumene*. This task of transposing is always fraught with profound difficulties and pitfalls, as the history of any missionary endeavor amply reveals. On the other hand, thanks to Divine Providence, this is also a task wherein the root tradition receives great riches in return, as the new is grafted into the old, producing hybrids possessing astonishing power and insight. Today's far-flung endeavors at "indigenizing the Gospel" can attest to that. At any rate, that is what happened in this case. Luke introduced Hellenistic philosophical concepts into the very heart of the early Christian apocalyptic kerygma, eventually producing tremendous results in western religious history.

Finally we noted that neither Matthew's apocalyptic tradition nor Luke's philosophical tradition had any place for the attested tradition of Jesus' anguish and grief as he faced torture and death. I have no other recourse but to suggest that here we may have a most poignant historical reminiscence, one which jars against both kinds of triumphalist image, describing Jesus' actual anguish when confronted by I do not know what terrors. Not least traumatic would have been the cowardice and treachery of his own closest friends. Choosing the path of nonretaliation opens one to fearful risks.[44] Perhaps we can glimpse, in spite of the Gospel writers' impressive faith portraits, Jesus' own fear and trembling.

---

[44]My father used to tell this story about the time when he came the closest to getting shot in all his years as a missionary. It was 1941, and he was still in China although the rest of the family had gone home a year earlier. He was free to roam about since the Japanese had not yet declared war on America. One day he was on his way to deliver a message or some medicines through Japanese lines in Shanghai to another part of the city. The errand was not entirely without danger, since foreigners were being shot without provocation. As he walked along, he happened to glance into a store window and admired the carvings inside. Then he noticed in the glass of the window that a Japanese soldier had started across the street toward him, and was cocking his rifle. "For a split second, I felt terrified. Then I remembered Jesus' example. I turned around, looked the Japanese soldier straight in the eyes and said in Chinese, "Peace, brother." He faltered and a startled look appeared on his face. "You are Christian?" he asked. "Yes," said my father. "Peace, brother," the Japanese soldier said, and held out his hand in greeting.

AGAPE AND IMITATION OF CHRIST

Birger Gerhardsson

It is rather common today for systematic theologians and moral philosophers to complain about those of us who are biblical scholars. In their sight we are very good a taking the biblical texts apart but not much interested in what to do with the pieces.

To a certain degree this reaction is understandable. The great word within modern biblical scholarship is analysis, not synthesis. We find it natural to study the individual books of the Bible, the individual blocks within the different books, and the individual texts within the blocks. This work must be done. Harmonizing has been one of the most characteristic features of Bible interpretation ever since the Early Church; Christian theology of an earlier day has not taken the pluralism of the Bible seriously enough. This we try to do today, and we must do it; the task is inescapable. And—if I may turn from duty to reward—we can also see with our own eyes how much exegesis can be enriched if we respect the diversity of the material and make it really show.

On the other hand, we must also listen to the accusation that we walk away, leaving nothing but pieces on the table. Every university discipline has a duty to seek the cooperation of other disciplines. There are important aspects of knowledge that can only be gained through cooperation between two or more disciplines. Furthermore, we must make sure that we do not leave lacunas between the disciplines or neglect borderline areas. Moreover, we all share a common responsibility for the world outside universities and seminaries.

It is hardly unreasonable to expect exegetes to bear in mind such broader concerns and to make their own contribution, both in synthesizing the results of their narrowly focused studies so that they can become parts of a larger whole, and in making suggestions as to how those results can be given practical effect.

It is my firm conviction that all *basic* research must be totally free, including research within the biblical field. Scholarship must acknowledge the ideal of working without control and inhibitions from any ideology, be it religious or non-religious. This ideal can, of course, never be reached totally and fully within the *Geisteswissenschaften,* but we must do what we can; and there is, in fact, a very great difference between those who strive to reach this ideal and those who do not even acknowledge it.

Because of the hard rules of the game, however, basic research leaves much undone. Therefore it must be supplemented by applied research and by other types of intellectual work on religious and existential questions; and it is a reasonable demand that even we as biblical scholars try to make our contribution to this wider area of work.

This article is dedicated to my old friend Bill Farmer. He has never been a dusty closet-scholar, isolated from the world outside the academy. Therefore I think my subject will be of some interest to him.

Unifying Elements in New Testament Ethics

In what follows I will try to say something about the contribution New Testament scholarship can make to the synthetical work on normative ethics, primarily Christian ethics. The New Testament material is not at all as diverse as the Old Testament material, but it is still diverse enough. Can we find unifying elements?

There are, of course, in the New Testament books themselves topics and patterns which overarch, and are capable of bringing order to, the disparate material. When Paul, for example, provides a list of positive qualities and activities and calls them "the fruit of the Spirit" and a further list of qualities and activities—this time negative—and calls them "the works of the flesh" (Gal 5:19-23), he indicates that these qualities and activities (together, presumably, with others like them) are closely linked with each other and can be classed together under overarching, unifying principles. Thus the text material itself contains synthesizing and structuring elements. Our task is to study such elements and examine case by case both their content and their extent; we may then discover how they relate to each other, how they can be seen and worked together to provide a complete picture. There is, it seems to me, no need to end up with a baffling plurality when we take seriously the diversity found in our texts.

In what follows I intend to discuss two of the synthesizing elements in the ethical teaching of the New Testament: "agape" (love) and "imitation of Christ." Both motifs are basic, central and comprehensive; both can be used as systematizing factors. Furthermore, they are not theoretical principles; each represents a kind of *total attitude,* if I may use the word "attitude" as the psychologists do to refer to a general inner disposition, by which feelings, willing, thinking, and doing are integrated so that a person's reactions and actions gain a characteristic coherence. Moreover, while both agape and imitation of Christ are individual attitudes, they are at the same time eminently social: fellowship, community, and society are part of the picture. Finally, both are in one way firm—they have a set of typical features—and in another way very flexible—they may vary from individual to individual and from situation to situation, within some limits. This means that they do not counteract variety; rather they inspire variety, an organic variety.

Agape

Let me start with the agape-synthesis; I am going to dedicate most of my space to that. Agape—"love"—is a rather difficult conception, but reflections and discussions about this attitude started early, and so did attempts to find useful linguistic expressions to indicate what this attitude meant. The teaching about agape in the New Testament writings and in Early Christianity ties into an ongoing debate on love among Jewish scribes and sages already at the beginning of our era.

I shall mention some of the *different attempts at presenting the agape-attitude* to be found in the New Testament writings.

We can begin with what is elementary, for love: the verb "to love" (*'ā-hab*, ἀγαπᾶν), and the noun "love" (*'ahăbāh*, ἀγάπη). Early Christianity could adopt these terms from the holy scriptures and a rich Jewish expositional tradition; they were embodied in sentences commanding the right attitude toward God and fellow human beings.[1]

There are indications that Jewish teachers at the beginning of our era had started discussing what in fact "love for God" means. As reflections became more intense, the need was felt for being more precise and for making distinctions on points where the usage of the ancient biblical texts was rather vague. Attempts were now made at defining, for instance, the difference between "to love God" and "to fear God."[2] Such Jewish debates preceded the New Testament teaching about agape.

As a *second* attempt at describing agape I would like to mention a number of "agape-definitions" or "agape-paraphrases" which we find in the Pauline writings (the genuine ones!). These include negative expressions:

μὴ ζητεῖν τὸ ἑαυτοῦ σύμφορον, "not to seek one's own advantage," 1 Cor 10:33,
μὴ ζητεῖν τὸ (τὰ) ἑαυτοῦ, "not to seek one's own (good)," 1 Cor 10:24, 13:5;
cf. Phil 2:21,

---

[1]On "love" in the Old Testament material, see G. Wallis et al., "אַהֲבָה, אָהֵב," *Theologisches Wörterbuch zum Alten Testament* (Stuttgart: Kohlhammer, 1973) 1:108-28; ET: *Theological Dictionary of the Old Testament*, vol. 1, rev. ed. (Grand Rapids MI: Eerdmans, 1977) 99-117.

[2]See R. Sander, *Furcht und Liebe im palästinischen Judentum*, BWANT 4, 16 (Stuttgart: Kohlhammer, 1935); A. Buechler, *Studies in Sin and Atonement in the Rabbinic Literature of the First Century* (New York: KTAV, 1967) 119-211; A. Nissen, *Gott und Liebe im antiken Judentum*, WUNT 15 (Tübingen: Mohr, 1974) 192-219.

μὴ σκοπεῖν τὰ ἑαυτοῦ, "not to look to one's own (interests)," Phil 2:4,
μὴ ἑαυτῷ ἀρέσκειν, "not to please oneself," Rom 15:1-3.

Such negative expressions are normally followed by a positive contrasting
element: "but to seek the good of others (as well)," or something similar.
Even the formula

τῷ πλησίον κακὸν μὴ ἐργάζειν, "to do no wrong to the neighbor," Rom 13:10,

and

ἀλλήλων τὰ βάρη βαστάζειν, "to bear one another's burdens," Gal 6:2,

might belong to this category.

These formulas describe the right attitude toward one's fellow-beings.
They seem to be used by Paul to define or paraphrase the command about
love for one's neighbor. It would be an interesting task to trace the genetic
background of these formulas in Hellenistic and Hellenistic-Jewish thought
on ethical duties—I do not think this has been done properly to date[3]—but
I cannot do this now.[4]

The *third* attempt is the familiar device of juxtaposing the two ancient
biblical commandments about love as a piece of catechism. From the wel-
ter of commandments in the Torah one lifts out the two commands about
love for God (Deut 6:5) and love for neighbor (Lev 19:18), and uses these
two as a general summary. This combination seems to begin within Hellenistic Judaism and to be inspired by Hellenistic thought. The Greeks had
a neat formula for human duties toward the gods and one's fellow humans:
"piety and righteousness" (εὐσέβεια καὶ δικαιοσύνη) or "piety and
love for humans" (εὐσέβεια καὶ φιλανθρωπία).[5] Once one has heard
this handy combination, one can easily lift the two commandments about

---

[3]It is quite remarkable how little attention these "definitions" receive not only
in the commentaries ad locibus but also in works on the love commandments or
on New Testament theology.

[4]See further my book, *The Ethos of the Bible* (Philadelphia: Fortress Press, 1981)
63-92. For the theme "the law of Christ," cf. H. Schürmann, "Das Gesetz des
Christus (Gal 6,2)," *Neues Testament und Kirche* (Wien: Herder, 1974) 282-300.
From the vast literature about love in the New Testament, I want to mention A.
Nygren, *Den kristna kärlekstanken genom tiderna. Eros och agape,* 2 vols.
(Stockholm: Diakonistyrelsen, 1930-1936) 1; and C. Spicq, *Apapè dans le Nou-
veau Testament. Analyse des textes,* EBib, 3 vols. (Paris: Gabalda, 1957-1959).

[5]See K. Berger, *Die Gesetzesauslegung Jesu. Ihr historischer Hintergrund im
Judentum und im Alten Testament,* WMANT 40 (Neukirchen-Vluyn: Neukirchener Verlag, 1972) 143-66.

love for God and love for neighbor out of the Torah and make a corresponding summary.

A striking fact is that we do not find these two commandments expressly put together—expressly quoted together—in the rabbinic literature or in other Hebrew or Aramaic writings extant from antiquity. That may be an accident, however (and one which a discovery of new texts might alter), because there was a good basis for this combination. Both impressed the same attitude, agape. And they had a characteristic term in common. The learned scribes and rabbis used to combine scriptural commandments which had an important term in common and interpret them together. In this case we can see for ourselves in the Hebrew text that the two commandments both contain the consecutive form *wĕ'āhabtā,* "and you shall love." In the whole Hebrew Bible this consecutive form is to be found only in the commands of love for God (Deut 6:5, 11:1) and for one's neighbor (Lev 19:18)—as well as in Leviticus 19:34, where the sphere within which love is to be shown is extended to include "the stranger who sojourns with you." Therefore I do not think that Jesus was the first in Israel to make this combination.[6] In any case, when this combination was made, the result was a very useful thumb-rule for the right attitude of life: agape.

This attempt we find in all three of the synoptic Gospels (Mark 12:18-34; Matt 22:34-40; Luke 10:25-28). Moreover, in the case of Matthew, the rule has been extended still further; we will return to this point.

Among the synoptics, Matthew is most given to ethical reflection. In his Gospel we can find many different approaches to the problem: what is agape? I want to draw the reader's attention to three of them. In my own presentation they make up items 4, 5, and 6.

My *fourth* example is the so-called "golden rule," as we find it in the Sermon on the Mount, Matthew 7:12: "Whatever you wish that men would do to you, do so to them" (RSV). (The saying is preserved in Luke as well, but there [6:31] as one rule among others.)

We ourselves would hardly connect this sentence with the agape-motif spontaneously, but we know that the scribes and the rabbis did so, and we

---

[6]B. Gerhardsson, *The Good Samaritan—the Good Shepherd?,* ConNT 16 (Lund: Gleerup, 1958) 6. Note that in Luke 10:27 it is the "lawyer" who combines the two commands. For the discussion about this among Jewish scholars, see D. Hagner, *The Jewish Reclamation of Jesus. An Analysis and Critique of Modern Jewish Study of Jesus* (Grand Rapids MI: Zondervan, 1984) 143-44.

know why.[7] They took the golden rule as an exposition of the commandment, "You shall love your neighbor as yourself" (Lev 19:18). It was not
very farfetched to do so, especially since they sometimes chose to read the
Hebrew text: "You shall love your neighbor; (he is) as you" (*wĕ'āhabtā
lĕrēă'kā - kamokā*). If one reads it in this way it is quite natural to borrow
the golden rule, which is known in much ancient wisdom,[8] and use it as a
practical explication.[9]

Even the version of the golden rule in Matthew 7:12[10] may have been
conceived as a practical exposition of the commandment about love for
one's neighbor. Moreover, it is meant as a handy summary of the holy
scriptures as well; the verse continues: "for this is the law and the prophets." In other words, this is what the holy scriptures are all about. Such a
claim provides a link between this statement and the declaration about agape
in Matthew 22:37-40 (my next example).

The *fifth* attempt in my list is the hermeneutic program we find in Matthew 22:37-40. What we have in this Matthean text is not just a popular,
catechetic summary of the sacred scriptures, but rather a very sophisticated program for how, according to Matthew, the innumerable individual
items in the ancient holy books are to be interpreted and applied in the
Church. What the Matthean Jesus is saying here about agape is (a) that the
command about love for God is first in rank, (b) that the command about
love of neighbor ranks second, and (c) that "all the law and the prophets"
depend (κρέμαται) on these two commandments. This is a deliberate sophisticated hermeneutic program, formulated with the aid of technical terms
from the scribal-rabbinic tradition. The meaning is that the individual

---

[7]See *Targum du Pentateuch,* trans. R. Le Déaut, SC 245, 256, 261, 271, 282;
6 vols. (Paris: Cerf, 1978-1981) 2.443 ad Lev 19:18. Cf. I. Abrahams, *Studies in
Pharisaism and the Gospels,* Library of Biblical Studies (New York: KTAV, 1967)
18-29. Pertinent rabbinic material in H. L. Strack, P. Billerbeck, *Kommentar zum
Neuen Testament aus Talmud und Misrasch,* 6 vols. (München: Beck, 1922-1961)
1:353-63, 905-908.

[8]Cf. A. Dihle, *Die goldene Regel. Eine Einführung in die Geschichte der antiken und frühchristlichen Vulgärethik* (Göttingen: Vandenhoeck & Ruprecht,
1962).

[9]Another factor as well invited reflections along these lines: the rationale for
loving the stranger given in Lev 19:34, which reads: "And you shall love him as
yourself; for you were strangers in the land of Egypt" (RSV). See also Deut 10:19.

[10]For further literature on the golden rule—and for a good interpretation as well—
see most recently U. Luz, *Das Evangelium nach Matthäus,* EKK 1/1 (Zürich:
Neukirchener Verlag, 1985) 387-94.

commandments in the Torah (and in the prophetical writings) are to be interpreted as concrete expressions of the love demand—*descendants,* as it were—of the two love commandments.[11]

We can see this program put into practice in the Sermon on the Mount, in the so-called antitheses (Matt 5:17-48). Here, we may observe what follows when specific demands from the Old Testament are interpreted as "depending on" the two love commandments. The Matthean Jesus quotes a series of individual, concrete commandments from the Torah in their traditional, plain meaning: "You have heard that it was said to the men of old . . . " Then his own declaration follows: "But I say to you that . . . , " and we get a new, profound interpretation in which the command has been transformed into a demand for a total attitude, governed by an unreserved love for God and for one's neighbor: agape. Jesus not only sharpens the commandments; he changes their character, and makes them into agape-demands.[12]

What is remarkable about this synthesis is that it takes into account *all the concrete commands in the books of the Old Testament*—both the wealth and the specificity of the material—without falling into the trap of casuistic atomism. The demands are all placed under an overarching principle which changes their character without, however, rendering them abstract or undefined.

My *sixth* example is a midrashic interpretation of the commandment about love for God with heart, soul, and strength (Deut 6:5). This command has a plain meaning, which is not difficult to grasp: you shall love God without restrictions, with your whole being. Jewish interpreters had, however, even before New Testament times, started on a fascinating way of "deep-reading" the scriptures and scrutinizing their wording in order to find additional teaching, secrets hidden in the details of the texts—in short, midrashic exegesis. In the case of the commandment about love for God, questions such as the following were discussed:[13]

---

[11]See further my article, "The Hermeneutic Program in Matthew 22:37-40," *Jews, Greeks and Christians* (Leiden: Brill, 1976) 129-50.

[12]See "The Hermeneutic Program," 141-43. For other aspects, cf. H. D. Betz, "The Hermeneutical Principles of the Sermon on the Mount (Matt 5:17-20)," *Essays on the Sermon on the Mount* (Philadelphia: Fortress Press, 1985) 37-53.

[13]I allow myself a good deal of simplification here. See further my book, *The Testing of God's Son (Matt 4:1-11 & Par),* ConBNT 2:1 (Lund: Gleerup, 1966) 71-76; and my article "The Parable of the Sower and its Interpretation," NTS 14 (1967-1968) 167-93.

a. What does it mean, more exactly, to love God "with your whole heart" (*bĕkol lĕbābĕkā*)? The answer was given: it means that your heart—the center of your personality—must not be divided before God or "smooth," that is, hypocritical. Even the evil inclination in your heart—the animal instincts—must obey the will of God. Hunger and thirst, lust for procreation or sensual pleasures, etc., must not seduce you to transgress the commandments of God.

b. What does it mean to love God "with your whole soul" (*bĕkol naphshĕkā*)? The usual answer was: "even if he takes away your soul (your life)." The danger or threat of death must not lead you to apostatize. Here the duty of martyrdom was expressed.

c. "With your whole strength" (*bĕkol mĕ'ōdĕkā*)—what does it mean? Answer: It means "with your whole *māmôn*," i.e., your possessions, your wealth, your might, all your assets apart from your life and your body. Thus you must submit even your strivings for wealth and power to the will of God. *Mamon* must not separate you from God.

This kind of exegesis had produced a profound and learned interpretation of the ancient commandment about love for God. This particular interpretation seems to have been cultivated especially by Pharisaic scribes and their successors, the rabbis.[14] Jesus and Early Christianity probably derived it from this source.

We find in the New Testament many vestiges of this more sophisticated interpretation of the commandment about love for God. Jesus seems to have been familiar with it and to have made use of it in his teaching. Paul knew about it and used it in an independent way. In Mark and Luke a number of pericopes appear in which this interpretation is formative, but one gets the impression that neither Mark nor Luke was himself aware of this pattern. John has nothing but fragments of it. It is above all in the Matthean tradition that this scribal interpretation of the greatest commandment in the Torah has been used in a fascinating way as an instrument for deep reflection and intelligent revision of many texts in the Gospel tradition.[15]

---

[14]Cf. *The Testing*, 71-76. It is, however, possible that the triad *da'at, kôaḥ, hôn* in the Dead Sea Scrolls (1QS 1:11-13, 3:2; cf. CD 13:11) reflects a similar interpretation of the Shema'; it is hard to see whence it could have been derived otherwise. Thus M. Miyoshi, "Das jüdische Gebet Šema' und die Abfolge der Traditionsstücke in Lk 10-13," *Annual of the Japanese Biblical Institute* 7 (Tokyo: Yamamoto Shoten, 1981) 77-84.

[15]For literature, see my *The Origins of the Gospel Traditions* (Philadelphia: Fortress Press, 1979) 93-94.

This particular attempt at indicating what agape is provides us with a more comprehensive and synthetic picture of its essence than the other ones do. Here we can see that numerous logia and parables in the teaching of Jesus—and not only those in Matthew—belong together and that it is possible for us to arrange them in a certain order, grouping many of them around a center and extracting from them an ethical teaching which we would hardly see otherwise. Most of the synoptic logia and parables involve a concern for elucidating the ideal attitude toward God and humankind and in the light of this interpretation we can organize them in an organic way, if not into a system at least into a kind of mosaic. Or, we might say that the interpretation provides a set of spotlights, illuminating a common area. Heart, soul, and *mamon* each attract a cluster of sayings of Jesus, and all of these can now be seen to elucidate agape. With this pattern in mind we may try to use even the individual concrete sayings of Jesus as building blocks for New Testament ethics and as an aid for our work in the field of normative ethics for today. We do not need to end up in incurable atomism. Furthermore, many of the narrative texts in the gospels can be read as illustrations of the agape which stands the test when heart, soul, and possessions are measured. Nor, for that matter, is there anything to keep us from organizing many of the admonitions in the epistles by the same principles. And, naturally, this applies as well to parts of the ethical material of the Old Testament.

The *seventh* attempt is the Johannine contribution: we may call it "God-love."[16] Ethical reflection in the Johannine writings does not show much interest in concrete ethical questions. Everything is concentrated in a great, focused pondering of the secrets of agape, which is here understood as "God-love": a mysterious intertwining of God's own love and the love for God. Themes like the Father's love for the Son and the Son's love for the Father, their love for us and our love both for them and the brethren are interwoven. Sharp distinctions cannot be made here, but I want to mention three characteristics.

---

[16]On the ethical dimension of the Johannine views, see, besides the commentaries, L. Dewar, *An Outline of New Testament Ethics* (Philadelphia: Westminster Press, 1949) 183-219; R. Schnackenburg, *Die sittliche Botschaft des Neuen Testaments,* Handbuch der Moraltheologie 8, 2nd ed. (München: Heuber, 1962) 247-80; T. B. Maston, *Biblical Ethics: A Guide to the Ethical Message of the Scriptures from Genesis through Revelation* (1967; reprint: Macon GA: Mercer University Press, 1982) 211-44; H. D. Wendland, *Ethik des Neuen Testaments. Eine Einführung,* GNT 4 (Göttingen: Vandenhoeck & Ruprecht, 1970) 109-22; J. T. Sanders, *Ethics in the New Testament: Change and Development* (Philadelphia: Fortress Press, 1975) 91-100.

a. The strong God-centering of agape. It is only in the Johannine tradition that the step has been taken to the statement "God is agape" (1 John 4:8, 16). For the Johannine circle the secret of agape is a vital part of the questions who God is and how God works: God's very essence is agape.[17]

b. Agape's character of a deep, "mystical" fellowship, a pulsating unity between the Father, the Son and believers; they "are" in one another, they "abide" in each other.[18]

c. The clear expressions for the conviction that God's love precedes our love and is its source and driving force. Here Christ is not primarily a demanding model for imitation but the highest expression of God's love for us; here we meet the clearest New Testament statements about the primacy of God's love: "In this is agape, not that we loved God but that he loved us . . . " (1 John 4:10). I think it is fair to say that none of the other models is *intrinsically* guarded against legalism, but the Johannine "God-love" is. Of course, the Pauline ethical teaching—taken as *a totality*—is well guarded against legalism; but as to Matthew, I am afraid that his ethical teaching is rather susceptible to this danger.[19] In comparison with Paul and John he is weak in this regard.

Since these seven examples all relate to agape, it can hardly be illegitimate to combine them—and other statements about agape as well—into a larger synthesis, provided one is aware of and sensitive to the problems involved. Such a synthesis can then be related to other syntheses, such as Paul's talk of the "fruit of the Spirit" (which, in turn, is linked with other New Testament texts discussing the role of the Spirit in the Christian life). Here, however, I will discuss only one of the other syntheses and see how it relates to agape.

Imitation of Christ

Now to this second synthesis: "imitation of Christ." I am a Lutheran and we in the Lutheran tradition have an inherited mental reservation against

---

[17]Cf. Nygren, *Den kristna* 1:122-26.

[18]Cf. J. Heise, *Bleiben: Menein in den johanneischen Schriften*, Hermeneutische Untersuchungen zur Theologie 8 (Tübingen: Mohr, 1967) and M. L. Appold, *The Oneness Motif in the Fourth Gospel*, WUNT 2,1 (Tübingen: Mohr, 1976).

[19]A revealing symptom is that Matthew can say about "the golden rule" that "this is the law and the prophets" (7:12) and about the two love commandments that "all the law and the prophets" depend on them (22:37-40). In both cases not only the law but also the prophets are summarized in *commands about human behavior.*

the motif "imitation of Christ."[20] Martin Luther saw two great dangers with this motif:

First, it can easily displace the adequate Christian attitude to Christ. If one takes Jesus primarily as a model and sees one's own role as imitating him, then one's own struggle of faith and ethics becomes paramount. In that case the decisive message of the New Testament has been obscured; the insight that the gospel is first of all a *gift* to us, not a demand, and that Christ is our Savior, not primarily our teacher or inspirer. That is why Luther saw the Gospel itself threatened by the imitation motif.

The second risk is that the task of imitation hardens into stereotyped forms; a set of specific virtues and actions make up the imitation of Christ, while we lose sight of other important attitudes, perhaps including even the most important point in Christian ethics: the heart's living openness to God. Luther saw how such a selective program can in fact become a refined means for our *defense* against God, a defense against God's total claim, and against his basic offer as well.[21]

It has been common since Immanuel Kant to formulate a similar objection in this way: imitations are never the same as the genuine article. An imitative ethos is an ethos of second rate. A blameless ethical action must have its start within the acting subject itself; it must be autonomous. To imitate somebody else, even if it is the Christ, is to take on a borrowed dress; it is not genuine moral action.

We do not, I believe, escape from this dilemma by drawing (with many theologians) a distinction between a (dubious) "imitation" and a (justified) "discipleship" (*Nachfolge*). On the other hand, I believe that we can counteract misinterpretation and misuse of this kind if we see that the New Testament references to Christ's example as a rule are references to his *agape*. To imitate Christ is to make his *agape-attitude* one's own.

---

[20]Especially among Lutheran exegetes and theologians it is customary to make a clear distinction between the motif of discipleship in the gospels and that of imitation in Paul. See especially H. D. Betz, *Nachfolge und Nachahmung Jesu Christi im Neuen Testament,* BHT 37 (Tübingen: Mohr, 1967). Like E. Larsson, *Christus als Vorbild. Eine Untersuchung zu den paulinischen Tauf- und Eikontexten,* ASNU 23 (Lund: Gleerup; Copenhagen: Munksgaard, 1962), I believe the two motifs can and should be seen together.

[21]For literature, see E. Larsson, *Christus,* 9; and cf. G. Wingren, "Was bedeutet die Forderung der Nachfolge Christi in evangelischer Ethik?" *TLZ* 75 (1950): 385-92.

Let me mention some telling examples from Paul, beginning with Philippians 2:6-11, the so-called *kenōsis*-passage.[22] There Christ is presented as a model for imitation, the one who made his choice already in a preexistent state and then carried out his decision on earth, even unto death. In the sentence which precedes this reference to this example of Christ, Paul says expressly what he has in mind here: the principle "to look not only to one's own interests, but also to the interests of others" (v. 4). That is—again—a paraphrastic description of agape. Christ's obedience in the *kenōsis*-passage in Philippians 2 is thus an example of exemplary agape. For that reason Christ's work can be taken as a model for the apostle and for other Christians, although they themselves are certainly no saviors.

In Romans 15:1-3 Paul makes use of another agape-paraphrase and illustrates it with the behavior of Christ: we ought "not to please ourselves; let each of us please his neighbor for his good, to edify him. For Christ did not please himself . . . " (RSV).

Even in 1 Corinthians 10:33-11:1 we find an agape-paraphrase side by side with a reference to the example of Christ: "not seeking my own advantage . . . Be imitators of me, as I am of Christ" (RSV).

These examples from Paul may suffice.[23] He is not the only one in the New Testament to present Christ as a model to be imitated. This way of conveying ethical wisdom and ethical exhortation we find in most New Testament books: Matthew, Mark, the Lukan and Johannine writings, 1 Peter. In these books as well we can see that this motif is not anchored in accidental features of Jesus' behavior or way of life, but that it is concentrated on Christ's agape-attitude, even though this is not stated so clearly as in Paul.

I think my examples have shown that agape and imitation of Christ are not two unrelated elements in the ethical teaching of the Bible. They belong together; in one sense they are identical. This must be kept in mind for the exposition of each of these motifs in the New Testament texts: they can mutually elucidate each other. The result will be an ethical model which is both quite concrete and governed by one simple basic principle. And, as we have already noted, such a model can be further developed when

---

[22]Against a rather massive opinion among scholars H. Riesenfeld has recently pointed out, in my opinion correctly, that Phil 2:6-11 is not a proper "hymn" but rather "ein rhetorisch geformter christologischer Lehrstück," Unpoetische Hymnen im Neuen Testament?, *Glaube und Gerechtigkeit,* Rafael Gyllenberg in memoriam (Åbo, 1983) 155-68.

[23]See further *The Ethos,* 72-74 and 122-26.

other New Testament syntheses, such as the role of the Spirit in the Christian life, are taken into account.

Concluding Remarks

I have spoken out of a tradition which has reservations about the imitation motif—theological hesitations, transmuted into Kant's stress on autonomous acts versus heteronomous ethics. Hence it is important for me that the two syntheses—that of agape and the imitation of Christ—can be shown not only to cohere but actually to safeguard one another against misinterpretation and misuse. For it is the concrete—we might say "incarnate"—*manifestation of agape in Jesus Christ* that makes the two commandments more than attitude-producing; and the concrete model elicits a devotion with overtones and undertones. Imitation means to try on a role, exemplified in an actual life of an actual person. But the concrete model does not confront us as something *which is not us* (heteronomous); it has its resonance in the agape which is part of all human existence.

Thus if we interpret the imitation as an imitation of Christ's agape, then it cannot be characterized as a foreign pattern pressed from without upon the imitator, a heteronomous norm. It is a total attitude, which must be internalized in a person so that it is governed from within: it becomes one's "I-ideal." In that way the imitation comes to maturity and becomes an independent, creative attitude, in which thinking and decisions of one's own are necessary.

And further, if imitation is interpreted in this way we do not give free reign to our general tendency to make selected ethical decisions, confining ourselves to a set of virtues which are easily practicable. The central demand in the imitation program is now that the heart shall love God and fellow human beings actively. Of course the tendency toward routinization is always there, but now the very program of imitation is constantly enlived by the agape-synthesis.

What about the risk of legalism? Is there not a risk that such a program in the final analysis is "under the law"—to use Pauline language—so that the central message of the New Testament, the Gospel of Grace, has lost its dominance and Christ has become an even more severe law?

I think this is not a specifically Christian problem; intrinsically it is a risk which threatens *all* serious ethical programs, inside and outside Christianity. High ethical ideals become easily a program for an intellectual and moral élite. As to Christianity, we have in the New Testament ethical ideals which reach to the skies and demand everything. The problem of "overdemands" *is* a real problem in Christian ethics.

It belongs to the insights of classical Christian theology that ethical questions largely remain problems of *practical reason,* and that therefore discussions of ethics are largely possible without reference to specific Christian beliefs (I say largely, not totally!). I agree with that; still I think it is important that in the discussions every religion and every ideology also presents its *total* program with all its arguments for its positions—whenever this is possible. In this way we make ourselves better understood, and some point of the program may enrich even people of other persuasions; in any case it widens the spectrum for the listener.

This means that we Christians should not hide our *internal* ethical arguments in our dialogues with outsiders. And in this connection I think that one of our most urgent tasks is precisely to point to the Gospel, to Christ as the *Savior,* to forgiveness and grace behind all demands. Perhaps we should start all serious ponderings and reasonings about ethics by reminding ourselves that there is grace in the world, forgiveness for our shortcomings, and permission to begin again. This is, all things considered, a fundamental presupposition in Christian ethical thinking. There was a deep existential wisdom in Israel expressed when the ten commandments were preceded by a sentence about the God who has saved his people, and when the Shema' with its profound love commandment started with the magnificent words that there is a Lord, one Lord. As to the New Testament, we find there such reminders as the following: "In this is agape, not that we loved God but that he loved us and sent his Son to be the expiation for our sins" (1 John 4:10).

If this perspective is kept in view, the Bible's talk about agape and the imitation of Christ becomes not simply a program for the "mature"—to use Pauline language—but also a meaningful goal for the church as a whole and the individual Christian, and an ideal which may prove acceptable to ordinary mortals as well.

THE GRAVAMEN AGAINST JESUS

C. F. D. Moule

The charge for which Jesus was crucified was that he claimed to be King of the Jews. Does this indicate the real reason for his being put to death? If not, what was the real reason? It must seem foolhardy to reopen this endlessly debated question, and over-optimistic to imagine that new light may be thrown on it by a reconsideration of the familiar data. It is my intention, however, to bring to this brief discussion of some of those data two principles which are not always observed. They will become evident in due course. The essay is dedicated with admiration to the recipient of this volume, a friend and scholar who has been conspicuously courageous in his insistence on looking afresh at familiar scenery; and it owes much to the searching challenge contained in the works of another friend and scholar, namely its editor.

A Jewish student, now a Rabbi, once asked me what historical thesis would need to be established or destroyed in order to undermine my Christian convictions. Part of an answer to that question might be that it would need to be proved that the death of Jesus was not due to anything in him which threatened the Judaism of his day. The relation of Jesus to Judaism is at the heart of the matter. This is why, in the debate about the death of Jesus, the disputants do, in fact, fall roughly into the two classes of those who deny that conflict with Judaism was a significant factor[1] and those who affirm that it was. Let it be added, in parenthesis, that there is nothing necessarily anti-Semitic in the latter conclusion (to which I subscribe), although it has too often been exploited with anti-Semitic intent.

At the start, there is a certain amount of common ground between the two opposing views. Probably neither side will doubt that purely prudential considerations were at least among the motives for putting Jesus to death. Even those who believe that the charge of being an aspirant to messiahship (in the popular sense) was a false charge, although undoubtedly the official charge, are still bound by the evidence to recognize that at least it could be made to seem plausible. Herod Antipas, according to Josephus

---

[1]Bibliography in E. Bammel, "The Revolution Theory from Reimarus to Brandon" in *Jesus and the Politics of His Day,* ed. E. Bammel and C. F. D. Moule (Cambridge: Cambridge University Press, 1984) 11-68.

(*Ant*. 18.118), feared that John the Baptist's influence over the crowds might lead to a revolt, and in the same way Jesus might well have seemed to be a potential danger, even if nothing was further from his own intentions (cf. John 11:48). As E. P. Sanders remarks, "anyone who claimed to speak for God and who attracted a following would alarm those who wanted to maintain the somewhat precarious *status quo* with Rome."[2] Similarly C. H. Dodd wrote: "The Pharisees and Herodians, we are told, formed a coalition against Him (Mark 3:6). No doubt the two parties objected to His proceedings on different grounds, but for both the danger lay in His appeal to lawless and irresponsible elements in the population."[3] Whatever may be thought about the suggestion that the Pharisees were involved, the principle holds good—and antagonism from at any rate Highpriestly and Sadducean quarters would certainly be likely on such grounds.

Again, it is easy for both sides to the debate to agree that among those who called for the death of Jesus there are likely to have been some who were smarting under the lash of his moral indignation against abuses within Judaism. Outspoken prophets are seldom popular with everyone, least of all at a time when patriotism and solidarity are at a premium. This holds for prophets from Jeremiah through Jesus of Nazareth to that other Jesus, the crazy son of Ananias, who went about shouting doom on Jerusalem during the Jewish war until, ironically, a missile from a Roman ballista silenced him (Josephus, *Bel*. 6.300-309). No Jewish or Christian community can ever have been without its insincere worshippers and its mere ritualists, and attacks by Jesus on such abuses are well authenticated, no matter how much their extent and style may have been exaggerated by later antagonism between Synagogue and Church. The parable of the wicked husbandmen (Mark 12:1-12 and parallels), with its echoes of Isaiah 5, belongs without much doubt in the context of Jesus' own time and is likely to be substantially authentic. There would be no lack of antagonists among those who were the target of such an attack.

Another by no means negligible factor is the sheer envy that may well have been aroused by the success of an unorthodox wandering healer and by his popularity. This is made explicit in Mark 15:10, Matthew 27:18, and quite plausibly.

It is when one asks whether there were not other motives besides those of political diplomacy and of resentment against moral castigation and of envy, that the two main schools of thought part company, one denying that

---

[2]E. P. Sanders, *Jesus and Judaism* (London: SCM Press, 1985) 288.

[3]C. H. Dodd, *History and the Gospel* (London: Nisbet, 1938) 129n1.

Judaism as such had any substantial complaint against Jesus, the other maintaining that, on the contrary, there is evidence for collision between Jesus and the essential Judaism of his day. In order to maintain the former position, it has to be shown that the relevant conflict-stories in the Gospels are unhistorical or seriously distorted. It has been suggested that the Jewish Christianity of which we seem to get glimpses in, for instance, some of the Matthean material was nearest to the real thing, but that the disciples who were closest to Jesus' own outlook and who might be represented by that strain of tradition were virtually eliminated in the Jewish war, and that the Pauline Christianity that dominates the New Testament represents an atypical, Hellenized, Gentile Christianity very far from the Founder's mind and from historical truth.

Such was the view of S. G. F. Brandon,[4] who proposed[5] that St. Mark's Gospel was a deliberate attempt to distance Christianity from its Jewish origins—an attempt occasioned by Vespasian's triumph which brought home to Christians in Rome, with a sudden shock, that their antecedents were uncomfortably bound up with *Judea capta,* and that, if they were to escape molestation by the Roman authorities, they had better get it believed that Jesus was the victim of Jewish malice, when Pilate wanted to let him off. Hence the conflict-stories and the treatment of the trial narratives by the Evangelists. It is totally unlikely, it is said, that a notoriously brutal prefect like Pilate should be concerned to free Jesus.[6] Whether Jesus was guilty or not, what political harm could his death do? Even violent

---

[4]S. G. F. Brandon, *The Fall of Jerusalem and the Christian Church. A Study of the Effects of the Jewish Overthrow of A.D. 70 on Christianity* (London: SPCK, 1957): " . . . the Jerusalem Church fell together with the Jewish nation in the catastrophe of A.D. 70, because the Church in its principles and the loyalties of its members was essentially one with the nation" (180). Till then, the authority of the Jerusalem Church, Brandon thought, had successfully surmounted the Pauline movement (which aimed to transcend the barriers of nationality), as is shown by hints in the Synoptic Gospels, Josephus, and Hegesippus. For a critique of Brandon, including his *Jesus and the Zealots,* see M. Hengel, *JSS* 14 (1969): 231-40, and *Was Jesus a Revolutionist?* (ET: Philadelphia: Fortress Press, 1971); and Bammel and Moule, *Jesus.*

[5]S. G. F. Brandon, "The Date of the Markan Gospel," *NTS* 7 (1960-1961): 126ff.; cf. *Jesus and the Zealots* (Manchester: University Press, 1967) 221ff. *Contra* F. F. Bruce, "The date and character of Mark" in Bammel and Moule, *Jesus,* 69-89.

[6]A recent brief restatement of this opinion is to be found in F. Watson, "Why was Jesus Crucified?" *Theology* 88 (1984-1985): 105ff.

protest from his followers could easily be dealt with by the army. And what likelihood is there, in any case, of the historicity of the alleged custom of releasing one prisoner at Passovertime?[7] Directly evidenced nowhere but in the Gospels and Acts 3:13f., it sounds like fiction designed to exculpate Pilate and incriminate the Jews. In such ways as this it is sought to eliminate any genuinely Jewish gravamen against Jesus.

It is not my intention here to offer a detailed defense of the conflict-traditions in the Gospels, though I shall underline the case made by others for the authenticity of some of them. What I want mainly to do is to apply to the question about the real gravamen against Jesus two principles. The first is that, to understand a historical situation, its sequel and consequences must be taken into account. This is firmly asserted by E. P. Sanders. He observes that "with regard to Jesus' intention and his relationship to Judaism," a good hypothesis "should meet Klausner's test: it should situate Jesus believably in Judaism and yet explain why the movement initiated by him eventually broke with Judaism."[8] Again, Sanders believes "that the evidence shows that . . . there is substantial coherence between what Jesus had in mind, how he saw his relationship to his nation and his people's religion, the reason for his death, and the beginning of the Christian movement."[9] Or, once more, " . . . the only way to proceed in the search for the historical Jesus is to offer hypotheses based on the evidence and to evaluate them in the light of how satisfactorily they account for the material in the Gospels, while also making Jesus a believable figure in first-century Palestine and the founder of a movement which eventuated in the church."[10] "Does the persecution of the early Christian movement," he pertinently asks, "shed light on the opposition to Jesus?"[11]

---

[7]See, for instance, R. L. Merritt, "Jesus Barabbas and the Paschal Pardon," *JBL* 104 (1985): 57-68, arguing that, whether or not the Evangelists have created two persons out of one (for some hold that "Barabbas" was another name for Jesus of Nazareth), they have invented the episode on the basis of comparable customs known elsewhere in the ancient world (Babylon, Assyria, Greece, and perhaps Rome). For a critique of attacks on the plausibility of the Johannine portrayal of Pilate and of the offer of amnesty to a prisoner, see J. A. T. Robinson, *The Priority of John* (London: SCM Press, 1985) 254ff.

[8]Sanders, *Jesus and Judaism*, 18, referring to J. Klausner, *Jesus of Nazareth: His Times, His Life and His Teaching* (ET: 1925) 369.

[9]Ibid., 22.

[10]Ibid., 166f.

[11]Ibid., 281.

Applying this principle, Sanders observes, for instance, that there is a total lack of evidence that any of Jesus' followers turned out, after his death, to have cherished a militant nationalism. Jesus was a king, but not of this world: his followers were a messianic movement, but not one looking for territory.[12] Perhaps it is significant that this seems to be true even of that very Jewish Christian, James, the Lord's brother. According to Josephus (*Ant.* 20.200f.), when he and others with him were condemned to be stoned for law-breaking (*paranomein*), this offended the strictly observant Jews (*peri tous nomous akribeis*). That is to say, he had a reputation for being himself observant. But there is no hint of any violent nationalism; and according to Hegesippus (*apud* Eusebius, *H.E.* II.23), whatever this tradition may be worth, he disappointed the nationalists by refusing to confirm that Jesus was leading the people astray, and by, instead, confessing Jesus as the Son of Man—which I believe stands for passive, not violent, resistance in the name of God.

In the same way, B. F. Meyer appeals to early Christian self-understanding for confirmation of his interpretation of Jesus;[13] and, in a broader context, M. Hellwig follows the same principle when she speaks of the "attempt to see the past event in the fulness of meaning which its impact on later history has been and still is unfolding."[14]

Following this principle of taking into account the sequel when interpreting the antecedents, I want to call attention in particular to the evidence of the Pauline epistles for interpreting Jesus of Nazareth;[15] and it is there that the second principle to which I referred comes into view. The estimate of Jesus in Paul is a religious estimate; and the second principle is that the religious claims of Christians—in the case in point, these are Christological claims—must not be assumed to be groundless or fictitious merely because they relate to what the historian, as such, cannot investigate; neither ought the historian to overlook the fact that he may find that the hypothesis that such claims correspond to reality enables him to make better

---

[12]Ibid., 294.

[13]B. F. Meyer, *The Aims of Jesus* (London: SCM Press, 1979) 239, cf. 253.

[14]M. Hellwig, *Jesus the Compassion of God* (Dublin: Dominican Publications/ Wilmington DE: Michael Glazier, 1983) 71.

[15]The significance of Pauline Christology for interpreting the origin of early Christian belief is pursued in more detail in C. F. D. Moule, *The Origin of Christology* (Cambridge: Cambridge University Press, 1977); and the question of Paul's relation to Judaism, in Moule, "Jesus, Judaism, and Paul" in Festschrift for E. E. Ellis (ed. G. F. Hawthorne, forthcoming).

sense than assuming their fictitiousness does, of what, as a historian, he can perceive. In other words, what is beyond the purview of a historian as such (e.g., the object of a religious conviction) may nevertheless positively illuminate the scene which, as a historian, he does examine. This is not to deny the danger of religious prejudice;[16] but the danger of the misuse of a hypothesis must not preclude its use. The Jesus of Paul is a transcendent presence: what if it was real, and what if Jesus of Nazareth was that same presence? May a historian not find his strictly historical work illuminated by this hypothesis?

But before the Pauline sequel to the life of Jesus is considered, some recent work on the conflict-stories in the Gospels calls for comment. E. P. Sanders has demonstrated that some of the reasons for conflict between Jesus and Judaism alleged by many Christian scholars are groundless.[17] It is manifestly false to paint a picture of Judaism as essentially a "book-keeping" religion that anxiously reckoned up profit and loss in its merit-ledger, and then to contrast this with the glorious freedom of Christianity, and so to claim that the reason why Jesus fell foul of Judaism was that he offered good news of the graciousness of God. On the contrary, a prophet proclaiming the graciousness of God would, as Sanders says, have met with enthusiastic assent. Professor Sanders, indeed, questions whether the main attack launched by Jesus was against self-righteousness in any case.[18] To pursue this point in detail it would be necessary to ask whether Sanders, while correctly pointing to the free grace of God in the belief of Judaism, may not have underemphasized other ingredients in it—for instance, the danger of "legalism" resulting from the doctrine of staying within the covenant by law-abiding, and the danger of élitism springing from doctrines of the election of Israel. But, be that as it may, he has also exposed other errors in respect of Judaism, into which some Christian writers, insufficiently intimate with the nature of early Judaism, have fallen, such as equating the Pharisees with the *Ḥaberim*, lumping together the *ʿamme ha-*

---

[16]Pilloried by E. P. Sanders in *Jesus and Judaism*, 278f.

[17]See *Paul and Palestinian Judaism* (London: SCM Press, 1977); *Jesus and Judaism;* and "Judaism and the Grand 'Christian' Abstractions: Love, Mercy, and Grace," *Int* 39 (1985): 357-72.

[18]*Jesus and Judaism*, 281. It must not be forgotten that the "bookkeeping" mentality is not absent from Jewish literature (or, for that matter, from Christian literature). K. R. Snodgrass, "Justification by Grace—to Doers: an Analysis of the Place of Romans 2 in the Theology of Paul," *NTS* 32 (1986): 72-93, names some instances, n. 48.

aretz with sinners, and imagining that Jesus' concern for ordinary people must have alienated him from Pharisees. In any case, it is the chief priests, he points out, and not the Pharisees, who seem to have been the prime movers when it came to action against Jesus.[19] Sanders has questioned, further, the extent of the evidence that Jesus disparaged the Law, pointing out that this is not reflected, as a principle, among his followers in the sequel.[20]

In many respects, then, Sanders challenges what might be called the standard Christian explanation of the clash between Jesus and observant Jews that is depicted in many of the Gospel traditions. But, if he shows that the conflict has often been wrongly located, he does not deny the fact of conflict. Indeed—faithful to the principle of taking the sequel into account—he notes that Jewish persecution of Christians itself points in this direction.[21] At certain points he does find well authenticated grounds for serious hostility. Three points in particular are named. Jesus promised access to the Kingdom of God to sinners without first requiring of them restitution;[22] he bade one whom he called to follow him to leave the dead to bury their dead;[23] and he attacked the Temple system.[24] Regarding this last matter, the so-called "cleansing" of the Temple was nothing of the sort. There was, Sanders maintains, no cleansing to be done, since the traders were only performing services essential to the maintenance of sacrifices, and the charges against their honesty implied in the Gospel narratives find virtually no support elsewhere. Rather, Sanders holds, what Jesus did in the Temple was a prophetic gesture connoting doom to the existing Temple system with a view to its replacement by a renewed Temple of God's making—an eschatological renewal. Among others who have reinterpreted this episode along the lines of a prophetic threat against the Temple are D. R. Catchpole[25] and M. J. Borg.[26] The latter maintains that the charge

---

[19]Ibid., 287f., 291f.

[20]Ibid., 268f.

[21]Ibid., 295.

[22]Ibid., 326, etc.

[23]Ibid., 252ff.

[24]Ibid., 61ff.

[25]D. R. Catchpole, "The 'triumphal' entry" in Bammel and Moule, *Jesus,* 319-34: "the action of Jesus in the Temple is an anticipatory sign carried out in prophetic fashion" (334)—anticipatory, that is, of an eschatological order of the fu-

against the traders for turning the Temple into a *spēlaion lē(i)stōn* (Mark
11:17 and parallels) does not refer to sharp practice or mercenary-mindedness, but means that the Temple has become a stronghold of the resistance movement, *lē(i)stai* being "freedom-fighters" (*lē(i)stēs*, it has been
observed, never means a "swindler"),[27] and resistance to Rome being part
of the quest for exclusiveness ("holiness" in that sense), which Borg sees
as Israel's disastrous mistake: not exclusive "holiness" but all-embracing
mercy, even towards the Romans, is God's design for Israel. Borg is followed in this respect by N. T. Wright.[28]

It is questionable—to pursue the Temple affair a little further—whether
any of these interpretations of it is entirely satisfactory. Is it not possible
that the charge of mercenary-mindedness is, after all, to be taken seriously
(made explicit as it is in John 2:16)? However that may be, that the incident, if it took place, caused deep, perhaps deadly, resentment is, in any
case, hard to doubt—resentment that would not be confined to the high
priests but would be felt alike by the leaders, the pious, and the populace
in general.[29] And that it is not a fabrication is supported by precisely the
fact that Jesus' intention is not made altogether clear. The story has neither
been suppressed as embarrassing to the Christian cause, nor yet clearly exploited as an attack on the Temple system itself, as it might have been, had
it been artificially devised by Christians who had come to believe that the
sacrificial death of Jesus superseded the sacrificial system (1 Cor 5:7; Heb
10) and that the veil of the Temple had been rent (Mark 15:38 and parallels, Heb 10:20), and, indeed, the Temple made redundant (Acts 7:48; Rev
21:22).[30]

As for the saying "let the dead bury their dead" (Matt 8:22; Luke 9:60),
there seems to be little doubt that this must have been grossly offensive.

---

ture associated with Zech 14:21. Cf. J. D. M. Derrett *apud* Sanders, *Jesus and
Judaism*, 367 n. 46.

[26]M. J. Borg, *Conflict, Holiness and Politics in the Teachings of Jesus* (New
York/Toronto: Edwin Mellen Press, 1984) 163ff.

[27]A. E. Harvey, *Jesus and the Constraints of History* (London: Duckworth/
Philadelphia: Fortress Press, 1982) 132 and notes, *apud* E. P. Sanders, *Jesus and
Judaism*, 66.

[28]N. T. Wright, "Jesus, Israel, and the Cross" in memorial volume for G. B.
Caird (ed. L. D. Hurst and N. T. Wright, forthcoming).

[29]Sanders, *Jesus and Judaism*, 287f.

[30]Ibid., 86.

M. Hengel, in his monograph on the theme,[31] makes a good case for its being a signal instance of something highly distinctive and disturbing in Jesus' style of leadership. There are, Hengel finds, no close parallels to this style in Judaism: " . . . Jesus' relationship to his disciples simply cannot be derived from the analogy of the teacher-pupil relationship such as we find it among the later rabbis. And, despite stronger points of contact with the apocalyptic prophets of his day than with the rabbis, Jesus is also fundamentally different from them too . . . Neither the misleading term 'rabbi' nor the designation 'eschatological prophet' . . . can adequately characterize his activity.'' Hengel finds a similar lack of parallels among the Greek philosophers and teachers. Accordingly, ''Jesus' 'charisma,' '' he continues, ''breaks through the possibilities of categorization in terms of the phenomenology of religion. The very uniqueness of the way in which Jesus called individuals to 'follow after' him is,'' Hengel concludes, the expression of an ''underivable'' authority.[32] E. P. Sanders, with knowledge of Hengel's observations, deems that the incident shows that ''at least once Jesus was willing to say that following him superseded the requirements of piety and the Torah.''[33] Similarly C. C. Rowland speaks of ''the harsh saying to repudiate an important religious obligation (to bury a corpse, *M. Nazir* 7.1) . . . ''[34]

Regarding the fraternizing of Jesus with tax collectors and others who were reckoned as blatant sinners, Sanders may well be right that Christian commentators have assumed too readily that this in itself must have been offensive to observant Jews. ''If Jesus, by eating with tax collectors, led them to repent, repay those whom they had robbed, and leave off practising their profession, he would have been a national hero.''[35] (The story of Jesus' doing this in the case of Zacchaeus, Luke 19: 1-10, is regarded by him as a secondary construction.) He concludes that Jesus' practice was offensive to Pharisees not because he was ready to associate with sinners, but only because he offered sinners access to the Kingdom of God without

---

[31]M. Hegel, *The Charismatic Leader and His Followers* (ET: Edinburgh: T. & T. Clark, 1981).

[32]Ibid., 87.

[33]Sanders, *Jesus and Judaism,* 255.

[34]C. C. Rowland, *Christian Origins: an Account of the Setting and Character of the Most Important Messianic Sect of Judaism* (London: S.P.C.K., 1985) 144.

[35]Sanders, *Jesus and Judaism,* 203, cf. 272.

requiring formal restitution. Even his followers, he believes, did not maintain this practice.[36]

Without denying the scandal, it is important not to interpret failure to require statutory restitution as failure to require repentance. There are convincing indications in the Gospel traditions that Jesus did not always insist on formalities. He does appear to have sat loose to conventional religious practices. "Indeed," writes Rowland, "there is a case to be made for regarding Jesus' teaching as a kind of eschatological Torah, whose emphasis on the inward motives may find its antecedent in the prophetic hope of the new Law written on the heart . . . "[37] It is true that Jesus is shown directing a leper to secure the statutory authorization of his cleansing (Mark 1:44 and parallels; Luke 17:14), but this might be for the leper's sake; otherwise, as J. Bowker puts it, "Jesus was claiming that relatedness to God depends on the condition of faith, not on the conditions in the covenant."[38] But none of this means that he did not call the sinners to repentance. Moreover, while it may be true that in theory an observant Jew would see nothing wrong in accepting table-fellowship with a sinner, if it was with a view to bringing him to repentance, how much evidence is there that Pharisees did in fact go out after sinners and take the risk of consorting with them with evangelistic intentions, without any prior guarantee of their intention to repent, and that they would not have suspected the integrity of one who did?[39]

It seems to me that there are good grounds for believing that observant Jews would have regarded Jesus' behavior as irregular, even if, as seems to me overwhelmingly probable, he did summon the sinners to repentance, if not to the conventional signs of it; but whether his practice in this respect would, by itself, have led to an attempt on his life is another matter. What does seem to be clear is that, taken together, the incidents thus far reviewed constitute a very strong case for the unacceptability of Jesus to the Judaism of his day.[40]

---

[36]Ibid., 209, 323f.

[37]Rowland, *Christian Origins,* 143.

[38]J. Bowker, *The Religious Imagination and the Sense of God* (Oxford: Clarendon Press, 1978) 161.

[39]For Jewish attitudes to proselytism, see P. Bowers, "Paul and Religious Propaganda in the First Century," *NovT* 22 (1980): 316-23 (320n7).

[40]On the question how far the message of Jesus included a national call to repentance, see G. B. Caird, *Jesus and the Jewish Nation* (London: Athlone Press, 1965). Sanders, *Jesus and Judaism,* 108, 112f., 116, is inclined to estimate the evidence for this as less convincing.

But I believe that it was on a deeper level that the fundamental gravamen lay. Does Sanders perhaps hint at this when he alludes to Jesus' extraordinary self-claim,[41] and when he sees the disciples' belief in the resurrection of Jesus as decisive for launching the sequel and recognizes that this could not have happened in a vacuum?[42] That is to say, however dramatic and unexpected the phenomenon of the birth of the Easter-belief was, to be convincing the belief had to be congruous with what the disciples knew of Jesus himself. The transforming belief was not just belief in a resurrection, but belief in the resurrection of the Jesus they knew. However, Sanders draws a line at this point. He grants that "in the Anglo-Saxon world it has often been argued . . . that something about Jesus could be inferred from, in fact was necessitated by, the faith which sprang up among his disciples," but he declares that, for his part, he does "not consider it likely that the link between Jesus and the consolidation and persecution of his followers lies in a common view of his *person*." It is enough, he thinks, that Jesus "was God's spokesman, knew what his next major action in Israel's history would be, and could specify who would be in the kingdom."[43] The basic question, round which not mere ideas but specific issues revolved was "who spoke for God?"[44]

I believe, however, that Paul's understanding of the "person" of Jesus is relevant to the inquiry about the circumstances of the death of Jesus. The Jesus of Paul, I have said, is a transcendent presence: what if Jesus of Nazareth was the same? Consider the facts. Paul of Tarsus is our earliest datable witness to the sequel to the life of Jesus. Those who object to treating the letters of Paul as primary evidence for that sequel are not justified in deeming him either ignorant of Judaism or not interested in Christian origins. Even if one ignores Acts 22:3 (the claim that he was trained by Gamaliel the Elder) as secondary, there are his own statements in Galatians 1:13f. and Philippians 3:4-6 about his training in Pharisaic Judaism; and there is the evident conflict of loyalties reflected in Romans 9-11 and elsewhere;[45] while, for his concern for Christian tradition, there is clear

---

[41]For references, see index of Sanders, *Jesus and Judaism,* under "Jesus, self-claim."

[42]Ibid., 21, 240, 320, etc.; 129, cf. 95.

[43]Ibid., 12; 280.

[44]Ibid., 280, 281, cf. 288. For a summary of this and other views, see W. D. Davies and E. P. Sanders, "Jesus: from the Semitic Point of View," in *The Cambridge History of Judaism.*

[45]See E. P. Sanders, *Paul, the Law, and the Jewish People* (Philadelphia: Fortress Press, 1983) 80, etc.

evidence in Galatians 1:18ff. (in a context where it was not to his advantage to acknowledge dependence on tradition) and in 1 Corinthians 7:10, 11:23ff., and 15:1-11. It cannot be denied that Paul is rooted both in Judaism and in early Christian tradition.

What light, then, do the Pauline epistles throw on the causes of the crucifixion? On the external level, the earliest known reference to it anywhere is in 1 Thessalonians 2:15f., which attributes it to the bitter antagonism of certain Jews. That passage contains a venom that is almost unparalleled in the Pauline corpus (though Phil 3:2ff. is not far off) and it was evidently written in the heat of anger; but it is difficult to believe that the charge could at any stage and in any circumstances have been gratuitously invented by one who was subsequently to write the passionately patriotic Romans 9-11. Besides, in attributing the death of Jesus to certain Jews, Paul is only saying what non-Christian Jews were later to say in the much-quoted *baraitha* in T B Sanhedrin 43a, before it became popular to claim that Jesus was turned into an embarrassment to Judaism only by subsequent Christian falsification.

This makes it initially difficult to believe that Jesus gave no offence to Judaism; but the nature of the offence begins to become visible only when one takes into account the remarkable fact that Paul, and with him practically all the other writers in the New Testament, assume the transcendent figure of their religious experience to be continuous with the historical figure, Jesus of Nazareth. Even discounting the "I am Jesus" of the heavenly vision in Acts 9:5, 22:8, 26:15, it is Paul himself who can speak of mystical union with one of whom, in the same breath, he speaks historically (using aorists) as "the Son of God, who loved me and sacrificed himself for me" (Gal 2:20). The one whom Paul found in his religious experience was assumed by him to be continuous with the one who was known as a historical individual, crucified in Judaea only the other day. The historian can observe, within the limits set by the data, both the historical figure and the symptoms of the subsequent religious experience; but if he is both properly inquisitive and honest, he is bound to pay attention also to what is implied by the religious symptoms, although this itself belongs outside the strictly historical purview.

Of course, nothing is simpler than to dismiss the implied claims as the product of fantasy. The historian's instinct, and indeed his duty as a historian, is to see whether he can rationalize the continuity between the historical figure and the transcendent Lord in the mind of the Christian worshipper by assuming that it is the spurious result of religious imagination. Given time and enthusiasm, a Euhemeristic process of evolution can produce a god out of a hero easily enough. But in this instance there are considerations that tell against this instinctive explanation.

One is that the understanding of Jesus as a transcendent presence appears full-blown in the earliest datable documents available. Some of the deductions, such as that Jesus is divine, may wait to be spelt out explicitly by later writers;[46] but all the implications are there from the first, in the Pauline epistles. There is not, in the New Testament documents, the progressive development that an evolutionary theory would expect. Even when C. C. Rowland adduces evidence for more "deification" of heroes within Judaism than one might expect in so monotheistic a tradition,[47] it still remains very remarkable that a contemporary figure, recently crucified, should have been viewed as Jesus is viewed very early in the development of New Testament devotion.

Assuming, for the time being, that the continuity deserves serious attention as perhaps reflecting reality, not fantasy, it is relevant to the present quest to inquire how Paul understands the relation between Jesus and Judaism. Paul says that Jesus was put to death by Jews. Is there any light thrown, in Paul's understanding of Jesus, on the reasons for this? One matter at least immediately presents itself in reply. The Jesus of Paul's experience is understood to have inaugurated a new covenant that superseded the Mosaic covenant. It is true that Paul never speaks of Israel itself as superseded: "new Israel" is a term that occurs nowhere in Paul, or, for that matter, in any part of the New Testament. Neither does Paul or any other New Testament Christian, unless it be those represented by Stephen (Acts 6, 7), explicitly propose to disregard the Mosaic Law.[48] But Paul does see the new covenant as superseding the Mosaic covenant, and says so clearly in 2 Corinthians 3, as the writer to the Hebrews does also with almost brutal explicitness in Hebrews 8:13 (and passim). Whatever Paul meant by *telos nomou* in Romans 10:4,[49] that he regarded the covenant inaugurated by Jesus as transcending the Mosaic covenant is clear not only from 2 Corinthians 3, but from the polemic contained in Galatians. Paul is there passionately opposing the requirement that uncircumcised Christians be circumcised, and the reason for so heated a repudiation seems to be that the requirement would impugn the sufficiency of Jesus Christ as what might be called "the covenant area." That is to say, in Paul's belief,

---

[46]Certainly Rom 9:5 is no sound basis for a contrary conclusion.

[47]Rowland, *Christian Origins*, 38. Cf Ezekiel the Tragedian's picture of Moses as ruling from heaven, cited by J. H. Charlesworth, *The Old Testament Pseudepigrapha and the New Testament* (Cambridge: University Press, 1985) 85.

[48]This point is insisted on by Sanders, *Jesus and Judaism*, 268f.

[49]For a recent discussion, see Sanders, *Paul*, 38ff.

a Gentile who has been baptized "into" Jesus Christ is *ipso facto* within the covenant: nothing further may be required of necessity to make him a member of God's People. Conversely—such appears to be the logic of the situation—a circumcised Jew who does not, in addition, confess Jesus as Lord (and, no doubt, submit to baptism in his name, cf. Acts 2:38), while he certainly cannot cease to be an Israelite, has not yet gone forward into the full destiny designed by God for his People—into "God's Israel" (Gal 6:16).

That, no doubt, is deeply offensive to a Jew; but it seems to follow from Paul's understanding of Jesus. Jesus fulfills and transcends the Mosaic covenant and includes and transcends Israel-of-the-old-covenant, fulfilling Israel indeed, rather than superseding it, but doing so by inaugurating a new covenant which does positively supersede the old. Jesus, rather than Torah, is seen by Paul to be now supremely the way into covenant with God. Christian life is lived "in" Christ, as in a magnetic field of energy. Grace, mercy, and peace come from God-and-Jesus—an astonishing formula for a monotheistic Jew to use.

It is easy to understand that if Jesus of Nazareth was, all along, in such a relationship with God—not necessarily (indeed, probably not) proclaiming it in so many words, but simply occupying such a position, in relation to God and to Israel—he must have been felt by many observant Jews to be intolerable and to constitute a blasphemy. If the Jesus of New Testament devotion corresponds with reality, and is not fiction, and if his continuity with the historical Jesus of Nazareth represents fact, not fantasy, then conflict between that historical figure and the Judaism of his day becomes as inevitable as conflict was for Paul who understood Jesus in this way, even if Jesus' attitude was not explicitly hostile to the law, and even if his behavior had not been as unorthodox as it seems, in certain respects, to have been.

Returning, then, to the Synoptic Gospels, it is possible to see numerous indications of just such a situation. Jesus is often portrayed as evincing a startling immediacy in his relation to God. E. P. Sanders speaks of "Jesus' extraordinary self-claim."[50] G. Bornkamm speaks of "the character of unmediated presence."[51] E. Fuchs writes "Jesus dares to make God's will effective as if he himself stood in God's stead."[52] C. H. Dodd wrote:

---

[50]See n. 41 above.

[51]G. Bornkamm, *Jesus of Nazareth* (ET: London: Hodder and Stoughton/New York: Harper & Row, 1960) 62, quoted by Sanders, *Jesus and Judaism*, 30.

[52]*Ges. Aufsätze* 2, 154, 156, quoted by Hengel, *Charismatic Leader*, 68.

"There must have been something about the way in which Jesus spoke and acted which provoked" the charge of blasphemy.[53] Such impressions are based, not on the questionably historical statements that he actually made the sort of claims that (by "hindsight," perhaps) he is represented as making in the Fourth Gospel, but on Jesus' quiet assumption, unmediated by appeals to Scripture or tradition, that he knew God's mind and was doing God's work.

Admittedly, it is well enough known that Judaism did recognize as authentic a certain degree of such intimacy with God. To claim to be spokesman for God was not, in itself, generally offensive.[54] If the average devout believer sought access to God's mind and will through the Torah and its traditional interpretation, through prayer and, while the Temple stood, through sacrifice and the mediation of the priestly system, yet there were the prophets and the charismatics who claimed more direct access to God, who had stood in his council (cf. Jer 23:22, etc.) and overheard his words, and who might even evince a startling familiarity with God. G. Vermes has familiarized us with this last phenomenon, when he adduces, for instance, the cases of Honi the Circle-Drawer (a saint of the first century BCE) and Rabbi Hanina ben Dosa (a wonder-worker of the first century CE). Such charismatics, he says, showed an "informal familiarity with God and confidence in the efficacy of their words" which was "deeply disliked by those whose authority derived from established channels."[55] But at least Judaism knew about them and did not put them to death. Vermes concludes that Jesus belonged "in the venerable company of the Devout, the ancient Hasidim." He "did not belong among the Pharisees, Essenes, Zealots or Gnostics, but was one of the holy miracle-workers of Galilee."[56] Rather similarly, but less precisely, P. Lapide places Jesus in the category of the great spiritual leaders of Israel.[57]

But even these charismatic figures had to be subject to tradition, as C. C. Rowland points out,[58] whereas Jesus, at least on certain occasions, seems

---

[53]C. H. Dodd, *The Founder of Christianity* (London: Collier-Macmillan, 1970) 78.

[54]Sanders, *Jesus and Judaism,* 271.

[55]G. Vermes, *Jesus the Jew: A Historian's Reading of the Gospels* (London: Collins, 1973) 81.

[56]Ibid., 223.

[57]P. Lapide, *The Resurrection of Jesus: A Jewish Perspective* (ET: Minneapolis: Augsburg Publishing House, 1983/London: S.P.C.K., 1983).

[58]Rowland, *Christian Origins,* 228.

to have flouted it. Still more striking is the vast difference between the jo-
cular, "Don Camillo" style of intimacy with God which characterized these
Jewish charismatics and the Abba-prayer of Jesus (Mark 14:36) which
combines intimacy with total devotion and reverence. Jesus does not really
match any of the suggested parallels. "Even within the characterization
. . . of an 'eschatological charismatic,' " writes Hengel, "he remains in
the last resort incommensurable, and so basically confounds every attempt
to fit him into the categories suggested by the phenomenology or sociology
of religion."[59] Perhaps the nearest analogy in pre-Christian Jewish thought
is in the Scriptures themselves. In Numbers 12:8 Moses is placed in a class
far above that of a prophet, by reason of his unique closeness to the Al-
mighty in face to face confrontation. The passage is taken up by Philo in
Leg. All. 3.103 and *Her.* 262 (the latter citing also Deut 34:10); and Rowland cites *Sifre* on the passage,[60] where the analogy is used of a king's agent
who is virtually identified with the king. "In all his utterances," says Josephus of Moses, "one seemed to hear the speech of God Himself" (*Ant.*
4.329; Loeb translation). But was such a phenomenon as is described in
Numbers 12:8 anything more than theoretically conceived? It is hard to believe that any devout Jew would have remained unshaken if he had actually
encountered such immediacy of access to the divine in a contemporary at
close quarters, bringing what J. Bowker calls the "effect" of God into dis-
concerting proximity. "Jesus," writes Bowker, " . . . insisted, first maybe
on the edges, but then at the very centre of Israel, eventually in the Temple
itself, that what he knew, and what could be discerned in his life and word,
of the nature and effect of God, was an authentic representation of that nature and its effect in the world of God's creation."[61] The Fourth Gospel
makes explicit the position of Jesus in this respect which was implicit in
his life and words. In the end, it is a choice between Moses and Jesus. E. P.
Sanders, categorizing Christian authors who, in effect, declare that Jesus
died "for the truth of the gospel" defines one group among these as believing that Jesus died "for his own christology, . . . because he set himself at least by implication above Moses . . . ''[62] I accept that as a
description of my belief, and I think that it is dictated by the evidence, and
not by Christian prejudice. In none of the traditions in the Gospels does
Jesus appeal to any human authority, unless it be in John 5:33, where it is

---

[59]Hengel, *Charimatic Leader,* 69.

[60]Rowland, *Christian Origins,* 177.

[61]Bowker, *The Religious Imagination,* 129.

[62]Sanders, *Jesus and Judaism,* 331.

revoked in the next verse. The appeal to the baptism of John the Baptist (Mark 11:30 and parallels) is best interpreted as an appeal not to the Baptist's authorizing Jesus, but to the divine commissioning which was evident in the Baptist's case, and—so Jesus implies—is a parallel to the origin of his own authority. Jesus, with no authentication from the orthodox sources, simply pronounces what he assumes to be God's words and does what he assumes to be God's deeds—and his words and deeds "succeed." He does not use a prophetic formula such as "Thus says the LORD": he says "I say . . . " He pronounces forgiveness (Mark 2:5 and parallels), and appeals for evidence of its validity to the visible cure that follows. It is true, of course, that absolution may be effectively pronounced in the name of God by any minister of God formally authorized or even authenticated by his personal standing (cf. Matt 16:19);[63] and Luke 7:48 (if it is interpreted in line with vv. 41ff.) shows that the Evangelist knew what was meant by the confirmation of a pardon already bestowed by God. But the incident in Mark 2 and parallels seems to be intended to represent a declaration made by Jesus as straight from God.[64]

There are at least two further matters that seem to imply an exceptional character in what Jesus does and says. These are the Son of Man sayings and the traditions of the Last Supper. I have written at length on "the Son of Man,"[65] and need here only state my conclusions. The fact that, almost without exception, the sayings-traditions, whether of Jesus, of Stephen (Acts 7:56), or of James the brother of Jesus (Euseb. H.E. II.23, these two both alluding to Jesus), present the phrase with the definite article is difficult to explain unless, in the Aramaic originals of these traditions, there was some locution which was unambiguously deictic (probably *not,* therefore, *bar nasha* but rather some unambiguous phrase), and which meant "the (well known) Son of Man." If so, the most likely object of reference would have been the human figure—"what seemed a son of man"—of Daniel 7, for Daniel was known and popular at the time.[66] Daniel's figure,

---

[63]Ibid., 240. But he also allows (301, cf. 273f.) that "If Jesus pronounced forgiveness of sins (Mark 2. 9-12), he might also have been arrogating to himself the prerogatives of the priesthood."

[64]I am indebted to Dr. W. Horbury of Corpus Christi College, Cambridge, for notes and references on this question. He believes that what provokes the verdict of blasphemy here is that one who had no formal authorization spoke thus confidently.

[65]E.g., "Neglected Features in the Problem of 'the Son of Man'," *Neues Testament und Kirche,* ed. J. Gnilka (Freiburg/Basel/Wien: Herder, 1974) 413-28.

[66]Josephus, *Ant.* 10.267.

in its turn, in some way represents (whether as a symbol or as a heavenly champion) the loyal, observant Jews who were prepared to part with their lives rather than transgress the will of God as they understood it. It is plausible, therefore, to conclude that Jesus used Daniel's human figure as a symbol for his vocation of total obedience, and for the vocation of those whom he summoned to share it—the vocation to be the very heart of true, renewed Israel, with the confident expectation of vindication ultimately in the heavenly court. But, if so, Jesus is himself always assumed to be the heart of that heart. Whereas he chooses a symbolic Twelve to represent renewed Israel but does not include himself within the number, standing, instead, over and above them, with the Son of Man a similar supremacy is expressed by his holding a special quintessential position within and at the very heart of the symbol. In the Synoptic traditions of the Sanhedrin trials, Jesus is equated with the Son of Man as vindicated before the heavenly tribunal. Sanders rightly observes that "the claim to be the Son of man, or to know that he was coming, is not blasphemy";[67] but here is the use of the claim with a difference. Independently of whether or not the Sanhedrin trial is historical, and independently of the debated question whether "the Son of Man" is in any way messianic,[68] the Son of Man sayings seem to reflect the affirmation of an obedience to the design of God of a quality which, because of its absoluteness, is not surprisingly called blasphemy.

The other set of traditions that must be mentioned as reflecting something of Jesus' extraordinary self-claim is that belonging to the Synoptic accounts of the Last Supper.[69] These of course belong to what was private to the disciples, and subsequent liturgical developments have no doubt left their mark upon them. But there is every reason to believe in the authenticity of the tradition that, in the upper room, Jesus claimed to be inaugurating a new covenant. Indeed, there seems to be no plausible explanation, otherwise, of the fact that the new covenant is, as we have seen, a significant factor in Paul's thinking.

Here, then, is evidence, additional to the impression of "immediacy" already discussed, for two startling claims—that Jesus was destined by his death to enter upon the eternal kingship referred to in Daniel 7 as given in heaven to one like a son of man, and to have inaugurated the new covenant

---

[67]Sanders, *Jesus and Judaism* 55.

[68]See, e.g., W. Horbury, "The Messianic Association of 'the Son of Man'," *JTS* n.s. 36 (1985): 34-55; W. Bittner, "Gott-Menschensohn-Davidssohn," *FZPT* 32 (1985): 343-72.

[69]Cf. Sanders, *Jesus and Judaism,* 324.

of Jeremiah 31. No doubt the Fourth Gospel makes explicit, by "hind-sight," much that was only implicit in the words and deeds of Jesus; but when that Gospel locates the gravamen against Jesus in a claim to oneness with God that seemed blasphemous (5:18, 10:30ff.), this appears, in the light of the evidence, to be a fair summary of the implications of his pres-ence; and what is reflected in Paul's epistles and other parts of the early Christian writings seems to match what may be gathered from a critical sifting of the traditions about the life of Jesus. If one disallows either of these, one causes difficulties for both. As Sanders asks (referring to what Jesus himself seems to have stood for), "Unless the entire scheme—which is a complete scheme, including a Messiah and extending to the final act, the inclusion of the Gentiles—was imparted via the resurrection appear-ances [an option which he justly questions], where did it come from?"[70] B. F. Meyer, at the end of his *The Aims of Jesus,* remarks that "it is above all in the tradition generated by Jesus that we discover what made him op-erate in the way he did . . . "[71] Something similar may be said, if the ar-gument of this essay is on the right lines, about discovering what caused Jesus to be crucified.

The conclusion of this essay amounts to a distinctively Christian under-standing of Jesus; and that, of course, relates to matters outside what a his-torian, as such, can investigate. But the question the essay is intended to pose is whether the hypothesis that this Christian estimate corresponds with reality does not make better sense of a larger number of data such as a his-torian can investigate, both in the traditions of the life of Jesus and in the evidence for the nature of its sequel, than a more "reductionist" estimate does: in other words, whether it is not right and proper to hold the histor-ical and the "trans-historical" together in a single continuum, albeit with-out any blurring of the respective limits and frontiers of the two.

---

[70]Ibid., 129.

[71]Meyer, *Aims of Jesus,* 252f.

HEROD ANTIPAS
AND THE DEATH OF JESUS

Pierson Parker

At Acts 4:24-31 a group of Jesus' followers are praying in Jerusalem. After quoting Psalm 1:1-2, they continue,

Truly in this city there gathered together, against your holy servant Jesus whom you anointed, both Herod, and Pontius Pilate with the Gentiles, and people of Israel. . . .

This is commonly taken as an echo of Luke 23:7-12, where Pilate sends Jesus to Herod Antipas.[1] No doubt that incident was in the worshipers' minds. I should like to propose, however, that their prayer reflects a great deal more than that. Specifically, (1) Jesus' death was determined *in advance* by Herod Antipas, Pilate, and the Jerusalem Sanhedrin acting *in concert;* (2) this three-way alliance was *instigated by Herod Antipas.*

A Tripartite Alliance

That the three governing bodies decided jointly to kill Jesus, and decided before he was arrested, fits many New Testament passages.

1. The Acts prayer itself points that way: (a) The Greek verb *sunēchthēsan,* above translated "gathered together," implies a deliberate, planned meeting. Some versions render it more vividly: "made *an alliance*" (JB), "made *common cause*" (NEB, Knox), "*joined forces* together" (Schonfield), "*mustered* together" (Moffatt), "*met and plotted* together" (Amplified), "*met to conspire*" (NIV); (b) The Herod of Acts 4:27 is of course *Antipas,* tetrarch of Galilee and Perea (cf. Luke 23:6-7); (c) He and Pontius Pilate, we read, joined forces with "people of Israel."[2] The only people of Israel who could thus consort with Pilate and Herod would be *the Sanhedrin.* Further, the prayer is itself elicited by grievous trouble which Peter and John have just had with the Jerusalem Sanhedrin.

---

[1]See, e.g., C. S. C. Williams, *A Commentary on the Acts of the Apostles* (New York: Harper & Row, 1957) 86; F. F. Bruce, *The Acts of the Apostles* (Chicago: I.V.C.F./Grand Rapids MI: Eerdmans, 1952) 127-28.

[2]RSV reads "*the* people of Israel," but the Greek has no article.

2. At Luke 20:19-20,

The scribes and the chief priests [i.e., the Sanhedrin] . . . watched him, and sent *spies* who pretended to be righteous, so that they might catch him in some statement, *so as to* (hōste) *deliver him up to the rule and authority of the governor.*

In Matthew and Mark these "spies" are *Pharisees from the Sanhedrin* together with *Herodians.*[3] The word "Herodians" may at one time have meant supporters of Herod the Great;[4] but that can hardly be the meaning here, for (a) Herod the Great was now long dead; (b) in the New Testament, the earliest Herodians we meet are in Galilee where Antipas rules (Mark 3:6);[5] (c) Josephus explicitly connects the Herodians with Herod Antipas, not as a sect but as the tetrarch's friends and supporters.[6] Here, then, associates of the Sanhedrin and of Antipas *together* seek evidence to take to *Pilate.*

3. Luke 22:3-4 says that

Judas who was called Iscariot . . . went away and consulted with the chief priests and captains (*stratēgois*), how to deliver [Jesus] to them. And they were glad. . . .

In the singular, *stratēgós* meant the *sagan,* captain of the Temple police and second in rank to the high priest (cf. Acts 4:1; 5:24, 26). But *stratēgoi,* plural, designated officers of the *Roman occupation.* This was the usage, e.g., at Philippi, Pergamum, Sardis.[7] In that case, Judas met with both Sanhedrin and Roman officials (whether jointly or separately we are not told).

4. At John 18:3, for Jesus' arrest a *speira* accompanies, rather precedes the Sanhedrin officers (*hupērétai*). A *speira* is not just "a band" or "detachment of soldiers" (KJV, RSV, NEB, NIV). It is, quite unmistakably, a *Roman cohort* (NASB, JB, NAB).[8] A full cohort would be 1,000 men;

---

[3]Matt 21:45-46; 23:15-16; Mark 12:12-13.

[4]Cf. J. C. Fenton, *Saint Matthew* (Baltimore: Penguin, 1963) 352.

[5]For a possible second mention, cf. the variant *tōn Herōdianōn* at Mark 8:15 ($\mathfrak{p}^{45}$ W Θ $f^1 f^{13}$ etc.). Jesus has just left Galilee at Mark 8:13.

[6]Ant 14.15.10.450.

[7]Walter Bauer, *A Greek-English Lexicon of the New Testament and Other Early Christian Literature,* 4th ed. rev., trans. and ed. W. F. Arndt and F. W. Gingrich (Chicago: University of Chicago Press, 1957) 778, where this is the *primary* definition of the word.

[8]F. F. Bruce thinks the failure of many translators, to render *speira* correctly, stems from their disposition to blame only Jews for Jesus' tragedy; cf. *The Gospel of John* (Grand Rapids: Eerdmans, 1983) 355n2.

but if only part of them came, it still means that (a) the Sanhedrin and Pilate have acted in concert; and (b) they fear armed resistance when Jesus is captured.

In the last two items Antipas and his Herodians do not appear. This is doubtless because, however much trouble they may stir up, they have no *legal* authority in Jerusalem.

5. The three-way conspiracy, Antipas-Pilate-Sanhedrin, clarifies a long list of items which, without it, appear bizarre or incomprehensible: (a) The Sanhedrin has got itself entangled with a band of Herodians, of all people, and this on the verge of Passover. (b) These Herodians once, and the Sanhedrin twice,[9] seize on *Roman taxation* as an issue to entrap Jesus. Surely that is more understandable if the topic was first proposed by Pilate or his aides. (c) The Sanhedrin clearly *know in advance* that they will have access to Pilate and can take Jesus before him.[10] (d) Just as clearly (Luke 23:2), Pilate *knows in advance* that Antipas will see the prisoner (Pilate must also know, beforehand, where Antipas is lodged; but as evidence that is less weighty. Both rulers may in fact be using Herod's palace on the western wall, or else the Antonia fortress northeast of the Temple; or Pilate may be in one and Antipas in the other).[11] (e) Sanhedrin members stand ready and willing to conduct Jesus to Antipas (Luke 23:7, 10). (f) The last two items (d, e) are the more remarkable since Antipas lacks jurisdiction in Jerusalem and Judea. Without prearrangement, it is hard to see how *both* Pilate and the Sanhedrin have got prepared to devote all this time to the tetrarch from the north.

6. Strangest of all, unless there was prior collusion, is Pilate's behavior when Jesus stands before him. (a) The instant Pilate sees Jesus, he asks, "Are *you*[12] the king of the Jews?" Yet *no such phrase has been used by Jesus' accusers.* Indeed, the wording "king *of the Jews*" or "*of the Judeans*" (*tōn Ioudaiōn*) would not have been used by these plaintiffs at all. In all the New Testament, only non-Jews ever employ the phrase: magi at Herod the Great's court (Matt 2:2), Roman soldiers,[13] and Pilate;[14] and Pi-

---

[9]Here and at Luke 23:2.

[10]Matt 27:1-2; Mark 15:1; Luke 23:1; John 18:28.

[11]Each building has its champions as Pilate's Jerusalem headquarters. Cf. Bruce, *Acts,* 356-57 and attendant references.

[12]*Su,* emphatic, Matt 27:11; Mark 15:2; Luke 23:3. On John 18:33, cf. item (c) below.

[13]Matt 27:29; Mark 15:18; Luke 23:37; John 19:3.

[14]Matt 27:11, 37; Mark 15:2, 9, 12, 26; Luke 23:3, 38; John 18:33, 39; 19:19.

late thereby arouses emphatic Sanhedrin objections (John 19:21). But neither, when Pilate speaks, have the accusers used the indigenous term "king of Israel." Even that label they do not taunt Jesus with, until he is on the cross (Matt 27:42; Mark 15:32). In fact only at Luke 23:2 do Jesus' accusers so much as mention kingship—"Christ a king"—and for this they give Pilate no explanation. Now elsewhere, Jesus has in one parable seemed to call himself a king (Matt 25:35, 40); Nathanael is said once to have dubbed Jesus "king of Israel" (John 1:49); at the triumphal entry the disciples *perhaps* call Jesus "king" (Luke 19:38; John 12:13), though by other accounts it is the Evangelists' own quotation from Zech 9:9 (Matt 21:5; John 12:15). In any case, those utterances were days, weeks, months or years ago, and there is no sign that, when they occurred, Pilate took any notice.

Therefore when Pilate, on confronting Jesus, pounces *at once* on the charge of kingship, it *has* to be because somebody has coached him beforehand. Presently I shall suggest who the coach may have been.

(b) Other details of the Pilate trial point still more decisively to collusion. At Mark 15:1-4,

Pilate asked him (*epērōtēsen autón*), "Are you the king of the Jews?" And he answering him said, "You say so (*sù légeis*)." And the chief priests accused him of many things. And Pilate *again* asked him, "Have you no answer to make?"

Sù légeis is sometimes taken as an affirmative, meaning "Yes" or "I acknowledge it." But in that case there would be no point in the accusers continuing, *and no sense to Pilate's demand*, "Have you *no* answer to make?" Greek, however, uses the same sentence structure in questions as in statements. Furthermore Jesus, a Jew, would neither use nor acknowledge the title, "king of the Jews." His reply to Pilate is no affirmation. It is a question, "Do *you* say so?" At Matthew 26:64, to a different demand from the high priest, Jesus answers similarly, *Sù eipas*, "*You* said this?" "Was this *your* word?"[15] Jesus seems clearly aware of a conspiracy.

(c) At John 18:33-34 he voices this awareness emphatically:

Pilate summoned Jesus and said to him (*eipen autō*),[16] "You are the king of the Jews." Jesus answered, "Are you saying this on your own (*apò seautou*) or *did someone else say it to you about me?*"

---

[15]Westcott and Hort, margin, punctuates both replies, to Caiaphas and to Pilate, as questions: see *The New Testament in the Original Greek* (New York: Macmillan, 1881) 65n, 110n.

[16]Not "asked him," *epērōtēsen autón*.

Like the worshippers of Acts 4:24-30, Jesus perceives that Pilate has already planned with others, to do him in.

7. Two further passages, which do not flatly assert a tri-partite conspiracy, may nonetheless hint at it:[17]

"Our chief priests and rulers surrendered (*parédoken*) him to the judgment of death. And they crucified him." (Luke 24:20)

Of course "chief priests" and "rulers" and "they" do not have to be three distinct bodies; but they might be. And "surrendered" suggests that the "chief priests" (Sanhedrin?) and "rulers" (Antipas's retinue?) bowed to a more potent authority.

The dwellers in Jerusalem and their rulers . . . finding nothing whatever that deserved death, nonetheless besought Pilate to have him done away with (*anairethēnai*). (Acts 13:27-28)

Again "Jerusalem dwellers" and "rulers" and "Pilate" need not be three separate entities, but they might be. Further, while the words "besought Pilate to have him done away with" make you and me think of the trial, *anairethēnai* is in fact indefinite and tentative, and would better fit an earlier conference with the governor.

8. A final point is not without interest. Herod, Sanhedrin and Roman rule are the very forces that Jesus warns against, when he quits Antipas's territory and goes to Bethsaida and Caesarea Philippi:

Herod (or Herodians), Mark 8:15;
Sanhedrin, Matt 16:6 par., 11, 21 par.;
Roman crucifixion, Matt 16:21 par., 24 par.

And immediately after these discourses Jesus himself sets out for Jerusalem where the three enemy groups will come together.

Instigated by Herod Antipas

Consider that (a) the Jerusalem worshippers of Acts 4:24-31 are not under Antipas's rule, but under Pilate and the Sanhedrin. (b) Psalm 2:1-2, which they cite as prophecy, lists the Lord's foes as, first, Gentiles and peoples, then kings and rulers. (c) Peter and John have just come from a severe Sanhedrin harassment. Yet despite these things, the prayer names "Herod" first, then "Pilate along with the Gentiles," then "people of Israel."[18] This would be appropriate if Antipas himself instigated the con-

---

[17]Cf., in addition, Luke 13:31-33; 23:12, discussed in the next section.

[18]Syntactically, "Herod" here is clearly separate from "people of Israel" but he is *not* clearly distinct from "the Gentiles." Cf. n. 32 below.

spiracy. That he was in fact the prime mover is congruent with many other features.

1. The enmity of the Herods, against Jesus' family and associates, was evidently of long standing. Julius Africanus found that Herod the Great had tried to suppress the Davidic genealogy of Joseph, but was thwarted by Joseph's relatives.[19] Matthew 1:13-14 says that the same Herod the Great sought to kill the child Jesus, thus forcing Joseph, Mary and Jesus to flee to Egypt. Later (Matt 2:22-23) Joseph so dreaded Herod's son Archelaus that he moved north to Galilee; we are not told *why* Joseph feared Archelaus (nor, actually, that Mary and Jesus went with him this time). Decades afterward (Acts 12:1-3), Herod Agrippa I slew one of Jesus' closest companions and imprisoned another.[20]

2. Jesus after his baptism spent at least six weeks, probably longer, in Judea.[21] But when Antipas jailed John the Baptist, Jesus at once transferred (*anechōrēsen*) to Capernaum in Galilee, close to Antipas's seat of government at Tiberias (Matt 4:12-13 par.). Thereafter, his ministry so resembled the Baptist's that Matthew puts almost identical words on the two men's lips.[22] After John's death, many thought that Jesus was in fact the Baptist come back to life (Luke 9:17; Matt 16:14 par.).

3. John inveighed against doings in Antipas's household (Luke 3:19; Mark 6:18 par.). Jesus made inroads into that same household, including Antipas's boyhood chum Manaen (Acts 13:1) and Antipas's steward's wife Joanna (Luke 8:3; 24:10).

4. Antipas had John beheaded. Jesus thereupon withdrew into Herod Philip's tetrarchy (Matt 14:13 par.). There Jesus fed the five thousand (Matt 14:14-22 par.; John 6:5-19). And there the Fourth Gospel describes an incident which C. H. Dodd dubbed one of the most assuredly reliable in that Gospel.[23] Most of the multitude, too, had come over from Galilee (John

---

[19]Africanus wrote ca. A.D. 200. He is quoted by Eusebius, *Eccl. Hist.*, 1.7.

[20]But perhaps they were more cordial toward Paul. Though Agrippa II did not get Paul released, he was otherwise kindly toward him (Acts 25:13-26:32). Indeed, Paul may himself have been related to the Herods: he had a kinsman named Herodion, and a friend named Aristobulus (Rom 16:10-11).

[21]Matt 3:17-4:11 par.; cf. Matt 23:37; Luke 13:34. The Fourth Gospel makes it much longer, John 1:29-51; 2:13-3:36.

[22]Cf. Matt 3:2 with 4:17; 3:7 with 12:34; 3:8 with 12:33; 3:10 with 7:19; and 3:12 with 13:30.

[23]*Historical Tradition in the Fourth Gospel* (Cambridge: Cambridge University Press, 1963) 213-17.

6:2; cf. Matt 14:12-14 par.). On witnessing Jesus' deed, the crowd sought *to take him by force and make him king* (John 6:15). Jesus avoided them. The next day the crowd took boats which had come *from Tiberias,* and went in them *back to Capernaum* (6:24). It is the most open, most seemingly seditious move to enthrone Jesus that the Gospels record. News of it was bound to reach Antipas. And not long afterward Antipas himself went to Jerusalem, where he would find Pilate and the Sanhedrin.

5. However, much other news about Jesus reached Antipas. Indeed, Mark 3:6 says that Jesus aroused Herodians' enmity soon after he got to Galilee, so that they joined with some Pharisees to try to destroy him (*hopōs autòn apolésōsin*). No other gospel puts Herodian opposition so early. But the Synoptics all agree that, after the Baptist's death, Antipas heard more and more about Jesus, and became more and more exercised. Jesus so reminded him of John that he thought Jesus *was* John returned from death (Matt 14:1-2; Mark 6:14-16). Or perhaps, as Carl Kraeling surmised, Antipas feared that Jesus was using John's ghost to practise necromancy.[24]

6. Jesus' last journey took him through Perea, Antipas's southern domain. There Jesus learned that Antipas purposed to kill him (*thélei se apokteinai,* Luke 13:31).[25] Jesus' life seems already to have been menaced several times;[26] but in the Gospels this is only the second *decision by a governing power* to put Jesus to death—the first being by Antipas's father when Jesus was a child (Matt 2:13).

So Antipas too was now in Perea, evidently en route to Jerusalem. Jesus' rejoinder calls Antipas a "fox." In Jewish parlance "fox" meant not so much "crafty" as "nasty, inferior." Jesus' contempt for the tetrarch is plain. And he sends back word, not that Antipas's purpose will be thwarted, but that it will have to be accomplished in Jerusalem.

7. On reaching Jerusalem, almost Jesus' first word is a long expression of sorrow and anger over John the Baptist (Matt 22:23-32 par.). There follows an excoriation of the Sanhedrin which recalls the one by the Baptist, even to using the Baptist's own words.[27]

---

[24]"Was Jesus Accused of Necromancy?," *JBL* 70 (1940): 147-53.

[25]Greek *thélein* often denotes purpose or intent; cf. Bauer-Arndt-Gingrich, *A Greek-English Lexicon,* 355 ¶2.

[26]Matt 12:14 = Mark 3:6; Luke 4:29; John 5:18. But has Luke placed this attempted lynching too early? It resembles John 10:31-39. Also Luke 4:21 and 25-26 recall events that occurred much later in Jesus' career.

[27]Cf. Matt 23:2-38 with 3:1-11; and in particular, Matt 23:33 with 3:7. Cf. also Matt 23:39 with John 1:26b-27; and Matt 22:21 par. with Luke 3:12-13.

8. Thus it becomes exceedingly interesting to compare two passages, one from Josephus, the other from our Fourth Gospel:

Josephus, *Ant.* 18.5.2[28]	John 11:46-53
When everybody turned to John—for they were profoundly stirred by what he said—Herod feared that John's so extensive influence over the people might lead to an uprising (for the people seemed likely to do everything he might counsel). He thought it much better, under the circumstances, to get John out of the way in advance, before any insurrection might develop, than for himself to get into trouble and be sorry not to have acted, once the insurrection had begun. So because of Herod's suspicion, John was sent as a prisoner to Machaerus, the fortress already mentioned, and there put to death.	The chief priests and the Pharisees gathered the Sanhedrin, and said, "What are we to do? For this [Jesus] performs many signs. If we let him go on thus, everybody will believe in him, and the Romans will come and destroy both our place and our nation." And one of them, Caiaphas, who was high priest at that time,[29] said to them, "You know nothing at all. Nor do you consider that it is expedient for you that one man should die for the people, and that the whole nation not perish." . . . So from that day on, they took counsel how to put [Jesus] to death.

In other words,

According to Josephus	According to the Fourth Gospel
Herod Antipas feared	The Sanhedrin feared
that John would stir up the populace,	that Jesus would stir up the populace,
and that this might	and that this might
start an insurrection	start an insurrection
and bring down on him	and bring down on them
the wrath of higher authorities.	the wrath of Rome.
To avoid this,	To avoid this,
Herod Antipas concluded,	the Sanhedrin concluded,
it was necessary	it was necessary
to put John to death.	to have Jesus put to death.

There can be no question of literary dependence here, of the Gospel on Josephus or Josephus on the Gospel. Well, this Sanhedrin meeting will almost certainly have taken place after Antipas got to Jerusalem. If the Sanhedrin disquiet, and its decision, owed nothing to the tetrarch, we have a remarkable string of coincidences. If, on the other hand, *Antipas's urg-*

---

[28]Following the translation of H. St. John Thackeray in the Loeb Classical Library (London: Heinemann, 1930).

[29]*Tou eniautou ekeínou* is often translated "that year"; but *eniautós* means any considerable period from 1 to 600 years. (Cf. Bauer-Arndt-Gingrich, *A Greek-English Lexicon,* 265.) The high priesthood was not an annual office.

ings led to the Sanhedrin action, this would fit everything else we have learned about Antipas's stance toward Jesus.

9. Luke 23:6-7 seems to make Antipas's intervention more fortuitous than Acts does:

> Pilate . . . asked if [Jesus] was a Galilean. And having learned (*epignous*) that he was from Herod's jurisdiction, he sent him to Herod, who was himself also in Jerusalem during those days (*en tautais tais hēmérais*).

But we have already seen how this cannot have been a chance occurrence: (a) Before reaching Jerusalem, Antipas had already resolved on Jesus' death—and Jesus knew it. (b) Acts 4:27 says that Herod and Pilate were in collusion. (c) Pilate obviously knew both where the tetrarch was, and that he was prepared to examine the prisoner.

There are other reasons. (d) The accusers have said that Jesus carried his activities "right into this place" (*heōs hōde,* Luke 23:5). While they *might* mean merely "into Jerusalem," *hōde* has normally a more restricted sense. They *seem* to be saying, rather, that Jesus has reached into Pilate's own precincts. And indeed Matthew 27:19 indicates that Jesus has affected Pilate's own wife. Since he affected members of Herod's household too, this makes one more ground for the two rulers' common concern.

(e) And immediately before *that* phrase, the accusers use words almost identical with those attributed to Peter, later, at Caesarea:

Accusers before Pilate, Luke 23:5	Peter at Caesarea, Acts 10:37
. . . teaching	. . . the word spread
through the whole of Judea	through the whole of Judea
(*kath' hólēs tēs Ioudaías*)	(*kath' hólēs tēs Ioudaías*)
and beginning (*kai arxámenos*)	beginning (*arxámenos*)
from Galilee (*apò tēs Galilaías*).	from Galilee (*apò tēs Galilaías*).

Archomai, "begin," commonly signifies that the person has, up to this point, engaged in something else, and *his activity now takes a new turn.*[30] Thus both Peter and the accusers point first to a wide ministry in Judea, but after that to a new and critical start in Galilee. That change was, we saw, precisely because Antipas had arrested the Baptist. It can hardly be accidental that Luke recalls this sequence at the very moment when Jesus is to come for the first time face to face with this Herod.

Thus Luke 23:5-7 does not stand in the way of our previous findings. The hearing before Antipas was anything but fortuitous. Pilate's decision to send Jesus to Herod, the Sanhedrin's cooperation, and their words to Herod (Luke 23:10) were all according to plan.

---

[30]Cf. ibid.

10. The story of the Antipas hearing is brief, but full of interest.

When Herod saw Jesus he was very glad. For he had for some time wanted to see him, because of having heard about him. (Luke 23:8a-b)

The curiosity, and desire to see Jesus, are noted earlier at Luke 9:9. But at Matthew 14:2, Mark 6:14 the tetrarch expresses not just curiosity but positive *dismay* that Jesus is so like the Baptist.

And he hoped to see some sign from him. (23:8c)

No doubt Antipas would have enjoyed a bit of spine-tingling entertainment; yet this cannot have been the main, and certainly not the sole reason he was glad to have Jesus before him. He had declared that Jesus was John the Baptist *redivivus*. Jesus had stirred up Galilee. Antipas wanted him out of the way.

And he questioned him at length (*en lógois hikanois*). (23:9a)

This again indicates that the ruler wanted more than just to witness a "trick" or two. The questions doubtless dealt with matters long in the tetrarch's mind.

But he himself answered him nothing. (23:9b)

At the Sanhedrin and Pilate hearings, Mark and Matthew say Jesus spoke a little. In Luke he engages in extended colloquy with the Sanhedrin. In John he converses with both Sanhedrin and Pilate.[31] Therefore when Jesus refuses to speak to Antipas at all, it looks like one more expression of his disdain for that ruler.

But the chief priests and the scribes stood vehemently accusing him. (23:10)

What they hoped to gain from this is hard to say. The whole appears, again, to reflect prior arrangement, to accommodate both Antipas and Pilate.

Herod and his soldiers treated him as a despised thing (*exouthenēsas*). And he arrayed him in gorgeous apparel and sent him back to Pilate. (23:11)

In the other Gospels it is Pilate's soldiers who put the kingly garment on Jesus. By ascribing the act to Herod, Luke underscores Herod's part in Jesus' tragedy. The gorgeous (= royal?) apparel suggests that *Herod regarded Jesus as a political rival*. Indeed, as we saw, the most open move to make Jesus king had been next door to Antipas's capital, and by Antipas's own people. To be sure, some of this is in Luke only, and some in

---

[31]Matt 26:57-27:31; Mark 14:53-15:20; Luke 22:67-70; John 18:19-23, 33-38; 19:10-11.

John only. Nevertheless, *when Pilate leaps instantly on the issue of kingship, the obvious candidate for having initiated that charge is Antipas himself.*[32] And when Herod sends Jesus back to Pilate royally arrayed, it reads like a sequel to Antipas's earlier monitions.

> So (*dé*) Herod and Pilate became friends with one another that day. For hitherto they had been at enmity with each other. (23:12)

Luke does not say why they had been foes, whether for Pilate's murder of some Galileans (Luke 13:1), or because Pilate had set up imperial votive shields in Antipas's father's former palace,[33] or for some other reason. Nor are we told whether the new friendship began after, during, or before the trial. Certainly, however, it required more communication that just a shuttling back and forth of their prisoner.

> Pilate, calling together the chief priests and rulers and the people, said to them, "You brought me this man as one who misleads the people. And behold, after examination I do not find this man guilty of the things you charge against him. Neither does Herod, for he sent him back to us." (23:13-15a)

That last is not accurate. (a) Antipas could not and did not issue a judgment.[34] (b) In Perea, however, Antipas *had* determined that Jesus must die.

The Antipas hearing is an interruption. The simplest explanation for it is, I submit, that Pilate acted in response to Herod who had set the whole process in motion.

All four Gospels (and Acts 3:13-14) make Pilate temporize, and let himself be overruled by the Sanhedrin. Yet had he been as undecided as these writers imply, he had every right, and duty, to consult Rome before issuing judgment. He did not. In truth Pilate was no puppet, nor was he kindly disposed. He was stupidly cruel. *He* proceeded to find Jesus guilty of subversion or insurrection.[35] *He* formally sentenced him; here Luke 23:24 uses the technical formula *kaì Pilatos epékrinen*. He, Pilate, assigned the mode of execution. Yet if the Gospels are easier on Pilate than he deserved, if they as it were "whitewash" him, Luke 23:15 "whitewashes" Herod Antipas also.

---

[32]It is hard to say whether Antipas would resort to the phrase "king of the Jews/Judeans." Though he observed Jewish religious customs, he was in fact half Idumean, half Samaritan.

[33]Philo, *Leg.*, 299-305.

[34]In the apocryphal *Gos. Pet.*, Antipas does condemn Jesus. That author evidently did not know the legal situation.

[35]Matt 27:37-38 par.; John 19:18-20.

Finally, if the foregoing analysis is right, consider how astutely Antipas touched the most sensitive nerves, first of the Sanhedrin, then of Pilate. Jesus, Antipas concluded, was John the Baptist returned; and John, he had feared, would endanger Antipas's own freedom vis-à-vis Rome; so the Sanhedrin was made to fear lest Rome take away their freedom likewise. The issue that roused Pilate was related, but of different focus, namely, that some of the populace sought actually to enthrone Jesus.

In sum, in the agonies of Jesus' closing days Herod Antipas played a far greater role than is sometimes realized. His enmity against Jesus was of long standing. Of the three rulerships (Pilate, Sanhedrin, Antipas), Antipas was the first to decide that Jesus must die. But to get Jesus executed, Antipas had to enlist those other authorities who had jurisdiction. This, Acts 4:27 seems to say, is what Antipas did. And the core of Pilate's own information will have come most readily from this Herod. Finally, the tripartite conspiracy explains a great deal that otherwise is highly bizarre in the Gospel accounts.

Antipas got his wish.

THE HISTORICAL SETTING
OF JOHN'S BAPTISM

Bo Reicke

Luke has indicated that John the Baptist began to preach in the fifteenth year of emperor Tiberius' government (Luke '3:1), which corresponds to A.D. 28. The notice was probably based on popular recollections without support in documents, but it can give a general impression of the time in which the Jews were first confronted with the Baptist's demand to repent and receive baptism.[1]

In the *Antiquities* of Josephus there is a report of the circumstances under which John the Baptist was finally killed by Herod Antipas, the te-

---

[1]Some general studies of John the Baptist and his movement: J. Thomas, *Le mouvement baptiste en Palestine et Syrie, 150 av. J.-C.—300 ap. J.-C.* (Gembloux: Duculot, 1935); C. H. Kraeling, *John the Baptist* (New York: Scribner's, 1951); P. D. van Royen, *Jezus en Johannes de Doper* (Leiden: Luctor et Emergo, 1953); J. Steinmann, *St. Jean Baptiste et la spiritualité du désert* (Paris; Ed. du Seuil, 1955); W. H. Brownlee, "John the Baptist in the Light of Ancient Scrolls," in *The Scrolls and the New Testament*, ed. K. Stendahl (New York: Harper & Row, 1957) 33-53; O. Betz, "Die Proselytentaufe der Qumransekte und die Taufe im Neuen Testament," *RevQ* 1 (1958): 213-34; J. Gnilka, "Die essenischen Tauchbäder und die Johannestaufe," *RevQ* 3 (1961): 185-207; J. Daniélou, *Jean Baptiste, témoin de l'agneau* (Paris; Ed.du Seuil, 1964); Hartwig Thyen, "Baptisma metanoias eis aphesin hamartion," in *Zeit und Geschichte: Danksbegabe an R. Bultmann*, ed. Erich Dinkler (Tübingen: Mohr, 1964) 97-125; *Studien zur Sündenvergebung im Neuen Testament und seinen alttestamentlichen und jüdischen Voraussetzungen* (Göttingen: Vandenhoeck & Ruprecht, 1970) 131-45; R. Schütz, *Johannes der Täufer* (Zürich: Theologischer Verlag, 1967); W. Wink, *John the Baptist in the Gospel Tradition* (Cambridge: Cambridge University Press, 1968); J. Becker, *Johannes der Täufer und Jesus von Nazareth* (Neukirchen: Neukirchener Verlag, 1972); R. B. Gardner, *Jesus' Appraisal of John the Baptist* (Würzburg: Theol.Fak., 1973); A. Poppi, *L'inizio del Vangelo: Predicazione del Battista, battesimo e tentazione di Gesu* (Padova: Messagero, 1975); L. F. Badia, *The Qumran Baptism and John the Baptist's Baptism* (Lanham MD: University Press of America, 1980); G. Barth, *Die Taufe in frühchristlicher Zeit* (Neukirchen: Neukirchener Verlag, 1981) 17-43; J. Ernst, "Öffnet die Türen zum Erlöser. Johannes der Täufer—seine Rolle in der Heilsgeschichte," *TGl* 74 (1984): 137-65.

trarch of Galilee and Perea (Jos *Ant* 18.109-119). This passage deals with political history and does not contain any reference to Jesus and the Christians, so it cannot be a Christian interpolation. As a discussion of the details will show below, the historian's report implies that John was executed around A.D. 32.

The baptism preached by John may therefore be supposed to have been practiced from around 28 to around A.D. 32. On the basis of this tentative chronology, the present article will deal with the following questions: (1) What was the central *purpose* of John's baptism? (2) Against which historical *background* was it developed? (3) How was the *relationship* between John and Jesus understood?

I

With regard to the *purpose* of the Baptist's activity, one has to observe that in the Gospels as well in Acts and in the *Antiquities* of Josephus the emphasis is always on the *conversion* which John required of the candidates for baptism. Conversion is called *metánoia* in Greek, and it means change of mind (*noûs*). According to the fourth Gospel the Baptist ascribed perfect remission of sin to Jesus, the Lamb of God (John 1:29), but also declared that he baptized in order to let the redeemer be revealed (1:31). Since writers of so different kind as the synoptic evangelists, the fourth evangelist, and Josephus indicate that John had the reputation of preaching repentance and conversion when baptizing people, the conclusion must be that a baptism of conversion was really the central point of his program.

This has to be illustrated more in detail by quotations of relevant texts.

(a) Matthew represented the Baptist as a voice who cried in the wilderness: *metanoeîte* (Matt 3:2), and he was said to have characterized his activity in these words: "I baptize you in water (*eis metánoian*, 3:11).

Mark and Luke simply used the technical expression *báptisma metanoías* to characterize John's baptism (Mark 1:4, Luke 3:3). The latter evangelist repeated the expression when letting Paul, in synagogues of Asia Minor, remind the audience of John's baptism (Acts 13:24, 19:4). In the letters of Paul no reference to John is found, but the apostle may very well have spoken of the Baptist in Jewish synagogues, as Luke has asserted in his second book.

A saying of the Baptist quoted by Matthew and Luke, representing a double tradition of the category generally called Q, indicates which practical consequence this *metánoia* was supposed to have. John was said to expect that all people baptized should bear "a fruit", or "fruits", corresponding to their conversion (*karpòn áxion tês metanoías*, Matt 3:8; *karpoùs axíous tês metanoías*, Luke 3:8), and that otherwise they would not be saved from the imminent wrath of God. The point was obviously that conversion should not only be a momentary act or a superficial ceremony, but lead to a permanent change of the person's moral attitude.

Certainly this saying of John was transmitted by disciples of Jesus who connected the preaching of the Baptist with the coming of the Saviour. However, their emphasis on John's moral demand was also based on historical circumstances, for exactly the same demand is what the historian Josephus found characteristic of John the Baptist.

(b) Josephus mentioned the Baptist in connection with a war, in which Herod Antipas was defeated by the king of the Nabateans and only rescued through an intervention of Roman troops in A.D. 36 (Jos *Ant* 18.116-118). The reason why the Nabatean king attacked the Galilean tetrarch around A.D. 35 was that a few years earlier Antipas had divorced a Nabatean princess in order to marry Herodias, his sister-in-law who had dissolved her marriage with his brother Boethus. John the Baptist condemned the marriage of Antipas and Herodias as incestuous, for according to the Law she was to be regarded as his sister (Lev 18:16) while her former husband was still alive (Matt 14:3-4 ‖ Mark 6:17-18, Luke 3:19). Josephus concentrated his narrative on the great success of the Baptist in Perea, a country which belonged to Antipas and was close to Nabatean territory. He said the success caused Antipas to fear a revolt, wherefore the tetrarch kept John a prisoner in the Perean fortress of Machaerus east of the Dead Sea, and beheaded him there.[2] This execution can be dated to around A.D. 32, some years after the beginning of John's public ministry in 28 (Luke 3:1), but not too long before the Nabatean war against Antipas about the year 35. It must also be dated before the crucifixion of Jesus which, for other reasons, probably took place in the year 33. Josephus indicated that many people regarded the defeat of Antipas in that war as a punishment for the murder of John.

The synoptic evangelists have told about the decapitation of John the Baptist without referring to the Nabatean war and Perea (Matt 14:3, Mark 6:16-17, Luke 3:20, 9:9). Since neither Matthew nor Luke have localized the event, there is no contradiction between their reports and the reference of Josephus to Machaerus in Perea. Mark, however, allowed his readers to believe the drama had taken place in Galilee (Mark 6:21). Another mistake of his is the statement that Herodias had been married to Philip, the brother of Antipas (6:17). In reality the ambitious woman had been mar-

---

[2] Reports on John the Baptist and recent excavations of Machaerus, written by V. Corbo, S. Légasse, S. Lofreda and F. Manns, are found in *SBFLA* 27 (Jerusalem 1977) and subsequent volumes.

ried to another brother of Antipas, the above-mentioned Boethus, whereas Philip was the husband of her daughter Salome (Jos *Ant* 18.137).[3] At least the original texts of Matthew and Luke do not contain these errors. It was Mark who inserted the names of Galilee and Philip in order to vivify the narrative, which has also been decorated by him with several picturesque details. The opposite is not probable, namely that Matthew and Luke would have abolished the names in order to correct the story of Mark, for their concern was not at all to collect facts about Antipas. It must therefore be admitted that Matthew's and Luke's versions on the death of the Baptist were more directly based on available traditions than Mark's.[4] At any rate the reports of Matthew and Luke on the execution of the Baptist are not in conflict with that of Josephus, and both traditions actually supplement one another.

Independently of the synoptic Gospels, the *Antiquities* of Josephus also contain a characteristic of John's baptism which confirms the Matthean-Lukan tradition about the conversion required by the Baptist, as quoted above. Josephus was concerned with political faults committed by Antipas, and it was only in this context that he referred to the execution of John. He wanted to point out that John had been an honest man who practiced baptism on moral grounds and that his punishment by the tetrarch had rightly upset many people (Jos *Ant* 18.116-117):

> To some of the Jews it seemed the army of Herod (Antipas) had been destroyed by God, so that he was rightly punished for the execution of John, surnamed the Baptist. Herod killed this honest man, who exhorted those Jews, who practiced virtue and who acted in righteousness toward each other and in piety toward God, to come together for baptism. Thus it seemed to him that baptism was acceptable with reference to peo-

---

[3]Matthew and Mark did not mention the name of that daughter of Herodias who is said to have danced at the court of Antipas (Matt 14:6; Mark 6:22). According to Mark she was a young girl (*korásion*). Possibly the evangelists meant another daughter of Herodias and not exactly Salome, whom Josephus has mentioned as the wife of Philip (Jos *Ant* 18.137). This brother-in-law of Herodias died in A.D. 34 (18.106), and though he left no children behind, Salome may already have been his wife in the year 32 when the martyrdom of John the Baptist seems to have taken place.

[4]The same conclusion is drawn from literary points of view by W. R. Farmer, *Jesus and the Gospel: Tradition, Scripture, and Canon* (Philadelphia: Fortress Press, 1982) 116 (referring to F. P. Badham, *St. Mark's Indebtedness to St. Matthew* (London: Kegan Paul, 1897): "The text of Matthew is less developed. To reverse the process and have Matthew create out of Mark's text his concise but dramatic statement is more difficult to explain."

ple who did not use it as an excuse for certain sins, but as a consecration of the body provided that before it the soul had been thoroughly purified by righteousness.

This statement does not include any reference to Jesus and cannot be a Christian interpolation. On the contrary it must be treated as a historical testimony based on personal knowledge of the relevant circumstances. For although the Baptist had been killed some five years before Josephus was born in A.D. 37, the historian was able to receive local information about John when he was a teenager. This was the case during the years 54-56 which Josephus spent in the Judean desert as the disciple of a baptist leader by the name of Bannous (Jos *Vit* 11-12a):

> I heard that somebody named Bannous lived in the desert. He wore cloths stemming from trees, he ate food growing of itself, and for purity's sake preached frequent ablutions day and night. I became his devoted adherent, and stayed with him for three years. Having fulfilled my desire, I returned to the city at the age of nineteen.

In striking analogy to John the Baptist in the desert, the baptist teacher of Josephus called Bannous thus rejected all food prepared by man, and only accepted natural products found in the desert.[5] Concerning his clothing he was even more ascetic than John the Baptist, and seems to have represented a radicalized criticism of established society. It is uncertain whether there was a real connection or a mere analogy between the two baptists, but as Josephus lived for such a long time with Bannous, the curious and intelligent young man was certainly able to pick up information about the baptist John. Therefore his portrait of the latter must be supposed to depend on historical recollections, even if he used Hellenistic expressions to describe the moral demands of John the Baptist.

Thus, both in the Matthean-Lukan tradition and in the witness of Josephus, the ethical requirements of John the Baptist prove to have been what impressed the contemporaries more than anything else. Without any doubt the primary meaning of John's baptism was to impose a serious change of mind and a righteous way of life upon those baptized.

Another element common to both sources is the localization of John's activity. The evangelists said that Jewish people went out to the Baptist in the wilderness near the river Jordan, and the historian knew that John was successful in Perea and eventually imprisoned there. In both cases the evidence implies that his activity was concentrated in the Jordan valley and the Dead Sea region, and in both cases the candidates for baptism were supposed to have been Jews (Matt 3:5 || Mark 1:5, Matt 3:9 || Luke 3:8, Jos *Ant* 18.117a).

---

[5]Observations on the diet of John the Baptist in S. L. Davies, "John the Baptist and the Essene Kashruth," *NTS* 29 (1983): 569-71.

II

Seeking for the historical *background* of John the Baptist's movement in earlier forms of baptismal practice, one has to pay attention to the fact pointed out at the end of the foregoing paragraph, that is, the concentration of John's preaching on Israel. Because of its Jewish orientation the Baptist's practice must in the first instance be explained on the basis of traditions found in Judaism.

(a) In this connection scholars have sometimes referred to baptism of proselytes in Judaism as described for example in a rabbinic treatise preserved in the Talmud and which is called *Gerim*, "Foreigners".[6] However, there is a considerable difference between the baptism proclaimed by John and the proselyte baptism known from this and other rabbinic texts. John's baptism was offered to Jews. The evangelists have reported that he was visited by people from Jerusalem, Judea and the Jordan valley (Matt 3:5 ‖ Mark 1:5), and required conversion from Pharisees and Sadducees (Matt 3:7) using the argument that God would be able to change even stones in the desert into children of Abraham (Matt 3:9 ‖ Luke 3:8). Josephus, too, has explicitly spoken of a purification and baptism offered to Israel (as mentioned above). Accordingly the Baptist's intention was to create a new community within Israel, a congregation of individuals purified and justified. Unlike this, *Gerim* and the other rabbinic texts have presented ritual stipulations for the incorporation of foreigners into the Jewish people.[7]

(b) On the other hand, exactly the Baptist's approach to Israel justifies the question whether there was not a relationship between him and the *Essenes*, that group of pious baptists described by Philo and Josephus, now also known from the Qumran scrolls. Above all the Essenes wanted to re-establish the legitimate Jewish priesthood, and they adopted children to be educated as their novices (Jos *Bell* 2.120). To a great extent they lived in the desert of Judea, where they built a monastery at Qumran and ended during the Jewish war as refugees in the fortress of Masada. It is certainly not possible to show that John was a member of the Qumran colony, but there are reasons to believe in some contacts between him and the Essenes.

---

[6]References to rabbinic sources treating proselyte baptism in P. Billerbeck, *Kommentar zum Neuen Testament aus Talmud und Midrasch* (München: C. H. Beck, 1922) 1:102-12.

[7]Billerbeck (ibid., 112) regarded the external form of proselyte baptism as the model of John's baptism, but also pointed out the difference between the ritual stipulations of the rabbis and the moral requirements of John.

John's father and even his mother belonged to priestly families (Luke 1:5), and the significance of this fact may be realized by a comparison with the high esteem of the sons of Zadok in the Qumran community (1QS 5.2, CDC 4.1). As a child John was brought up in the Judean wilderness (Luke 1:80) where Qumran is also found; as a preacher and baptist he was active in parts of Judea and Perea surrounding Qumran. Just as the Qumran community was said to prepare for the coming of the Lord in the desert according to Isa 40:3 (1QS 8.14), so John was reported to have fulfilled this scripture (Matt 3:3 with par.), or even to have quoted it (John 1:23). In both cases the members of the relevant baptist movement came from the people of Israel and went out into the desert. Certainly there is a difference in so far as the Essenes regarded their baptisms as lustrations to be repeated, whereas John's baptism is described as a definitive, non-recurring, and eschatological ceremony. In spite of this difference, however, John the Baptist must be supposed to have been influenced to some extent by the Essene movement, for several characteristics which cannot be understood as coincidental are common to both groups.[8]

Therefore it is also legitimate to use the exhortations to conversion, which characterized the Essenes, to illustrate what John the Baptist had in mind when he preached *metánoia*. Philo and Josephus have emphasized the asceticism of the Essenes, pointing out how they wanted to avoid city life, sensual lust, and material wealth (Philo, *Omnis probus,* 75-87, *Hypoth* 11.1-18, Jos *Bell* 2.119-158). Their moral training was said to depend on the study of the Bible (Philo, *Omnis probus,* 80-82, Jos *Bell* 2.136,145). With the aid of the Qumran scrolls, this picture offered by Philo and Josephus can be confirmed and specified. To be included as full members of the Qumran community, the believers had to confess and to practice honest, profound and total conversion of their attitude toward God and the world. Otherwise they would be cursed (1QS 2.11-15), and no water of ablution would help them (3.4-6). It was a question of conversion from evil (5.1) to the will of God as defined in the Law of Moses (5.1,8). Thus conversion meant accepting the covenant that was established by God in the past and is now represented by the elect people (5.22). Life should be controlled by what is absolutely true and right, that is, the Law of God (6.15). Moreover, conversion from sin was said to be not only the precondition, but also the consequence of this return to God's covenant (1QH 6.6, 14.21,24), for it was regarded as the work of God's grace and love (1QS

---

[8]Since the discovery of the Qumran caves in 1949, similar observations have been made by numerous scholars, and some of them are quoted above in n. 1.

1.8, 4.4, CDC 8.17). Forgiveness of sin and the justification of man were expressly said to be the free gifts and works of God (1QS 2.1, 11.2-5). Several of these points are reminiscent of what can be established about the preaching of John the Baptist.

In accordance with the emphasis on God's initiative, the Qumran believers also expressed their conviction of having received the Holy Spirit of God enabling them to practise knowledge and obedience. This topic is especially found in the last part of the Qumran Book of Psalms (1QH 15.22-17.26 passim, Fragm 2.9,13). Every member of the Qumran organization was expected to praise God for having been elected and purified by the Holy Spirit and thus being allowed to join the community (1QH 16.12). Conversion was therefore understood as something more than a decision of man to change his mind. It was also supposed to imply a divine regeneration of man based on his participation in the Holy Spirit which had been sprinkled on him like water (1QS 4.21, 1QH 17.26).[9] The persons reborn in the desert were described as trees of life having permanent connection with the water of life in paradise (1QH 8.4-20).

Seeing that such advanced ideas of the Holy Spirit are found in Qumran texts, one is prompted to raise the question whether there was not a difference at this point between John the Baptist and the Essene pietists. Deviating from the Qumran witnesses, the New Testament reflects the view that John the Baptist and his followers did not offer more than a baptism in water, ascribing the distribution of the Holy Spirit to a coming authority of whom John only claimed to be the forerunner (Matt 3:11 with par., John 1:33, Acts 1:5, 11:16, 19:2).

However, although early Christian writers had reasons to relativize the pre-eminence of the Baptist maintained by his disciples whom they still found in their environment (Luke 3:15, Acts 1:5, 11:16, 18:25, 19:3), the New Testament picture of John's restriction to a baptism in water must not have been absolutely wrong. It may be assumed that John did actually baptize in water only, while reserving the distribution of the Holy Spirit to somebody that would bring the final consummation. This suggestion is based on an essential circumstance observed above: that John's preaching and baptism of conversion was not offered to an inner circle of exceptional sanctity and spirituality, but to the population of the Holy Land in general. Our four evangelists could not deny the fact that John the Baptist had given rise to a broad movement of spontaneous conversion in Judea and Perea, so that "all people" were said to have streamed together wanting by his

---

[9]Brownlee, "John the Baptist," 43; see n. 1 above.

baptism to be saved from destruction (Matt 3:5 with par., 11:7, Luke 7:24, Matt 21:26 with par., John 1:7; cf. Acts 13:24). Josephus also described this extraordinary popularity of the Baptist (Jos *Ant* 18.118). It is evident that John wanted to bring as many people as possible to conversion, and therefore was not able to impose spiritual exercises upon his adherents, like those required for two years from the novices of the Qumran monastic order (1QS 6.21). Just because of the expansion of his revival movement as compared with that of the Essenes, of which John was obviously aware, he may be supposed to have told people converted that his baptism in water had also to be completed by a baptism with the Holy Spirit. On this account it does not seem absurd to presume that he did expect somebody greater coming to make a general distribution of the Spirit possible. This would greatly correspond to what the evangelists have reported on the messianic prophecy of John (Matt 3:11 with par., John 1:33), although they could not avoid interpreting his declarations in the light of Christ's coming in Jesus.

According to Matthew and Mark, the endeavors of John to convert people in Judea and Perea were continued by Jesus in Galilee, after John had baptized him and become a prisoner (Matt 4:17 ‖ Mark 1:15). The fourth evangelist gave more generous information by stating that Jesus, after being proclaimed the Lamb of God by John, began to preach a new birth in water and spirit (John 3:5). Christ was even said to have practiced baptism himself (3:22), or at least to have permitted his disciples to baptize (4:2). In obvious analogy to John's parenetic activity, the Gospels of Mark and Luke have furthermore reported that Jesus sent out his apostles to preach *metánoia* (Mark 6:12, Luke 24:47), and in later contexts this preaching was explicitly connected with baptism (Acts 2:38, Heb 6:1-2).

Yet there was probably a difference between John the Baptist and Jesus or his apostles in so far as the reason and the result of man's conversion were hardly supposed to be the same. John was a prophet who preached repentance before the imminent judgment (Matt 3:7 ‖ Luke 3:7; cf. Matt 11:18, Luke 7:33), and since he appears to have been influenced to some extent by the Qumran movement, he may be supposed to have required a conversion back to the Law of the Old Covenant (as mentioned above). Jesus and his apostles, on the other hand, are consistently said to expect a more forward-looking, eschatological attitude of conversion: Man's interest should be controlled by the divine energy and reality now proclaimed in the New Covenant (Matt 4.17 ‖ Mark 1:15, Matt 18.3, Luke 24:47, John 3:5, Acts 2:38, 3:19, etc.).

(c) Beside the analogies here emphasized concerning the Essenes of Qumran, the baptismal movement initiated by John and continued by Jesus may, in a wider context, be compared with religious ideas and rites found in other Jewish traditions. Religious ablutions were practiced very early in Egypt, Sumer, and other parts of the ancient world, but it does not seem possible to derive John's baptism or Christian baptism from any civilization so remote. Even attempts to explain the baptismal movements of John and Jesus with the aid of Hellenism are to be rejected, since the region of the Jordan was not exactly a center of hellenistic piety. It is only possible to adduce certain Jewish traditions based on the Old Testament, which may have been of importance for the baptismal practice of the Essenes and consequently inspired John to some degree.

Ezekiel's reference to a water of purification, which God will sprinkle upon the elect people (Ezek 36:25), can be supposed to have inspired Jewish pietists to develop baptismal ceremonies. But this prophecy does not alone explain the ritual practice in question.

It seems that a more concrete explanation is found in priestly traditions. Since the Essenes wanted to represent the legitimate priesthood and the genuine people of Israel (CDC 4.2-3), the ritual bath which the High-Priest took in the Temple on the day of atonement (Lev 16:24) may have contributed to their baptismal ceremonies. A similar baptism was required from all priests before eating of the sacrifices, if they had been polluted by anything unclean during the day (Lev 22:5; the expression *rāḥaṣ* means "to wash, bathe"). Rabbinic traditions applied this stipulation to every priest before he took on the white garments and began his temple service (Mishna Yom 3.2b-7a, Bab Talm. Ber 2b,2; the expression *ṭābal* means "to dip, bathe"). In the Mishna and Tosephtha a special treatise was devoted to the question what degree of uncleanness was still clinging to a person who had taken a ritual bath the same day, and the text in question is called *Tebūl jōm* ("Somebody cleansed the same day"). Other rabbinic traditions mention sectarians characterized as Morning-Baptists because they required a ritual bath from everybody before the morning-prayer (Jos Yad 2, Bab Talm. Ber, 22a). A similar expression found in Christian traditions is *hemerobaptistaí,* which means Daily Baptists and was used to indicate several Jewish and Christian sects (Just *Dial* 80, Eus *Hist* 4.22.7, Can *eccl apost* 6.6.5, Epiph *Haer* 17). John the Baptist was also counted among them, a mistake perhaps based on the attitude of his later disciples (Ps Clem *Hom* 2.23).

The picture given by these Jewish and Christian texts may not be quite exact, but so much is evident that communities of pietists among the Jews wanted to represent the genuine Old Testament priesthood. In so far as they applied the ritual baths and water ablutions of the priests to all believers, they developed into different groups of baptists. The water ceremony was either regarded as being an initiation of the believers once for all, or a purification to be repeated on special occasions and in some cases daily.

In the New Testament, John the Baptist represents the first type of baptism, a unique, nonrecurring ceremony of initiation. This makes him differ from the Essenes and other Jewish baptists, though partial connections between him and the Qumran believers may be assumed.

Jesus was also baptized once and for all in the river Jordan, and never repeated the ceremony which is described as implying his initiation to a life guided by the Spirit (Matt 3:16 with par.). He rejected the repeated ablutions practiced by Jewish pietists (Matt 15:2 || Mark 7:5, Matt 23:25, Luke 11:39), and restricted such rites among Christians baptized (John 13:10). Post-apostolic tradition has further emphasized the uniqueness and singularity of Christian baptism, though inclinations to adopt the repeated baptisms of Jewish groups were found in the Orient.

III

Another question to be treated is the historical and theological *relationship* between John the Baptist and Jesus Christ. It is reflected and interpreted by New Testament documents in different ways.

(a) The first point to be considered is a historical circumstance unanimously attested by the evangelists: that John the Baptist had been visited by Jesus at the place where people were gathered to receive his baptism (Matt 3:13 || Mark 1:9a || Luke 3:21a, John 1:29). According to the synoptic Gospels, John then *baptized Jesus* (Matt 3:16a || Mark 1:9b || Luke 3:21b). This is not mentioned in the fourth Gospel, but indicated there by the Baptist's observation of the Spirit upon Jesus (John 1:32). No doubt the apostles knew that John had baptized Jesus.

In the synoptic reports on the baptism of Jesus, the Saviour is said to have experienced how the heaven was opened, the Spirit came upon him and the voice of God proclaimed him as the Son (Matt 3:16b with par.). This was especially reported with regard to similar experiences to be made by his disciples, for even if Christ's baptism was supposed to be a unique event, the Christians were also meant to be confronted with a heavenly reality by receiving spirit and sonship at their baptism. In the Johannine report, however, it is the Baptist who proclaims Christ's sonship (John 1:34). He enforces this proclamation by identifying Jesus with the Lamb of God which brings remission of human sin (1:29), and by observing the coming of the Holy Spirit on him like a dove (1:32) which indicates that Christ will be the one who offers the expected baptism in spirit (1:33).

(b) Christ's adoption of John's baptism led the Christians to portray the Baptist as the *forerunner* of the Saviour. Thus the Baptist was understood as that voice in the wilderness, of which Second Isaiah had said that it would be sent to prepare the way of the Lord (Isa 40:3). Remarkably enough the Qumran community had already used the same prophecy to explain its own activity in the wilderness (1QS 8.13-14): "They shall go out in the desert to prepare His way there, as is written: Prepare the way . . . (scil., of the Lord) in the desert, straighten the road of our God in the wilderness" (Isa 40:3). Just as the Essenes living in the desert motivated their messianic expectations by quoting that passage of Isaiah, so the evangelists interpreted John the Baptist in the light of the same prophecy. In the latter case, however, an interesting difference between the Gospels occurs: The synoptic evangelists have remarked that John fulfilled the prophecy in question (Matt 3:3 with par.), while the fourth evangelist has stated that John quoted it himself (John 1:23). John's function of a forerunner was further illustrated by his declaration that he felt unworthy to unbind the sandals of the Coming One (Matt 3:11 with par., John 1:27), that is to do the humble service of washing his feet.[10] Another expression of his subordination is found in connection with the image of Christ as the bridegroom, and here again that characteristic difference between the Gospels can be observed. The synoptic evangelists have quoted Jesus as saying that John's penitential rules should belong to the past, because the presence of the bridegroom implies joy (Matt 9:15 with par.). According to the fourth Gospel the Baptist had declared himself that he was sent as the forerunner of Christ and the best man of the bridegroom (John 3:28-29).[11]

(c) John's function as Christ's forerunner was also understood against the background of *salvation history*. In this context the four Gospels share the conviction that John the Baptist had been sent by God (Matt 21:25 with par., John 1:6). With regard to details, however, particular aspects of each Gospel have to be observed.

Matthew has especially mentioned that John first hesitated to baptize Jesus, and then did it after having been told: "In this way it is proper for us to fulfill all righteousness" (Matt 3:14-15). The argument implies that God had sent his Son to undergo John's baptism, thus letting the righteousness preached by the Law, the Prophets, and finally by the Baptist, be sublimated in the person of Jesus. The interest of Matthew in the conception of

---

[10]P. Proulx and L. A. Schökel, "Las sandalias del Mesías Esposo," *Bib.* 59 (1978): 1-37. The authors combine the washing of the feet with the below-mentioned traditions concerning Christ as bridegroom.

[11]R. Infante, "L'amico dello sposo figura del minstero di Giovanni Battista nel Quarto Vangelo," *RevistB* 31 (1983): 3-19.

righteousness is reflected in the Sermon on the Mount (5:6,10,20, 6:33), and in a later utterance of Jesus the Baptist is said to have come in the way of righteousness (21:32). In the Sermon on the Mount, Jesus also emphasizes that he fulfills the Law and the Prophets (5:17). A double tradition of Matthew and Luke dealing with the importance of the Baptist (Matt 11:7-19, Luke 7:24-35) contains an explicit declaration that John's preparation of Christ's coming (seen in the light of Mal 3:1) implied the culmination of Old Testament prophecy and law (Matt 11:9 and 13, Luke 7:26 and 16:16), though it is now surpassed by the children of the kingdom (Matt 11:11, Luke 7:28). Jesus was also said to have called the Baptist a new Elijah (referring to Mal 3:23), which equally indicates the culmination of the Old Covenant in John (Matt 11:14, 17:12 || Mark 9:12).[12]

In the Gospel of Mark there is less material dealing with John the Baptist than in the other Gospels. This can be explained by the assumption that Mark had such readers in mind as were believers, and had already received elementary information but appreciated concrete narratives. In fact his references to John the Baptist do not represent didactic but narrative interests, and the episodes depicted by Mark belong to synoptic triple and double traditions all found in contextual parallelism (Mark 1:2-11 and 14, the appearance of the Baptist; 2:18, the question of fasting; 6:14-29, the death of the Baptist; 9:13, Elijah already come; 11:30, John's baptism sent from heaven). Mark's more narrative and less didactic orientation is apt to explain why he left out several Baptist traditions preserved by Matthew and Luke. He found it sufficient to demonstrate that John had been the forerunner of Christ (a topic enforced in Mark 1:2 by the insertion of Mal 3:1 treated as if it were the beginning of Isa 40:3). Then he dramatized the intrigues of Herodias against the Baptist (Mark 6:17-29) in order to clarify their analogy with the hatred of Jezebel against Elijah (1 Kgs 19:2), understood to be a prophecy on the passion of John as Elijah redivivus (Mark 9:13, "as written about him," pointed out by Mark alone). John thus appears in Mark as preparing the way of the Lord (1:2) under two special aspects, that of a forerunner and that of a martyr.[13]

Luke was especially concerned with the ministry of John as the forerunner of Christ. This interest has found an expression in the prologue where

---

[12]M. M. Faierstein, "Why Do the Scribes Say that Elijah Must Come First?" *JBL* 100 (1981): 75-86; D. C. Allison, "Elijah Must Come First," *JBL* 103 (1984): 256-58.

[13]C. Wolff, "Zur Bedeutung Johannes des Täufers im Markusevangelium," *TLZ* 102 (1977): 857-65.

Luke indicated his ambition to describe everything from the beginning (Luke 1:3), and therefore he started his report with narratives illustrating the birth and the childhood of John. It appears that Luke took over the relevant stories and hymns from early Christians in Jerusalem who, using Baptist traditions but focusing them on Christ, emphasized the coherence of salvation history but superseded an inclination found in baptist circles to glorify John as the one expected to fulfill the hope of Israel (Luke 1:14, 68, 3:13, Acts 13:25a). To begin with, Luke admitted that John came from the tribe of Levi, both parents being of priestly descent (Luke 1:5), and that his birth depended on a revelation in the Temple, the center of the Old Covenant (1:9-13). But then he pointed out that Jesus came from the tribe of Judah and was born in the city of David (1:27, 2:11). This concern for the family background of both may be a reflection of the Essene belief in two Messiahs, one from Levi and one from Judah (1QS 9.11, 1QSa 2.12,14,20, CDC 12.23-24, 14.19, 19.10-11, 20.1, 4QTest 12,14).[14] At any rate Luke has further emphasized the parallelism of John and Jesus by his remark that their mothers were relatives (Luke 1:36) and met shortly before the children were born (1:40), but then has underlined the superiority of Jesus by telling how the mother of the Baptist welcomed the mother of the Lord (1:42). It is further remarkable that Luke has preserved the above-mentioned double tradition about the culmination of the Law and the Prophets in John (Matt 11:7-19, Luke 7:24-35), the central point of which Luke has taken up again in a later context (Luke 16:16).

In the fourth Gospel the reader is also confronted with the preliminary function of John the Baptist at the very beginning, but the evangelist John has then preferred to characterize the position of the Baptist in salvation history with the aid of personal quotations and theological conceptions. Thus the prologue includes a solemn declaration that John the Baptist was sent to witness about the incarnation of the eternal Logos and the authentic Light (John 1:6-8), and several testimonies of this kind are quoted in subsequent passages. Since the presentation of the Baptist in the prologue is directly continued by references to the incarnation of the Logos and Light (1:9-11) as well as by indications of the sonship and new birth granted to his believers (1:12-13), the practical framework of the prologue can be understood as baptismal preaching. At any rate the evangelist found it essential that John the Baptist had come to witness about Christ as the Logos and Light in this dark world. For in what follows the author has taken spe-

---

[14]K. G. Kuhn, "The Two Messiahs of Aaron and Israel," in *The Scrolls*, ed. Krister Stendahl (New York: Harper & Row, 1957) 54-64.

cial care to quote personal testimonies of John on Jesus. He has presented a series of five such testimonies in his first chapter (1:15-36), and a sixth testimony in his third chapter (3:27-36). The topics of these Baptist testimonies may be defined as follows: (1) Jesus has existed from eternity and inspired all preachers from Moses to the Baptist, although he began his own preaching after the latter (1:15-18; cf.1:30). (2) John only claimed to be the voice in the wilderness, and to baptize in water (1:19-28). (3) He recognized Jesus as the Lamb of God which removes the sin of the world (1:29-31). (4) John also said that he saw how the Spirit came down upon Jesus, so that he realized that Christ as the Son of God would replace John's baptism in water by a baptism in holy spirit (1:32-34). (5) When proclaiming Jesus as the Lamb of God, John the Baptist also brought two of his disciples over to Jesus (1:35-37). (6) He explained again that he should not be regarded as the Messiah. This title ought to be reserved for Jesus as the heavenly bridegroom, whereas John wanted to be Christ's best man and to rejoice over the success of his superior (3:27-36).[15] In a later context the evangelist has related that Christ, just before his passion began, returned to the place near the Jordan where the Baptist had been active, and that people found the latter's proclamations about Jesus confirmed (10:40-41).

These different pictures of John the Baptist, offered by the four evangelists, are theological interpretations of his role in the history of salvation. It is not fair to call them unhistorical, although they are neither uniform nor based on direct biographical information. They imply historical truth in so far as they depict the relationship between the movement of John and the activity of Jesus.

Seen in a general soteriological perspective, the Gospels may be said to indicate that John's task was to bring about the culmination of the Old Covenant represented by the Law and the Prophets. This has explicitly been ascertained in passages referred to above: in a Matthean-Lukan tradition containing declarations of Jesus on the Baptist (Matt 11:11a, 13, Luke 7:28a, 16:16) and in a Johannine tradition quoting words of the Baptist about Jesus (John 1:16-17). Implicitly, however, John's function as an intermediary between the Old and New Covenants is reflected in other Gospel passages as well. His announcement of the approaching judgment and his baptism of conversion in the desert and in the river at the border of civilized life were understood as a continuation of the Law's elenctic function. It had to bring everybody to realize that he is a sinner and must be converted in order to avoid the judgment. At the same time, John's prophetic

---

[15]J. Wilson, "The Integrity of John 3:22-36," *JSNT* 10 (1981): 34-41.

utterances on the Coming One have to be considered. When the Gospel was preached by Jesus, it had in this way been prepared by the Law under its elenctic and prophetic aspects. Corresponding to the functional difference between the Law and the Gospel, the message of John was different from that of Jesus and yet its forerunner. This is theologically what the four Gospels were to show in four individual ways.

JESUS AND THE KINGDOM:
THE RESTORATION OF ISRAEL
AND THE NEW PEOPLE OF GOD

E. P. Sanders

Not very long ago more or less everyone supposed that the primary relationship between Jesus and his contemporaries in Jewish Palestine was one of hostility, so that, if one asked about his views on "Israel," the answer would be that he was against it—or, at least was against it as it had always been conceived. The answer might then continue that other Jews of his day had a narrow and nationalistic view of Israel and consequently of God, and that Jesus had fallen into conflict with his contemporaries partly because of this. He wanted to take the message of God's love beyond the confines envisaged by his contemporaries.

It has usually been regarded as self-evident that Jesus could not have agreed with the doctrine of the election, or have thought favorably about the nation of Israel as such. Christian NT scholars—Gentile to the core— have tended to think that being Jewish did not matter much to Jesus. To illustrate the dominant view of four generations of mainline NT scholarship, I quote Günther Bornkamm:

> Jesus has by no means substituted the idea of a kingdom of God embracing all men for the hope of the coming of the kingdom of God to Israel alone. But it is no less clear that through Jesus' words and actions the illusion of the inalienable, as it were, legal rights of Israel and its fathers is attacked at the root and shaken to pieces.[1]

I shall not discuss here the first part of Bornkamm's statement, which denies universalism to Jesus. This is an important and interesting question, specially in view of Jesus' attitude towards the tax collectors and sinners. If they are in the kingdom, who is excluded? But, as I said, I leave this aside in order to focus on the denial that Jesus could have seen the election of the nation of Israel positively. In arguing that he did not, NT scholars have seen themselves as following not only Jesus, but also many of the prophets, down to and including John the Baptist, who spoke against Jewish complacency and reliance on the election.

---

[1]Günther Bornkamm, *Jesus of Nazareth,* trans. Irene and Fraser McLuskey with James M. Robinson (New York: Harper & Brothers, 1960) 66.

We are in the midst of a serious problem, as a moment's reflection will show. Everyone agrees that Jesus proclaimed something which he called "the kingdom of God." Yet we are told he did not offer it indiscriminately to one and all, but neither did he offer it to the descendants of Abraham as such. Then to whom? The problem is not just with modern Christian scholars who have their own agenda. The problem is actually in the gospels themselves. There we find passages in which Jesus is critical of aspects of Judaism, but also passages in which he shows himself reluctant to go to Gentiles. What, then, was he up to? Did he wish, for example, to put himself at the center, and to assert that *only those* who followed him would be in the kingdom? That is also a problem, since it attributes to Jesus a more exclusive view than the doctrine of the election.

There are four principal ways of responding to the question of to whom did Jesus direct the proclamation of the kingdom.

1. He addressed people as individuals. He intended to confront every hearer in her or his own individuality. He addressed neither humanity as such, and certainly not the nation of Israel as such, but each individual who encountered him met the challenge to give up self-striving and to be open to God's future. Thus his message, individualistic, could readily be universalized; since individualism and universality go together. All individuals make up the human universe. This was Bultmann's view, and we have just seen that it was Bornkamm's, and it has been one of the chief scholarly interpretations. It denies any special status to Israel: special status, rather, is "shaken to pieces."

2. He addressed all Israel and intended *reform*. He attacked only abuses or individual aspects of Judaism.

3. He wanted to establish the *true Israel* that is a remnant of the especially pious and loyal. Remnant or true Israel theology is well known from the biblical prophets.

It is quite easy, of course, to combine *reform* and *remnant*. If reform is preached, and not all accept, those who do accept will be the righteous remnant. In traditional remnant theology the rest will be physically destroyed by God's avenger (e.g., the Assyrians).

4. Jesus addressed all Israel, but he did so only pro-forma. He shared a common view, that Israel should be restored before the end, and that then Gentiles would enter the kingdom. He held this view, but he knew in advance that Israel would reject his preaching, and he offered the kingdom to them only so that their destruction would be justified.

Let us cast our eye back over these four possibilities. Number four strikes us as a bit strange. Why would Jesus spend his time and energy on Israel if he thought that Israel would be destroyed and that his message would go to the Gentiles? In that case, why did he not just start to preach to Gentiles? There were lots around. Number one makes sense to moderns: Jesus shared our preoccupation with our own existential individuality. He addressed individuals then, his message addresses them now.

Numbers 2 and 3, or 2 and 3 combined, are the ones which make best sense to moderns: Jesus was a reformer, and he thought that Israel would, when the kingdom came, consist of those who reformed. Remnant thinking usually had in mind a reform and survival of the few, but it need not do so. Perhaps Jesus thought of a righteous remnant—those who reformed—as being very numerous. Perhaps he expected large success. In this case he would be a reformer, and he would expect a remnant, but we could avoid the thought that he anticipated the destruction of the majority.

The combination of reform and remnant has another very great appeal. It can explain how the movement started by Jesus ended up, after his death and resurrection, largely Gentile. The explanation runs like this: Jesus called on Israel to reform, but too few heeded the call, either when it was presented directly by him or by his followers. The followers—or at least the close followers—appear to have numbered no more than about 500 (see 1 Cor 15:6). That is *too small* a remnant. In that circumstance, it was reasonable for his call eventually to make its way to the Gentiles, who heeded it. We see this presentation of early Christian history in Acts—Paul preaches to the Jews, who heed not, and he then goes to the Gentiles, and it makes good sense. Thus the notion of a call to reform, and the gathering of a remnant, which eventually became a Gentile majority (1) corresponds more or less to what happened after Jesus' death and (2) agrees with modern notions of religious movements and their development. This turns out to be another way of asserting the *individualism* of Christianity: it addresses each individual in his or her own circumstances. National boundaries do not matter much, and individuals who wish to accept may. This is all very appealing. The question is, of course, whether or not this fits with the way in which Jesus saw his own mission.

Once we reach this stage, in which modern assumptions about individualism and freedom of choice determine what views we attribute to ancients, we know that we had better pause and examine the matter more closely. It seems so self-evident to most of us that a worthwhile message should be *universal and individual* that it is hard to imagine another. Further, it is so easy for us to think of growth and progress, spread and development, that we can readily imagine how a message which began locally could spread. Still further, we know that Jesus' followers did in fact develop a world-wide vision. But here scholars are unanimous in denying to Jesus the view that his message of God's grace and love should gradually spread throughout the civilized world. We keep coming back to a problem: he addressed only Israel. The question is, with what end in view?

After considerable debate with myself, I have decided not to make many negative arguments with regard to "Jesus as reforming prophet." I would have to go through passage after passage, showing why it should be taken in some other way, or—most often—why it should be attributed to Luke rather than Jesus. That is tedious, and it would consume our time while doing no more than raising question marks. I want instead to address no. 4, and then to put my own view vis-à-vis nos. 1 and 4. First, to recall no. 1: Jesus had nothing positive to say about the national hope of his people. This gives him a curiously remote position if he was a Bible-reading Jew. Scripture is full of promises to Israel. The position which I have numbered 4 has the merit of taking very seriously Jesus' standing in his actual history, and his belief in the God of the scripture, and even his place within the prophetic and eschatological tradition within Israel. It seriously takes Jesus, in other words, as a first-century Jew. Thus it requires attention.

First, again, to summarize it: Jesus preached to Israel, but did so knowing that he would be rejected, and he did so in order that the election of Israel would be honored as a matter of form. He acted thinking that Israel in fact would be destroyed, and the kingdom would pass to the Gentiles.

This is a strange view, and it seems to attribute to Jesus such cynicism, that you may be inclined to reject it out of hand. It was, however, the view of Joachim Jeremias, one of the most influential NT scholars of this century. He was a man of great personal piety, and he gave himself out to be, and was generally regarded as being, a great expert in the Judaism of Jesus' time. Thus his view, or aspects of it, has been widely accepted. His proposal, in more detail, runs like this:

1. *Jesus limited his own mission, and that of his disciples during his lifetime, to Israel.*[2] This rests upon Matthew 10:5-6 and 15:24. According to 15:24, Jesus said, in response to a request to heal the daughter of a Canaanite woman, "I was sent only to the lost sheep of the house of Israel." According to 10:5-6, he sent forth his disciples with the charge, "Go nowhere among the Gentiles, and enter no town of the Samaritans, but go rather to the lost sheep of the house of Israel."

2. *The end of the present order would come, but before it did, the gospel would be preached to the Gentiles, not by human missionaries, but by God's angel.*[3] This rests upon combining the view that the end was near (and thus

---

[2] Joachim Jeremias, *Jesus' Promise to the Nations,* trans. S. H. Hooke (London: SCM Press, 1958) 19-39.

[3] Ibid., 46-51, 69.

did not allow time for a world-wide mission by humans) with Mark 13:10 and 14:9: "the gospel must first be preached to all nations"; "truly, I say to you, wherever the gospel is preached in the whole world, what she has done will be told in memory of her." These references to "preaching the gospel to the whole world," Jeremias assures us, refer to angelic activity, and thus he retranslates Mark 14:9: "Amen I say unto you, when the triumphal news is proclaimed (by God's angel), to all the world, then will her act be remembered (before God), so that he may be gracious to her (at the last judgment)."

3. *The present generation of Israel would be excluded from the kingdom, but Gentiles would come in.*[4] This rests upon Matthew 12:41-42 and 8:11-12:

> The men of Nineveh will arise at the judgment with this generation and condemn it; for they repented at the preaching of Jonah, and behold, something greater than Jonah is here. The queen of the South will arise at the judgment with this generation and condemn it; for she came from the ends of the earth to hear the wisdom of Solomon, and behold, something greater than Solomon is here.
>
> I tell you, many will come from east and west and sit at table with Abraham, Isaac and Jacob in the kingdom of heaven, while the sons of the kingdom will be thrown into the outer darkness; there men will weep and gnash their teeth.

To these passages Jeremias needed to add only two more points in order to achieve his result. One is the theological principle, "to the Jew first, then to the Gentile." This is actually stated by Paul (e.g., Rom 1:16), not by Jesus. But, Jeremias proposed (not without reason), Paul only reflects common Jewish opinion.[5] Thus, he thought, Jesus himself held this view, and saw himself as achieving the first part, preaching to Israel, so that God's angel could take care of the important part, proclamation to the Gentiles. The second further ingredient was the theory that in Jesus' day Judaism was uniformly hostile towards Gentiles. Jesus, he said, removed the general Jewish theory of vengeance and inserted the idea of mercy to Gentiles.[6] All Jews, he proposed, hated Gentiles and longed only for their destruction. Jesus harked back to second Isaiah, and thought that God's love would be extended to Gentiles. In order to achieve this extension, to be sure, Jeremias's Jesus predicted the destruction of the present generation of Israel, but that can be seen as a minor matter, compared to the much larger inclusion of all those Gentiles. Thus Jeremias, in his pious way, made a vicious and vindictive view sound like the introduction of love and mercy.

---

[4]Ibid., 55-73.

[5]Ibid., 71f.

[6]Ibid., 41-46.

I can say to Jeremias's credit that he was prepared to attribute to Jesus the view that he was acting out part of a scenario which had been scripted in heaven. To understand the ancients, we need to be able to attribute to them non-modern ways of thinking. The ideas of a rigid sequence required by God, and proclamation by an angel, are certainly non-modern. The idea of the destruction of a whole generation of Jews, alas! is all too modern.

Is anything wrong with Jeremias's view? I mean apart from attributing such a deplorable attitude to Jesus? Well, one thing leaps to the eye: the theory that Jews contemporary with Jesus had a uniformly hostile view of the Gentiles. This aspect of the theory has been greatly influential, and it largely determines the recent book by John Riches, *Jesus and the Transformation of Judaism*.[7] It is, however, completely erroneous, and it rests upon a complete distortion of the evidence. The distortion is so great that it must have been intentional. It would be easy to say just that Jeremias's paraded knowledge of Jewish literature was not actually adequate. That would be easy, though too generous. It was bogus. He in fact seems not to have been able to read Rabbinic literature, and his knowledge of it was entirely confined to the handbook of snippets compiled in German by Paul Billerbeck. But on the present issue we see more than simple ignorance. He simply altered the evidence. I offer one example: He quotes one-half of a rabbinic text, T. Sanhedrin 13.2, in order to assert that the Rabbis all thought that all Gentiles would be destroyed. The other half of the passage, which is in Billerbeck in German, says that there are righteous Gentiles who would be saved.[8] Were one to read on, one would discover that the favorable view predominated—even after and despite two gruesome wars with Rome. Here Jeremias simply created a fiction and handed it down to those who admire his learning and piety.

Anything else? What about the gospel evidence? On one point Jeremias again resorted to complete distortion of the evidence. Luke 4:22 says this: "And all spoke well of him [or testified about him], and wondered at the gracious words which proceeded out of his mouth. . . . " Here Jesus is described as being praised by the people of Nazareth. Jeremias forces even here his view that Jews uniformly lusted for the destruction of others. He translates the verse thus: "They protested with one voice and were furious, because he (only) spoke about (God's year of) mercy (and omitted the words

---

[7]John Riches, *Jesus and the Transformation of Judaism* (London: Darton, Longman & Todd, 1980).

[8]Hermann L. Strack and Paul Billerbeck, *Kommentar zum Neuen Testament aus Talmud und Midrasch* I (Munich: C. H. Beck 1926) 360f.

about the Messianic vengeance)."[9] Thus it was not only Jewish literature which he was prepared to beat out of all semblance to what it actually says.

What about the other New Testament passages which are basic to his hypothesis? Here, of course, we enter uncertainty. The other passages which Jeremias quotes are there. The question is the standard twofold one which always arises when we study the sayings of Jesus: did he really say it? If he did, did it mean what it now means in the context of the gospel accounts? There is one thing on which all NT scholars are in agreement: the various gospel writers, and before them the people who passed on sayings of Jesus, used them in their own, later, contexts. The passage about the woman at Simon the leper's house is a perfect example. According to the story the woman anointed Jesus with oil. The disciples protested, saying that the oil could have been sold and the money given to the poor. Jesus, however, said that she had anointed him beforetime for burial, and predicted that what she had done would be told "wherever the gospel is preached in the whole world" (Mark 14:3-9). In its present context it clearly refers to preaching by human missionaries and apostles, on the widest possible geographical scale, and obviously over a long period of time. That is, in Mark and Matthew, Jesus is taken to be predicting the Christian missionary activity which in fact followed his death and resurrection. Jeremias accepts the final saying, about preaching in the whole world, as authentic, but denies that the gospels correctly understand it. It must refer, he proposed, to the end of the age. He accepted as authentic the passages in the gospels in which Jesus says, in effect, that the end is imminent, and he understood the saying about preaching the gospel in the whole world in their context.

Thus there are two separate acts involved in interpreting this saying, and the same two acts must take place in interpreting **any** saying by Jesus. Here I do not criticize Jeremias, except for lack of methodological control and a surfeit of bad judgment. He gives no principles by which he can decide that the saying is authentic and comes from another context than the one the gospels give it. But the two interpretive steps are necessary: to understand Jesus, we must decide which parts of the gospels really refer to his lifetime, and then gain an overall view of him and his life which will give a context in which events and sayings can be understood.

The sayings themselves, it is clear, are treacherous. Make the right selection from them, and you can prove almost anything. The establishment of some context is necessary for understanding them. The context in which

[9]Jeremias, *Jesus' Promise to the Nations,* 44f.

Jeremias interpreted passages bearing on the question of "Jesus and Israel" was a certain understanding of Jewish history and religion—an understanding which is actually a theological judgment against it which is well-known and which I have described elsewhere: In Jesus' day Judaism had greatly declined. It had become a legalistic religion, one which stiffled all true piety, one interested only in the compiling of petty merit, and one which systematically denied the grace of God. Jesus had nothing to do with this debased religion.[10] He came to change it: he wished to reintroduce the love and mercy of God. Jeremias, then, unfortunately had him re-introduce it by predicting the destruction of Israel.

I shall not repeat arguments against the context which controlled Jeremias' interpretation of Jesus—and most of New Testament scholarship for decades. I wish instead to propose that we can reconstruct from the gospels the context in which Jesus actually lived and worked. This context, once established, will allow us fruitfully to reconsider Jesus' attitude towards his own people.

The context of Jesus' life and work can be summarized by presenting eight more-or-less incontrovertible facts about him, his message, other aspects of his activity, and the outcome of his career. I shall first list them and then explain both how we know each one to be a "fact" and what light this context throws on the question of "Jesus and Israel."[11]

1. Jesus began his work in close association with the movement begun by John the Baptist.
2. Jesus was a Galilean who preached and healed.
3. He called disciples and spoke of there being twelve.
4. He confined his activity to Israel.
5. He engaged in a controversy about the temple.
6. He was crucified outside Jerusalem by the Roman authorities.
7. After his death, Jesus' followers continued as an identifiable movement.
8. At least some Jews persecuted at least parts of the new movement.

1. How do we know that Jesus got his start under John the Baptist? By the classical method of cross examination. All four gospels represent Jesus as starting off under John, but it is not their agreement which establishes this as a rock-hard fact. It is, rather, their insistence that John himself pub-

---

[10]Ibid., 62: "Jesus was not influenced by late Jewish exegesis, but by the Old Testament itself."

[11]These facts are derived from my *Jesus and Judaism* (Philadelphia: Fortress Press, 1985).

licly and deliberately subordinated himself to Jesus. The fifth time that the Gospel of John has John the Baptist say, in effect, "I am not the one, he is, he is, he is," we begin to see what is going on. The dependent position of Jesus on John has been altered, so that John effaces himself before Jesus. The popularity and success of the movement initiated by John the Baptist, we know from Acts, gave the early Christian movement a bit of trouble. Why did not the early Christians just say there was no relation? Well, they could not. It was well known. Jesus even protected himself once by appealing to the authority of John the Baptist (Mark 11:27-33). So, in short, I conclude that Jesus started off as a member of John's movement.

What do we learn? We know what sort of movement John's was. John was an eschatological preacher of hell-fire and damnation if repentance were not forthcoming. I shall not repeat the details and how they are confirmed by comparing what is told of John by Josephus. It can be shown to be a fact that Jesus got his start in close association with a prophet who said that the end is near, that the axe is laid to the root of the tree, and that Israel must return to God. By threatening destruction, of course, John the Baptist intended to encourage repentance and reform.

2. I shall not undertake to prove *that* Jesus was a Galilean who preached and healed. I take the bare fact to be beyond dispute. What does it tell us? It tells us that Jesus had more than one way of drawing a following—and thus that he sought one. I think that Morton Smith is correct in proposing that the miracles drew bigger crowds than the teaching. The teaching attributed to Jesus is engaging and demanding. It has its own compelling character. But the healings certainly attracted crowds.[12]

Crowds are important to the story. They help to account for the execution. A loner who draws no one after him will not be much of a disturbance and may even find it difficult to get into trouble. Not so one who rouses a crowd.

And what if he rouses a *rabble*? What sort of people leave off the day's work to follow an itinerant preacher and healer? Seldom the prosperous burghers and large landowners. Further, and most important, we note that one of the major themes of Jesus' teaching coheres with his life as itinerant healer: the theme is that the wicked, those who do not live within the fairly tolerant limits of the law, will inherit the kingdom of God. Tax collectors, at least suspect of corruption, if not of treason, as ultimately servants of

---

[12]Morton Smith, *Jesus the Magician* (New York: Harper & Row 1978) 9, 11, 23f.

Rome,[13] Jesus said, would enter the kingdom. Prostitutes and the wicked would enter. These, the offscourings of society, were attracted by the miracles, often healed by them, and then promised the kingdom.

We see here a difference from John the Baptist. The note of threat and impending doom—if it is present at all in the authentic teaching material—is in any case in a different context. The context is promise, promise to the poor, the despised, the weak—both physically and morally. So, Jesus looked for the coming kingdom, as did John, but gave a different turn to the message, both by what he said and by what he did.

3. That Jesus called 12 disciples is the weakest of the 8 facts which I offer you. The difficulty is straightforward: we have more than 12 names. There are slightly different ways of assessing the names which we are offered in the gospels and Acts, but the simplest way of counting gives 15 names to be included in the 12. There is no dispute about the meaning of the number 12: it points to the inclusion of the 12 tribes of Israel in the kingdom. The question is whether or not Jesus thought of there being 12, or whether the disciples, after the crucifixion and resurrection, made up the number because of its symbolic value.

If the number was made up, it was made up very early, for Paul gives it as a tradition which he had learned that Jesus appeared to "the twelve." I think that the conception of 12 goes back to Jesus for two simple reasons. (1) If the disciples had immediately sat down and made up the number, they must have split up before agreeing on who was included. That is, an invented number should have been backed up by a firm name list. The variations in the lists, which seem at first to call the number into question, actually point to its going back to Jesus. (2) If the disciples made the number up, and passed it on to such early converts as Paul, they should have told him: "Jesus appeared to the 11 who were left"—since, according to Matthew and Acts, Judas, the betrayer, was dead. Even if he was not dead, but only hiding in disgrace, the disciples would hardly have told Paul, "he appeared to 12 including Judas."

The simplest explanation is that Jesus himself thought up the number and spoke of "the twelve" as his special followers, those who would judge the 12 tribes of Israel (Matt 19:28). All the evidence is saved if we think that Jesus himself used the number symbolically. There were not always just twelve with him, and maybe the close followers did number 15 or so. But if he himself thought of there being 12, we can understand the varia-

---

[13]Tax collectors for Rome were probably often considered collaborators. The common attitude towards Antipas's tax collectors, however, cannot be recovered with certainty.

tions in the lists and Paul's saying that he appeared to "the twelve." It was Jesus who used the number symbolically. *He himself intended to say that his movement represented the restoration of all Israel, including the lost tribes.*[14]

4. I shall not say anything about 4, that Jesus confined his activity to Israel. Jeremias argued that as well, proposing that he did so pro-forma. The question why he did so must be settled on other grounds.

5. The controversy about the temple was almost certainly the immediate cause of Jesus' crucifixion. There are three sorts of traditions about the temple:

a. One is the so-called "cleansing" (Matt 21:12-13 and par.). Jesus went into the temple courtyard and turned over one or more tables used for converting the money of pilgrims into a coinage acceptable by the temple priests—one not showing an "image."

b. Jesus predicted that the temple would be destroyed. He said that not one stone would be left on another (Matt 24:2 and par.).

c. Jesus threatened that he himself would destroy the temple (Matt 26:61 and par.; Matt 27:40 and par.).

Of the two sayings, one predicting, one threatening destruction, the Evangelists wish us to believe that the former is authentic, the latter inauthentic. That is, all three tell us that Jesus did make the prediction. Matthew and Mark say that at his trial he was accused of making the threat, but that the witnesses were false. Luke does not mention the threat in his account of the trial. The threat, however, reappears. According to Matthew and Mark passersby taunted Jesus while he was on the cross: You who would destroy the temple, save yourself. Luke does not mention the taunt. Yet in volume 2 of his work, Acts, Luke has to refer to the threat. The accusers of Stephen say that he, Stephen, had said that Jesus would destroy the temple (Acts 6:14).

It is probable that we should reverse the Evangelists' preference, and think that he threatened rather than just predicted. They protest too much that he did not really threaten. Luke tries to ignore the threat, but is finally unable to do so. He has to tell the story of Stephen, or the rest of Acts will not work. It is difficult to imagine any Christians making the threat up, for they very badly wanted to deny it.

But whether Jesus threatened or predicted, we must take it that he did say something about the temple's being destroyed. I think that we should

---

[14]On the symbolism of the twelve there is a substantial consensus. See Sanders, *Jesus and Judaism*, 98-106 and further literature cited there.

interpret the overturning of tables in light of the saying. Probably the over-turning represented the coming destruction of the temple. Usually the action is understood as a gesture towards "cleansing." But if he thought that it was too impure for God's habitation, why did the disciples, after his death, continue to worship there? But I do not here wish to carry this debate on, for finally it does not matter. Let us take it that Jesus thought that the temple would be destroyed and that it should be at least cleansed. What does this tell us about what he was up to, and his stance towards Israel?

I think that it points towards a positive stance. Destruction may not sound positive, but it is part of a well-known positive theme: the old must be destroyed in order to make way for the new. We see this thinking applied to the temple in I Enoch, a well-known book in Jesus' day, and in the recently discovered Temple Scroll from Qumran. God himself would destroy the temple, in order to replace it with his own perfect temple.[15]

We are here at the crunch point. Either Jesus wanted to do away with the central institution of the religious life of Israel, or he wanted to say that it would be restored by God, in order all the better to serve Israel. I think that it is the latter. We have already seen positive gestures towards all Israel—the restoration of the 12 tribes, the inclusion even of the outcasts—but the most telling points lie just ahead.

6. Jesus was crucified by the Romans, and crucified on a specific charge: he claimed to be king of Israel. According to Matthew, Mark and Luke that was precisely the concern of the high priest in interrogating him: are you God's Messiah, the coming king? According to John, Pilate ordered that the inscription which gave the cause of crucifixion should read, "Jesus of Nazareth, king of the Jews." There is lots of other evidence that Jesus in effect considered himself "king," though he was hesitant to say it directly. We recall another symbolic gesture, riding into Jerusalem on an ass—as Zechariah had predicted the coming king would do. Further, there is the strong inference from the calling of the 12: if they represent Israel, what does he, their leader, represent? Now, I do not for a moment think that Jesus plotted revolt and insurrection. He thought of himself as king in some other sense. But, still, as king. *And one does not wish to be king of an entity about which one does not care.*

7 & 8. I shall take numbers 7 and 8 together. They say that after Jesus' death and resurrection his followers continued as a movement which was identifiable and which was at least occasionally persecuted by some within Israel. These two facts combine to tell us something very important about

---

[15] 1 Enoch 90.28f.; 11QTemple 29.8-10.

Jesus' followers. They constituted a *movement which had a distinct programme*. They did not just gather, drink tea, and recall Jesus' marvelous message. Had they done only such innocuous things, there would have been no persecution. They had to get out into the streets, announce a message, and challenge others in order to be persecuted. Further, the challenge had to have some aspect which pushed the Jewish leaders into retaliation. The Jewish leaders, it is perfectly clear in the gospels, Acts, and the writings of Josephus, were not the Pharisees, but the chief priests. To the high priest, it was generally held, God had entrusted the government and oversight of the nation of Israel. The chief priests had numerous concerns, and a principal one was that they were in charge. They wanted badly to maintain their positions, and they wanted no nationalist movement to arise which would bypass them and either confront Rome or appeal to her directly. It appears that they thought that Jesus was enough of a trouble maker that he might inspire a crowd to demonstrate in favor of "the kingdom of God," and that this might lead the Romans to act against the crowd. The Romans did not like competing kingdoms, whether of God or humans, and they certainly would not tolerate a crowd gathering and listening to someone proclaim another kingdom. The chief priests, very reasonably from their point of view, had Jesus executed by the Romans. The Romans evidently were satisfied to leave it there, having killed the leader, and they did not go after the disciples. The chief priests were still worried about the followers of the Galilean, and they harried the movement. Eventually, I add, jumping ahead three decades, one high priest had the Jerusalem leader of the Christian movement executed. The high priest was then deposed on Roman orders. This shows the source of the opposition to Jesus and his movement: the chief priests.

Now, what have we learned? That Jesus' followers after his death had a definite programme, one which brought them into conflict with the spiritual and temporal leaders of Israel. We know pretty well what they proclaimed. It was that Jesus was the Messiah, the anointed king of Israel, that he would return, and that he would reign. It would follow that his followers would be in a privileged position.

Well here we have it. I think we have enough evidence in hand to give a firmly affirmative answer to the question: did Jesus favor the nation of Israel. A moment ago I said that the temple incident, devoid of context, could mean a negative position towards the central institution of Israel, or a positive one. When we see that the disciples thought of Jesus as the Messiah/king of Israel, that he probably thought in the same terms, that he thought of there being 12 followers, representing restored Israel, we are compelled *by context* to take the evidence about the temple in a positive

way. Jesus was not *just* against it. Maybe there were aspects or practices
which he opposed—we cannot now recover them, but maybe there were—
but he was not just against the temple.

Now we have a firm context. If one moves from John the Baptist, proclaiming the nearness of the end and the need to repent, to the earliest years
of the Christian movement, in which the return of Jesus and the establishment of the kingdom of God were proclaimed, we have a completely secure context. Further, we can then add in the chief symbolic actions of
Jesus' life—one of which I have barely mentioned, the other of which I
now name for the first time. Jesus not only said things, he performed symbolic actions. The ones we know about are these: he called disciples and
spoke of there being 12; he demonstrated the coming overthrow (or possibly cleansing) of the temple; he entered Jerusalem on an ass (Matt 21:1-
9 and par.); he shared a final supper with his disciples, a supper which almost certainly symbolized, in the traditional way, the joy of the messianic
age, and at which he spoke of drinking wine again only in the kingdom
which would come (Matt 26:26-29 and par.). Every one of these actions
points in the same direction: Jesus was a spokesman for the coming restoration of Israel, for the establishment of God's ideal kingdom *over the
nation of Israel as such*. We do not know, and I shall not here speculate
on, all the nuances of Jesus' view—such as whether the coming kingdom
would be in a transformed but still physical world or not. But we can answer our basic question in positive terms: *Jesus affirmed the value and per-
manence of the nation of Israel as a nation.*

Let us now recall the two principal positions which I described above.
Bornkamm, representing the vast majority over several decades, took the
view that Jesus said absolutely nothing "to confirm or renew the national
hopes of his people." Jeremias, speaking only for himself, but persuading
a very large number, said that Jesus went only to Israel and that he preached
the message of the coming of the God of Israel and of his kingdom, but
that he did so with his eye on the destruction of Israel and the entry of the
Gentiles.

Ideas such as these come all too readily in theological scholarship. In
general our field is marred in two substantial ways: NT theologians, teachers all, have a hard time imagining any evidence other than attributed
teaching. The gospels do not attribute to Jesus a chapter on "what I think
about the nation of Israel," and so it has been easy for the majority of
scholars, represented by Bornkamm, to say that Jesus did not confirm that
nation. Note that he says, "not a word does he say" to confirm Israel. The
only evidence that would count is prose. If we look at symbolic actions,
we see that they speak very clearly of Jesus' positive attitude towards the
nation of Israel.

The second blight on our field has been that the NT is usually taught about and written about in an air of theological abstraction. One looks for ideas which oppose other ideas. Jesus favored love; he had conflict with his contemporaries; therefore they opposed love: that sort of thinking. Jeremias was actually a good deal more realistic. He at least tried to put Jesus in the first century, not in a spiritual realm devoid of time and space. But he had his own theological abstractions to work out. God, whose spokesman was Jesus, was in favor of Gentiles and would destroy Israel.

Among principal scholars, W. D. Davies is closest to the view offered here, and he has also dealt with the implications of Jesus' positive affirmation of Israel in a very sensitive way. Davies would distinguish "the nation of Israel" from "the people of Israel," and he proposes that Jesus' positive stance was towards "the people," not "the nation."[16] I have argued that the positive stance was towards "the nation." I shall not here pursue the distinction, but only note it as important.[17] I wish to close by saying just one word about implication. I do not think that Jesus' positive position on the nation of Israel must govern thereafter every Christian stance towards every Jewish nation-state. We cannot easily leap from Jesus' view that in the coming kingdom God would restore Israel to, for example, the view that in the present the State of Israel must be unhesitatingly championed by Christians. Eschatological hope and practical politics are not necessarily the same.

On the other hand, however, Christians who are true to Jesus cannot say that their faith makes the nation of Israel a complete irrelevance—that we need think nothing at all about the national aspirations of Israel (as Bornkamm would have it). People often talk about the scandal of particularity in the Christian message: God fully revealed himself in one place and time. Judaism has its own scandal of particularity: God chose Israel as his own people. When it turns out that Jesus shared the second scandal of particularity, that he himself saw the full redemption of Israel as the goal towards which he directed his own efforts, those who accept the first scandal—that God spoke definitively through Jesus Christ—cannot deny the second—that he called Israel as people and as nation, to be his own.

---

[16]W. D. Davies, *The Gospel and the Land* (Berkeley: University of California Press, 1974) 336-54.

[17]Sanders, *Jesus and Judaism,* 116-19.

Part III

EARLY CHRISTIANITY

THE WORLD MISSION
AND THE EMERGENT REALIZATION
OF CHRISTIAN IDENTITY

Ben F. Meyer

This study deals with the relationship between the self-consciousness of early Christianity and the launching of the early Christian mission to the gentile world. From the standpoint of early Christian self-consciousness, the question is: what was it in the mind and heart of early Christianity that made the launching of the mission possible and reduced the possibility to act? From the standpoint of the history of the mission, the question is: what impact did the mission have on the self-consciousness of the early Christian Church?

Before taking up these two questions in turn (in parts two and three of this article), we shall sketch briefly the historical background and development of the launching of the mission, concentrating less on the detail of its episodes than on the conditions of its possibility.

Part one, then, is a historical sketch, which will begin with Jesus. Part two asks a set of "why?" questions. Why was there initially no mission to gentiles on the part of the community gathered around "Cephas and . . . the twelve" (1 Cor 15:5)? How explain, on the other hand, the willingness of Christian *hellēnistai* (Greek-speaking Jewish Christians) to speak the word of salvation to Samaritans (Acts 8) and gentiles (Acts 11)? What led the Antioch Christian community to sponsor a mission to the synagogues of Cyprus and south-central Asia Minor (Acts 14-15)? What explains the momentous agreement of the leaders of the Jerusalem Church with the Torah-free mission of Barnabas and Paul (Gal 2:1-10; Acts 15)? What freed Paul to launch out on his own, claiming a mandate for a worldwide mission to gentiles? Part three will raise the question: what in the end was the real impact of the mission on the self-consciousness of the first Christians?

I

Jesus understood his mission to comprehend the salvation of the world (Mark 14:24; par. Matt 26:28;[1] cf. Mark 10:45; par. Matt 20:28;[2] Matt 8:11;

---

[1] See Joachim Jeremias, *The Eucharistic Words of Jesus* (Philadelphia: Fortress

par. Luke 13:29;[3] Mark 4:30-32; par. Matt 13:31f.; Luke 13:18f.[4]). But how should we understand "salvation of the world"? What were the concrete, historical terms in which Jesus and his first disciples conceived of salvation for the world?

The appropriate place to begin is with Old Testament conceptions of salvation. In the consciousness of Israel, Yahweh had taken the initiative in choosing his own people out of the vast world of the peoples (Gen 11-12; Ex 19:5f.). He chose Israel and saved Israel. He entered into a covenant with Israel. By that fact Israel became liable to an economy of blessings and curses, of saving interventions and condemnatory judgments, as in the oracle,

> Only you have I known
> out of all the earth's tribes;
> therefore will I punish you
> for all of your crimes. (Amos 3:2)

Israel conceived good fortune and ill-fortune alike as convenantal judgments of God. But the covenant was no more *quid pro quo* arrangement. It expressed Yahweh's elective love. Israel's transgressions of the covenantal stipulations failed to cancel out this love. If application of the covenantal dynamic to Israel meant "therefore will I punish you for all of your crimes," this same covenant grounded the hope that, though the judgment would be terrible, some would be snatched from the lion's mouth (Amos 5:15). And these few, said Amos and Isaiah and Micah and Zephaniah and the late chapters of Zechariah, were the new bearers of election and the seed of Israel to be restored.[5]

Press, 1977) 179-82. Rudolf Pesch, *Das Abendmahl und Jesu Todesverständnis* (Freiburg: Herder, 1978) 69-125.

[2]See Peter Stuhlmacher, "Existenzstellvertretung für die Vielen: Mk 10,45 (Mt 20,28)," in *Versöhnung, Gesetz und Gerechtigkeit* (Göttingen: Vandenhoeck & Ruprecht, 1981) 27-42.

[3]See Joachim Jeremias, *Jesus' Promise to the Nations* (London: SCM Press, 1958) 55f. Jacques Dupont, " 'Beaucoup viendront du levant et du couchant . . . ' (Matthieu 8, 11-12; Luc 13, 28-29)," *SEcc* 9 (1967): 153-67. Of the attempts to break down the historical ascertainment yielded by this word of Jesus, namely, that he envisaged the eschatological pilgrimage of the nations at the consummation of time, none, so far as I can judge, has succeeded. An example is Dieter Zeller, "Das Logion Mt 8,11f/Lk 13,28f und das Motiv der 'Völkerwallfahrt,' " *BZ* 15 (1971): 227-37; 16 (1972): 18-95.

[4]See B. F. Meyer, *The Aims of Jesus* (London: SCM Press, 1979) 163f., 214f.

[5]See ibid., 224-35, esp. 225-29.

Such was the remnant thematic. Initially it was dominated by threats of punishment, but promises of restoration won out in the end.

> I know the thoughts that I think toward you, says Yahweh.
> They are thoughts of weal and not of woe,
> and they give you a future and a hope ('*ahărît wětiqwā*');
> then you will call upon me and come and pray to me
> and I will hear you; you will seek me
> and when you seek me with all your heart
> you will find me . . .
> and I will change the course of your destiny (*wěšabtî et-šěbûtěkem*). (Jer 29:11-14a)

The sense of the last phrase is: "I will restore your fortunes," or "I will bring about your restoration."[6] This epitomizes the hope of Israel.

Now, hope is a hoping for and a hoping in. As a hoping for, the hope of Israel was centered on the restoration of Israel. As a hoping in, it was centered on Yahweh, who was able to bring about this restoration, for he was Lord of the earth as well as Lord of Israel, and willing to bring it about, for to Israel he was father (Jer 3; 31; Isa 63; 64) and husband (Hosea), avenger and redeemer (Isa 40-55), like a suzerain committed to his liege (Exod 19-26; Deut 6; Josh 24) and like a mother bound to her children, for he had *raḥămîm*—a mother's compassionate tenderness—for his people (e.g., Pss 25:6; 79:8).

But Yahweh was the creator and Lord of the nations, too (Gen 1-12). In words addressed to Israel, he made promises for the nations, confirming that they had a share in blessings on Israel (Gen 12:3)[7] and, above all, in the climactic blessing of Israel's permanent restoration (cf. Isa 14:1; 56:3-7; Zech 2:15; Pss 46:10 [LXX v. 9] 96:7-10). The reign of Yahweh, celebrated in the great Autumn festival,[8] so impinged on the classical prophets' hope of restoration as eventually to make it include not only the ingathering of Israel, but of the nations themselves. Both, perhaps, are meant in the psalm verse that says:

> Of Zion they shall say, "One and all were born in her." (Ps 87:5)

---

[6]See Ernst Ludwig Dietrich, שוב שבות *Die endzeitliche Wiederherstellung bei den Propheten* (Giessen: Töpelmann, 1925). On the eschatology summed up in the words "the restoration of Israel," see now E. P. Sanders, *Jesus and Judaism* (London: SCM Press, 1985) 77-119.

[7]See the sagacious treatment of this text in Gerhard von Rad, *Genesis. A Commentary* (Philadelphia: Westminster Press, 1972) 159-61.

[8]See John Gray, *The Biblical Doctrine of the Reign of God* (Edinburgh: T. & T. Clark, 1979).

for everyone, no matter where he was born, would recognize in Zion his real home (Ps 87:7). Zion was the cosmic mountain and the navel of the earth (Ezek 5:5; 38:12).[9] It was the source of waters, hence of life, for all the world (cf. Gen 2:10-14; Ezek 47; Joel 4:18 [LXX 3:18]; Zech 14:8; Ps 46:5). Zion was the gate that divided this world from the netherworld (Ps 9:14f. [LXX vv. 13f.]). It was the site of the world sanctuary (Isa 56:7) and the goal of the world pilgrimage at the end of the days (Isa 2:2-4; 18:7; 25:6; 60:1-22; 66:18-23; Jer 3:17; Hag 2:7; Zech 8:20-23; 14:16-19; cf. Isa 14:1f.; 19:23; Ps 68:30 [LXX v. 29]). From Zion the Yahweh of Israel's future and hope would summon the whole earth "from the rising of the sun to its setting" (Ps 50:1) and the motif of Yahweh's reign conjured up the image of the princes of the peoples gathered together with the people of the God of Abraham (Ps 47:10 [LXX v.9]). The nations would bring their treasures as sacrifices to the temple court (Ps 96:8-10; cf. Ps 68:30 [LXX v. 29]).

Jesus of Nazareth presented himself to the Israel of the age of Tiberius as charged with a mission for the end of time. He announced, not a revolution, not a reform, but a fulfillment. He announced the reign of God, which the Israel of his time rightly understood to signify the divinely promised and long hoped-for restoration of Israel.[10] Moreover, by a series of stunning symbolic acts—cures and exorcisms, repeated initiatives toward notorious sinners and table fellowship with them, choice of twelve disciples (a symbol-charged number) and the sending of the twelve all over Galilee with the self-same proclamation of fulfillment, and finally a procession to the temple as the lowly and pacific "king" of Zech 9, and the many-faceted act of purging the court of the gentiles of merchants, parabolically judging the national cult and intimating its restoration—Jesus

---

[9]Shemaryahu Talmon, "הַר har; גִּבְעָה gibhᵉah," *Theological Dictionary of the Old Testament,* ed. G. Johannes Botterweck and Helmer Ringgren, vol. 3, trans. Geoffrey W. Bromiley and David E. Green (Grand Rapids: Eerdmans, 1978) 427-47, see 437-38, has urged that the navel motif is absent from the Hebrew Bible. If this should prove to be so, the thematic complex "navel of the earth" will have entered the tradition of Israel in the intertestamental period (see, e.g., LXX Ezek 38:12), complementing the already age-old complex of Zion themes. In the New Testament the entire thematic complex is attested by Matt 16:17-19; see Meyer, *Aims,* 185-97.

[10]See ibid., 133-35, 171-73, 220-22. For direct evidence of how the Israel of Jesus' time related "reign" and "restoration," see the relevant parts of the *Qaddiš* and *Tĕphilla, Aims,* 138; 289n34.

presented himself as fulfiller (cf. Zech 14:21) as well as announcer of fulfillment (cf. Isa 52:7-9).

Here, in short, was a restoration of Israel in process of realization, a restoration that confounded, dumbfounded, average expectations in Israel. It tore at the fabric of scribal authority. It violated taboos grounded in the Torah. In the cleansing of the temple, this impressive but baffling restoration lay violent hands on the untouchable. For all these things and, above all, for the claim to transcendent authority that they all implied, Jesus would pay with his life.

Unlike the Israel contemporary with him, Jesus renounced every hint of hope for vengeance on the gentiles.[11] Though he included the gentiles as beneficiaries of God's climactic and definitive saving act (of which he himself was the decisive agent),[12] he neither commanded nor commended a mission to gentiles. In accord with biblical tradition, he alluded to the salvation of the gentiles in the imagery of the post-historical pilgrimage of the peoples to restored Zion (Matt 8:11; par. Luke 13:29).[13]

Such was the inheritance of the Aramaic-speaking followers of Jesus (called *hebraioi* in Acts) who were gathered into an Easter community around Cephas and the twelve. According to Paul, in a text providing the earliest evidence of the self-understanding of this Jerusalem community, Cephas, James, and John were "pillars" (Gal 2:9)—pillars, that is, of the messianic temple of believers.[14] In its own view this eschatological sanctuary, together with the Zion on which it was established, constituted the nucleus of fulfillment of age-old hopes. This living sanctuary awaited the crowning events of history: the entry of all Israel into its appointed restoration, the return of the dispersed from all the countries to which the Lord had banished them (cf. Jer 32:37-40), the climactic hallowing of God's name, as the nations acknowledged the restoration of Israel (Ezek 36:23), and, finally, the pilgrimage of the peoples, when Zion would attain its destiny as the peak (Isa 2:2) and sanctuary (Isa 56:7) of the world. The Christian *hebraioi* of Jerusalem accordingly knew themselves as that sanctuary

---

[11]Jeremias, *Jesus' Promise to the Nations,* 40-46.

[12]See Meyer, *Aims,* 164, 167f., 171, 184, 247, 298, n. 30.

[13]See above, n. 3.

[14]See Ulrich Wilckens, "στῦλος," *Theological Dictionary of the New Testament,* ed. Gerhard Kittel and Gerhard Friedrich, vol. 7, trans. Geoffrey Bromiley (Grand Rapids: Eerdmans, 1971) 732-36, see 734-35; also, C. K. Barrett, "Paul and the 'Pillar' Apostles," in *Studia Paulina,* J. de Zwaan Festschrift, ed. J. N. Sevenster and W. C. van Unnik (Haarlem: Bohm, 1953) 1-19, see 12-16.

which Jesus was to build "in three days" (Mark 14:58; par. Matt 26:61; Mark 15:29; par. Matt 27:40; John 2:19; cf. Acts 6:14).

We thus find world salvation in the field of vision of the Aramaic-speaking Church of Jerusalem; but we do not find there the enabling conditions of a mission to the world. In the actuality of history, however, gentiles would not come into the legacy of the Jerusalem Church by a mass pilgrimage. Those who in fact came into this legacy did so thanks to an energetic missionary movement to the gentile world. According to Acts, this took place through the mediation of Greek-speaking Jewish Christians, probably converts to the first kerygma, whose distinctive horizons made a mission to non-Jews possible, and whose initiative and drive converted the possibility into action.

Acts provides seminal data on this dynamic element in earliest Christianity. They include the story of Stephen and his death by stoning (Acts 6-7); the story of Philip in Samaria (Acts 8); the story of Saul/Paul: his persecution (Acts 8), his conversion (Acts 9), and his proclamation of Jesus in Greek-speaking synagogues (Acts 9:19-21, 29); the arrival in Antioch of Greek-speaking refugees from Jerusalem, and their preaching to gentiles of Jesus as Lord (Acts 11:19f.).

These data derive, no doubt, from the *hellēnistai* themselves, via Antiochene literary sources.[15] Despite their lacunary and episodic character, the sources make it clear that the *hellēnistai* of Antioch were the initiators of a mission in gentile lands. What the sources of Acts do not tell us is how it was that a mission to the diaspora made little sense to one wing of early Christianity and made excellent sense to another. What this says about early Christian diversity is among the questions we shall entertain presently, in part two.

Paul of Tarsus looked back on his conversion experience on the road to Damascus as ordered from the start to his becoming Apostle of the gentiles (Gal 1:16). If (as is possible but not certain) Paul meant that right from the start he understood this "revelation" as a missionary mandate to win over the gentiles, perhaps he inaugurated his career immediately, in Arabia, i.e., the Nabatean kingdom (southern Transjordan, the Negev, and the Sinai peninsula) (Gal 1:17; cf. 2 Cor 11:32f.). But if so, it was an abortive ex-

---

[15]See Adolf von Harnack, *Die Apostelgeschichte* (Leipzig: Henrichs, 1908) 169-73; Joachim Jeremias, "Untersuchungen zum Quellenproblem der Apostelgeschichte," *ZNTW* 36 (1937): 205-21, reprinted in *Abba* (Göttingen: Vandenhoeck & Ruprecht, 1966) 238-55; with qualifications, Martin Hengel, "Between Jesus and Paul," in *Between Jesus and Paul* (London: SCM Press, 1983) 1-29, see 4.

perience. Paul would have learned from it that the actual fulfillment of his appointed career hinged not on personal initiative but on Church policy.

Paul may well have had something to do with the initiative of the Antioch community summarily described in the opening verses of Acts, chapter 13. In this enterprise Barnabas and Paul were partners. Their work came under attack by right-wing *hebraioi* from Jerusalem (Gal 2:4; Acts 15:1, 5), but it was affirmed by the pillars of the community: Cephas, James, and John (Gal 2:6-9; cf. Acts 15:7-19).

It may have been the so-called Antioch incident (Gal 2:11-21) and Luke's inheritance of the views of the Antioch community that together account for the distance between Acts' portrait of Paul and Paul's portrait of himself. Paul's real vocation—his independent mission to the gentiles (Gal 1:15f.; cf. 1 Thess 2:3f.; Gal 2:2, 7-9; Rom 1:5, 14; 11:13; 15:15-28)—took wing only after the dispute with Cephas and Barnabas (Gal 2:11-21), which was also the end of his special ties with Antioch. Thereafter he could unambiguously locate himself and his career in the missionary scenario sketched in Rom 9-11, which now accorded priority to the preaching to the gentiles. This reinterpreted, it did not sacrifice, the salvation-historical principle that went back to the policy of Antioch and, much later, found lapidary expression in Rom 1:16, "the Jew first, then the Greek." Paul now applied the principle to the divine plan as a whole. The present moment was concentrated on the salvation of the gentiles. The Apostle of the gentiles had come into his own. With the figure of Paul bent on the task of the world mission, we bring this summary sketch to a close.

II

What might account for the fact that the Greek-speaking Jewish Christians exhibited from the outset so striking an openness to Samaritans and gentiles? The charges against Stephen (Acts 6:13f.) offer a first clue. Stephen was hostile to temple and Torah, claiming "that Jesus the Nazorean will destroy this place and change the customs that Moses handed down to us" (Acts 6:14). The first part of the charge appears to reflect the word cited against Jesus in the trial before the Sanhedrin (Mark 14:58; par. Matt 26:61; cf. John 2: 19). The reference of the second part of the charge is less precise, but it probably relays in garbled fashion words of Jesus such as his claim to bring the Torah to its appointed completeness (Matt 5:17), or his abrogation (Mark 10:6-9; par. Matt 19.8f.; cf. Matt 5:32; Luke 16:18) of the Deuteronomic legislation on divorce (Deut 24:1-4) in favor of return to what he conceived as the original ideal of marriage (Gen 2:24), or his indifference to the current halakah on the Sabbath (cf. Mark 2:27) and other topics (e.g. Mark 7:15; par. Matt 15:11). The point is that the charge against

Stephen indirectly attests Stephen's appropriation of gospel traditions. Measured against the accent on the positive, the mood of confidence, the tone, the style, the bias of Cephas and the twelve as depicted in the first chapters of Acts, Stephen's interpretative retrieval and application of Jesus' words stand out as independent and distinctive. Whereas the Christian *hebraioi* were buoyed up by an optimism to which the heritage of Jesus' conflicts with his contemporaries and his harsh words on imminent judgment and ordeal, the ruin of the nation, the capital, and the temple were all very alien, the *hellēnistai* appear to have been strangely unaffected by this happy mood. Behind the charges against Stephen there probably stands an unvarnished appropriation by Christian *hellēnistai* of all Jesus' grim prophecies. The *hellēnistai* had come into possession of these traditions through the *hebraioi,* but the interpretation that they gave them was their own. If this is so, how are we to account for it?

The challenge is to account not only for a set of discrete interpretations, but for the horizon in which such moves took place. How describe and account for this horizon? A first set of indices relates to the break with the past of Jesus' historic words that the Easter event effected. In contrast to Jesus' own prophetic vision, his resurrection diverged *ex eventu* from the still future and climactic coming of the reign of God. What had not been foreseen was the single, isolated resurrection of Jesus from the dead, an event dissociated in time from the general resurrection and the judgment. The eschatological scheme that informed the authentic sayings of Jesus about the future[16] had posited two successive moments: that of the ordeal (Aramaic, *nisyônā';* Greek, *ho peirasmos*) to be ushered in by his own suffering and death and to include a set of dreadful disasters, and that of the swiftly following ("in three days")[17] resolution of the ordeal by the revelation of "the Man" (*bar 'ĕnāšā'; ho huios tou anthrōpou*), the pilgrimage of the nations, the judgment, the new sanctuary in its splendor, the banquet with the patriarchs. In this scheme the historic life of the messianic remnant or assembly (*cēdtā', hē ekklēsia*) was coterminous with the

---

[16]See Joachim Jeremias, "Eine neue Schau der Zukunftsaussagen Jesu," *TBl* 20 (1941): 216-22; the substance of this not easily accessible article is given in Meyer, *Aims,* 202-209.

[17]On the sense of the "three days" in Mark 14:58; par. Matt 26:61, see the whole essay of Joachim Jeremias, "Die Drei-Tage-Worte der Evangelien," in *Tradition und Glaube* [K. G. Kuhn Festschrift] ed. G. Jeremias, H.-W. Kuhn, H. Stegemann (Göttingen: Vandenhoeck & Ruprecht, 1971) 221-29.

ordeal; its *'abbā'* prayer was to be a prayer for the ordeal;[18] its distinctive cultic meal would not only commemorate the death of Jesus but also invoke it in calling on the Father to put an end to the ordeal.[19] There had been no room in this scheme for a single resurrection to take place in the course of historical time nor, consequently, for an interim between the resurrection of Jesus and his public manifestation at the coming of the reign of God ("the day of the [Son of] Man").[20] The Easter event shattered this eschatological scenario and required that the whole be reconstituted to allow for an indeterminate segment of time between the resurrection of Jesus and his public manifestation.

The *hebraioi* reconstituted the scenario as far as possible along lines that had been laid down by Jesus himself. Israel had arrived at its long hoped-for restoration in the disciples who celebrated his resurrection and now constituted the messianic community on Zion. While awaiting the consummation of time and the ingathering of the nations, this community would gather in its brethren by the power of the Easter kerygma. The categories of the community's self-understanding were grounded in the Jesus tradition: the eschatological sanctuary, the remnant of the last days, the assembly of the new covenant.[21]

But what did they make of their legacy of themes on the ordeal, such as the destruction of the temple? The opening chapters of Acts, as we have observed, suggest a conception of the present moment to which doom-laden prophecy was alien and irrelevant. Easter had unexpectedly inserted into the eschatological scheme of things a last moment of indeterminate (but surely brief!) duration that would accord Israel a last (and surely irresistible!) appeal to enter into its heritage of messianic blessings (Acts 2:38; 5:31f.).

The Christian *hellēnistai* did not share this vision of things. Evidently, it was their understanding of the significance of the Easter event that gen-

---

[18]See Meyer, *Aims,* 208. For greater detail both on the prayer and on the ordeal as its context, see Joachim Jeremias, "The Lord's Prayer in the Light of Recent Research," in *The Prayers of Jesus* (London: SCM Press, 1967) 82-107.

[19]Otfried Hofius, " 'Bis dass er kommt': I Kor xi. 26," *NTS* 14 (1968): 439-41, has shown that the temporal clause *achri hou elthē,* in 1 Cor 11:26 carries the nuance of a purpose clause. This attests eucharistic celebration as a cry for the parousia and the reign of God, in thematic parallel with the Our Father.

[20]In addition to the references in n. 16 above, see C. H. Dodd, *The Parables of the Kingdom* (London: Nisbet, 1935) 63.

[21]See B. F. Meyer, *The Church in Three Tenses* (Garden City: Doubleday & Co., 1971) 4-12.

erated the enabling conditions of their negative stand on Torah and temple and of their positive openness to Samaritans and gentiles. Contrary to the *hebraioi*, for whom Easter had reduced Jesus' prophecies of doom to provisional status, the *hellēnistai* interpreted Easter precisely as validating Jesus' woes on Israel, her capital and temple. The positive side of this view was a conception of Easter as radically transcending "this age." Its impact on those who shared in it by faith and baptism was transformative. Henceforward, life would be lived under the ascendancy of "the age to come." Temple and priesthood, Torah and halakah, were now all obsolete.

Moreover, textual indices to christology among the *hellēnistai* illuminate their missionary initiatives. The account of Stephen's trial supplies us with a reference to the Son-of-man theme (Acts 7:56), and in the story of Philip we meet a prophetic interpretation of the great Isaian passage on the suffering Servant (Acts 8:32-35). Both of these allusions to biblical sources are significant, for both sources strike the note of universalism. The salvation of the "many" (= the nations) in which the great Servant text culminates (LXX Isa 53:11; cf. 52:12) has as its only antecedent supposition the obedient suffering of the Servant. And the universal dominion of the "one like a son of man" ("all nations, tribes, and languages," LXX Dan 7:14) follows immediately on his ascent to the court of the Ancient of Days (LXX Dan 7:13). The *hellēnistai* need only have identified the Easter event with the reversal of the fate of the Servant (LXX Isa 53:10b-12) and with the ascent of the "one like a son of man" (LXX Dan 7:13) to have understood this event as grounding scripturally an explicit universalism now.

Again, there are liturgical compositions produced by the *hellēnistai* and preserved by Paul that point in the same direction. A satisfactory literary critique isolates, in my opinion, a pre-Pauline distich in Rom 3:25f.:[22]

hon proetheto ho theos hilastērion en tō, autou haimati
dia tēn paresin tōn progegonotōn hamartēmatōn en tē, anochē, tou theou.

This may be rendered:

whom God displayed as the [true] propitiatory in his own blood
for the remission of sins committed in [the time of] God's forbearance.

The primary effect of the text is to present Christ's bloody death as a divinely planned eschatological event. Its meaning had been limned in advance by the most solemn rite of the Day of Atonement, the sprinkling of blood on the propitiatory (Lev 16:14). This golden lid on the ark of the

---

[22]See B. F. Meyer, "The pre-Pauline Formula in Rom 3.25-26a," *NTS* 29 (1983): 198-208.

covenant had signified the presence of God, the locus of revelation, the forgiveness of sins; now these meanings were magnified by transposition to Golgotha where, for all to see, God displayed the fulfillment whose "type" had been hidden in the temple's innermost recess.

But it is a secondary aspect of the text that engages us here. The propitiatory—and, by implication, the whole economy of ritual Torah and temple—is reduced to the role of "type." The "true" propitiatory was the crucified Christ. In the perspective of this text the forgiveness of sins had awaited the climactic, definitive, unrepeatable *yôm kippur* of Golgotha. Once given this reality, temple and Torah could claim no independent significance. This sense of the text converges in approximate fashion with the accusation against Stephen.

The Philippians hymn (Phil 2:6-11) is likewise relevant to the recovery of the soteriology of the *hellēnistai*. The essential thrust of the hymn is to set the confession *kyrios Iēsous* ("Jesus is Lord!" 1 Cor 12:3; cf. Rom 10:9f.) in salvation-historical context. Resurrection, exaltation, installation as Lord were facets of the same event. The hymn gives the divine reason why (cf. v. 9, "therefore" or "this is why") of this event: it was a reward of obedience. In response to Jesus' selfless and flawless submission to God, God gave him the "name" by which he is acclaimed as divine Lord. Our present interest is in a secondary aspect of the text: the claim of the exalted *kyrios* to universal acclamation. Otfried Hofius is probably correct in understanding the full realization of the universal acknowledgement of the *kyrios* to be reserved for the end of time.[23] Still, the decisive moment, the turning point of the ages, has already taken place. In the view of the *hellēnistai* who composed this hymn[24] Easter had set the stage for the world mission.

Hebraioi and *hellēnistai* alike were convinced that the nations were rightful beneficiaries of eschatological salvation. The difference between the groups was established by a set of conceptions on the part of the *hebraioi* that the *hellēnistai* did not share: that the unexpectedly isolated vindication and glorification of Jesus created a new situation reducing his harsh prophecies of the ordeal to provisional status; that the regime of the Torah remained intact as in Jesus' day and with the radicalization that he brought to it; that (as to "when?") the entry of the gentiles into salvation would be

---

[23]See Otfried Hofius, *Der Christushymnus Philipper 2,6-11* (Tübingen: Mohr, 1976) 41-55.

[24]See the treatment of Reinhard Deichgräber, *Gotteshymnus und Christushymnus in der frühen Christenheit* (Göttingen: Vandenhoeck & Ruprecht, 1967) 128-31.

signaled by "the day of the Man" (cf. Luke 17:22, 26, 30) in accord with Jesus' own view; that (as to "how?") this would take place by the eschatological pilgrimage depicted in the scriptures, again in accord with Jesus; that the mission of his followers was consequently limited, as in his own lifetime, to the house of Israel. Given these conceptions, the disparity between the inclusion of the gentiles in God's saving act and, on the other hand, their present isolation from messianic salvation was not felt to be enigmatic or incongruous. But in the absence of this set of conceptions and in the face of contrary convictions—that the vindication of Jesus confirmed the doom of the temple; that his expiatory death rendered the temple cult superfluous; that the glorification of Jesus already laid claim to universal acknowledgement and celebration—the world's non-entry into messianic salvation was precisely an incongruity calling for resolution.

Thus, the distinct horizons projected by the *hellēnistai* comprehended an explicit universalism, not in the mode of Hellenistic humanism, but in that of realized eschatology. The Servant, now glorified, was seen to have served "many" well (LXX Isa 53:11; cf. the "many nations" of 52:15); now "all nations, tribes, and languages" (LXX Dan 7:14) were called on to serve him, the Son of man installed at God's right hand (Acts 7:56; cf. Ps 110:1). The history of man's sin and God's forbearance—the ever accumulating debt and the patiently postponed settling of accounts—had come to an end on Golgotha (Rom 3:25f.). The millenary horizon evoked by the theme of Yahweh and his people now yielded to a horizon evoked by the theme of God, Christ, and the whole human race. Paul would ask, "is God God of the Jews alone? Is he not also God of the gentiles?" (Rom 3:29). God had reconciled to himself through Christ (cf. 2 Cor 5:19) not only Israel but "the many" (Mark 10:45; par. Matt 20:28; cf. Mark 14:24; par. Matt 26:28). Now "every knee" and "every tongue" (Phil 2:10f.) was to acknowledge God in acknowledging Jesus as Lord (Phil 2:11).

If the *hebraioi* were the link of the earliest community with the past of Jesus, the *hellēnistai* by their self-understanding made themselves the link with the future: not as the vanguard of Israel but as the vanguard of a purified mankind.

III

We began by sketching the beginnings of the Christian mission to the gentile world. Then, in an effort to make these beginnings historically intelligible, we offered an account of the interpretative convictions that induced Christian *hellēnistai*, first, to welcome Samaritans and gentiles into salvation and, then, to sponsor a missionary initiative in the Greek-speaking diaspora. We evoked two phases in the missionary career of Paul. Together with Barnabas, he first worked as commissioned by the Antioch community. Soon, however,—and perhaps under the impact of "the Antioch incident"—he made his work depend exclusively on an unmediated divine mandate for a worldwide mission to the gentiles.[25] The Paul of the letters is already established in this second phase of his missionary career.

We turn now to the question: what impact did the mission have on the self-consciousness of the first Christians? Obviously, a full answer would be too large, too complex, too difficult to attempt here. All the more reason, then, to focus on the heart of the matter, namely, on the resolution of policy questions that the launching of the mission made acute. This will require that we return briefly to the sequence of historical events, for to speak of "policy questions" suggests a certain conscious unity on the part of Christians as well as a conscious capacity for authoritatively settling practical issues, and the historicity of both these implications has been contested.

Both, on the other hand, find historically cogent support in Paul and in Acts. Paul, for example, affirmed the unity of the Church by his writing of letters, which was an effort to achieve *koinōnia* and a practice of realized *koinōnia,* like "the collection" for the poor among the saints in Jerusalem. Moreover, he made unity within each Church (e.g., 1 Cor 1-4; 12:4-6, 12-31; Phil 2:1-18) as well as among the Churches (e.g., Rom 16:25-27; cf. 1 Cor 16:1-4) not only a vital supposition (Gal 1:6-9; 2:2; 1 Cor 9:19-21; 10:32), but also a fully articulate theme (1 Cor 10:16f.; 12:12-31; 13:1-13). He underscored the ultimate ground of unity as one Spirit, one Lord, one God (1 Cor 12:4-6), proclaimed in one gospel (1 Cor 12:4-6; 15:1-11; Gal 1:6-9; Rom 1:16f.), re-creating mankind through baptism (1 Cor 12:13; Rom 6:3f.; cf. 2 Cor 5:16-21) and the eucharist (1 Cor 10:16f.), and eliciting from this new creation and Israel of God (Gal 6:15f.) a corporate life lived in love (1 Cor 13:1-13). If Paul made his career a career-long pursuit of ecclesial unity, this interlocks substantially and easily with inherited data in Acts and Luke's own redactional themes in Acts.

Neither in Paul nor in Acts did the concern for unity inhibit, much less paralyze, initiative. The first fifteen chapters of Acts depict a dynamic,

---

[25]Gregory Dix, *Jew and Greek* (Westminster: Dacre, 1953) 31-32, 48-50, had the merit of attempting to reconstruct the way in which Paul's call as Apostle of the gentiles concretely impinged on the history of missionary policy. Whether Paul early initiated a missionary career among gentiles is unclear. If he did, he learned in time, as the letter to the Galatians indicates, to make it cohere with ecclesial policies and commitments.

pneumatic movement, its members venturing on one initiative after another. But the recurrent pattern was to follow up these initiatives with an effort of discernment, testing them for their coherence with the experiences, convictions, and commitments that the ecclesial community took to be normative.

Examples of this pattern of follow-up are the Jerusalem community's sending of Peter and John to Samaria in the wake of the baptizing of Samaritans by Christian *hellēnistai;* it was thus that the Samaritans "received the holy Spirit" (Acts 8:17). Again, once Peter had baptized the gentile Cornelius and his household, he was obliged by "the advocates of circumcision" (Acts 11:2) to present the rationale of this act to the Jerusalem community, which he successfully did (Acts 11:4-18). Furthermore, among the fugitives from persecution in Jerusalem there were "some men from Cyprus and Cyrene" who evangelized gentiles in Antioch. The Jerusalem community sent Barnabas to Antioch to test the legitimacy of this initiative (Acts 11:22-24). Probably in persuance of this mandate, Barnabas in turn called on Saul/Paul (Acts 11:25) to participate in the Antiochene leadership of "prophets and teachers" (Acts 13:1). Finally and climactically, the initiative of a missionary journey (Acts 13-14) was contested by Jerusalem advocates of circumcision, but legitimized by the leaders of the Jerusalem community (Acts 15; cf. Gal 2:1-10).

The simultaneous operation in primitive Christianity of three factors—spontaneous missionary initiatives, concern for ecclesial unity, and acknowledgement of apostolic authority—generated the phenomenon of a developing Christian consciousness. The "consciousness" in question refers, not to the views of just one wing or of one faction or of one or another party within Christianity, but rather to a development on the part of Christianity as a whole between 30 A.D. and 60 A.D. In that fast-moving thirty-year period there was among the mass of Christians, be they Jews or Greeks, a far-reaching change of horizons, of self-understanding, of conscious self-shaping.[26] For, even more significant than the changing self-definition of particular groups (say, of the *hellēnistai*) was the inter-group impact of such change (e.g., the dialectic of Jerusalemite and Antiochene self-definition). It is finally inescapable that the peculiar mix of missionary initiatives, concern for unity, and acknowledgement of authority powered and steered a general evolution of Christian consciousness. The last and main purpose

---

[26]These are the three moments that together constitute "self-definition" in my use of the term; see B. F. Meyer, *Self-Definition in Early Christianity,* ed. Irene Lawrence (Berkeley: Center for Hermeneutic Studies in Hellenistic and Modern Culture, 1980) esp. 6-9.

of this essay is to establish the fact of this change and to define its character.

The conviction that ecclesial unity was a divine imperative meant that the Jerusalem community gathered around Cephas, the twelve, and James, "the brother of the Lord," could not regard with indifference the work—which they themselves had neither initiated nor could in any way have seen their way clear to initiate—of evangelizing Samaritans and gentiles. The same conviction of unity as divine imperative meant that when the innovations of Christian *hellēnistai* driven out of Jerusalem to Damascus or Antioch were questioned or disallowed by critics among the Christian *hebraioi* of Jerusalem, the innovators did not feel free to sustain their course of action in the invulnerable conviction of being right. Rather, they sought to bring the conflict to authoritative resolution. Paul remained in this tradition. To be sure, he never doubted the authenticity of his own vocation; but neither did he think it meet and just that he go his own way without reference to the Torah-observant saints of Jerusalem (Gal 2:2).[27]

How was the religious and ecclesial consciousness of these Jerusalemites affected by the successes of Antiochene Christian missionaries in the diaspora of the Greeks? Some scholars have been willing to say: not at all.[28] The Jerusalemites (despite Paul's explicit testimony to the contrary respecting the "pillars") never really approved the Torah-free mission; "the two fronts remained" and they agreed "to differ."[29] But one may wonder about the historical plausibility of this view. For, while the Torah-observant life of the Jerusalemite Christians differed from the Torah-free life of their gentile brethren in the Pauline and other communities of the Greek-speaking diaspora, and while both wings of the early Church agreed to differ in this sense, neither interpreted the differences as divisions rupturing ecclesial communion. Unlike the minority of dissident reactionaries among the *hebraioi*, Cephas, James, and John could and did affirm both diversity

---

[27]This is explicit in Paul (e.g., Gal 2:2); it is also among the vital suppositions without which the data from both Paul and Acts for the reconstruction of what actually happened would lose their intelligibility. The identification of such indispensable suppositions was a basic and signally successful technique in Dix's account of the passage of Christianity into the gentile world. See Dix, *Jew and Greek,* 29-51.

[28]E.g., Rudolf Meyer, "περιτέμνω," *Theological Dictionary of the New Testament,* 6:72-84, see 83: "G1. 2:7 shows us, of course, that fundamentally freedom from *Ioudaïsmos* was simply noted in Jerusalem. . . . " This follows Eduard Meyer, Hans Lietzmann, and others.

[29]Rudolf Meyer, "περιτέμνω," 83.

and unity, as Paul and Barnabas did. They did not demand that gentile converts to the common Christian kerygma (1 Cor 15:11) be circumcised. Between Christian Jew and Christian Greek uniformity was not imperative; hence, there was unity amid diversity. On the side of the gentile converts in the Mediterranean basin this is amply attested and historically certain. On the side of the Christian *hebraioi* of Jerusalem it is, though less fully attested, still solidly probable, and surely more probable than the contrary hypothesis (e.g., that the Jerusalem Church flatly refused the Pauline collection, so signifying ecclesial rupture). True, a new chapter in Christian history was opened by the events of the decade in which Cephas, Paul, and James were executed, and revolt broke out among Palestinian Jews against the empire; henceforward, the Christian center of gravity would shift from Jerusalem to Antioch and Ephesus and, eventually, to Rome. These developments, however, go beyond the limit we have set for this essay (60 A.D.).

How are we to explain the will to unity among the leaders of the *hellēnistai* and the openness to new initiatives among the leaders of the *hebraioi*? The answer proposed here is that it derived on both sides from the cardinal experience of salvation, i.e., from what the kerygma theologians of our century have named "the Easter experience of the disciples" (*das Ostererlebnis der Jünger*). This experience was "cardinal" in the sense that on it, according to Paul, hinged the divine revelation of the gospel and the mandate to proclaim it (see, for example, 2 Cor 5:18f.).

It was on this basis, it seems to me, that Paul could mount an argumentative appeal to the *hebraioi* (represented by Cephas at a particular moment in Antioch): "we [i.e., you as much as I] . . . have come to know [i.e., by our encounter with the risen Christ] that man is made righteous not by works of the Law but through faith in Christ . . . " (Gal 2:15f.). The Easter experience, generative of the gospel and accordingly a normative index to the gospel, had totally bypassed the Torah, neither comprehending nor entailing it. Paul's appeal to Cephas had its counterpart in his appeal to the Galatians (Gal 3:2-5). They, too, had had an experience of salvation, a charismatic experience of the gifts of the Spirit of God. How had the Torah figured in this experience? In no way at all. It thus fell outside the sphere of the normative. Again, the appeal to the experience of salvation as principle of discernment was the linchpin in Peter's apologia for having baptized Cornelius and his household without requiring circumcision (Acts 11:15-17). In a word, the experience of salvation was an index to Christian identity.

"Identity" is what the core of one's allegiance makes one to be. The allegiance proper to the Christian is summed up in (to use a Pauline word) the "gospel" (*euaggelion*). They are Christians who commit themselves to the gospel, and Christian identity is what commitment to the gospel effects in those so committed. "Christian identity" and "gospel" are exact correlatives.

In the flesh-and-blood actuality of history, however, identity is realized in a cultural context. Christian *hellēnistai* differed culturally from Christian *hebraioi* already in Jerusalem of the early thirties. When identity is considered, not in abstraction from cultural context, but precisely in cultural context, I would call it self-definition. Self-definition, in other words, is identity culturally incarnated. Inasmuch as Torah piety belonged part and parcel to the horizons of the *hebraioi* of Jerusalem, they assimilated the experience of salvation in a way that left allegiance to the Torah intact. This is the point at which we must attend to the Pauline appeal differentiating between Torah piety and the heart of the Christian experience: "We [you and I] have come to know [by our encounter with the risen Christ] that man is made righteous, not by works of the Law, but through faith in Christ" (Gal 2:15f.).

We have said that "the Easter experience of the disciples" was the cardinal Christian experience, inasmuch as the gospel and its proclamation hinged on it (2 Cor 5:19; cf. 1 Cor 2:10-16; 9:1f.; 15:1-11). It was a charged experience: not only a revelation but a reconciliation—the reconciliation to God, through the communion offered by his risen and glorified Son, of men who had earlier rejected the claim of this same Son (James), or abandoned him (the disciples in general), or "denied" him (Peter), or "persecuted" him (Paul).[30] Neither the prescriptions of the Torah nor its remedies for transgression had had any role in this drama of acquittal and reconciliation. It had not named and condemned the transgressions nor, much less, mediated their cancellation. The Easter experience—exclusively, integrally, normatively—had been revelation and reconciliation and mandate. It had generated the content of the gospel and the charge to proclaim it.

As foundational, the Easter experience was not merely a first experience, soon left behind. It was a lasting resource, the full sense of which could come to thematic consciousness only with time and under pressure of experience. In the last century Carl von Weizsäcker argued that the persecution of the Jesus movement by Judaism (Acts 8:1) was the experience that "liberated the Christian faith." Persecution, that is, functioned as the

---

[30]See Peter Stuhlmacher, "Jesu Auferweckung und die Gerechtigkeitsanschauung der vorpaulinischen Missionsgemeinden," in *Versöhnung, Gesetz und Gerechtigkeit* (see above, n. 2) 71f.

means by which Christianity "came to a knowledge of itself."³¹ One aspect of this observation is surely right: the matrix of the social reality that is "meaning" is, as George Herbert Mead has urged, the dialectic of gesturer and respondent.³² The gesturer learns the meaning of his gesture by taking account of the respondent's response to it. Thus, the *hellēnistai* learned something of themselves from the persecution that greeted the expression of their views in the Greek-speaking synagogues of Jerusalem.³³ But Weizsäcker was less than right in thinking that it was just this that mediated the discovery of Christian identity. For, the *hellēnistai* were only one wing of the two wings that made up the Christian community. The persecution of the *hellēnistai* mediated, rather, the transition from the performative to the thematic self-definition of the *hellēnistai*.

Still, we have insisted that the inter-group dialectic of *hebraioi* and *hellēnistai*, of Jerusalem and Antioch, produced something of a common Christian consciousness. Moreover, we have already located the act that brought that dialectic to intensity. It was the launching of the Torah-free mission. This is what "liberated Christian faith." Here was the means by which it came to know itself. The mission drove the early Church to discover, laboriously, a selfhood irreducible to any and all cultural contexts. Christian identity was incarnated culturally, and that means that it was incarnated diversely. But it could not be exhausted nor swallowed up nor petrified in any of its cultural incarnations. As Paul put it, "neither circumcision nor uncircumcision is of any importance at all" (Gal 6:15; cf. 1 Cor 9:23). This inner Christian drama, set in motion by the Torah-free mission, was a drama of identity. Out of a crisis of conflicting self-definitions, Jerusalemite and Antiochene, one identity—the subjective correlative of one gospel—emerged into the light of thematic self-knowledge. A Greek adage founded on a line from Pindar bids us "Become what thou art!" Through the crisis instigated by the world mission, Christianity became what it already was: Israel restored, but far more than that, for the Israel of God was a new creation.

The figure that gave focus to this momentous self-realization was, of course, Paul of Tarsus.

---

³¹Carl von Weizsäcker, *The Apostolic Age of the Christian Church*, 2 vols. (New York: Putnam, 1897) 1:75.

³²On Mead's paradigm, see Gibson Winter, *Elements for a Social Ethic* (New York: Macmillan & Co., 1966) 17-29, 88-104.

³³On this topic and on the synagogues in question, see Hengel, "Between Jesus and Paul," 17-25, with the notes on 148-54.

Free from all, I made myself a slave to all,
　　to win over as many as I could.
To the Jews I became like a Jew
　　to win over Jews,
　　to those under the Law, like one under the Law
　　(though I am not myself under the Law)
　　to win over those under the Law;
　　to those free of law, like one free of law
　　(though I am not free of God's law
　　but am bound to Christ's law)
　　to win over those free of law. (1 Cor 9:19-21)

This remarkable flexibility respecting religious cultures or self-definitions is no isolated datum in Paul. When the gospel was at stake, neither circumcision nor foreskin had the slightest importance (Gal 6:15; 1 Cor 9:23). Having brought Christian identity to full consciousness, Paul could relativize all self-definitions. For example, he could put the gospel ahead of the self-definition, in itself fully legitimate, of "the strong" in Corinth and in Rome. It allowed him to differentiate between unity and uniformity. For, as we have already argued, there were two sets of opposites: unity versus division, and uniformity versus diversity. If division was incompatible with unity, and diversity with uniformity, still, there was no incompatibility of unity and diversity. Paul affirmed them both, but with this proviso: when diversity began to pose a threat to unity, he affirmed the priority of unity.[34] One gospel meant one self-identical Church, and the plurality of self-definitions, however legitimate, would not be allowed to subvert the oneness of the gospel and the correlative oneness of the Church.

From the moment of the Easter experience, the disciples became conscious of a new ecclesial, election-historical identity. But they moved from consciousness of identity to knowledge of identity only under pressure of the launching of the mission to the gentiles. The pressure was generated by theological conflicts, and the conflicts were rooted in cultural differences. The movement from mere consciousness of identity to thematic knowledge of identity concretely consisted in what Gregory Dix called "the

---

[34]Bengt Holmberg, *Paul and Power* (Lund: Gleerup, 1978) 25, cites with seeming approval a view of Traugott Holtz to the effect that the supreme value for Paul was not the unity of the Church but the truth of the gospel. The question, however, is whether Paul dissociated the two. "The strong" might be said to have had the better of their argument with "the weak," so far as the truth of the gospel was concerned; but Paul, invoking the reign of God, urged them to put up with the weak for the sake of "perfect harmony" with one another, "one heart and voice" in glorifying God (Rom 14:13-15:6).

'de-Judaisation' . . . of Christianity.''[35] The eschatological hope of Israel for definitive restoration was the chrysalis of an eschatological universalism when those hopes found fulfillment.

Publicly, Jesus proclaimed the reign of God and restoration of Israel. Privately, he taught his disciples what this meant for him: his death for the world and his glorification—to vindicate the meaning and value of that death as well as to undo its physical effects. If Jesus' death and glorification defined the gospel, the universalist thrust of that death and glorification somehow belonged to the definition. How? The world mission showed how. For, the mission brought into the light of day what had lain in the dark, a little under the surface of Israel's hopes, a little under the surface even of the Easter experience. The mission gradually but dramatically laid bare, not only to the world at large, but to Christians themselves, what the gospel was: the power of the salvation for all who believe. It was news of new creation and a new mankind. The gospel was a third force, irreducible alike to Judaism and to Hellenism.[36] The identity correlative to the gospel accordingly transcended Jew and Greek, slave and freeman, male and female. The mission let Christianity know itself as mankind made new by solidarity with a new Adam lately risen from the dead (1 Cor 15:45).

This epoch-making transition of Christianity from a Judaic to a catholic (*kath' holēn tēn gēn*) context has seemed to me a peculiarly appropriate theme for an essay meant to honor Bill Farmer. Among his contributions has been leadership over the past two decades in the Texas "Seminar on the Development of Catholic Christianity." As for the Church of martyrs celebrated in Farmer's *Jesus and the Gospel*:[37] from the stoning of Stephen to the climactic persecutions under Decius and Diocletian, Christianity paid in blood for the self-discovery mediated by the world mission. For, it was through the conception and realization of the mission that Christianity dis-

---

[35]Dix, *Jew and Greek*, 109.

[36]Dix makes a final point: the process by which Christianity ceased to be Jewish did not thereby make it Greek. "It became itself—Christianity." Or, "if we are to be positive, then [not the 'Hellenising of Christianity' but] the 'Catholicising of Christianity' must serve." *Jew and Greek*, 109. As the writer of Ephesians saw (Eph 3:1-21), Paul, by the divine gift of insight into "the secret" of salvation in Christ, became the mediator of this process.

[37]W. R. Farmer, *Jesus and the Gospel. Tradition, Scripture, and Canon* (Philadelphia: Fortress Press, 1982) 154-227.

covered itself to be intrinsically transcendent vis-à-vis historic Judaism and destined as news of salvation to a gentile world "without love, without pity" (Rom 1:31). In the transitions sketched above we see an emergent Christianity of martyrs—evangelical and orthodox in its fidelity to the traditions that it canonized as "the New Testament,"[38] catholic in its bold resolve to take the whole world for its mission field.

[38]W. R. Farmer, "A Study of the Development of the New Testament Canon," in *The Formation of the New Testament Canon: An Ecumenical Approach,* ed. William R. Farmer and Denis M. Farkasfalvy (New York: Paulist Press, 1983) 7-95, esp. 22-43.

AN IRENIC VIEW OF CHRISTIAN ORIGINS: THEOLOGICAL CONTINUITY FROM JESUS TO PAUL IN W. R. FARMER'S WRITINGS

Wendell Willis

New Testament scholarship in this century has been much concerned about tracing out theological development from Jesus through the early church. In so doing it is claiming and assessing the heritage of F. C. Baur and W. F. Bauer, both of whom sought to refute the picture given in classical dogmatics. Because William Farmer's work in N.T. theology is not as well-known as his study of the gospels and because it may be of interest to see an alternative view, I use this opportunity to sketch out his reconstruction to allow others to compare it with the more familiar ones of Baur-Bauer-Bultmann (and heirs). Space does not permit a full assessment of Farmer's model, much less the more familiar consensus view. I hope, however, by expounding it to make other scholars aware that Farmer's attack on the two-document hypothesis is not his most radical (in the literal meaning of the term) concern! I will show how this irenic thesis has been abiding in Farmer's writing, but will emphasize his recent book, *Jesus and the Gospel*,[1] which is really his New Testament Theology.

Since the provocative work of F. C. Baur, a century and a half ago,[2] there has developed and expanded a consensus that the earliest Christian church was characterized by partisan strife and dogmatic disagreement. While Baur's controversial presentation of Peter and Paul as leaders of op-

---

[1]W. R. Farmer, *Jesus and the Gospel: Tradition, Scripture, and Canon* (Philadelphia: Fortress Press, 1982).

[2]First published in Tübingen's *Zeitschrift für Theologie* in 1831. Baur continued and developed this thesis in a number of works including a book on Paul and on the development of Christian theology. An excellent discussion of Baur, especially as a theologian, but also with reference to his work in New Testament studies is Peter C. Hodgson, *The Formation of Historical Theology* (New York: Harper & Row, 1966). Hodgson (203), states that it was from this first Pauline study that Baur developed his understanding of the historical and theological framework of the first two centuries which are so well known.

posing wings of the Christian faith earned him the scorn of the German theological establishment, by the contemporary standards his views appear pretty tame. Baur argued only for a bipolar church in which Judaizers opposed Hellenizers, both of which were overcome and supplanted in the development of Catholic Christianity. His attempt to break the domination of dogmatic theology over biblical studies by insisting that the various *"Tendenzen"* within the New Testament preclude a single, normative dogma, has been subsequently taken up and pushed to its logical end, and beyond.

The thesis of a primitive Christian diversity that existed prior to what came subsequently to be the orthodox majority was subsequently renewed by the seminal work of Walter Bauer, *Orthodoxy and Heresy in Earliest Christianity*.[3] This study assumed the work of Baur but also modified it in two very important directions. Like his predecessor, Bauer found early Christianity characterized by internal divisions and mutual hostilities. But he argued also that the divisions in "earliest Christianity" were more manifold than had been previously thought. Second, Bauer sought to prove that Christianity in the

---

[3]Walter Bauer, *Orthodoxy and Heresy in Earliest Christianity* (Philadelphia: Fortress Press, 1971). The translation is based upon the 1964 edition, somewhat revising the 1934 original study. The English translation also contains important supplemental essays by Georg Strecker. It is interesting that Bauer's work evoked little discussion until a generation later.

Many scholars have accepted Bauer's thesis in basics, but sought also to find a common core to the diversity. An outstanding example is James D. G. Dunn, *Unity and Diversity in the New Testament* (London: SCM Press, 1977), which finds the sole unity in the Christians' belief that the man Jesus is now the exalted Lord. He documents this thesis in every strata of New Testament writings and with a reconstruction of pre-Pauline Christianity.

For a summary of reviews of Bauer's reconstruction see Strecker's supplement in the English version and also Daniel J. Harrington, "The Reception of W. Bauer's *Orthodoxy and Heresy in Earliest Christianity* in the Last Decade," *HTR* 73 (1980): 289-98; Robert Wilken, "Diversity and Unity in Early Christianity," *SCnt* 1 (1981) 101-10. Wilken notes these external factors which may have contributed to the recent revival of Bauer: the Nag Hammadi find, the social upheaval of American life in the 1960s, and the impact of Vatican II upon traditional theological alignments.

Helmut Koester in "The Structure and Criteria of Early Christian Beliefs," in *Trajectories through Early Christianity* (Philadelphia: Fortress Press, 1971) 206, alludes to the contemporary cultural crises in the western world which have impacted upon the concerns of reevaluating traditional views on "heresy" and "orthodoxy" as initiated in Bauer's study.

second and third centuries was really a great diversity of regional movements, where in many places, quite often the "heretics" outnumbered the "orthodox." Indeed, Bauer argued that in many places the *only* expression of Christianity was what came to be regarded as heresy.

A renaissance of Bauer in recent years was marked by the reissuing of this book and its translation into English. Amplifying it are contemporary presentations of New Testament history which continue the Baur-Bauer thesis of a divided and infighting Christian church for which both "heresy" and "orthodoxy" are meaningless and useless terms. The new consensus, developed from Bauer, pushes his reconstruction of Christian diversity back into the New Testament itself and argues that from the very beginning there were a number of interpretations of Jesus that can be traced back through varied "trajectories" to Jesus himself.[4] Thus Baur's model of Hellenistic Christianity led by Paul, opposed by a Judaizing view, which resulted in Catholic Christianity is so thoroughly fractured that its only remnant is the belief that the earliest church was divided and mutually hostile. It is over against this picture of a fragmentary, non-cohesive Christian history that Farmer's reconstruction can be seen as radically dissident when he pictures an early church which is characterized by a core gospel and an irenic attitude, traceable to Jesus himself.

Summary and Overview

Let me sketch briefly some ways in which Farmer's work is a provocative alternative to the Baur-Bauer consensus on the development of early Christianity. Then I will examine in some detail his reconstruction of this early irenic faith, with special reference to the encounter of Peter and Paul in Antioch.

---

[4]Alluding, of course, to James M. Robinson and Helmut Koester's collection of essays: *Trajectories Through Early Christianity* (Philadelphia: Fortress Press, 1971). This volume is the handiest access to recent applications of Bauer's thesis. In it, Koester, in "Gnomai Diaphoroi," 114-19 traces the indebtedness of his work to Bauer's thesis. He makes similar remarks elsewhere, esp. see his "The Theological Aspects of Primitive Christian Heresy," in *The Future of Our Religious Past,* ed. James M. Robinson (New York: Harper & Row, 1971) 65-66.

Of course this is also an interest from Koester's own teacher, Rudolf Bultmann. See his *Theology of the New Testament* (New York: Scribner's, 1955) 2:137-42.

Since this essay was completed and submitted Farmer has published "The Church's Stake in the Question of 'Q'," *PSTJ* 39 (1986): 9-19 in which he directly assesses the modern appropriation of Bauer by Koester and Robinson. In his critical treatment, Farmer shows how important his synoptic studies are in his reconstruction of Christian doctrine.

First, there is his view that the synoptic gospels were each one written to encourage and assist an ecumenical tendency in the first century. This stands in contrast with fairly dominant views in which Matthew and Luke are seen to be refuting the gospel which precedes them (as also does John).

Second, there is his view that this irenic and ecumenical tendency in early Christianity can be documented early in the basic *agreement* of Peter and Paul that preceded their encounter at Antioch (described in Galatians) and successfully sustained them through this faith crisis. Thus already Baur's proposal of antagonistic Petrine and Pauline wings is denied. Farmer argues that they were able to overcome this disagreement and to grow from it because both shared a *theo*-logy of God's gracious acceptance of the outsider (= sinners).

Third, Farmer argues that this irenic theological stance shared by Peter and Paul, and later manifested in the gospels, was derived from Jesus' own words and deeds. Thus he takes up the challenge of Bultmann which dominated New Testament studies until the 1960s, which denies that there is any essential connection between Paul and the historical Jesus. Not only does Farmer trace back the theology of Paul (and Peter) to Jesus, he thinks that this same theology was common and normative in the mainstream of the early church.

Fourth, pushing back yet farther, Farmer seeks to show that the theology of Jesus is related to his own historical situation and explains his decision to teach and act in awareness of God's gracious acceptance of sinners. Thereby Farmer also takes up the question of what it is possible to affirm as historical about Jesus and whether the gospel accounts permit or encourage a reconstruction of the life of Jesus. Perhaps most atypical here is his willingness to locate stages of development in Jesus' ministry and to assign synoptic material to those different periods of Jesus' life as well as his willingness to speak of his character.

Peter and Paul: Apostles of a Gracious God

A. The Crisis in Antioch. It might be anticipated that one would trace out Farmer's reconstruction of the formation and development of early Christianity either from its beginning (in Jesus' ministry) or its final written form (reflected in the shape of the New Testament canon). I have chosen rather to begin in the middle with the Antioch incident between Paul and Peter. This is really an appropriate entry point because it is this conflict which was a key factor for Baur's thesis of two conflicting wings in the early church. Indeed, this incident and Paul's reference to "parties" in Corinth are the most explicit textual evidence for Baur's reconstruction of partisan primitive Christianity—perhaps his most enduring and influential legacy for New Testament study.[5]

Farmer has no doubt that there were some antagonisms and conflicts, first between Jews and Christians, prior to the Antioch encounter. Proof of this is found easily in Paul's own letters which describe his persecution of Christians, as well as in later New Testament writings (especially in hostile sayings attributed to Jesus directed at the Pharisees, e.g. Matt 23:21-23).[6] Nor does he doubt that within the earliest Christian movement as well, there was first a period of sectarian rivalry, now partially obscured in the New Testament—especially in Acts.[7] Further evidence from Paul's letters and the gospels indicates that Antioch was the scene of a major internal conflict over the practice of the Christian faith. But the outcome of this encounter is not as certain as many have assumed.

At Antioch opposition to Paul's gospel "or what is tantamount to the same, opposition to some of the practical consequences of that gospel, was tolerated in the church."[8] This opposition, Galatians tells us, was directed at the practice of Jewish Christians eating with Gentile Christians. Even this separation Paul might have tolerated except when Peter and Barnabas, along with other Jewish Christians who had formerly shared table with the Gentile Christians, reversed their practice under pressure from outside. Then Paul regarded himself and his gospel as imperiled (2:14-16). While some might present their conduct as another gospel, Paul saw it as "no gospel at all."[9] It is important for Farmer's reconstruction of this event that we see both that it was a crucial event (it even explains the polarity within the gospel of Matthew as an Antiochian gospel)[10] and yet also one that was

---

[5]W. R. Farmer, "Peter and Paul: A Constitutive Relationship for Catholic Christianity," in *Texts and Testaments,* ed. W. Eugene March (San Antonio: Trinity University Press, 1980) 219, points to the pervasive power of Baur's views on twentieth-century criticism. Hodgson, *Formation,* 207f., points out that Baur thought that the accommodation between Petrine and Pauline elements in the early church was achieved by the time of Irenaeus and Tertullian. Bauer, also, is doubtful of any resolution before the late second century.

[6]W. R. Farmer, "The Post-Sectarian Character of Matthew and Its Post-War Setting in Antioch of Syria," *PRS* 3:3 (1976): 235-47.

[7]W. R. Farmer, "The Provenance of Matthew," in *The Teacher's Yoke* (Waco TX: Baylor University Press, 1964) 114.

[8]"Peter and Paul," 222.

[9]Ibid.

[10]Farmer, *Jesus and the Gospel,* 135-38.

resolved with Peter and Paul in agreement—as they had been prior to the encounter.

Farmer's reconstruction of the Antioch confrontation differs from the more common ones in significant ways. First, he accepts as accurate Paul's assertion that he and Peter agreed theologically on the teaching of justification by faith alone (Gal 2:16, as, incidentally, Acts claims in its picture of the two apostles). Paul then was not confronting Peter with a new or different theological position when he rebuked him. Not only does this accord well with what Paul says, it also makes it more understandable why Paul would have been emboldened enough for such a rebuke at all—he presumed on their prior agreement.

Second, and implicit in the first observation, is that in Paul's eyes Peter's failure was one of not acting on what he really believed, not a failure in belief.[11] Thus Peter's theological view was different from those of the circumcision party. This, in turn, explains why on his initial arrival in Antioch Peter was willing to have table fellowship with the Gentiles, although he later ceased to do so under external pressures. Peter usually could be counted on to walk in a manner consistent with the gospel.

Third, Farmer asks, what was the theological agreement that Peter and Paul shared prior to this event which supported (and in Paul's view, demanded) a shared table fellowship of Jewish and Gentile Christians? It was the same theology expressed in Jesus' parables of God's gracious love for all lost sinners set forth in his controversies with the Pharisees (Luke 18:9-14). This message Peter, as one of the disciples of Jesus, shared with Paul. In essence, though certainly not in verbal formulation, it agrees with the pre-Pauline kerygma. Here Farmer notes that one must distinguish between Paul's theology and his christology: "His theology appears to have been essentially the same as that of Jesus."[12]

What is not clear, according to Farmer, is to what degree Peter and Paul agreed christologically (as well as perhaps other details of their faith). What Paul says is that they agreed on God's justifying grace being found in faith in Jesus Christ and not by works of the law.[13] This faith, expressed christologically in the pre-Pauline kerygma of the early church (e.g., 1 Cor 15:1-

---

[11]Ibid., 82.

[12]W. R. Farmer, "The Dynamic of Christianity: The Question of Development Between Jesus and Paul," *ReL* 38 (1969-1970): 577. Bultmann, of course, also found continuity between Jesus and Paul, but it was in their eschatological vision. There was not a material continuity of theology.

[13]Farmer, *Jesus and the Gospel*, 56-57 = Farmer "Peter and Paul," 225.

11, note that Paul says that Peter and he preached the same message, 15:11) asserted that God's promises of salvation in the Old Testament (especially, Farmer thinks, in Isaiah) were manifested in a covenant of grace by Christ's death "for all."[14] This "gospel" transformed Jesus' particular eschatological message of monotheistic, forgiving love "into a dynamic (both personal and social) and intellectually integrating faith and fellowship open to all people."[15]

Finally, Farmer's reconstruction of the Antioch confrontation differs from many others in that he believes that Peter accepted Paul's rebuke as correct and repented of his "hypocrisy" on the question of open table fellowship (more later on this atypical assessment).

B. Peter and Paul Prior to Antioch. Galatians 2 describes two associations which Paul had with Peter before the Antioch encounter. The second and most fully discussed was the Jerusalem conference (2:1-10). But the first was a brief (two-week) visit that occurred three years after Paul's conversion (1:17-21). In Farmer's reconstruction these visits are vitally related to each other, and to the face-to-face encounter in Antioch. Farmer asks an important, rhetorical question in evaluating Peter's relationship with Paul: How was this Jerusalem conference arranged? "In the final analysis it appears to me that the only person Paul could have counted on to arrange for James and John to be in Jerusalem at an agreed-upon time and to agree to take part in the discussions of his gospel and to participate in the far-reaching decision that needed to be made was Peter. . . ."[16] But why would Peter be willing to assist in such a meeting? On the view of Baur it is difficult to answer this question—unless the events were otherwise than Paul affirms, and he was really summoned to Jerusalem by the earlier apostles.[17] Farmer suggests instead that it was in the previous fifteen-day visit

---

[14]W. R. Farmer, "Galatians and the Second-Century Development of the *Regula Fidei*," SCnt 4 (1984): 166-67.

[15]Farmer, "Peter and Paul" 226.

[16]Ibid., 221.

[17]E. L. Allen, "Controversy in the New Testament," *NTS* 1 (1954-1955): 146-47, insists that "one cannot accept Paul's reconstruction of the events at Antioch and the Jerusalem agreement about his mission because he too is biased." The obvious rejoinder is, what reconstruction is not? But who is more likely to be knowledgeable? At least, one would have to say that Paul intended to be accurate about his presentation, for he takes an oath to that effect. Moreover, any serious inaccuracies would, no doubt, have been called to his attention by opponents in

that Paul and Peter conferred and agreed in principle on "the fundamental apostolic faith, upon which the Christian church rests today. . . . ''[18]

In this fifteen-day visit Peter discussed with Paul the faith of Jesus which he shared with his twelve disciples and by which he had inspired them. Paul saw this same spirit of love which had transformed him and brought him into the community of faith present in Peter, and identified it as the spirit of Jesus Christ. Thus "Peter and Paul were in fact united in the same Spirit of Jesus."[19] There may have been details of the faith that were not discussed, or with full agreement not realized. However, more important than these were the mutual deep personal trust and fundamental theological agreement. This theological agreement of the fifteen-day visit was reaffirmed in the Jerusalem conference 14 years later and appealed to by Paul in Antioch.

In Farmer's reconstruction there is a place for division and hostility among early Christians, but there was a unity manifested in the apostolic acceptance of "two separate and mutually recognized missions in the Christian movement."[20] This is evidenced in the Jerusalem conference and its agreement among Peter, James and John with Paul and Barnabas.[21] Initially such a division of mission efforts had practical benefits by permitting the Jewish Christian mission a "peaceful coexistence within the wider Jewish community while at the same time extending the greatest degree of freedom to Paul and his co-workers in their missionary activity among the

---

Galatia.

J. D. G. Dunn, "The Relationship Between Paul and Jerusalem According to Galatians 1 and 2," *NTS* 28 (1982): 465, shows that it is both historically probable and textually faithful to say that Paul inquired from Peter about Jesus.

[18]Farmer, *Jesus and the Gospel,* 54.

[19]Farmer, "Peter and Paul," 227. Farmer also notes, *Jesus and the Gospel,* 57, that our confidence in such an agreement between Peter and Paul is increased because it rests on evidence given by Paul when he was seeking to show his independence from Peter.

[20]Farmer, "Post-Sectarian Character of Matthew," 241.

A similar solution is proposed by Lloyd Gaston, "Paul and Jerusalem" in *From Jesus to Paul* ed. Peter Richardson and John C. Hurd (Waterloo, Canada: Wilfrid Laurier Press, 1984) 61-72. He concludes, 71, "The theology of Paul and the theology of Jerusalem are completely different, and yet Paul can say that they are the same (1 Cor 15:11) and that each acknowledged the position of the other (Gal 2:1-10)."

[21]Farmer, "Post-Sectarian Character of Matthew," 237.

Gentiles.''[22] Thus in Farmer's view there was theological agreement between the two missions, even if they decided to follow independent lines for evangelism. It was inevitable, however, that difficulties should arise in places like Antioch where "a strict division of the two missions would have been difficult to maintain.''[23]

In his encounter with Peter at Antioch, Paul appealed to "the truth of the gospel" as he rebuked Peter. That action suggests that there was a common standard which he knew Peter would have previously accepted. It was something that had been agreed upon by Paul, Barnabas, Peter and James, as well as others at the apostolic conference in Jerusalem when the Pauline mission received full recognition.[24] At its core was the message of all persons being made acceptable to God on the basis of faith in Jesus Christ and not by keeping the law (Gal 2:16).[25] This gospel, although presented christologically in Pauline (and pre-Pauline) form, has continuity with Jesus' own preaching of God's gracious acceptance of sinners.[26]

As I have noted, Farmer asks whence Peter and Paul derived their apostolic faith that formed the basis of their mutual acknowledgment? He insists that for both apostles the source is Jesus—his teaching and life. It was Jesus' message of God's acceptance of those outside the accepted world of Jewish piety (i.e., "tax collectors and sinners") and his willingness to share table with them. This Paul first found so offensive that he persecuted Christians, but he later accepted and preached himself. Referring to the parables of the lost son and his elder brother (Luke 15:11-32) and to the laborers in the vineyard (Matt 20:1-15), Farmer argues "such a noble and heartfelt appeal did not go completely unheeded but rather lodged itself within the collective unconsciousness of the Pharisaic community, there to work its way inexorably . . . . One elder brother, a strict Pharisee, subsequently while persecuting the church,

---

[22]Ibid., 242.

[23]Ibid.

[24]W. R. Farmer, "Galatians and *Regula Fidei*," 160. Baur, *The Church History of the First Three Centuries* (London: Williams and Norgate, 1878) 53, suggests that the agreement was to divide! Each party recognized the other party would go its own way.

[25]Farmer, "Peter and Paul," 227. On the question of the ambiguities in the agreement, see F. F. Bruce, *Paul: Apostle of the Heart Set Free* (Grand Rapids: Eerdmans, 1977) 151-59.

[26]Farmer, "The Dynamic of Christianity," 576.

was won over by the powerful reality of God's love.''[27] This is the real source of Paul's theology—Jesus.[28]

C. Paul and pre-Pauline Christianity. Rudolf Bultmann is widely known for his insistence that Paul was converted to the kerygma of the pre-Pauline church and not to the teachings of Jesus.[29] Farmer's reconstruction, while recognizing the importance of the pre-Pauline church in shaping Paul's theology, argues for a different continuity between Jesus, the pre-Pauline church and Paul himself.

Farmer points to Paul's own testimony that he persecuted the church and the gospel he later preached (Gal 1:16). It is often supposed that what he found so offensive in the Christian movement was the *message* of the kerygma (1 Cor 15:1-11), namely Jesus' sacrificial death, his resurrection and his present lordship. However, as is now recognized, there were many messianic claimants in the first century and the idea of messiahship and even resurrection was not at all unprecedented. Even Pharisaic Judaism allowed for a great diversity of doctrinal ideology on messianic issues.[30] Farmer argues that it was the *practices* of the early Christians that Paul found so objectionable that he harassed the Christian movement (1 Cor 15:9).

---

[27]W. R. Farmer, ''The Theological Task and the Historical Jesus,'' *BTF* 11 (1979): 56-57.

[28]''The theology of the parables of Jesus is essentially the same as the theology of Paul,'' W. R. Farmer, ''Reply to Christopher Duraisingh,'' *BTF* 11 (1979): 73. Cf., W. R. Farmer, ''An Historical Essay on the Humanity of Jesus Christ,'' in *Christian History and Interpretation,* ed. W. R. Farmer, C. F. D. Moule, and Richard R. Niebuhr (Cambridge: Cambridge University Press, 1967), for a fuller statement of this thesis.

[29]Bultmann, *Theology of the New Testament,* 1:187-89. F. C. Baur, *Church History,* 47, located the continuity of Jesus and Paul in Paul's focus upon Jesus' death. ''He [Paul] lives only in contemplation of the Crucified One.''

A recent summary of the questions of the continuity between Jesus and Paul is S. G. Wilson, ''From Jesus to Paul: The Contours and Consequences of a Debate,'' in *From Jesus to Paul,* 1-21. Wilson assesses the attempts to find continuity based upon eschatology, Christology, view of the Law, and the idea of God's gracious love. However, he despairs of any avenue's success. On p. 20 he writes: ''The dilemma, in my view, is that while Jeremias and Käsemann are right in saying that it [establishing continuity] should be done, Bultmann is essentially right in saying that it cannot be done.''

[30]See for example, Josephus, *Jewish Wars* 2.254-66, for documenting the proliferation of Messianic claimants in mid-first-century Israel.

Specifically, it was the church's practice of righteous Jewish Christians accepting non-observant Jews and even Gentiles into their table fellowship.[31] Just as their master and lord ate with all who accepted his invitation to God's gracious love, so also did the early Christians. Just as earlier Pharisees were scandalized by this practice of Jesus, so was Paul the Pharisee scandalized by the same practice in the early church. This acceptance of the unrighteous on the basis of grace was then the faith that Paul first persecuted, and then preached.[32]

This reconstruction does not deny the development in the pre-Pauline church's preaching—so that this pre-Pauline church preached the kerygma rather than simply repeating Jesus' parables. But it insists that both Jesus' parables and the kerygma—although in different form—present the same message of God's gracious acceptance of sinners on the basis of faith. While recognizing this development, Farmer's reconstruction helps account for the continuity which historically does exist between Jesus, the pre-Pauline church and Paul by pointing to the *common practice* that accompanied their differing articulations of the faith. It also explains why Paul confronted Peter about his change of dining customs with the accusation that a "compromise on this matter was not a compromise of the *bene esse,* but of the *esse* of the fellowship of Jesus Christ.'"[33] By thus focusing on the practice, rather than the verbalizations, Farmer is able to account for the development of the Christian movement from Jesus to the primitive community to Paul. This same belief is expressed in the kerygmatic and confessional formulae of the pre-Pauline church in its insistence that the covenant established by the death of Christ proffered God's free salvation to "all" (both Jews and Gentiles).[34]

D. The Aftermath of Antioch: Peter's Conversion. Just as most reconstructions assume that prior to Peter and Paul's clash at Antioch they represented diverging theologies, so also many assume (or assert) that their

---

[31]Farmer, *Jesus and the Gospel,* 55 = Farmer, "Peter and Paul," 224-25. "Indeed, once it is recognized that Jesus was opposed by some Pharisees for eating with Jews who were living like Gentiles (with 'tax collectors and sinners'), it is not difficult to reconstruct the reasons Paul had opposed the church. As a Pharisee he could have been opposed to the church of Jesus Christ, as some Pharisees were to Jesus, only if the members of this postresurrection community continued the table fellowship practices Jesus had initiated."

[32]Farmer, *Jesus and the Gospel,* 56.

[33]Ibid., = Farmer, "Peter and Paul," 225.

[34]Farmer, "Galatians and the *Regula Fidei,*" 167.

face-off resulted in each apostle continuing in his own way and the gulf between them widening.[35] Farmer argues to the contrary, that Peter accepted Paul's rebuke and modified his actions in accord with it—in short, that Peter repented.

According to Galatians 2, Paul was able to expose Peter's conduct as hypocritical in that he could appeal to a fundamental theological agreement which he and Peter shared. This agreement was an emphasis on Jesus' death as the sole means of being righteous before God. It is true that we do not have anywhere an indication of Peter's response to Paul's accusation that his conduct was making ineffective Jesus' death. But Farmer feels sure that Peter "certainly would have been conscience-stricken to think that he had acted hypocritically by withdrawing from table fellowship."[36] Rather the result of Paul's argument was that "this confrontation with Paul was a growth experience for Peter in which his vision and understanding of the practical consequences of faith in Jesus Christ were enlarged and deepened, then it would have resulted in a change in Peter's thinking."[37]

As evidence for such a resolution to the Antioch crisis, Farmer notes three things: First, that Paul's view won the day in that his letters (including his account of the debate in Galatians) were decisive in the forming of the church canon.[38] Second, the story of the New Testament canon also includes a positive place for Peter, showing that his role was not displaced by Paul, but was affirmed. It is the apostolic concurrence of Peter and Paul

---

[35]Baur, *Church History,* 55, "Through all the Epistles of Paul we do not find the slightest indication that the apostles ever drew nearer to each other in after years." Citing the pseudo-Clementine Homilies, Baur suggests that they show the Jewish Christians never forgave Paul's harsh words to Peter.

C. K. Barrett, "Pauline Controversies in the Post-Pauline Period," *NTS* 20 (1978): 230, insists that the Antioch dispute is one of many Pauline conflicts of which we simply don't know the outcome.

[36]Farmer, *Jesus and the Gospel,* 62.

[37]Ibid.

[38]Farmer, "Peter and Paul," 222. This truism, it would appear, makes less credible any reconstruction in which Paul is left alone deserted by Peter, Barnabas and the Antioch church! (A reconstruction proposed by Koester, "Gnomai Diaphori," in *Trajectories,* 122-23., when he says that Paul's "theological rigidity, bare of all liberality, forced Paul to depart from Antioch, since he obviously lost in the showdown with Peter and Barnabas." Like Farmer's, this is a possible conclusion to the encounter, but it is equally undocumented in the primary sources.)

that is regarded as normative.[39] Finally, Farmer regards certain Petrine gospel stories (such as Luke 22:31-32; 5:1-11, and Matt 17:1-8) as legendary descriptions behind which stands Peter's conversion to a higher christology in which Jesus so transcended the law and the prophets that the Gentiles are admitted to the church apart from the law (cf. Acts 11:1-8). He takes these stories to be metaphorical for Peter's positive reaction to Paul's censure at Antioch when he turned fully to a policy of acceptance of God's grace through faith apart from legal rectitude.[40]

Jesus as the Source of Peter and Paul's Faith

A. Confidence in Speaking about Jesus. If F. C. Baur's view that apostolic Christianity was marked by internal divisions and quarrels has accelerated since his day to a consensus, his views on the influence of Jesus upon Christianity has received the reverse reception. Baur regarded Jesus as the founder of Christianity, primarily in the originality and radicalism of his teaching—and also his actualizing of his teaching in his own life.[41] As is well-known, subsequent kerygmatic theology emphasized rather the cleavage between Jesus' teaching and that of the earliest Christian church: in Bultmann's famous reduction of Jesus' life and teaching to a "*dass*" and Tillich's "picture of Jesus" (Tillich taught at Union seminary when Farmer was a student there).

However, there were critical scholars who never accepted such a disjuncture. Among them were C. H. Dodd in England (with whom Farmer studied) and John Knox at Union (Farmer's teacher and mentor). It is possible to understand almost all of Farmer's publications—including his well-known work on the Synoptic problem—as being related to his concern with the possibility and importance of knowing about the work and life of the historical Jesus. This is his major, often disputed, scholarly agenda.

The importance of knowing about the historical and theological continuity between Jesus and the earliest church is clearly seen in an article of

---

[39]Farmer, *Jesus and the Gospel,* 58. This is most skillfully crafted in Acts where Peter and Paul fulfill the roles of each other! Cf. Farmer, "Peter and Paul," 233.

[40]Farmer, *Jesus and the Gospel,* 77-86. This suggestion is dismissed in a recent review as "Jungian psychology." See the review by Royce Gruenler in *JBL* 104 (March 1985): 142.

[41]Hodgson, *Formation,* 223.

a quarter-century ago: "On the New Interest in Jesus."[42] In that essay Farmer assesses the now-famous 1950s publications by James M. Robinson, Ernst Fuchs, Günther Bornkamm, and Ernst Käsemann as signaling a rejection of the view that "all one needs is the picture of Jesus as the Christ in the New Testament."[43]

Farmer was especially interested in the post-Bultmannian willingness to speak of the continuity of the work and proclamation of Jesus and the earliest Christians and their acceptance of the theological validity of so doing. In Käsemann's view that what one can say with greatest certainty about Jesus is that he ate with sinners, Farmer finds confirmation for his own key to the reconstruction of the continuity between Jesus and the early church.[44] In Fuch's reconstruction Farmer applauds especially his willingness to speak of Jesus' "attitude" as it can be known from the parable of the prodigal son.[45]

Farmer's approach, while thoroughly critically respectable, has always been more confident about the historical knowledge of Jesus. He believes that the possibility of knowing about Jesus' thought and deeds was effectively established by Dodd's *Parables of the Kingdom* in 1935 and confirmed by Jeremias, *Parables of Jesus* in 1947.[46] In assessing the gospel materials, Farmer emphasizes the following criteria developed in parable research:

---

[42]W. R. Farmer, "On the New Interest in Jesus," *PSTJ* 14 (1960): 5-10. In his doctoral dissertation, *Maccabees, Zealots, and Josephus* (New York: Columbia University Press, 1956) 187, Farmer complained that the emphasis on the Risen Christ to the exclusion of the earthly Jesus then current in much kerygmatic theology, was a mistaken approach similar to the primitive docetists.

[43]Farmer, "On the New Interest in Jesus," 5. The "post-Bultmannian" shift away from Bultmann's disassociation of Christian faith from Jesus' preaching and self-understanding, marked a major reversal of the dominant trends in New Testament study from World War I until the 1950s.

[44]Farmer, "The Dynamic of Christianity," 573. He contrasts this with the Ritschlian (and Bultmannian, although in very much different ways!) view that what was most certain is that "Jesus preached the imminent coming of the Kingdom of God." This view of Jesus' preaching, Käsemann continued to share with his teacher.

[45]"W. R. Farmer and Norman Perrin, "The Kerygmatic Theology and the Question of the Historical Jesus," *ReL* 29 (1959-1960): 94. Farmer often takes this famous Lucan parable as a major source of understanding about both Jesus' teaching and conduct. Beyond this, he is impressed that Fuchs was willing to speak of Jesus' "attitude" at all.

[46]Farmer, "The Dynamic of Christianity," 573.

The environment of Jesus of Nazareth was physically Palestinian and temporally pre-Pauline. Therefore, whatever he did and said, however distinctive or even unique it may have been, would have been accommodated to those who shared this environment. . . . On the other hand, the environment of the evangelists was extra-Palestinian and post-Pauline. We can assume that what the evangelists wrote was accommodated accordingly. . . . Thus, Paul's writings are an important control in distinguishing between the environment of Jesus and that of the evangelists. . . . Basically, then, what is seen in Paul's letters is one way in which it is possible to adapt the gospel so that it was viable for the predominately gentile churches in Asia Minor and points west.[47]

Assessing the parables with these criteria, Farmer stresses those parables which teach the folly of postponing repentance and those which rebuke self-righteousness. "Both groups of parables reflect a theology of grace. It is precisely these parables of grace that are found neither in the Gospel of Mark nor the hypothetical source Q."[48] This observation explains why Farmer so strongly resists the two-document hypothesis "which in effect shunts the parables of grace to the side and into a critical limbo."[49]

Jesus' parables of grace, Farmer argues, were typically spoken in defense of his practice of freely accepting those non-observant Jews who accepted his call for repentance, when he was criticized by the Pharisees for so doing. Taken together, therefore, Jesus' teaching and actions (i.e., his life) are understood in how they impacted subsequent Christian history. Here Farmer appeals to Schleiermacher and Baur's contentions that part of each individual life is its impact on subsequent history.[50]

---

[47]Farmer, *Jesus and the Gospel,* 22-23.

[48]Ibid., 27-28.

[49]Ibid., 28. Cf. Farmer, "Reply to Christopher Duraisingh," 72.

[50]Farmer, "Historical Essay on the Humanity of Jesus Christ," 101. "For Schleiermacher and Baur, Jesus was the founder of Christianity, and not merely an historical presupposition of Christianity."

Hodgson, *Formation* 234, notes that Baur's confidence in the relative historicity of Matthew allowed him to have a more positive and really more orthodox picture of Jesus' self-awareness than most of his contemporary critical scholars.

While he does not often cite him, Farmer is clearly reflecting the strong influence of his teacher John Knox, who stressed the church as part of the work of Jesus and his abiding presence. See John Knox, *The Church and the Reality of Christ* (New York: Harper & Row, 1962/London: Collins, 1963).

In "Peter and Paul," 236n19, Farmer refers to John Knox's *The Early Church and the Coming Great Church* (New York: Abingdon Press, 1955), for the origin in his own thought of the question whether the unanimity of the early church pic-

B. Development in Jesus' Theology. This theology of grace was continued in the earliest church. And since Paul claims that he preached the faith that he once tried to destroy, it was also the faith of Paul. It is clear in Galatians that a major issue for Paul was his deep interest in the question of eating with Gentiles. Thus Farmer reconstructs the development of the doctrine of God's gracious acceptance of sinners from Jesus' own preaching and practice, to the pre-Pauline church (including Peter), to Paul, and to the gospels of Matthew and Luke.[51] What Paul contributed was to exposit this theological teaching christologically by attending to Jesus' death and resurrection,[52] but it is the same theology of grace as that which Jesus preached.

Farmer argues that not only is it possible to see continuity between the faith preached by the earliest Christians and the life and preaching of Jesus, it is also possible to discern stages in Jesus' own public ministry. In tracing out three major stages in Jesus' ministry, Farmer creatively argues that Jesus' own theology did not spring full-grown at the baptism by John, but advanced in stages and in relationship to his own life situation. The stages Farmer reconstructs are: Jesus' ministry before his baptism by John; from his baptism until the death of John; and subsequently his decision to accept the probability that his antagonism with the Pharisees would cost him his own life as well.[53]

Although frequently overlooked in studies of his life, Jesus' acceptance, endorsement and sharing of the prophetic preaching of John the Baptist came very near the end of his own life. It is possible, of course, that John's preaching awakened in Jesus for the first time a religious interest and a desire to teach. However, since John's work was regarded as an oddity, and since it required some inconvenience to witness, and was presented as a summons to renewal to true Israelites, it seems more reasonable that Jesus was already involved in his own teaching when he came to John for baptism. Thus preceding his affiliation with John, Farmer thinks that we should locate those "sayings of Jesus which bespeak a peaceful, tranquil and even idyllic life within a world where human existence is fraught with personal

---

tured in Acts was historical or fictional. "Knox saw no great defection or decline in this first or second century. What I propose here may be seen as supplementary to Knox's views."

[51]Farmer, *Jesus and the Gospel*, 28. Cf. Farmer, "The Dynamic of Christianity," 574.

[52]Ibid., 63.

[53]Ibid., 32-48.

anxiety.''[54] (Examples of this earlier stage of Jesus' ministry are easily found in the Sermon on the Mount.)

The next stage in Jesus' career was when he acknowledged the decisive commitment to God demanded by John and adopted John's preaching emphasis (repentance before the kingdom's coming) as his own.[55] In this step he issued a summons to repentance to ''sinners.'' To this period would be ascribed those parables teaching God's gracious love and the folly of delaying repentance. These themes were artfully presented by Jesus and resulted in a response in which sinners drew near to him and heard him gladly. Jesus affirmed their repentance by his willingness to accept them into the intimacy of his table fellowship.[56]

This decisive central stage is vital not only for Farmer's reconstruction of the life of Jesus, but also for his understanding of the continuity between Jesus and the early church. In order to appreciate its decisive character, we must remind ourselves of the social divisions in occupied Judea which were based upon religious beliefs.

The phrase, ''tax collectors and sinners'' referred to the vast majority of the Jewish populace in Jesus' surroundings, not to a small group of social outcasts. It meant all those people who were collaborators with the Gentiles in social associations and who thus failed to adhere to the strict observance of the law as demanded by the established world of Jewish piety (determined by the Pharisees).[57] A particularly decisive issue was their laxity in observing the kashrut laws and the purity codes.[58] It was to the majority (of ''sinners'') that Jesus issued his gracious call to repent (as John had).[59] But Jesus took an additional step of accepting them into his community of readiness for the Kingdom, without requiring a probationary period, as other religious associations in Judaism demanded. A ''scandalous feature of Jesus' admitting unrighteous Jews into the intimacy of his table

---

[54]Farmer, ''The Theological Task,'' 47.

[55]Ibid.

[56]Farmer, ''The Dynamic of Christianity,'' 575.

[57]Farmer, *Jesus and the Gospel,* 30-32.

[58]Farmer, ''The Theological Task,'' 52.

[59]Farmer, *Jesus and the Gospel,* 25-28. Farmer thinks that Jesus' willingness to eat with sinners marked a profound difference between himself and John the Baptist who came ''in the way of righteousness'' (Matt 11:16-19b), see Farmer, ''The Theological Task,'' 55.

fellowship was the absence of any fixed probationary period (the most liberal of the *haberim* required six months—and the Essenes two years).''[60]

The final stage of Jesus' ministry was a result of the second. When the religious outcasts accepted his preaching and in turn were fully accepted by him
(i.e., he ate with them) there developed a strong and effective opposition to
him in the religious establishment. The possible outcome of this opposition
Jesus had already witnessed with respect to John and his decision to continue
in the face of severe criticism from the religiously powerful would have represented a conscious decision to accept the probability that this life would be
taken from him.[61] In response to the criticisms of the Pharisees, Jesus' teaching turned to a rebuke of the self-righteousness of those who resented God's
mercy to the outcasts (e.g., Matthew 23:13, 29-31).

Both Jesus' teaching of the great mercy of God toward the religious outcasts and his rebuke of those who resented this mercy because they trusted
in their own righteousness, become themes of Christian preaching, both
for the first apostles and for Paul. It is this theology which Peter and Paul
share from Jesus that formed the basis for their initial concord in Jerusalem
and to which Paul successfully appealed at Antioch.

In summary, Farmer is confident that it is both historically possible and
theologically necessary to know about Jesus' earthly life and the development of his words and deeds. He claims as ''a peculiar merit'' of his
Jesus and the Gospel, that ''it goes beyond the simple reconstruction of
Jesus' message. . . . it serves in a modest way to demonstrate the possibility of a 'story of Jesus' acceptable to historians, a story which is not essentially different from the story of Jesus familiar to us from the Gospels.''[62]

This story, recoverable from the gospels, is essential to understanding
what meaning the Risen Lord had (and has) for faith. It identifies who is
the Christ whom God exalted. Indeed, Farmer argues, ''There is nothing
essential to Christian faith that is not fully present in the man Jesus.'' For
''it is to the humanity of Christ that we must look if we will see his divin-

---

[60]Farmer, ''The Theological Task,'' 52-53.

[61]Ibid., 49. That Jesus decides to stick by his practice of open table fellowship
in the face of hostile criticism, provides historical explanation of his rejection by
the religious authorities of the day, and his resulting execution. Thus his death
cannot be separated from his basic life behavior and teachings. ''Historical Essay,'' 103.

[62]Farmer, *Jesus and the Gospel,* 21.

ity."[63] This continuity between the historical Jesus and the developed Christian doctrine in the apostles and the early church is well summarized by Farmer with a rhetorical question:

> Jesus did do something with his life and did teach or preach something. Is it not reasonable to conclude that this something provided the Christian movement an initial impetus, that is, that authentic Christian life and faith, at one or more decisive points, is commensurate with the original intention of Jesus and the effect he had upon the life and faith of his disciples?[64]

Conclusion

In spite of many critiques, both of comprehensive[65] and selective[66] character, Bauer's paradigm has enjoyed continuing approval and made increasing impact on the reconstruction of early Christian history. A good example of this influence is Helmut Koester's recent two-volume introduction to the New Testament.[67] The lasting power of Bauer's thesis is probably, as Wilken says, because it provided a new framework for interpreting the explosion of new discoveries in early Christian writings in a time of cultural upheaval in western Christendom. He "created a new paradigm, a new model, from which sprang a coherent tradition of scholarly investigation."[68]

I have sought in this essay to show how Farmer's many publications manifest another, very different, paradigm on the development of early Christian thought and history. In conclusion, let me summarize as to how Farmer's view contrasts with that of a leading representative of Bauer's thought (as applied to the New Testament)—Helmut Koester.

---

[63]Farmer, *Maccabees, Zealots and Josephus,* 187. Here is clearly the influence of John Knox, who fully develops this thesis in *The Humanity and Divinity of Christ* (Cambridge: Cambridge University Press, 1967).

[64]Farmer, "Historical Essay," 107.

[65]In addition to the reviews cited in n. 3 see H. E. W. Turner, *The Pattern of Christian Truth* (London: Mowbray, 1954); H. D. Betz, "Orthodoxy and Heresy in Primitive Christianity," *Int* 19 (1965): 299-311.

[66]In addition to articles cited in the above works, see also Gary T. Burke, "Walter Bauer and Celsus: The Shape of Late Second-Century Christianity," *SCnt* 4 (1984): 1-8; and Fred Norris, "Ignatius, Polycarp, and 1 Clement: Walter Bauer Reconsidered," *VC* 30 (1976): 23-44.

[67]Helmut Koester, *Introduction to the New Testament,* 2 vols. (Philadelphia: Fortress Press, 1984).

[68]Wilken, "Diversity and Unity," 103.

First, there is the question of whether there was an early Christian "orthodoxy" shared by the apostles, from which "heretics" deviated. Koester argues that "distinctions between canonical and non-canonical, orthodox and heretical, are obsolete."[69] His reason is that the categories previously employed to make such distinctions (apostolic authority, kerygma, life and/or teaching of Jesus, primitive Christian cultus, or freedom from pagan influence) have lost their value as criteria.[70] Farmer, on the other hand, argues that there was continuity between the faith which Paul persecuted, the faith he preached as a Christian (and shared with other apostles), and that faith ultimately expressed in the *regula fidei*.[71] Farmer described this as the apostolic faith "not to be identified with either Peter or Paul per se, but with Peter *and* Paul. It is inclusive of both, but not limited or absolutely identical with either."[72]

Second, a corollary issue to whether there existed a conscious orthodoxy is whether the early church was composed only of warring factions, or whether there was harmony and agreement among the apostolic leadership. It was Baur who first influentially argued that "up to the time when the apostle [Paul] disappears from the scene of history, we have before us nothing but differences and oppositions, between which no certain way of compromise or reconciliation yet appears."[73]

Bauer then set forth a similar, more schismatic, picture of warring regional sects in post-apostolic Christianity. This view is continued and enlarged in Koester, so that each of the New Testament gospels—and their sources—represents conflicting understandings of Jesus. Farmer, how-

---

[69]Koester, "Conclusion: The Intention and Scope of Trajectories," in *Trajectories*, 270.

[70]Koseter, "Theological Aspects," in *The Future*, 66-72; Koester, "Gnomai Diaphoroi," in *Trajectories*, 116f.

[71]Farmer, "Galatians and *Regula Fidei*," 165. "The *regula fidei*, if it is to be properly understood, must be understood within the context of a certain development set in motion by the agreement reached by Paul and those who were apostles before him when he met in Jerusalem with Peter and James three years after his conversion and fourteen years later at the Jerusalem conference, when he and Barnabas were given the right hand of fellowship. The apparent breakdown of the agreement reached in the Jerusalem conference, reported by Paul in Galatians 2:11-21, was, in reality, a 'correcting' episode in this development. The composition of the account in Acts was a later 'correcting' episode in the same development."

[72]Farmer, *Jesus and the Gospel*, 54 = Farmer, "Peter and Paul," 219-20.

[73]Baur, *Church History*, 76.

ever, while recognizing some diversity in the earliest church nonetheless thinks that there was a "fundamental theological understanding and agreement shared by these apostles . . ."[74]

Third, there is the question of the influence of the historical Jesus upon the development of early Christian theology. This is an issue not addressed by Bauer; however, Koester argues that Jesus is the real source of the diversity in earliest Christianity—of both "orthodoxy" and "heresy"![75] In "Four Primitive Gospels"[76] Koester suggests four distinct, really contradictory, ways in which Jesus was significant for diverse groups in the early church.[77] It is accordingly inappropriate and illegitimate to try to locate an "orthodox" view of Jesus or his teachings.[78]

Farmer is of the opinion that the apostolic faith shared by Peter and Paul, reaffirmed at the Jerusalem council, shaped the canon and the *regula fidei,* is traceable to Jesus himself. Thus there is a correct view of Jesus, in the early church, and in Christianity today. That is why, since his student days at Union, Farmer has pursued the question: "What place is to be given to the historical Jesus in any systematic expression of the Christian faith?"[79]

The theology which comes to expression in the parables of Jesus, which is to be corrolated with the ministry of Jesus, is essentially the theology of Paul. And "since we learn from Paul himself that he preached the faith of the church he once persecuted, it follows that Paul preached a pre-Pauline faith. The historian has no alternative but to conclude that the theology that is common to Paul and to the two streams of parable tradition preserved separately in Matthew and Luke goes back to Jesus."[80]

Thus although both Farmer and Koester see primitive Christianity as derived both historically and theologically from Jesus, only Farmer believes that on the basis of Jesus' life and teaching is it possible to find a Christian

---

[74]Farmer, *Jesus and the Gospel,* 51.

[75]In his article, "Theological Aspects," in *The Future,* 78-79, Koester has a section entitled, "The historical Jesus as source of the problem of Orthodoxy and Heresy," in which he urged that Jesus had equal influence both on Paul and Paul's opponents.

[76]This influential article seeks to document Christian diversity in the period before the writings of the New Testament.

[77]"The Structure and Criteria of Early Christian Beliefs," in *Trajectories,* 211-29.

[78]Ibid., 205-11.

[79]Farmer, "Historical Essay," 106.

[80]Farmer, "Reply to Christopher Duraisingh," 73.

"orthodoxy" that can be traced through an apostolic faith from Jesus through the early church fathers.

Although Farmer's work on the synoptics has received some attention by colleagues, regrettably his reconstruction of early Christian development has not. I hope the present exposition of its main points will encourage others to examine it seriously as a comprehensive and important alternative paradigm to the Baur-Bauer-Bultmann reconstruction (one could also attend to its sources in John Knox, whose many works in New Testament theology no longer receive the attention they merit). Finally, I offer some points at which I think Farmer's reconstruction needs additional examination.

First, if Paul is so influenced by Jesus' parables of grace, and if he learned about Jesus' life and teachings from Peter during their fifteen-day visit, how does one account for Paul's non-use of this Jesus tradition in his letters? One would think, for example, that the parable of the prodigal son would have been as useful in Paul's argument with the Galatians as the rather obscure allegory of Sarah and Hagar.

Second, although kerygmatic theology has been eclipsed in recent years, and although the Bauer-Koester view has claimed there were keryg*mata* in earliest Christianity, there is still a focus in the New Testament writings, including Paul's, on the death and resurrection of Jesus and his lordship.[81] Has Farmer's focus upon the historical Jesus given adequate explanation for this emphasis upon the Risen Lord?

Third, Farmer does not seem to have dealt adequately with the diversity manifestly present in the New Testament itself (leaving aside that in extra-canonical writings). For example, the starting point for Baur's view of a divided Christendom, 1 Corinthians 1:11-17, needs to be explained in some way. Or one may consider the opponents of Paul in 2 Corinthians, who seem to have had adequate influence to threaten his work in Corinth (and from 2:17, one may consider if they are the majority there).

But beyond these or other particulars, Farmer presents scholars with the importance of the paradigms we start with, and performs the vital service of challenging us to examine them.

---

[81]See R. H. Fuller's article "New Testament Trajectories and Biblical Authority," *SE* 7 (1982): 189-99, for a suggestion that the New Testament writers exercised control of the "trajectories" with reference to the kerygma and the historical Jesus.

One of the key issues raised by kerygmatic theology, which Farmer neglects, is the question of the apocalyptic view of the Kingdom. Because of its importance to most reconstructions of early Christian thought, this topic really needs Farmer's consideration in his paradigm.